From The RED FOG 1

Mosae Nohara

Translation: Caleb D. Cook

Lettering: Chiho Christie

AKAI KIRI NO NAKA KARA Volume 1
©2020 Mosae Nohara/SQUARE ENIX CO., LTD.
First published in Japan in 2020 by SQUARE ENIX CO., LTD.
English translation rights arranged with SQUARE ENIX CO., LTD.
and Yen Press, LLC through Tuttle-Mori Agency, Inc.

English translation ©2022 by SQUARE ENIX CO., LTD.

Yen Press
150 West 30th Street, 19th Floor
New York, NY 10001

Visit us at yenpress.com · facebook.com/yenpress · twitter.com/yenpress · yenpress.tumblr.com · instagram.com/yenpress

First Yen Press Edition: February 2022

Yen Press is an imprint of Yen Press, LLC.
The Yen Press name and logo are trademarks of Yen Press, LLC.

Library of Congress Control Number: 2021949718

ISBNs: 978-1-9753-4120-6 (paperback)
978-1-9753-4121-3 (ebook)

10 9 8 7 6 5 4 3 2 1

WOR

Printed in the United States of America

D0595747

AFTERWORD

HELLO AND NICE TO MEET YOU.
I'M NOHARA. I CAN'T THANK YOU
ENOUGH FOR DECIDING TO PURCHASE
VOLUME 1 OF FROM THE RED FOG!!!
I'M GLAD WE HAVE A CHANCE TO MEET
LIKE THIS EVEN NOW, IN AN ERA WHEN
THE WORLD IS FULL TO BURSTING
WITH MANGA. I'M SO GRATEFUL.
DRAWING THIS SERIES STARTED OUT AS
MORE OF A HOBBY, BUT THANKS TO THE
SUPPORT OF A LOT OF PEOPLE, I MANAGED
TO GET IT SERIALIZED. NOW IT'S BEING
PUBLISHED AS SEPARATE VOLUMES TOO! THANK
YOU TO MY EDITOR, THE EDITOR-IN-CHIEF, AND
EVERYONE ELSE WHO HELPED ME ALONG
THE WAY. IT'S MADE ME SO HAPPY TO
RECEIVE ENOUGH SUPPORT TO
ACTUALLY PUT OUT A BOOK.
THE GOAL WITH THIS SERIES IS TO GET
READERS' HEARTS PUMPING AND
BLOOD RUSHING, SO REST ASSURED
THAT MY OWN HEART AND BLOOD WERE
WORKING JUST AS HARD WHILE
I WAS WRITING AND DRAWING IT.
I HOPE I KEEP ENJOYING THE FREEDOM
TO CRAFT THIS SERIES INTO SOMETHING A
LITTLE SCARY, BUT STILL LOTS OF FUN.
I'LL BE GIVING MY ALL, SO I HOPE
YOU'LL COME ALONG FOR THE RIDE.
SEE YOU AGAIN IN VOLUME 2!!

Thanks ♦
Assistant / Ken Sawada   Editor / Noritaka Shimizu

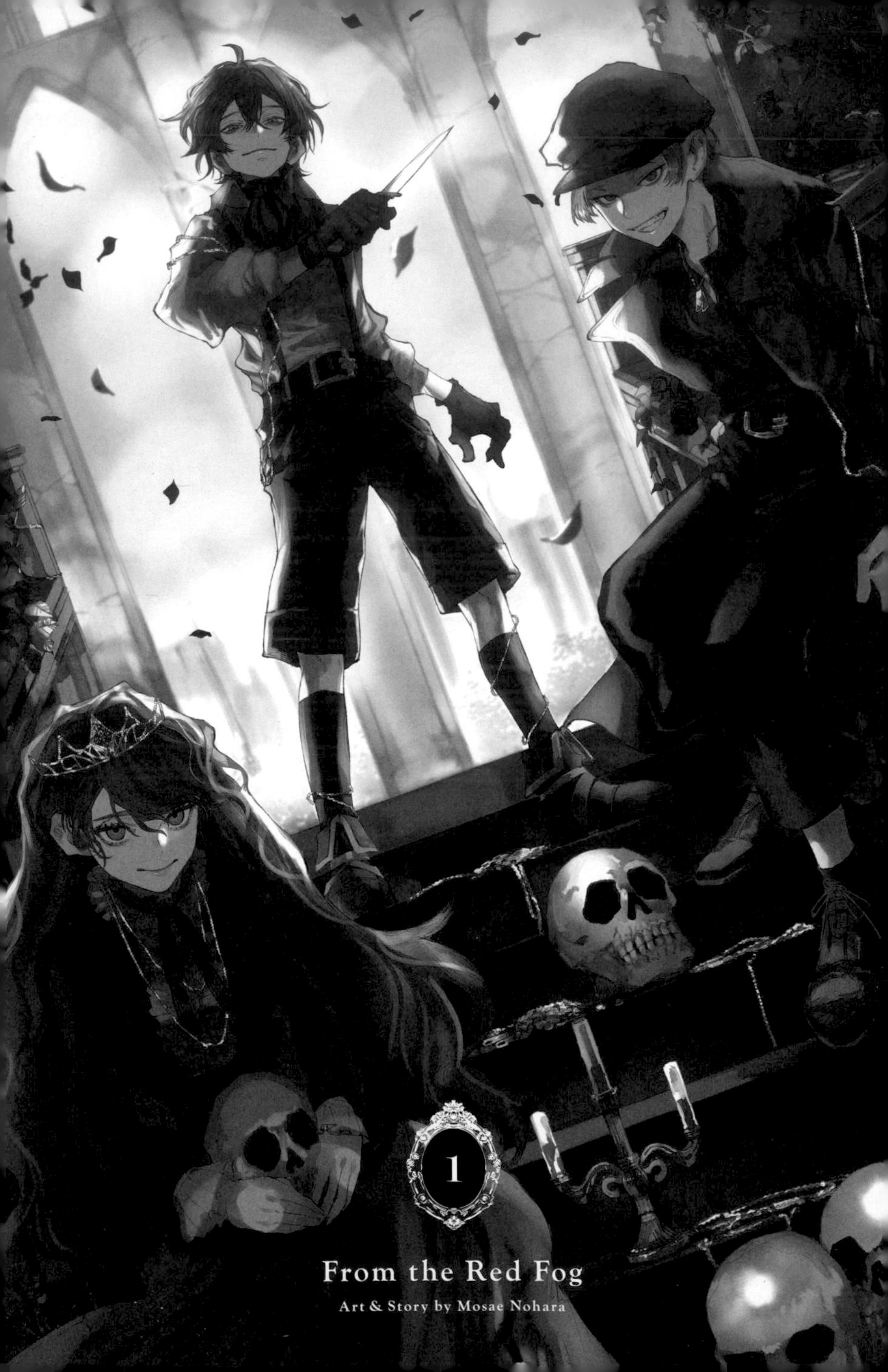
1
From the Red Fog
Art & Story by Mosae Nohara

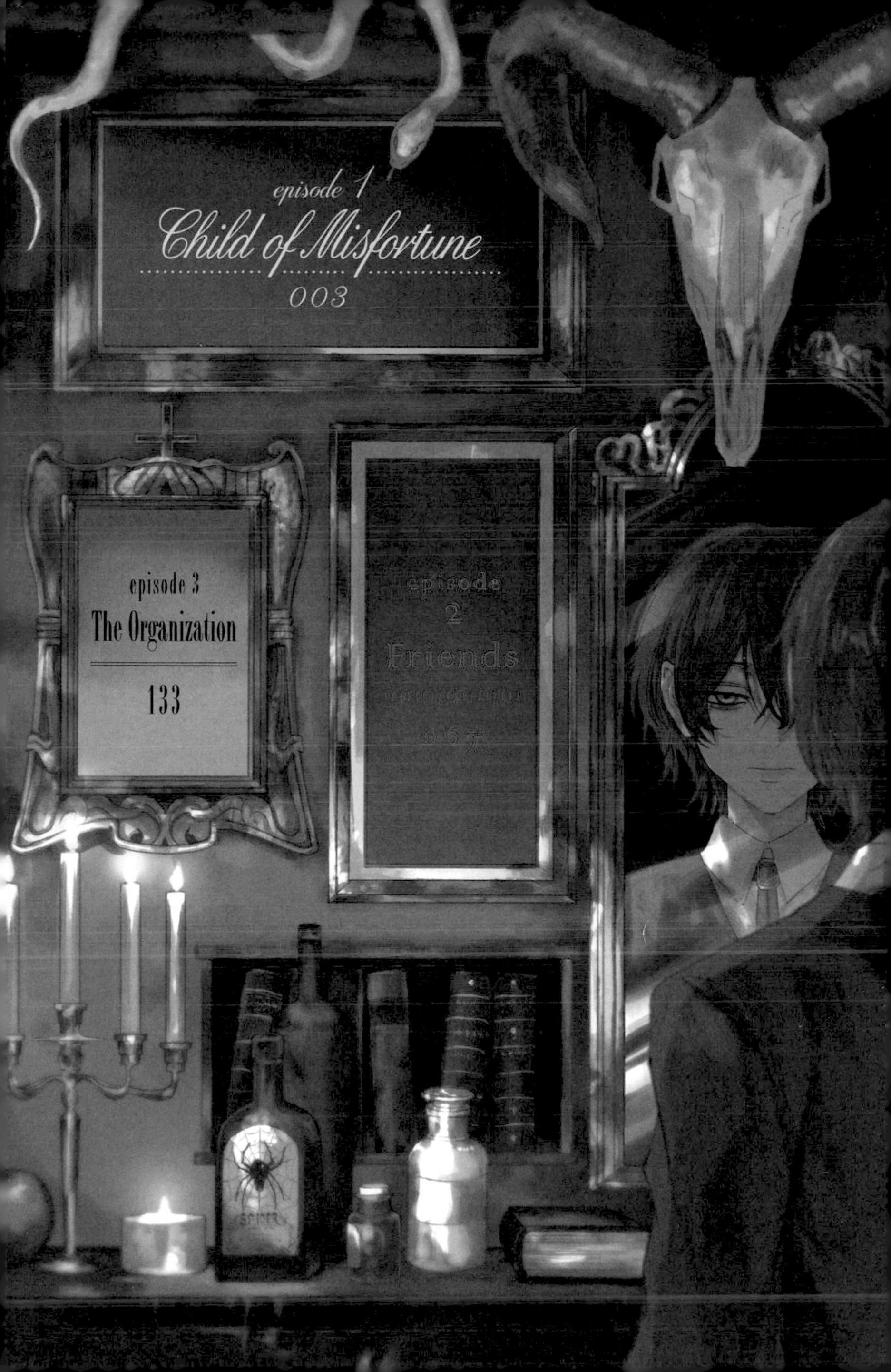
episode 1
Child of Misfortune
003
episode 2
Friends
067
episode 3
The Organization
133

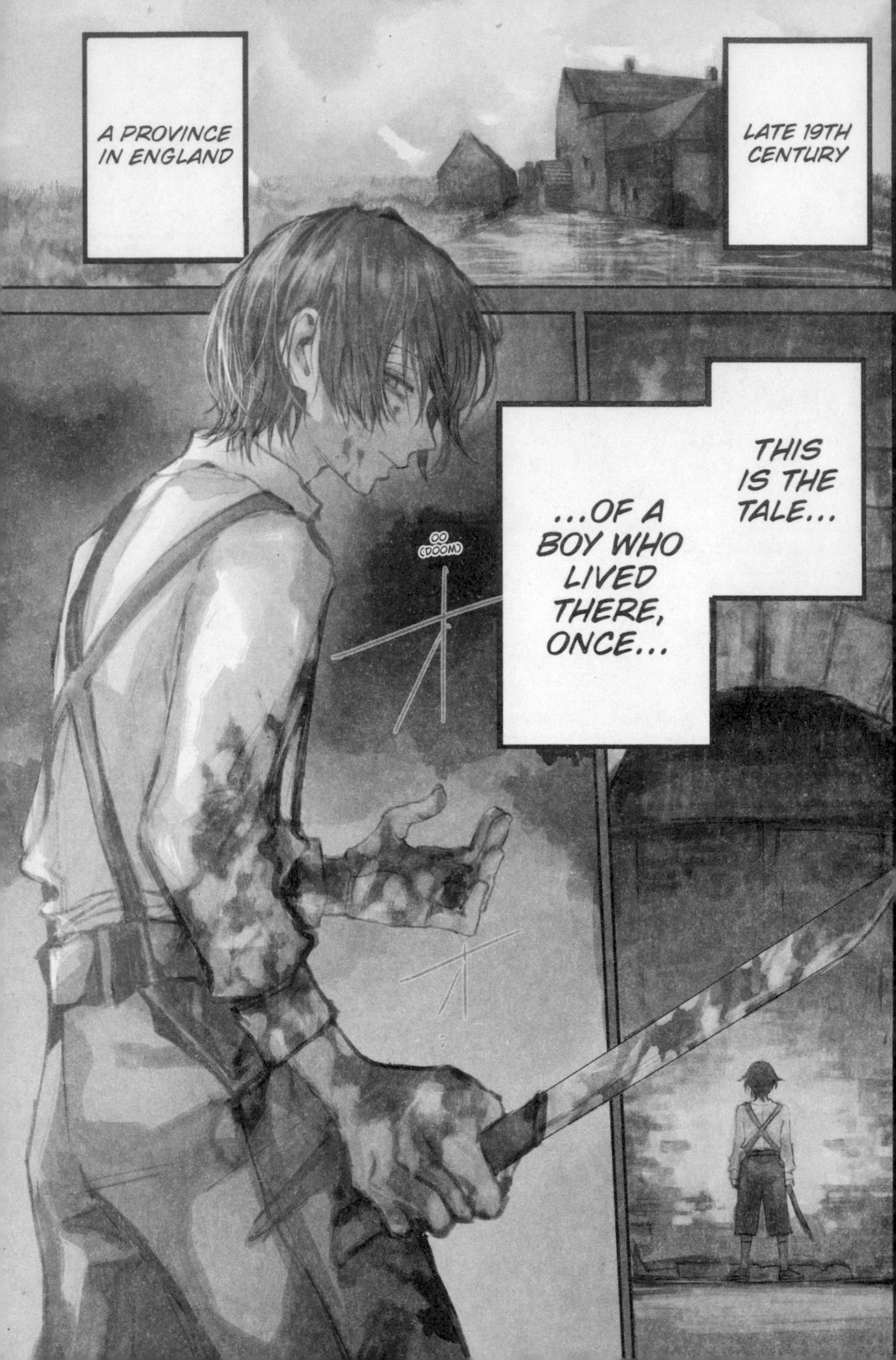
LATE 19TH CENTURY
A PROVINCE IN ENGLAND
THIS IS THE TALE...
...OF A BOY WHO LIVED THERE, ONCE...
(DOOM)

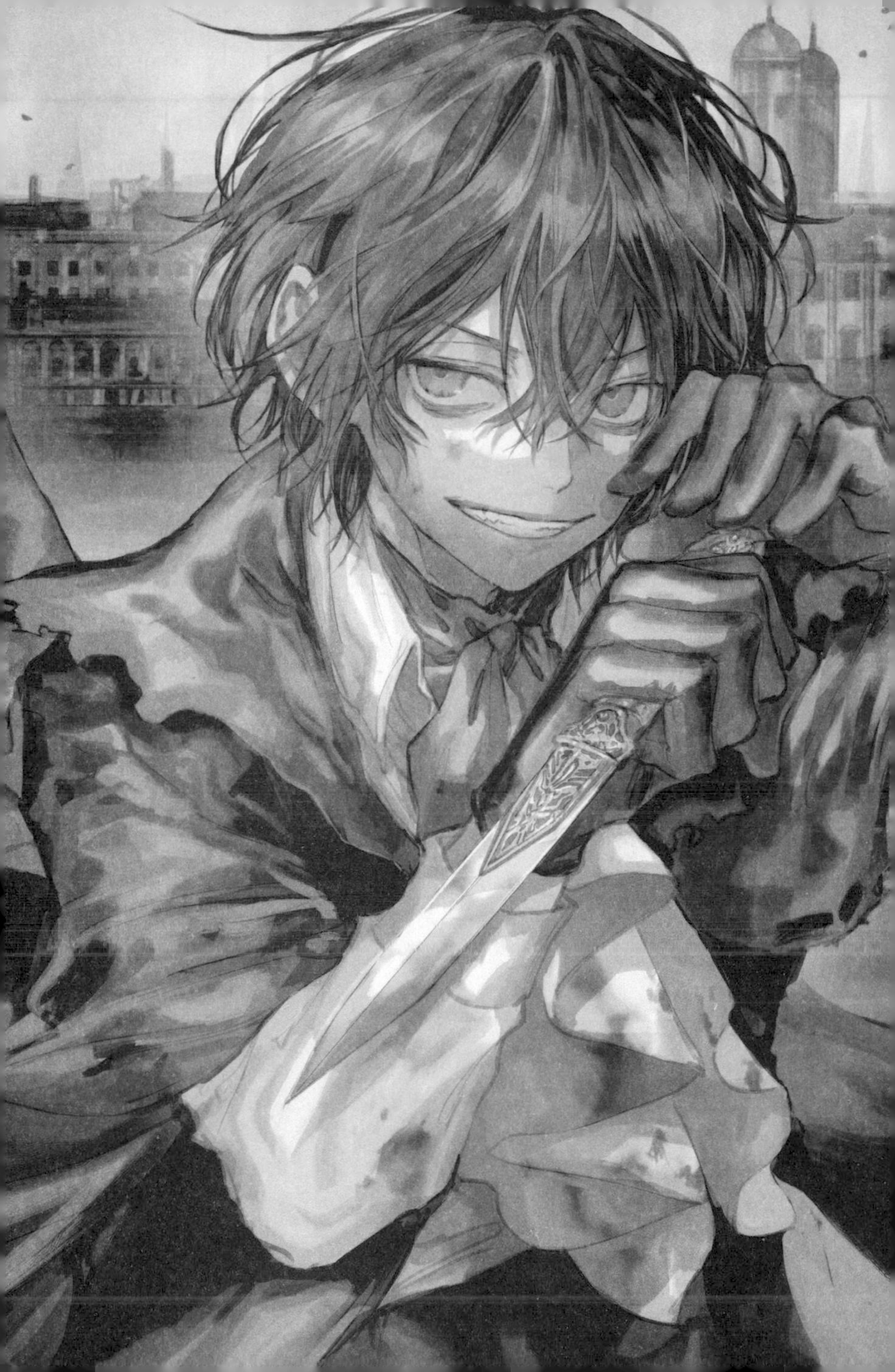

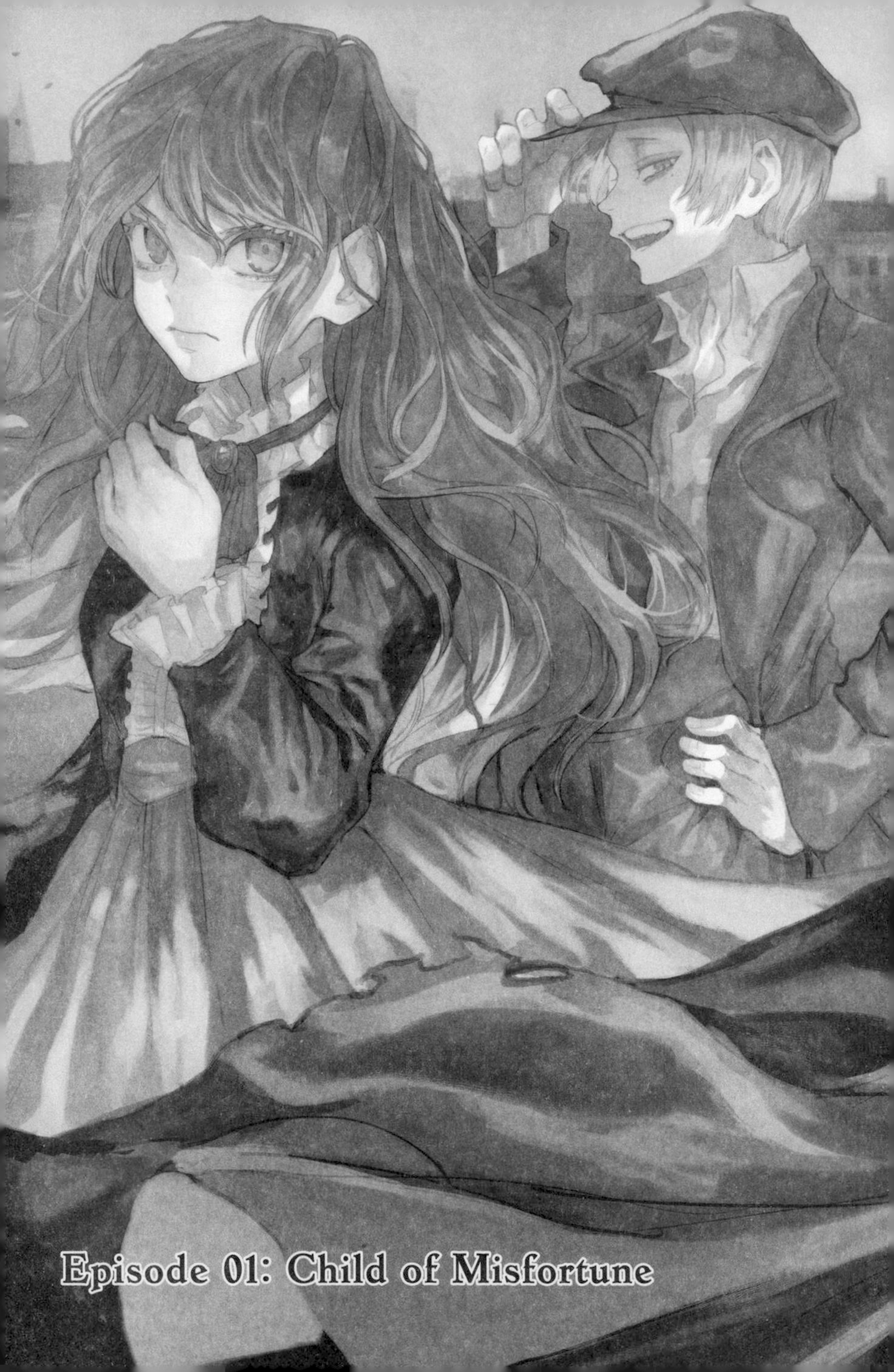

Episode 01: Child of Misfortune

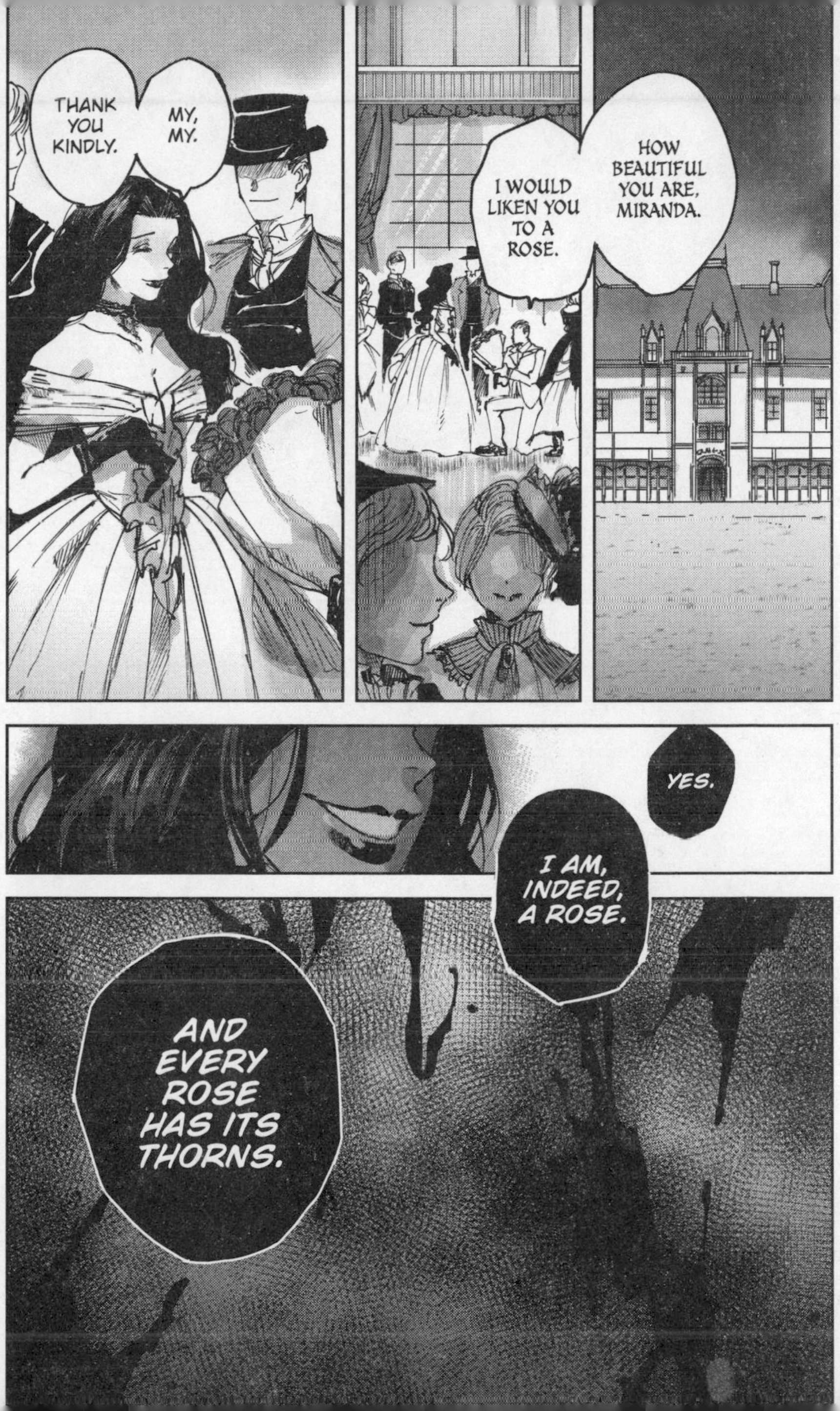
HOW BEAUTIFUL YOU ARE, MIRANDA.
I WOULD LIKEN YOU TO A ROSE.
MY, MY.
THANK YOU KINDLY.
YES.
I AM, INDEED, A ROSE.
AND EVERY ROSE HAS ITS THORNS.

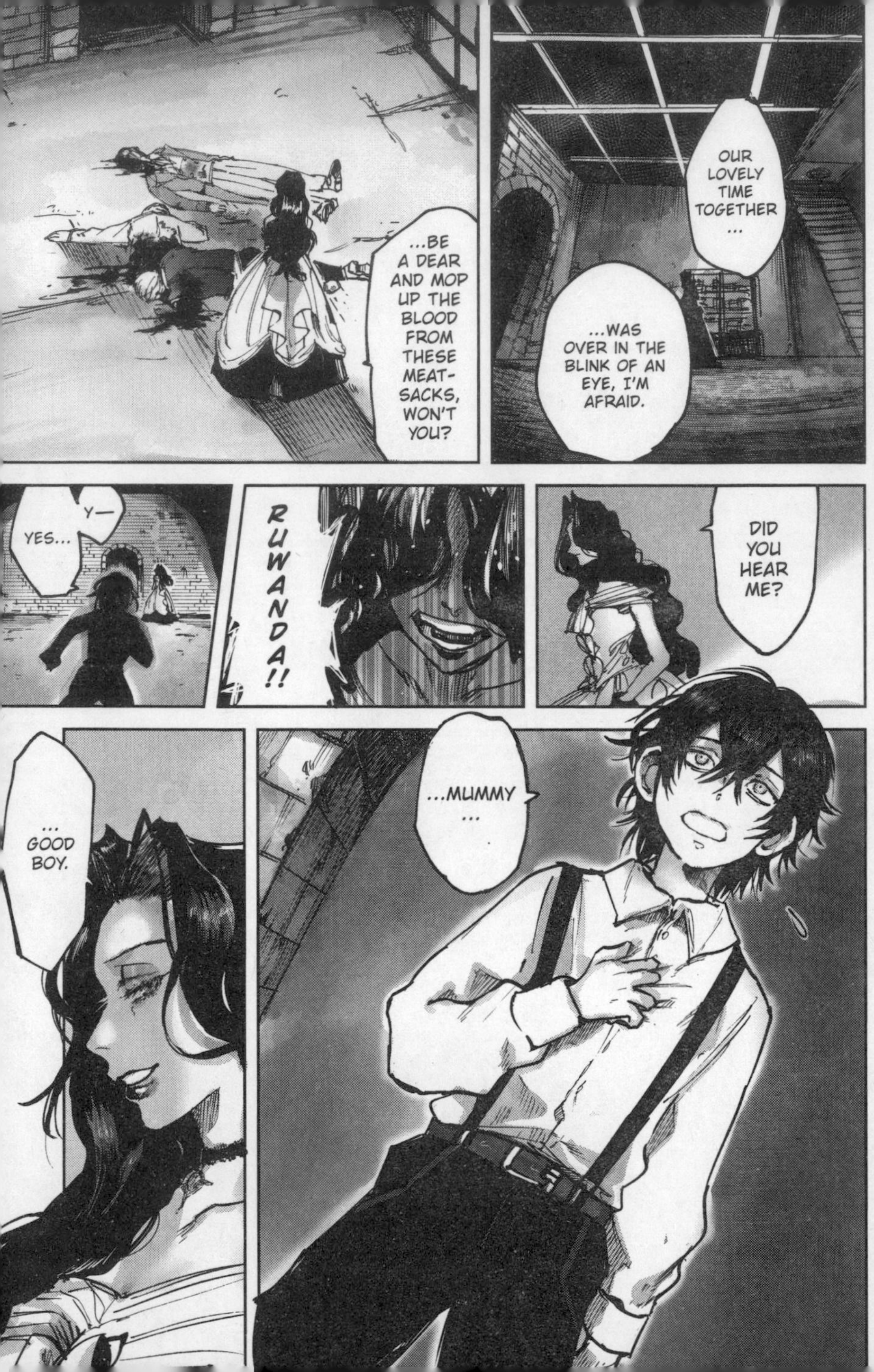
OUR LOVELY TIME TOGETHER ...
...WAS OVER IN THE BLINK OF AN EYE, I'M AFRAID.
...BE A DEAR AND MOP UP THE BLOOD FROM THESE MEAT-SACKS, WON'T YOU?
DID YOU HEAR ME?
RUWANDA!!
Y— YES...
...MUMMY ...
... GOOD BOY.

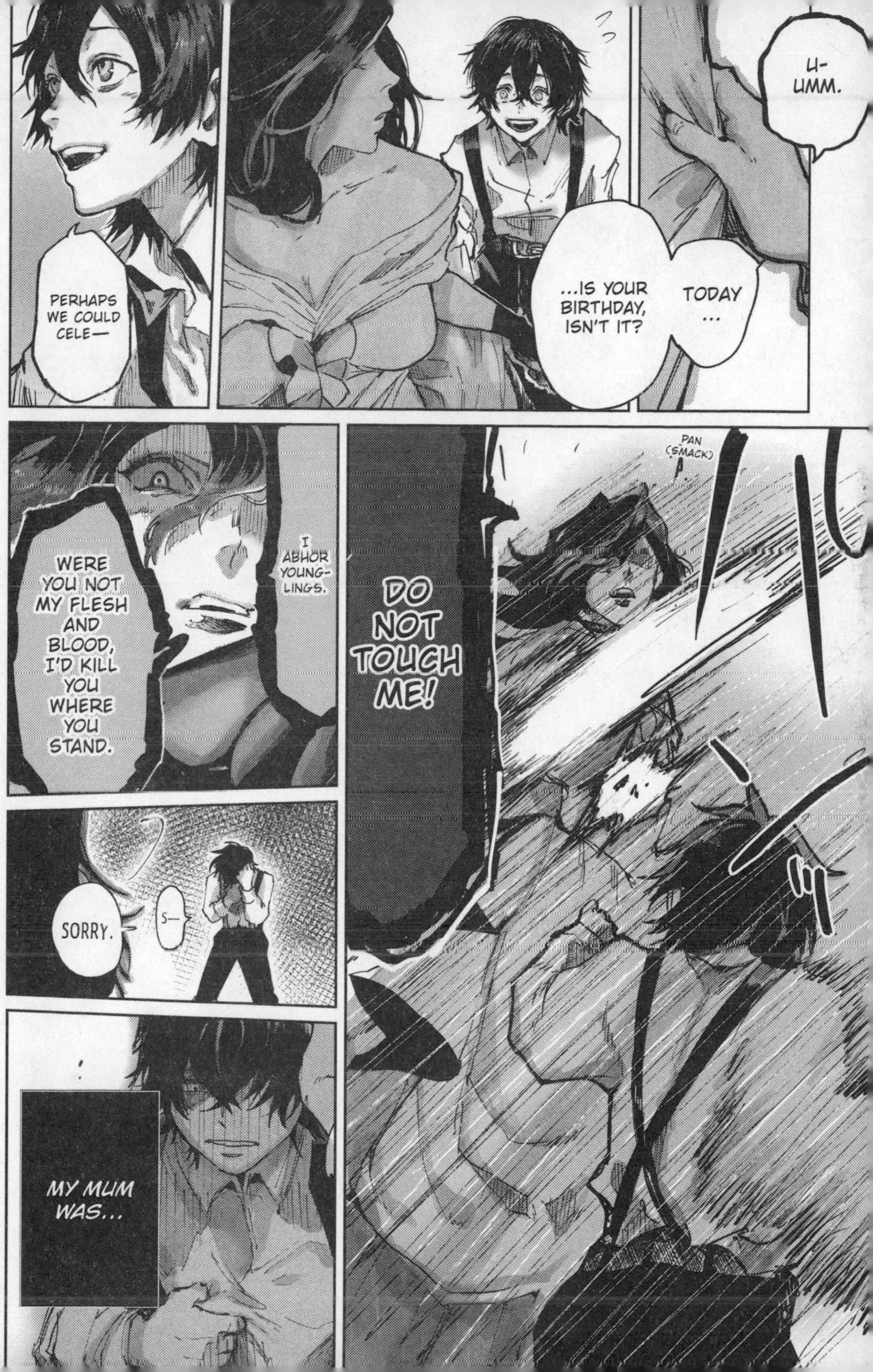
U-UMM.
TODAY...
...IS YOUR BIRTHDAY, ISN'T IT?
PERHAPS WE COULD CELE—
PAN (SMACK)
DO NOT TOUCH ME!
I ABHOR YOUNGLINGS.
WERE YOU NOT MY FLESH AND BLOOD, I'D KILL YOU WHERE YOU STAND.
S—
SORRY.
MY MUM WAS...

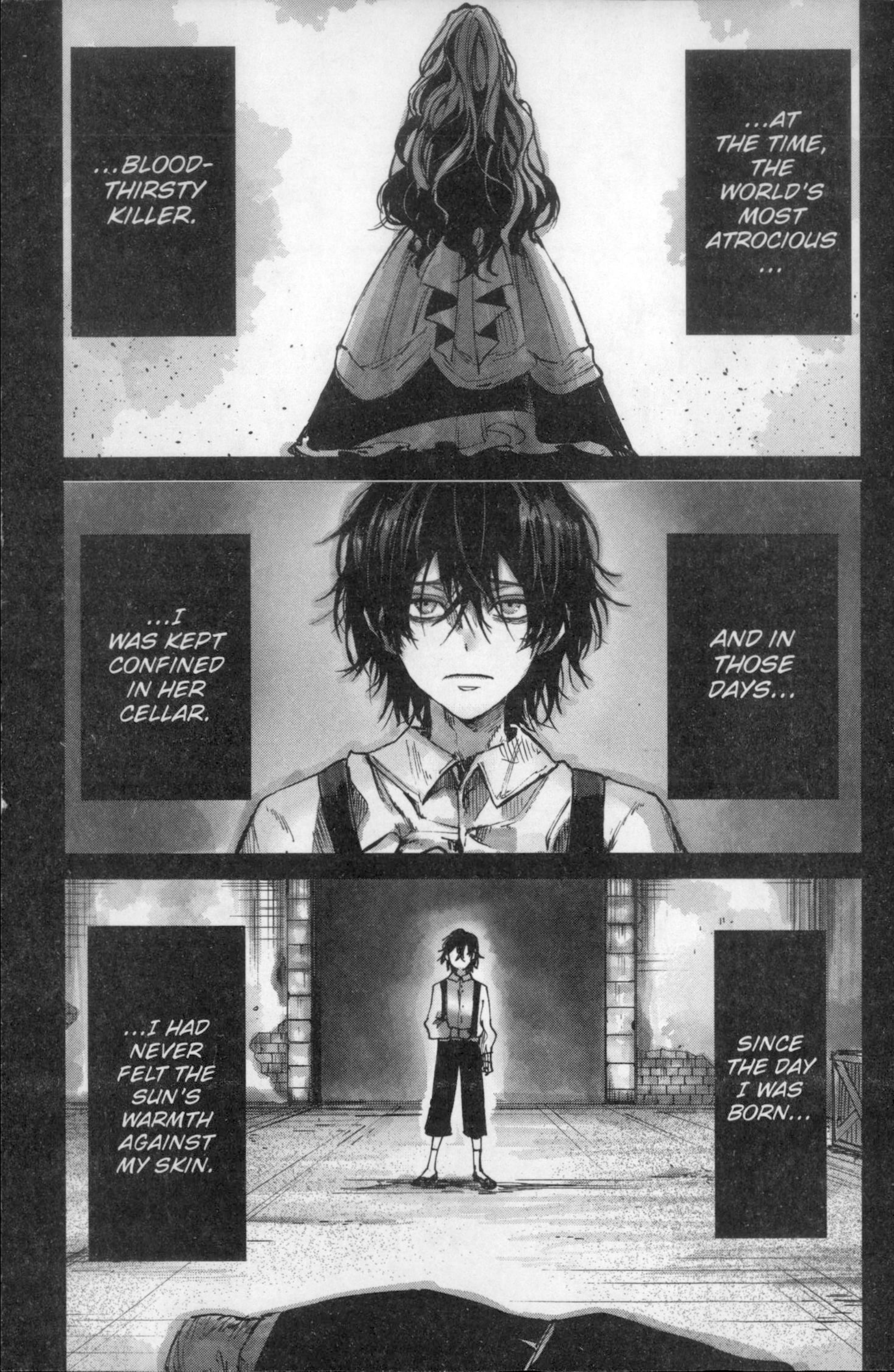
...AT THE TIME, THE WORLD'S MOST ATROCIOUS ...
...BLOOD-THIRSTY KILLER.
AND IN THOSE DAYS...
...I WAS KEPT CONFINED IN HER CELLAR.
SINCE THE DAY I WAS BORN...
...I HAD NEVER FELT THE SUN'S WARMTH AGAINST MY SKIN.

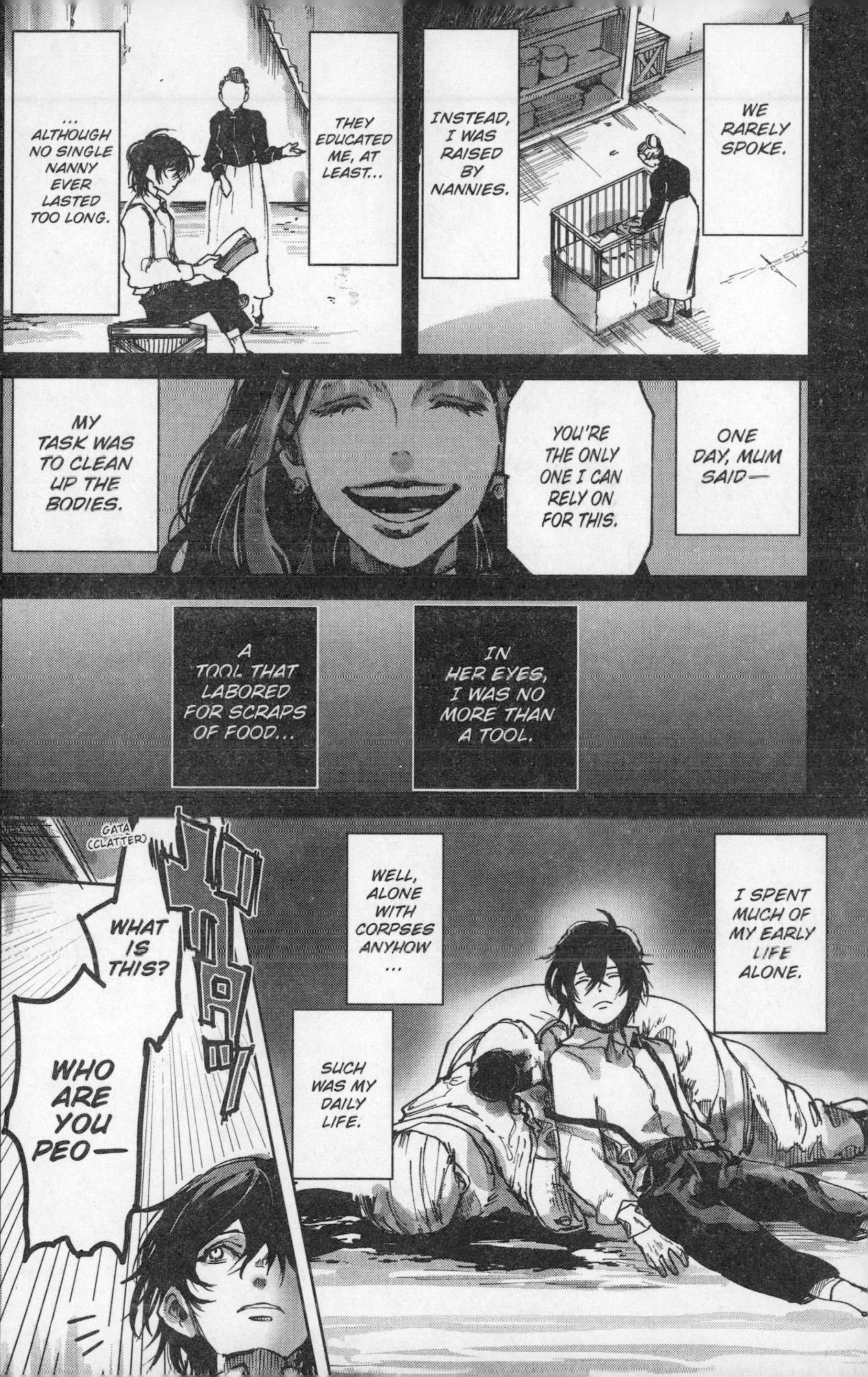
WE RARELY SPOKE.
INSTEAD, I WAS RAISED BY NANNIES.
THEY EDUCATED ME, AT LEAST...
...ALTHOUGH NO SINGLE NANNY EVER LASTED TOO LONG.
ONE DAY, MUM SAID—
YOU'RE THE ONLY ONE I CAN RELY ON FOR THIS.
MY TASK WAS TO CLEAN UP THE BODIES.
IN HER EYES, I WAS NO MORE THAN A TOOL.
A TOOL THAT LABORED FOR SCRAPS OF FOOD...
I SPENT MUCH OF MY EARLY LIFE ALONE.
WELL, ALONE WITH CORPSES ANYHOW...
SUCH WAS MY DAILY LIFE.
GATA (CLATTER)
WHAT IS THIS?
WHO ARE YOU PEO—

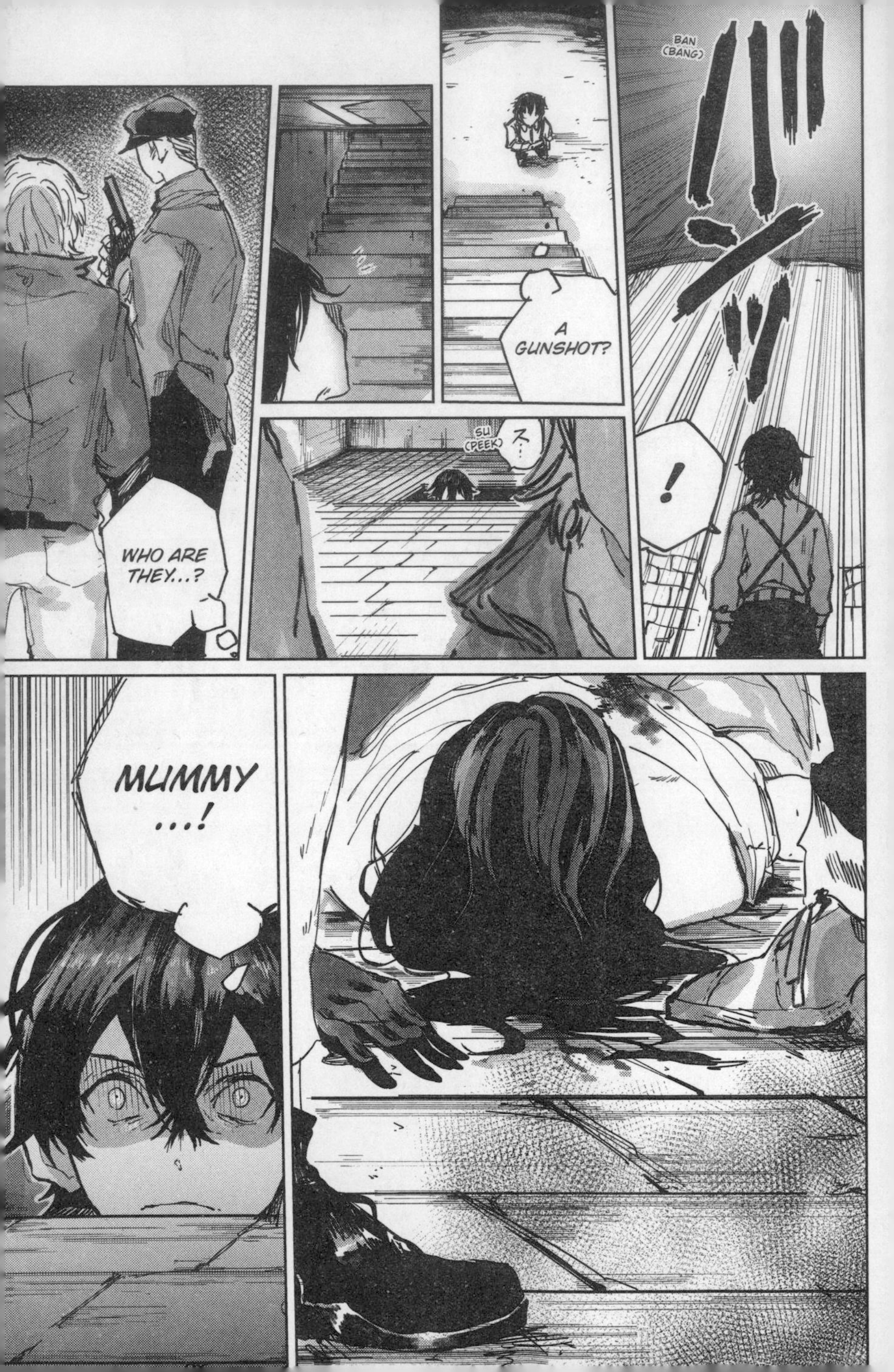
BAN (BANG)
!
A GUNSHOT?
SU (PEEK)
ス…
WHO ARE THEY...?
MUMMY ...!

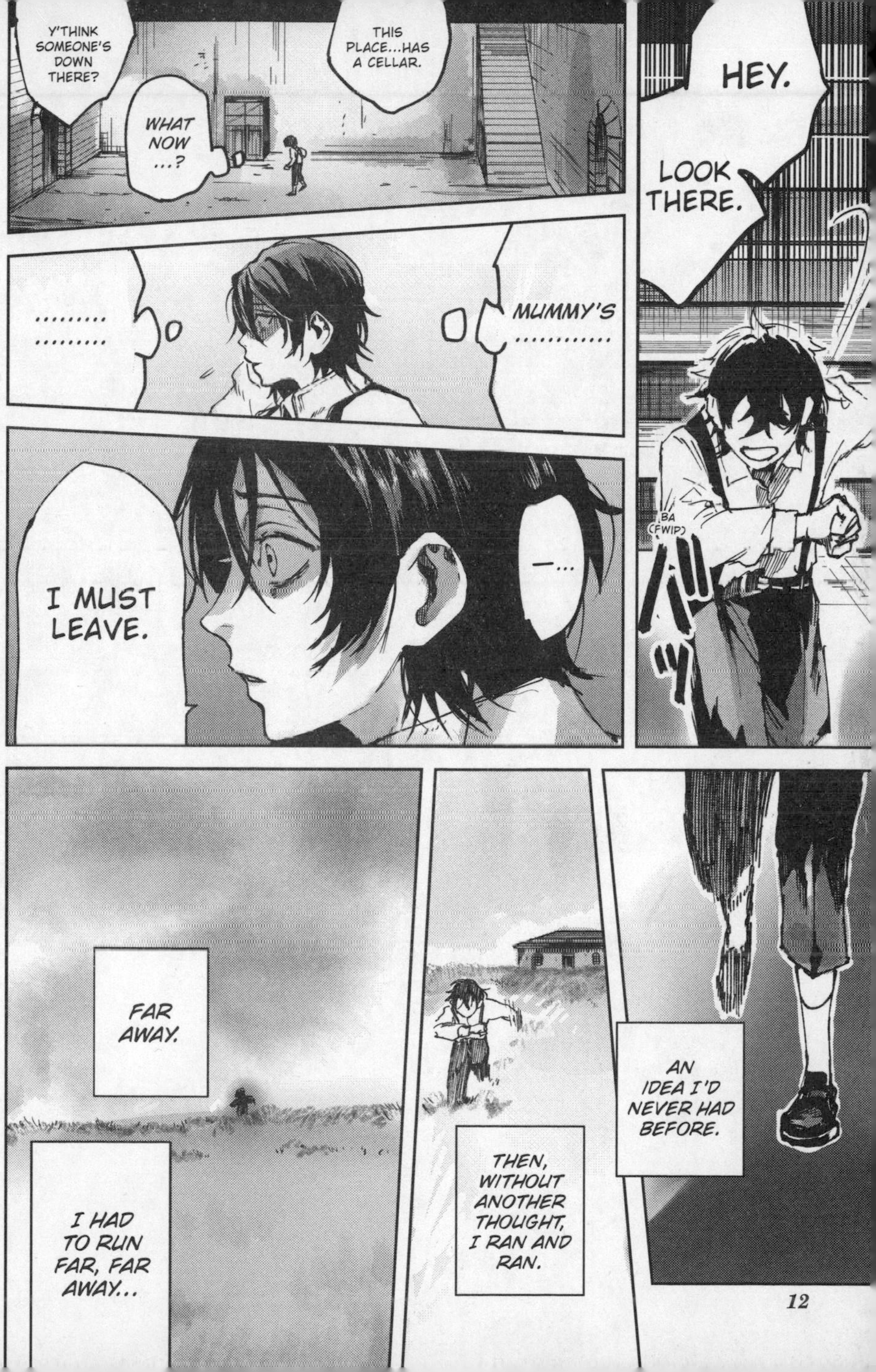

HEY.
LOOK THERE.
BA (FWIP)
THIS PLACE...HAS A CELLAR.
Y'THINK SOMEONE'S DOWN THERE?
WHAT NOW ...?
MUMMY'S ....
....
—...
I MUST LEAVE.
AN IDEA I'D NEVER HAD BEFORE.
THEN, WITHOUT ANOTHER THOUGHT, I RAN AND RAN.
FAR AWAY.
I HAD TO RUN FAR, FAR AWAY...

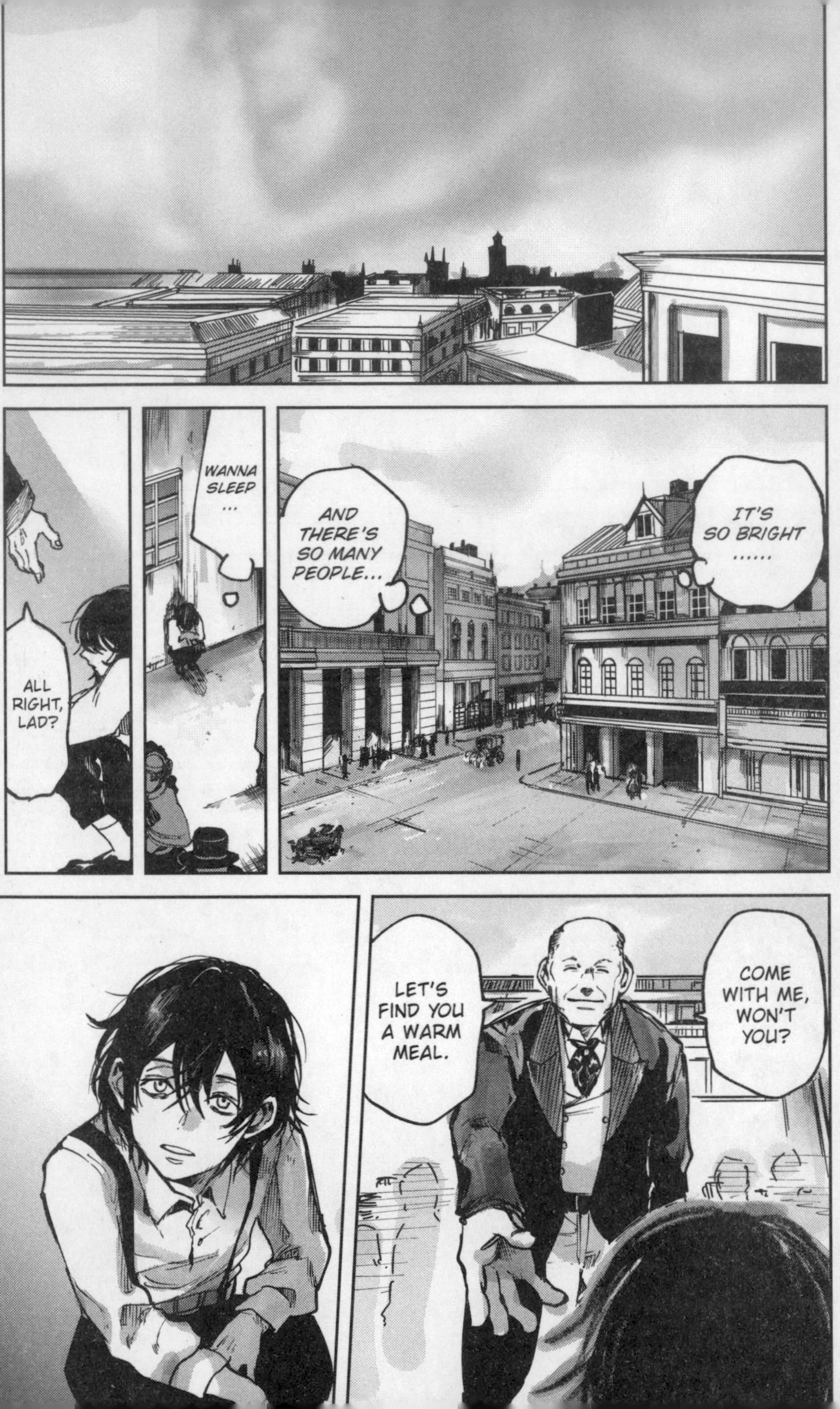
IT'S SO BRIGHT ......
AND THERE'S SO MANY PEOPLE...
WANNA SLEEP ...
ALL RIGHT, LAD?
COME WITH ME, WON'T YOU?
LET'S FIND YOU A WARM MEAL.

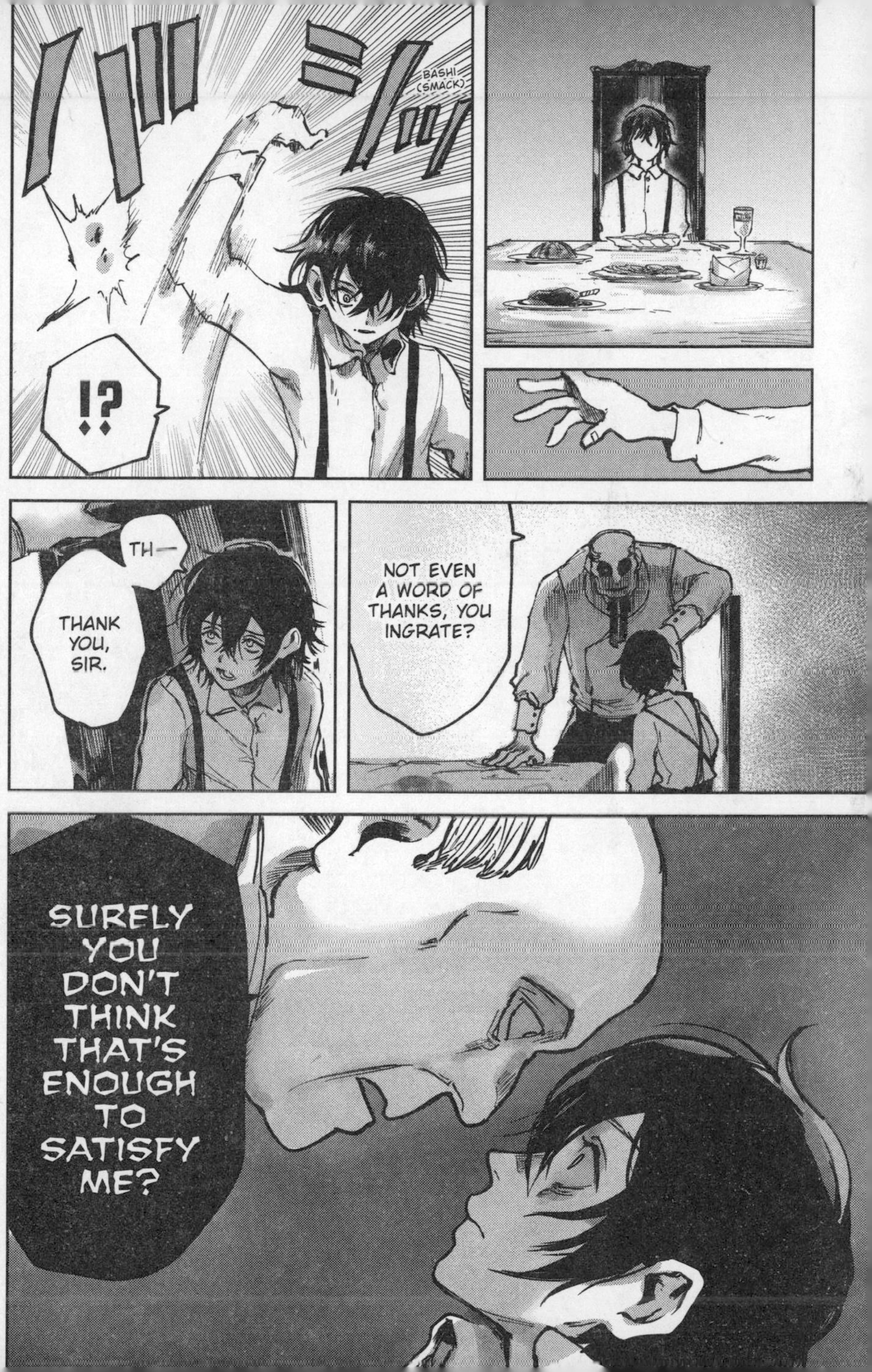
BASHI (SMACK)
!?
NOT EVEN A WORD OF THANKS, YOU INGRATE?
TH—
THANK YOU, SIR.
SURELY YOU DON'T THINK THAT'S ENOUGH TO SATISFY ME?

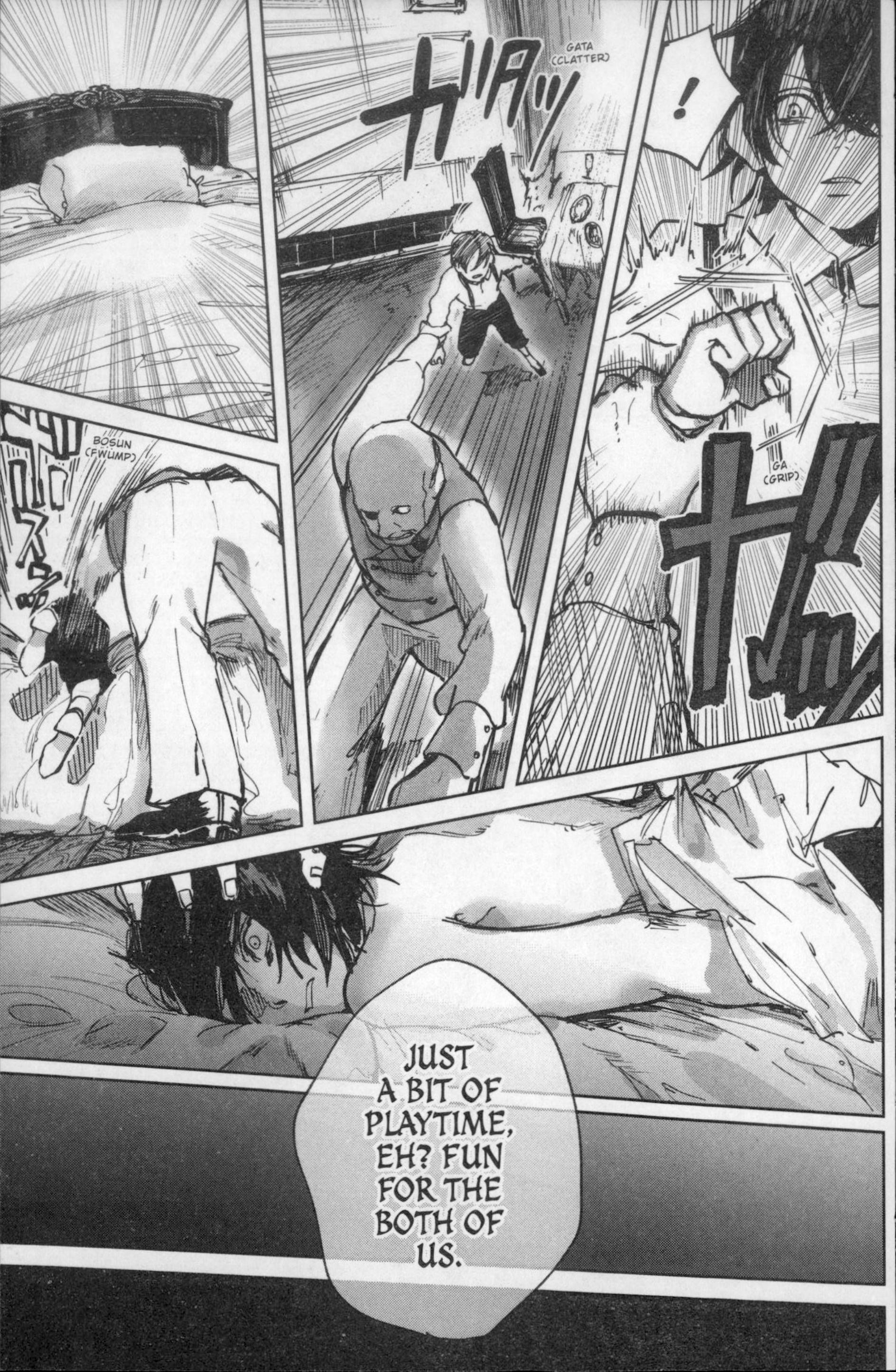
!
GA (GRIP)
GATA (CLATTER)
BOSUN (FWUMP)
JUST A BIT OF PLAYTIME, EH? FUN FOR THE BOTH OF US.

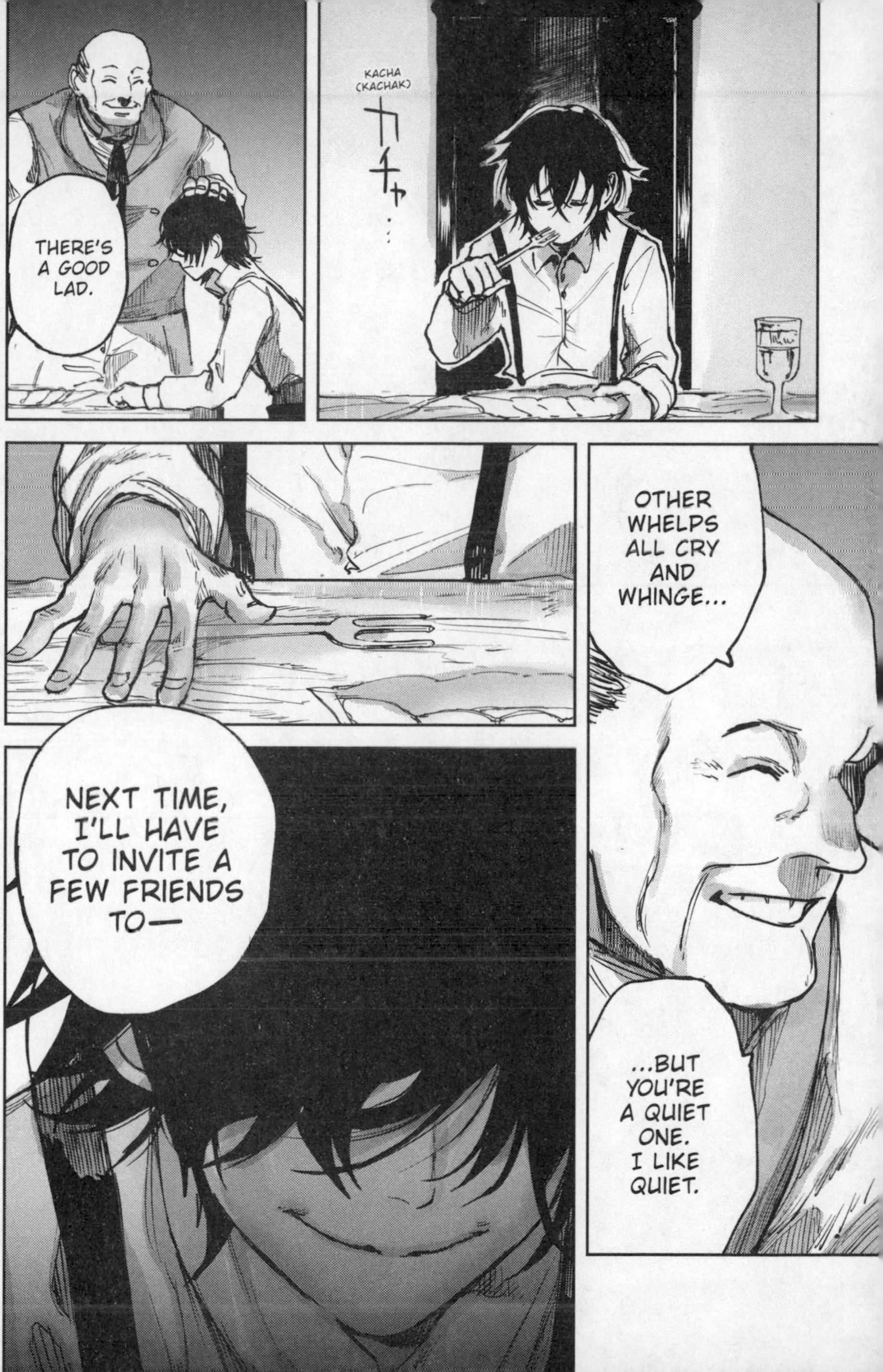
KACHA (KACHAK)
カチャ…
THERE'S A GOOD LAD.
OTHER WHELPS ALL CRY AND WHINGE...
...BUT YOU'RE A QUIET ONE. I LIKE QUIET.
NEXT TIME, I'LL HAVE TO INVITE A FEW FRIENDS TO—

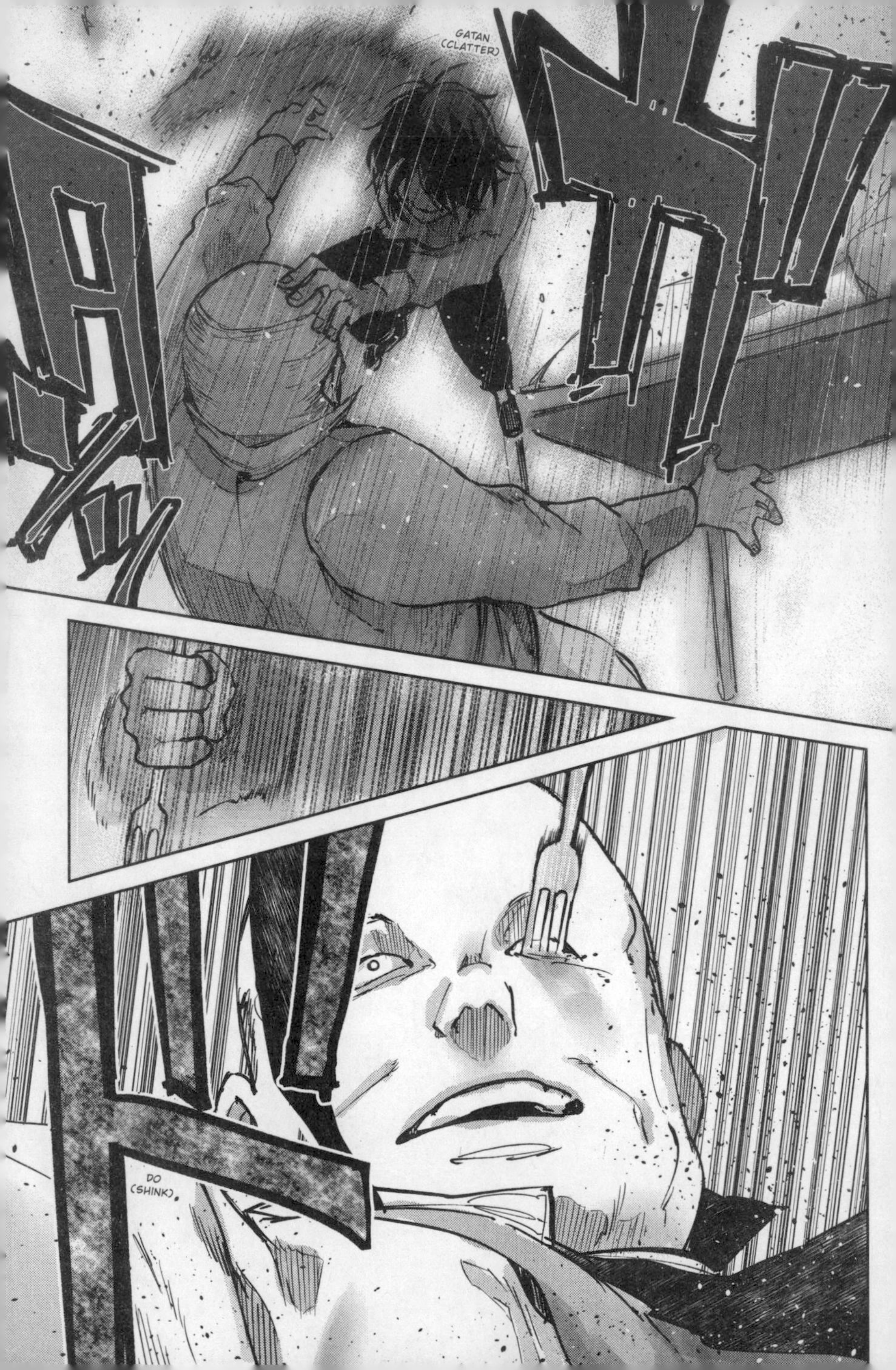
GATAN
(CLATTER)
DO
(SHINK)

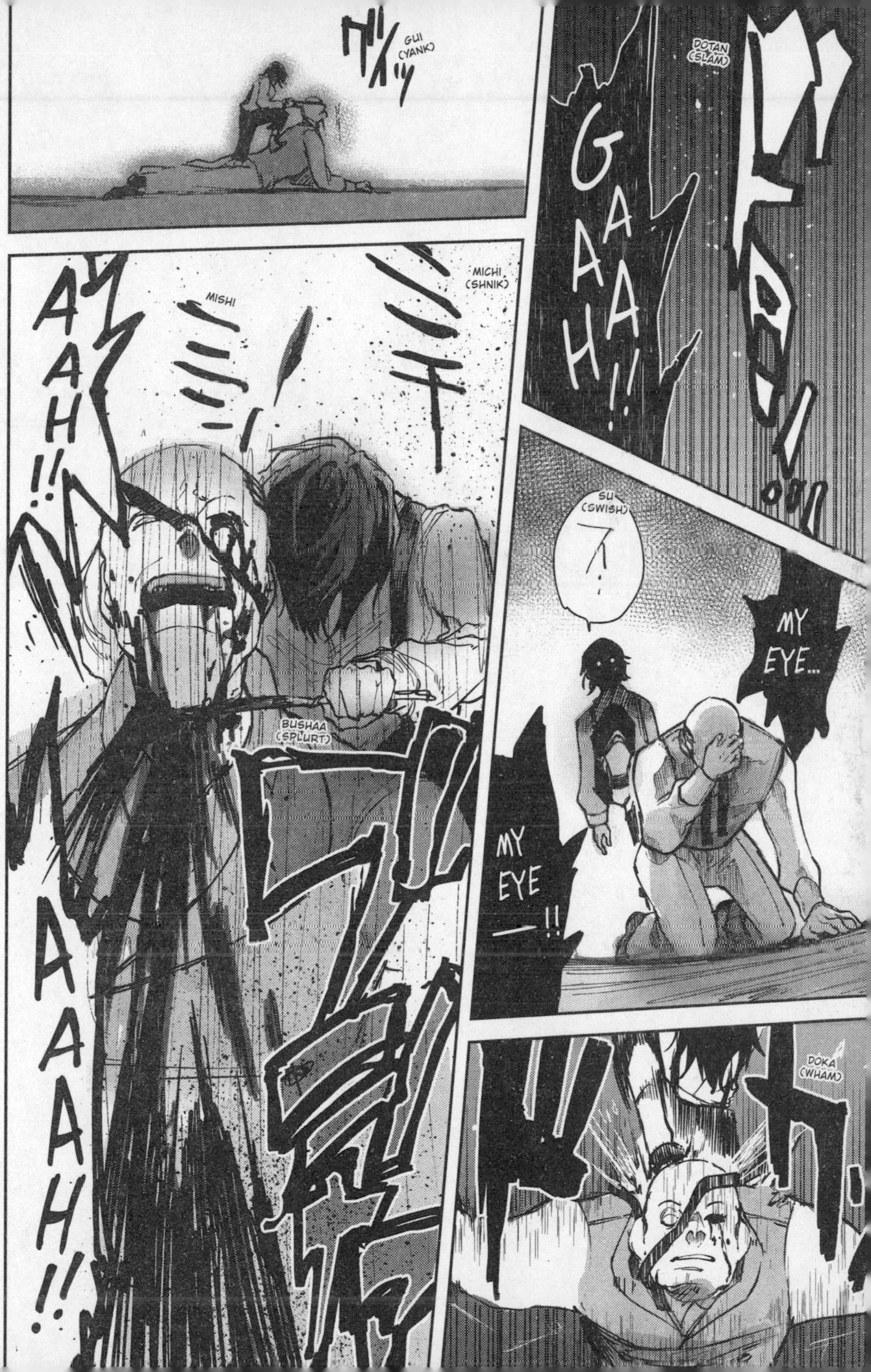

DOTAN (SLAM)
GAAAH!!
GUI (YANK)
SU (SWISH)
MY EYE...
MY EYE—!!
DOKA (WHAM)
MICHI (SHNIK)
MISHI
BUSHAA (SPLURT)
AAH!!
AAAAAH!!

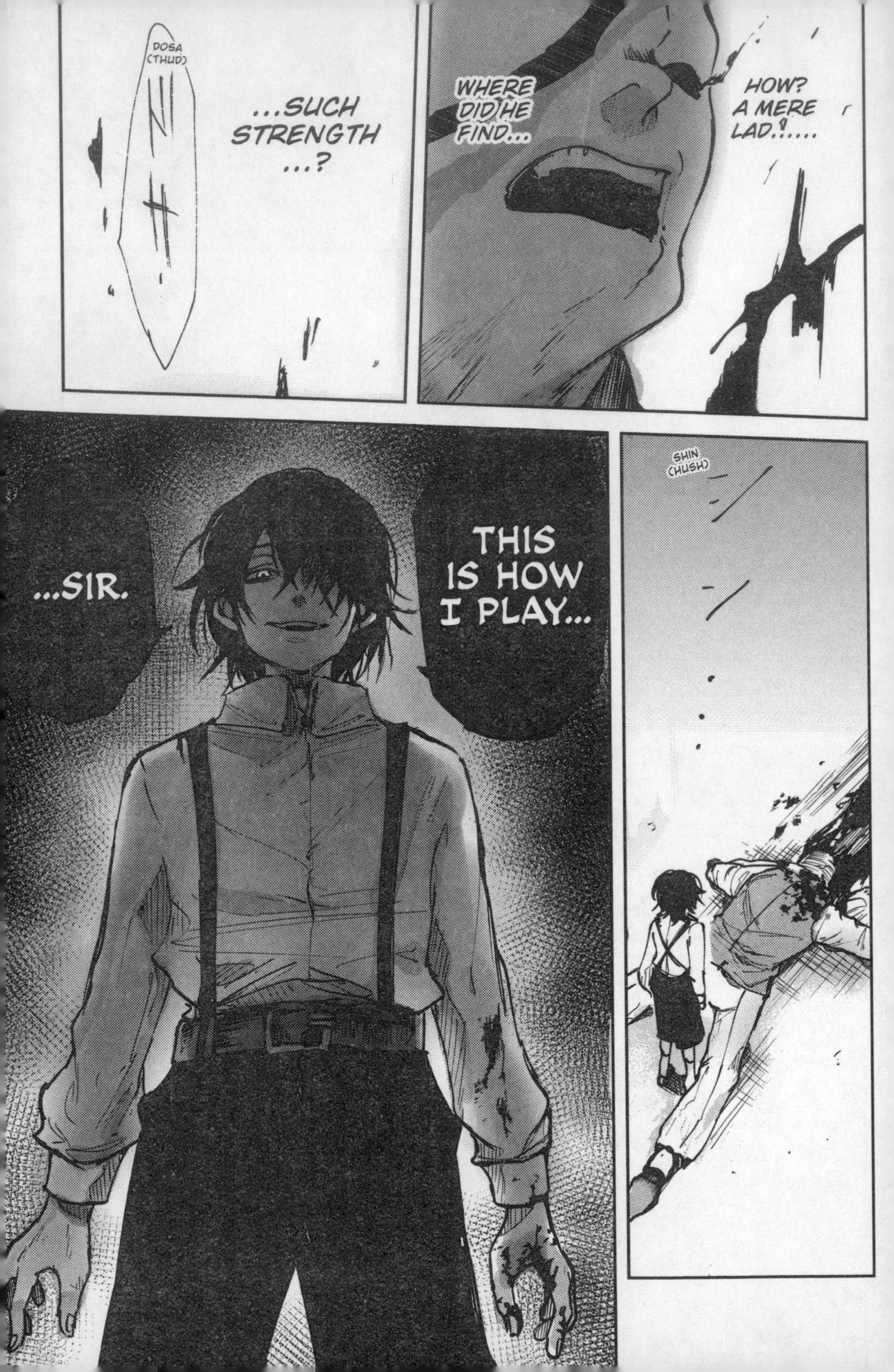
HOW? A MERE LAD!......
WHERE DID HE FIND...
...SUCH STRENGTH ...?
DOSA (THUD)
SHIN (HUSH)
THIS IS HOW I PLAY...
...SIR.

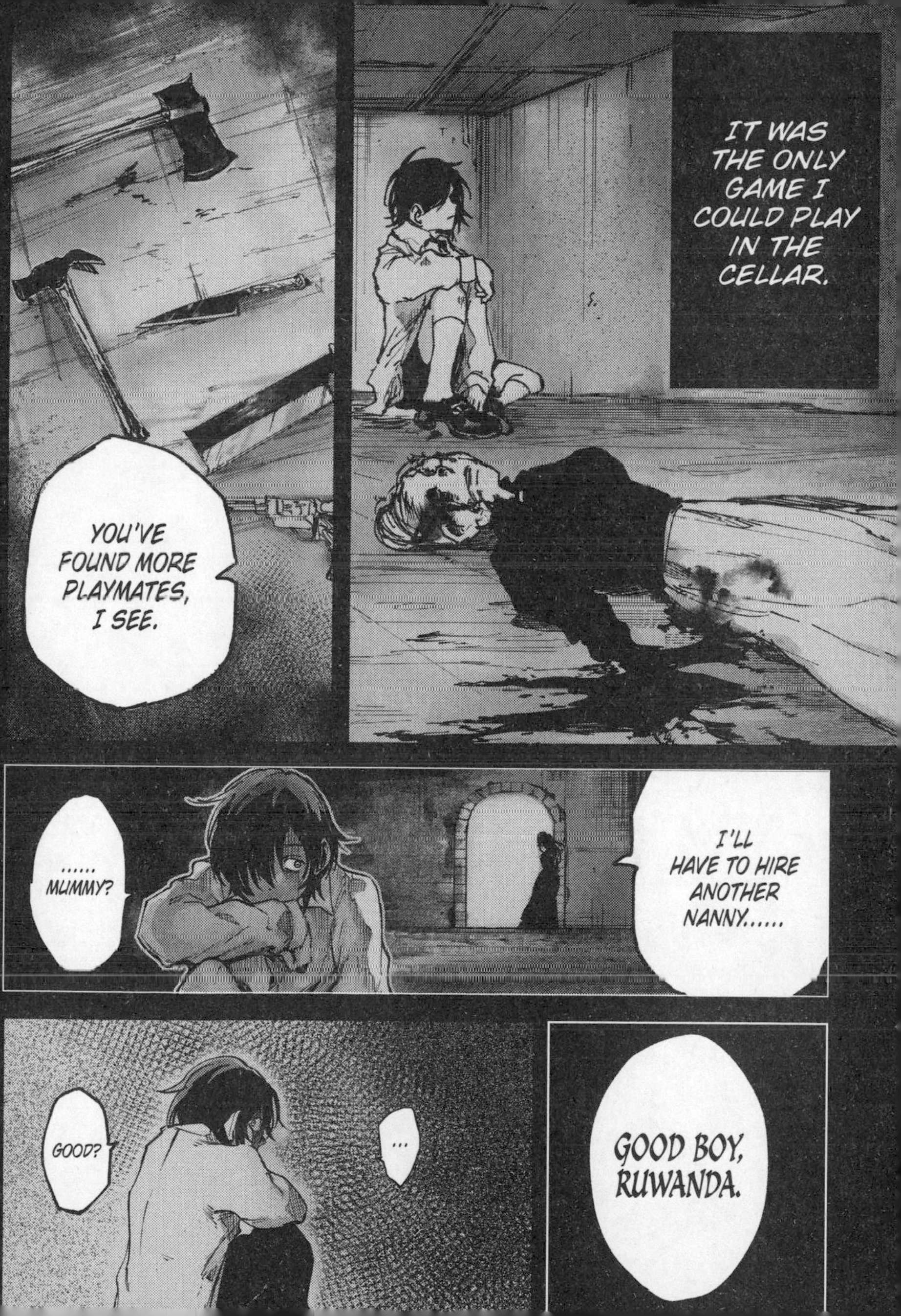
IT WAS THE ONLY GAME I COULD PLAY IN THE CELLAR.
YOU'VE FOUND MORE PLAYMATES, I SEE.
I'LL HAVE TO HIRE ANOTHER NANNY......
......MUMMY?
GOOD BOY, RUWANDA.
...
GOOD?

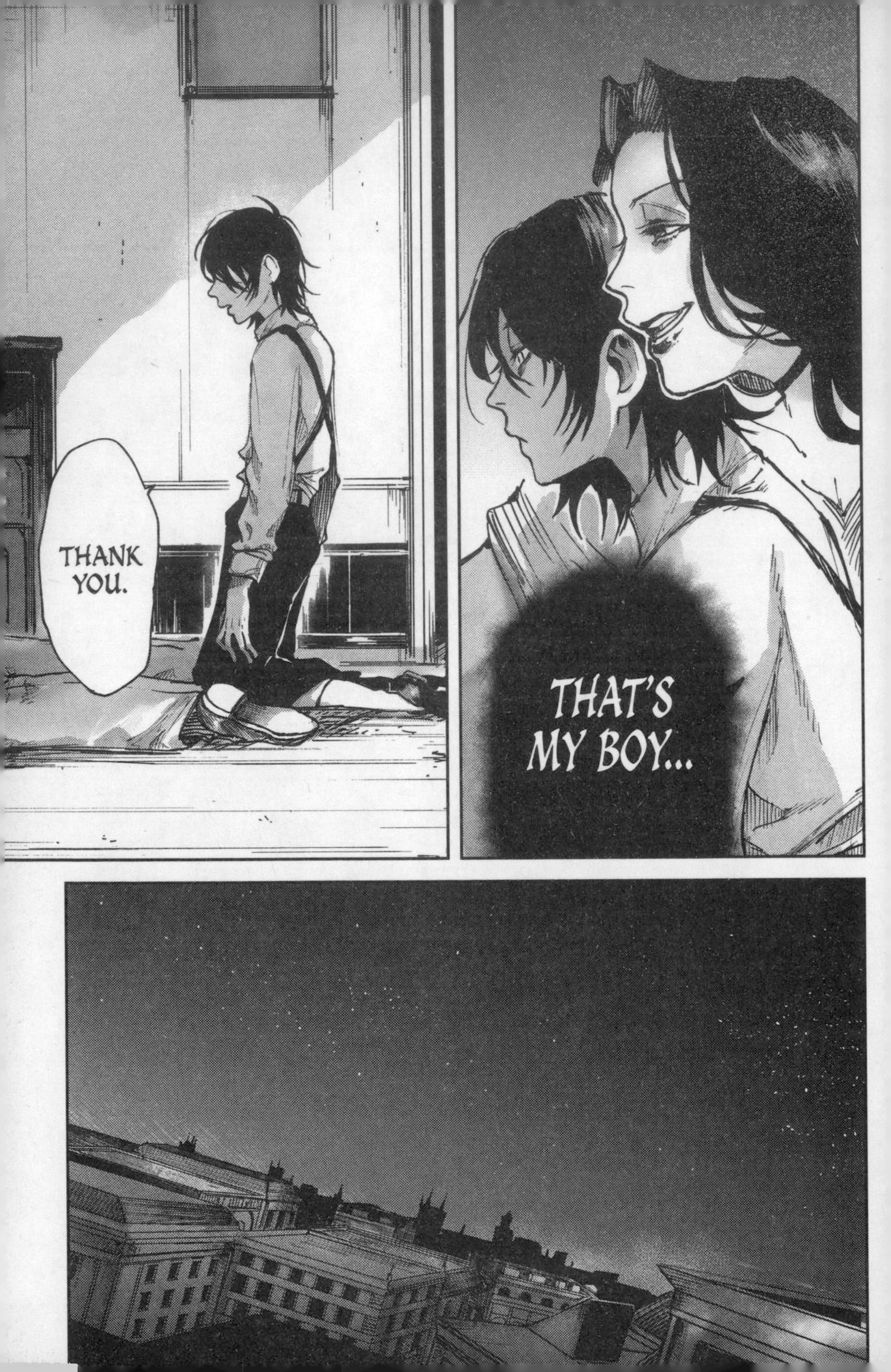
THAT'S MY BOY...
THANK YOU.

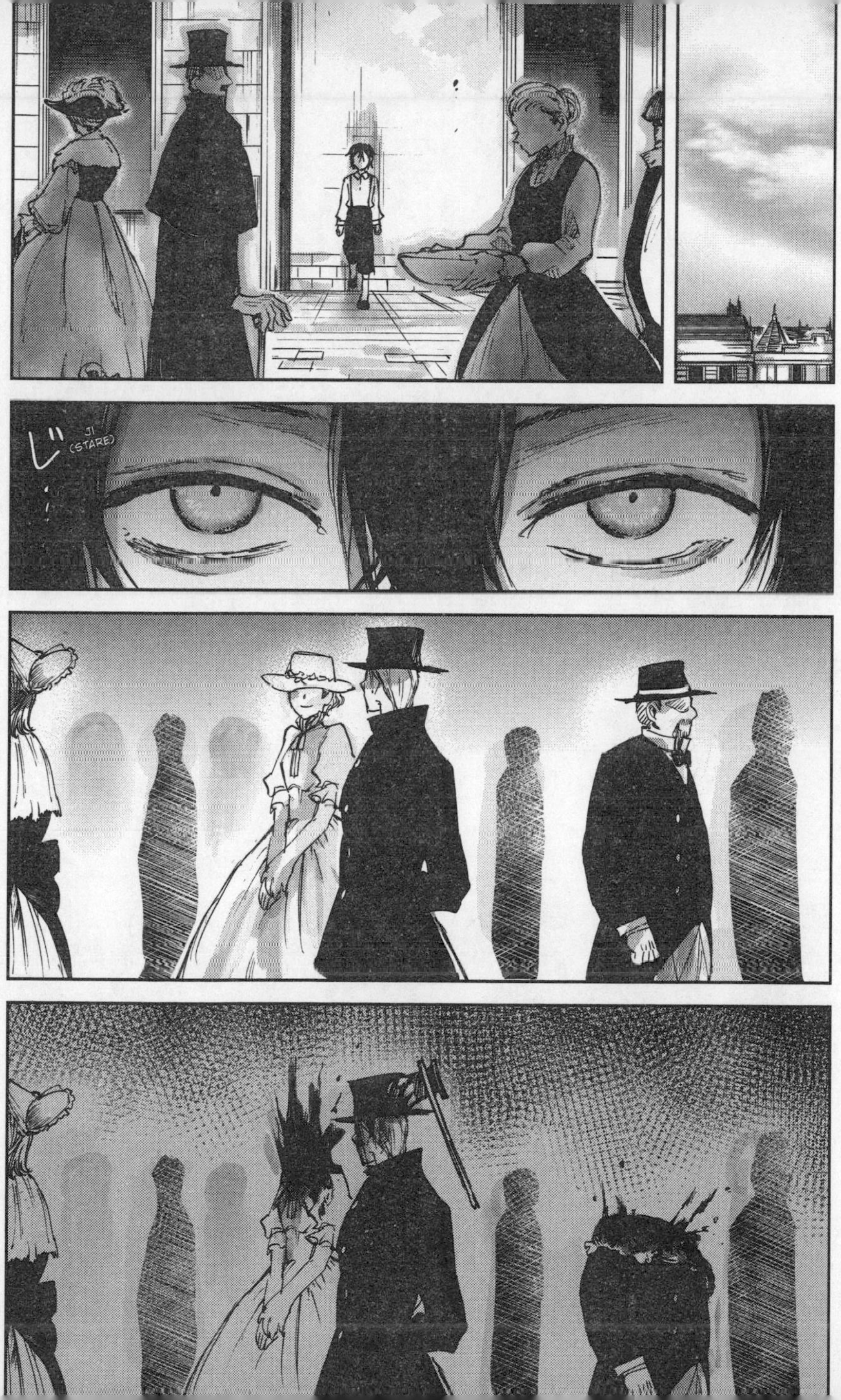
ジ…
JI (STARE)

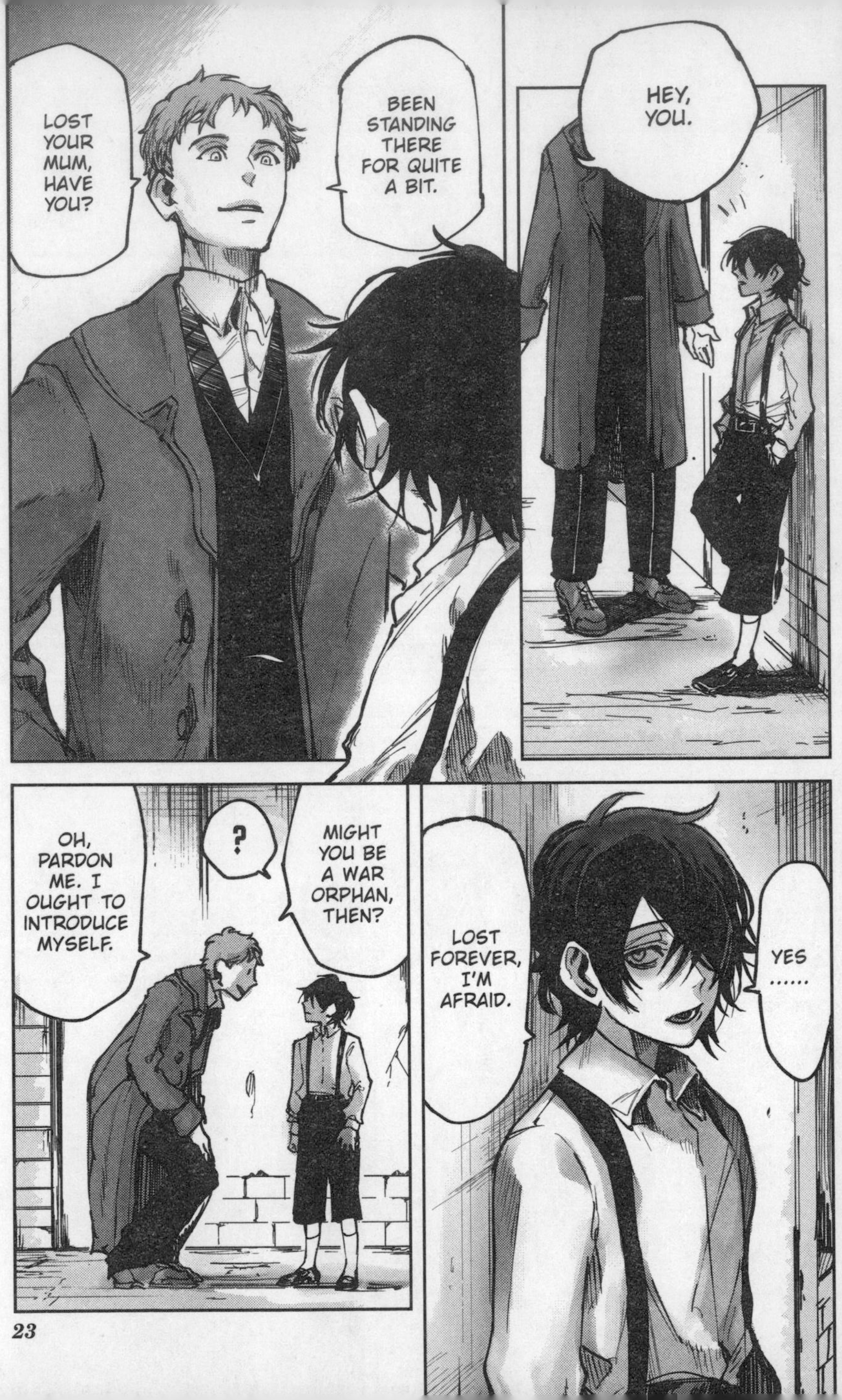
HEY, YOU.
BEEN STANDING THERE FOR QUITE A BIT.
LOST YOUR MUM, HAVE YOU?
YES ......
LOST FOREVER, I'M AFRAID.
MIGHT YOU BE A WAR ORPHAN, THEN?
?
OH, PARDON ME. I OUGHT TO INTRODUCE MYSELF.

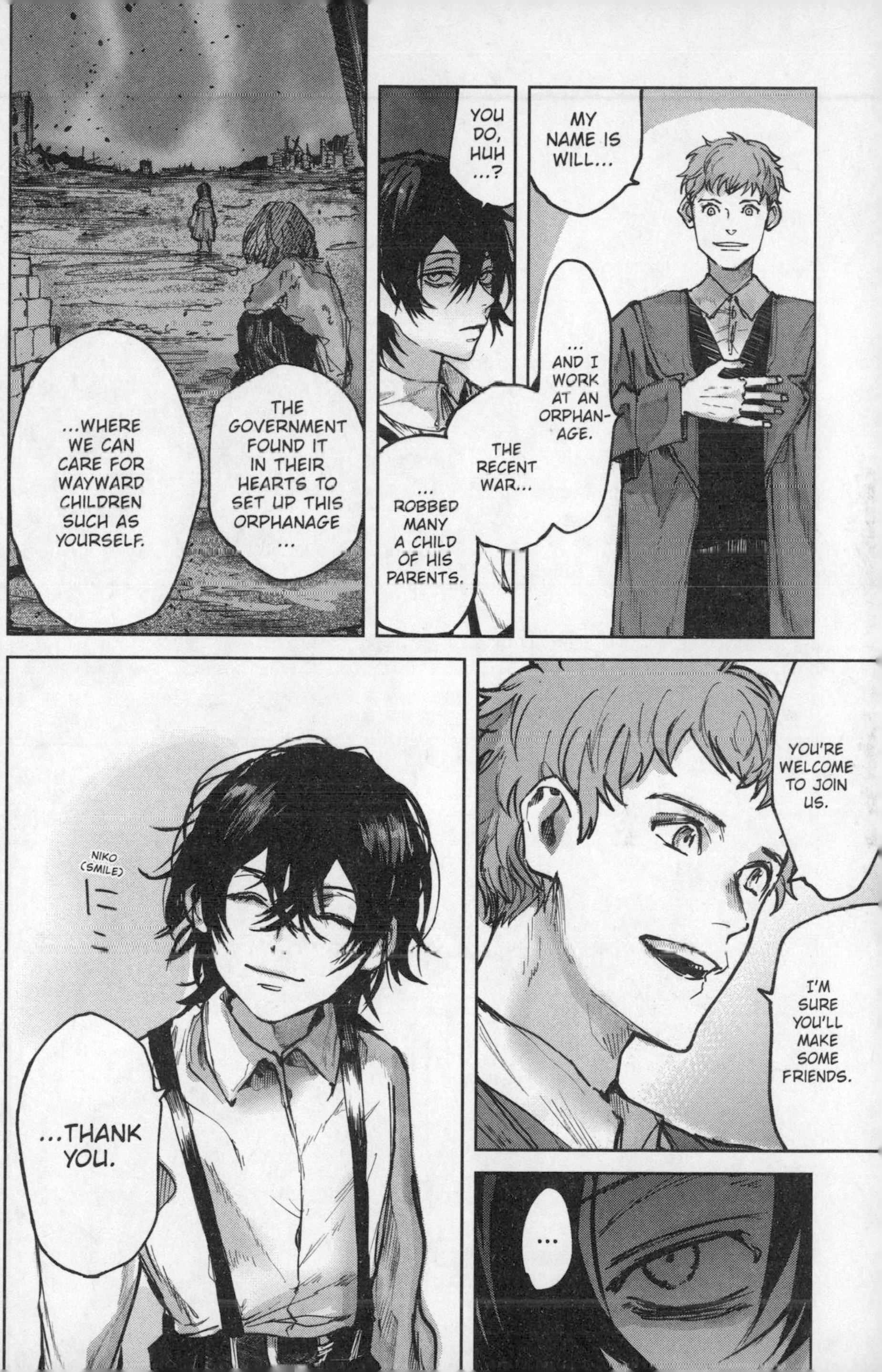

MY NAME IS WILL...
...AND I WORK AT AN ORPHANAGE.
YOU DO, HUH ...?
THE RECENT WAR...
...ROBBED MANY A CHILD OF HIS PARENTS.
THE GOVERNMENT FOUND IT IN THEIR HEARTS TO SET UP THIS ORPHANAGE ...
...WHERE WE CAN CARE FOR WAYWARD CHILDREN SUCH AS YOURSELF.
YOU'RE WELCOME TO JOIN US.
I'M SURE YOU'LL MAKE SOME FRIENDS.
...
NIKO (SMILE)
...THANK YOU.

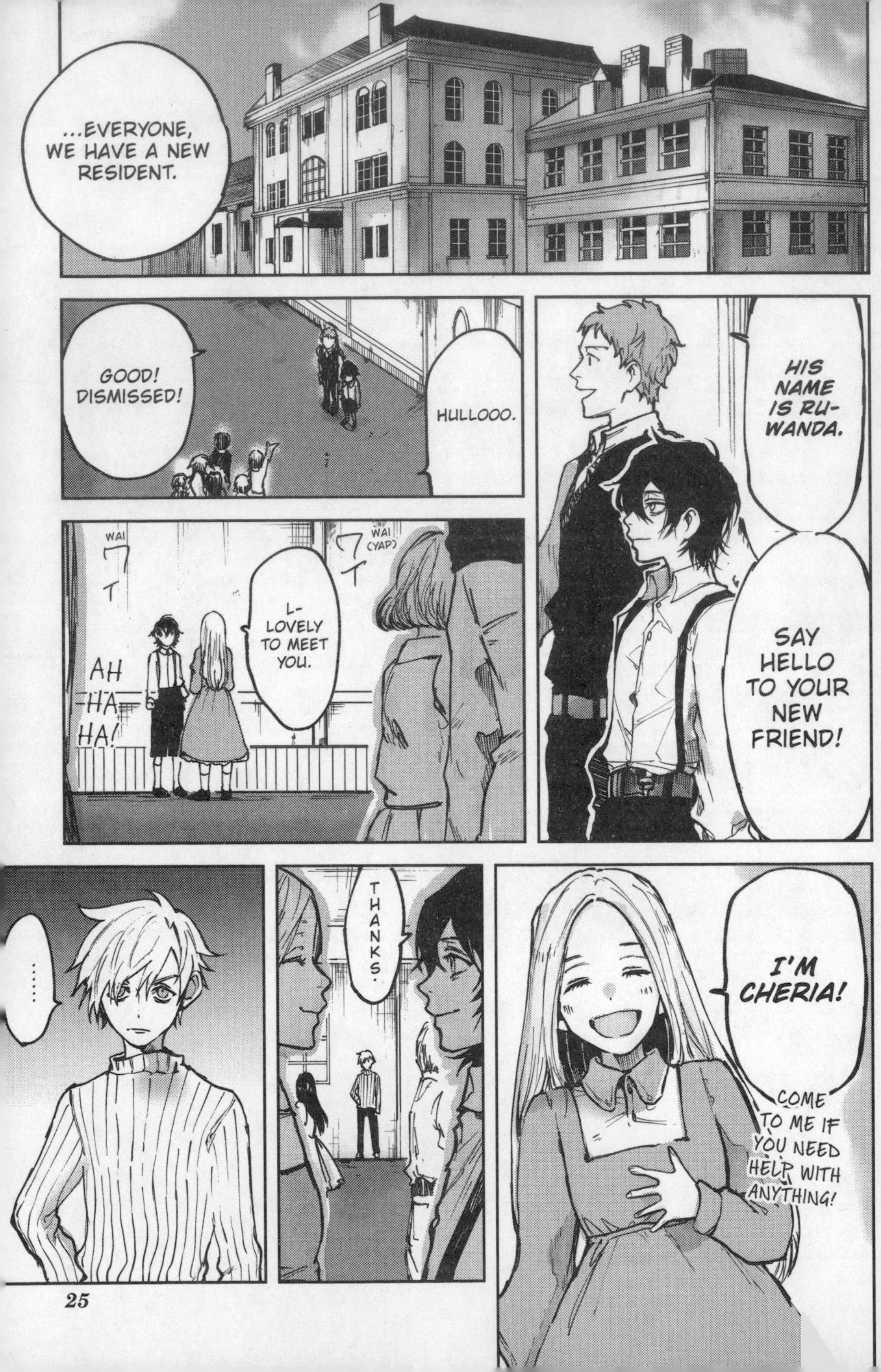
...EVERYONE, WE HAVE A NEW RESIDENT.
HIS NAME IS RU-WANDA.
SAY HELLO TO YOUR NEW FRIEND!
HULLOOO.
GOOD! DISMISSED!
WAI (YAP)
L-LOVELY TO MEET YOU.
WAI
AH HA HA!
I'M CHERIA!
COME TO ME IF YOU NEED HELP WITH ANYTHING!
THANKS.
......

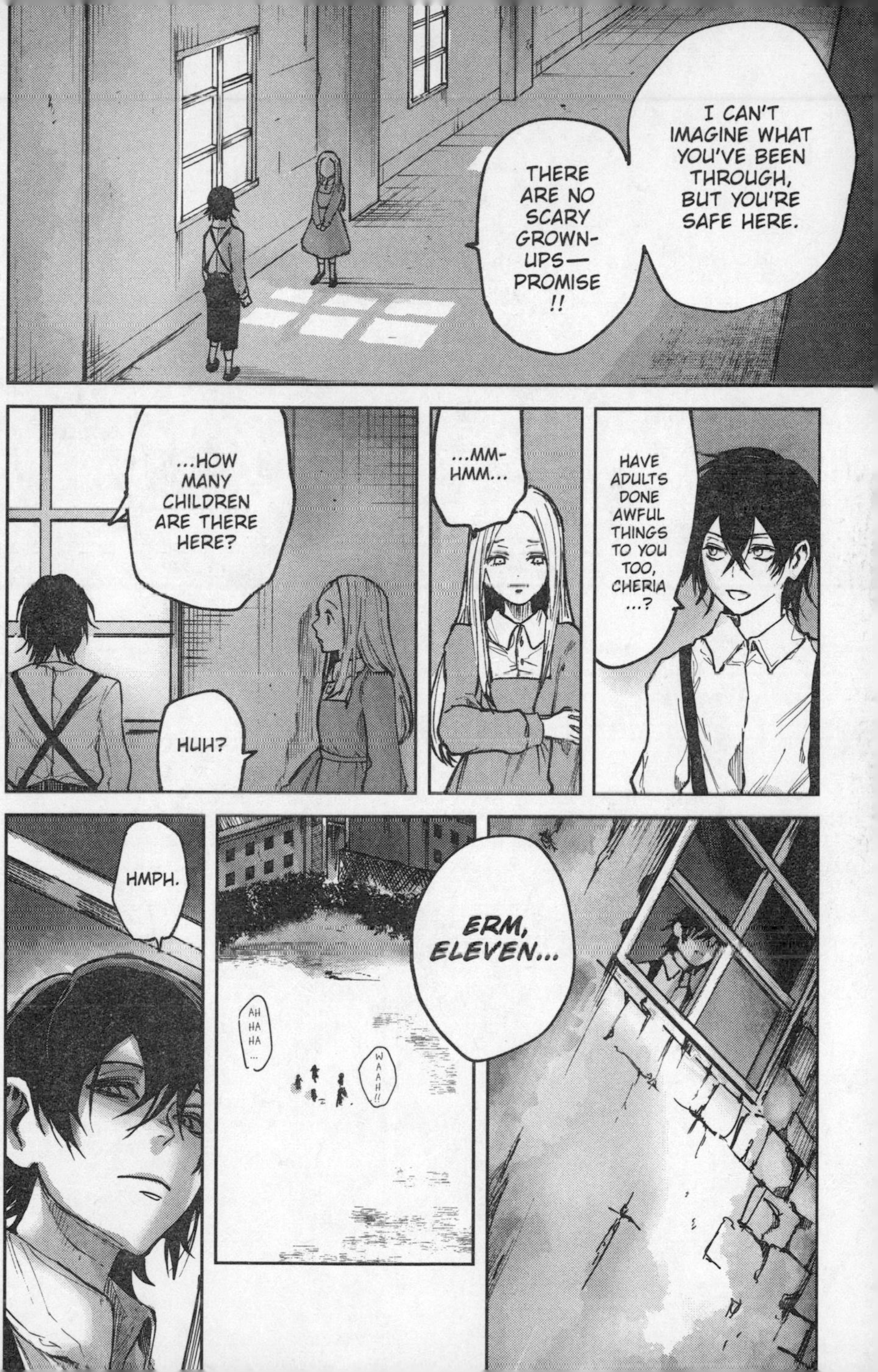
I CAN'T IMAGINE WHAT YOU'VE BEEN THROUGH, BUT YOU'RE SAFE HERE.
THERE ARE NO SCARY GROWN-UPS—PROMISE!!
HAVE ADULTS DONE AWFUL THINGS TO YOU TOO, CHERIA...?
...MM-HMM...
...HOW MANY CHILDREN ARE THERE HERE?
HUH?
ERM, ELEVEN...
WAAH!!
AH HA HA...
HMPH.

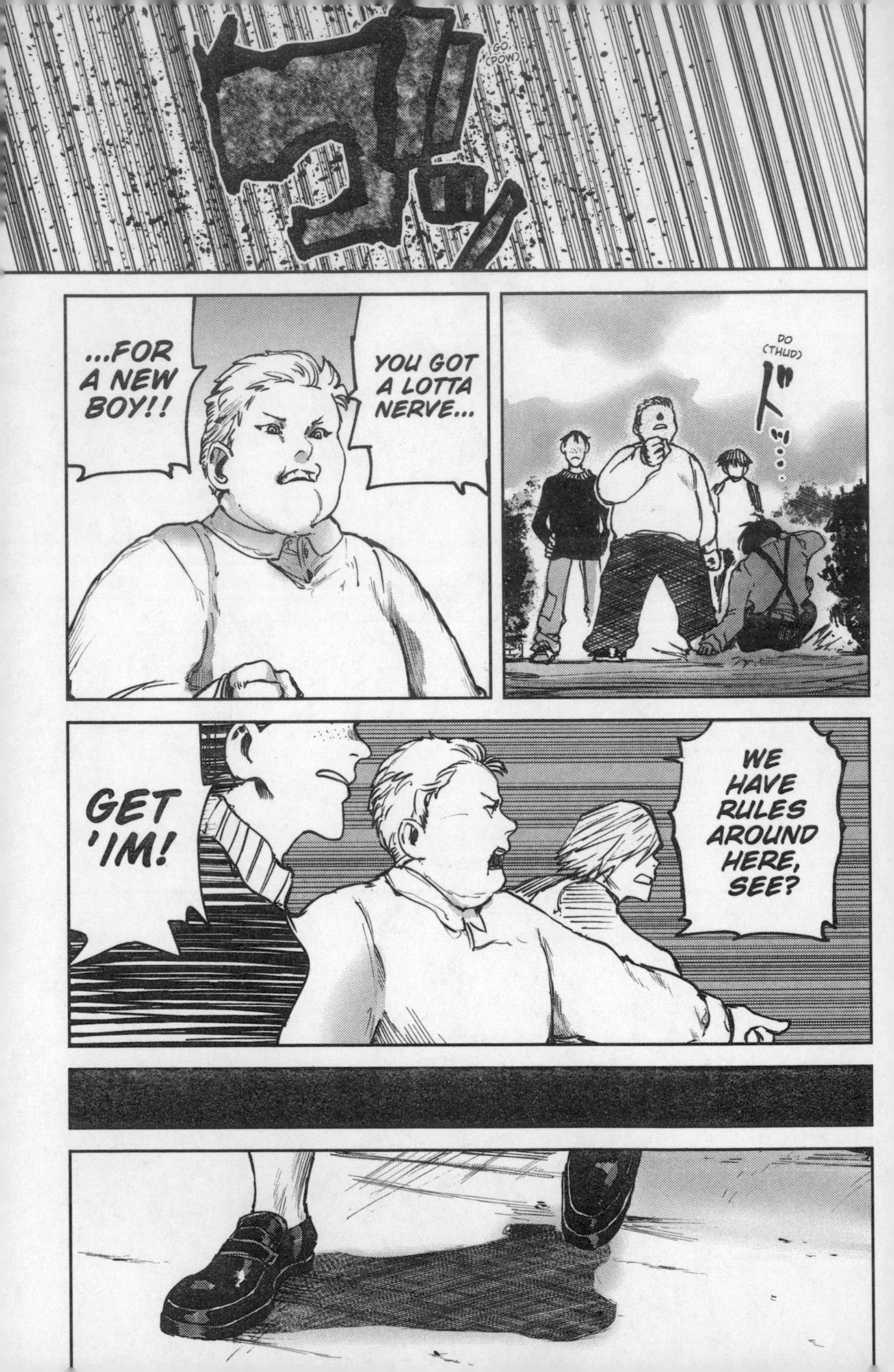
GO (POW)
DO (THUD)
YOU GOT A LOTTA NERVE...
...FOR A NEW BOY!!
WE HAVE RULES AROUND HERE, SEE?
GET 'IM!

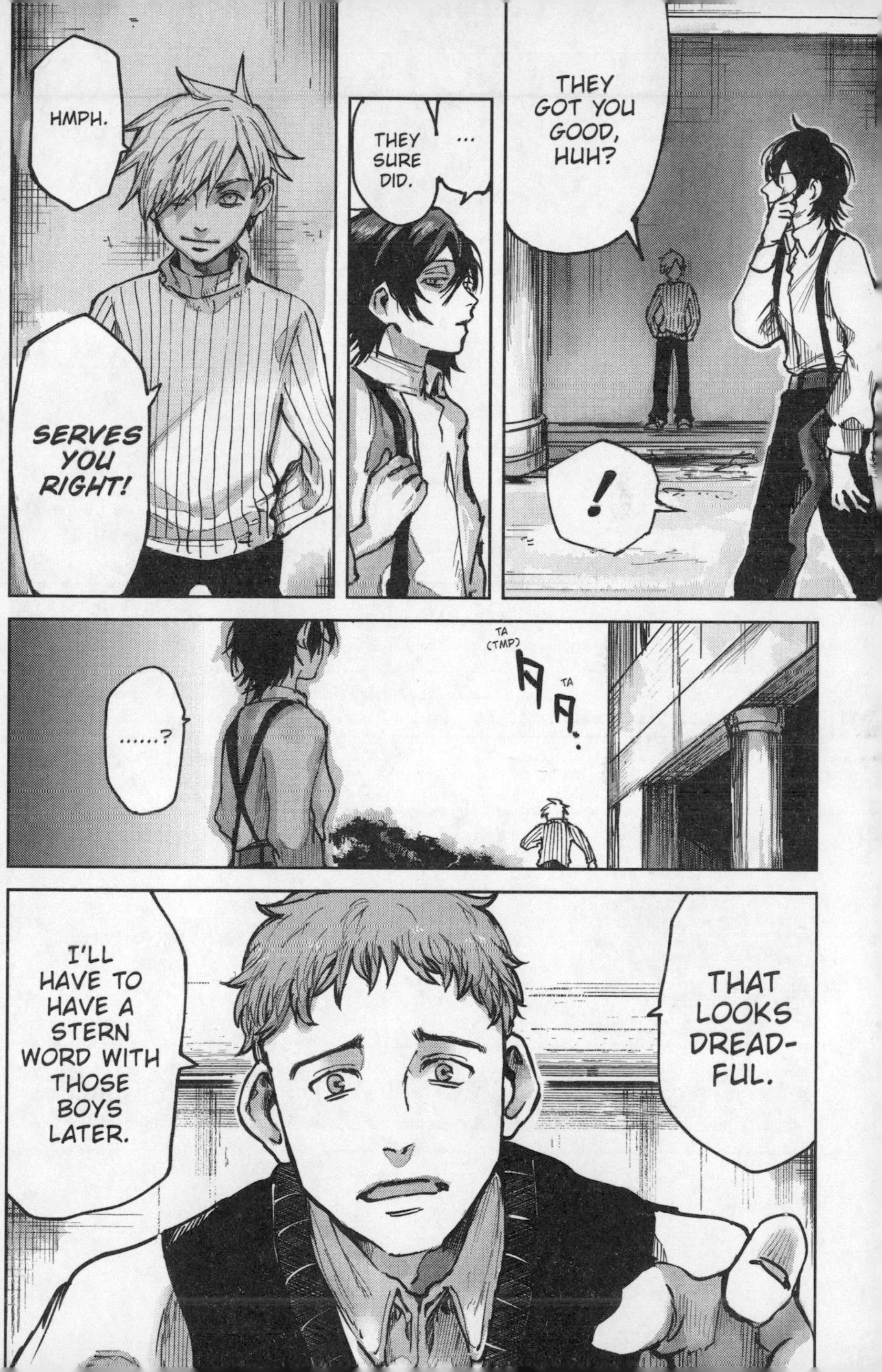
THEY GOT YOU GOOD, HUH?
!
...
THEY SURE DID.
HMPH.
SERVES YOU RIGHT!
TA (TMP) TA
......?
THAT LOOKS DREAD-FUL.
I'LL HAVE TO HAVE A STERN WORD WITH THOSE BOYS LATER.

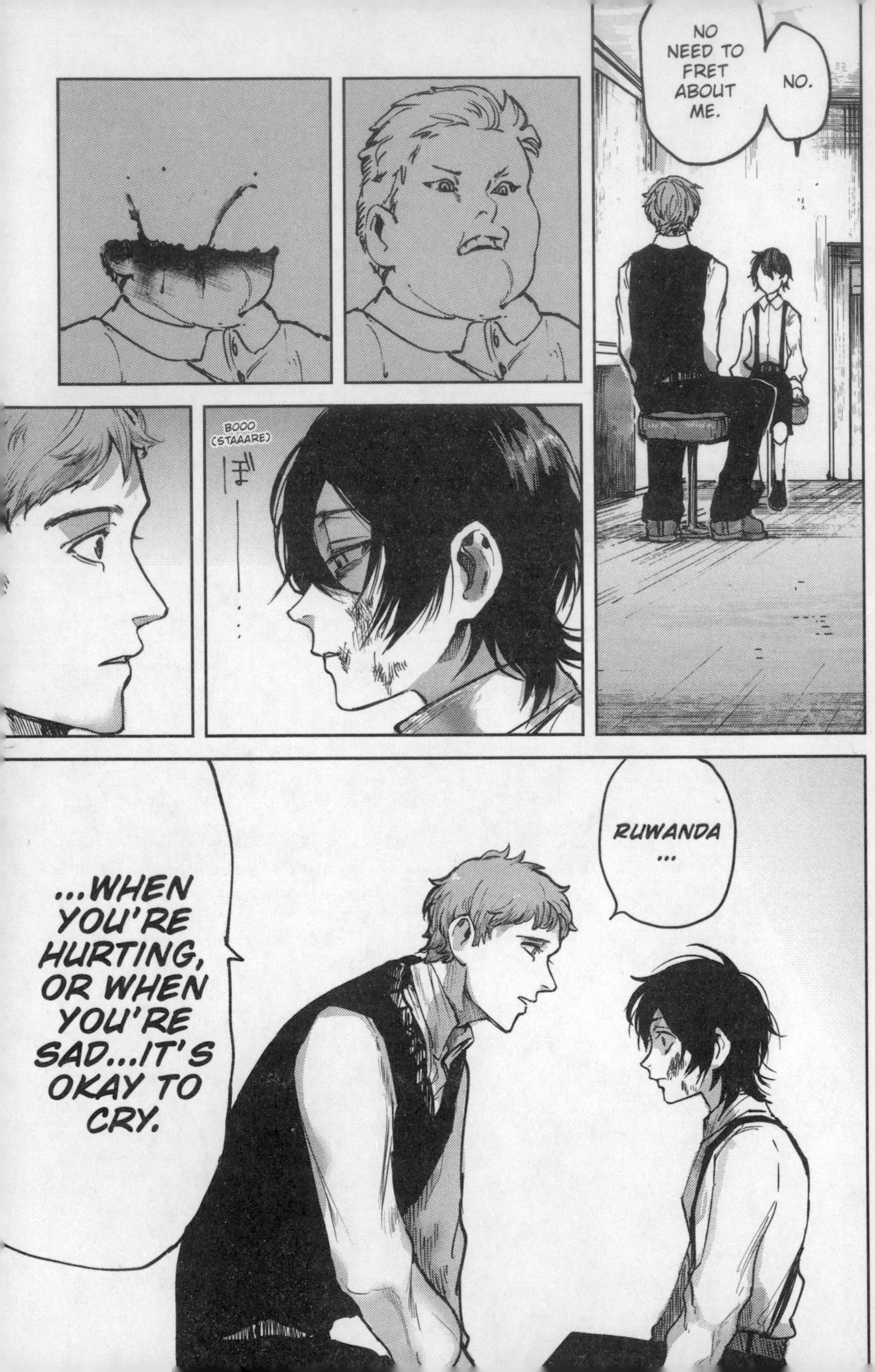
NO.
NO NEED TO FRET ABOUT ME.
BOOO (STAAARE)
RUWANDA ...
...WHEN YOU'RE HURTING, OR WHEN YOU'RE SAD...IT'S OKAY TO CRY.

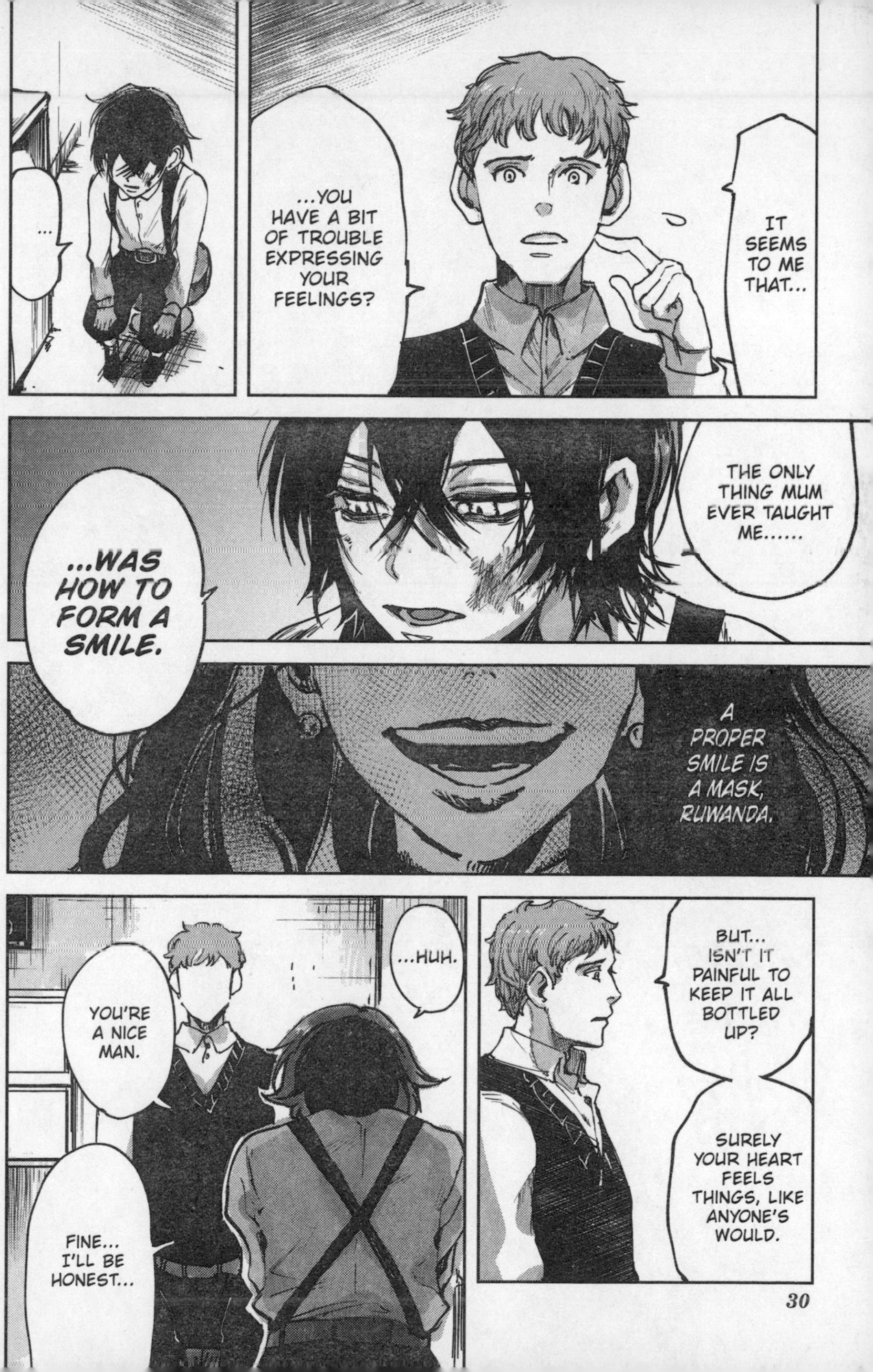
IT SEEMS TO ME THAT...
...YOU HAVE A BIT OF TROUBLE EXPRESSING YOUR FEELINGS?
...
THE ONLY THING MUM EVER TAUGHT ME......
...WAS HOW TO FORM A SMILE.
A PROPER SMILE IS A MASK, RUWANDA.
BUT... ISN'T IT PAINFUL TO KEEP IT ALL BOTTLED UP?
SURELY YOUR HEART FEELS THINGS, LIKE ANYONE'S WOULD.
...HUH.
YOU'RE A NICE MAN.
FINE... I'LL BE HONEST...

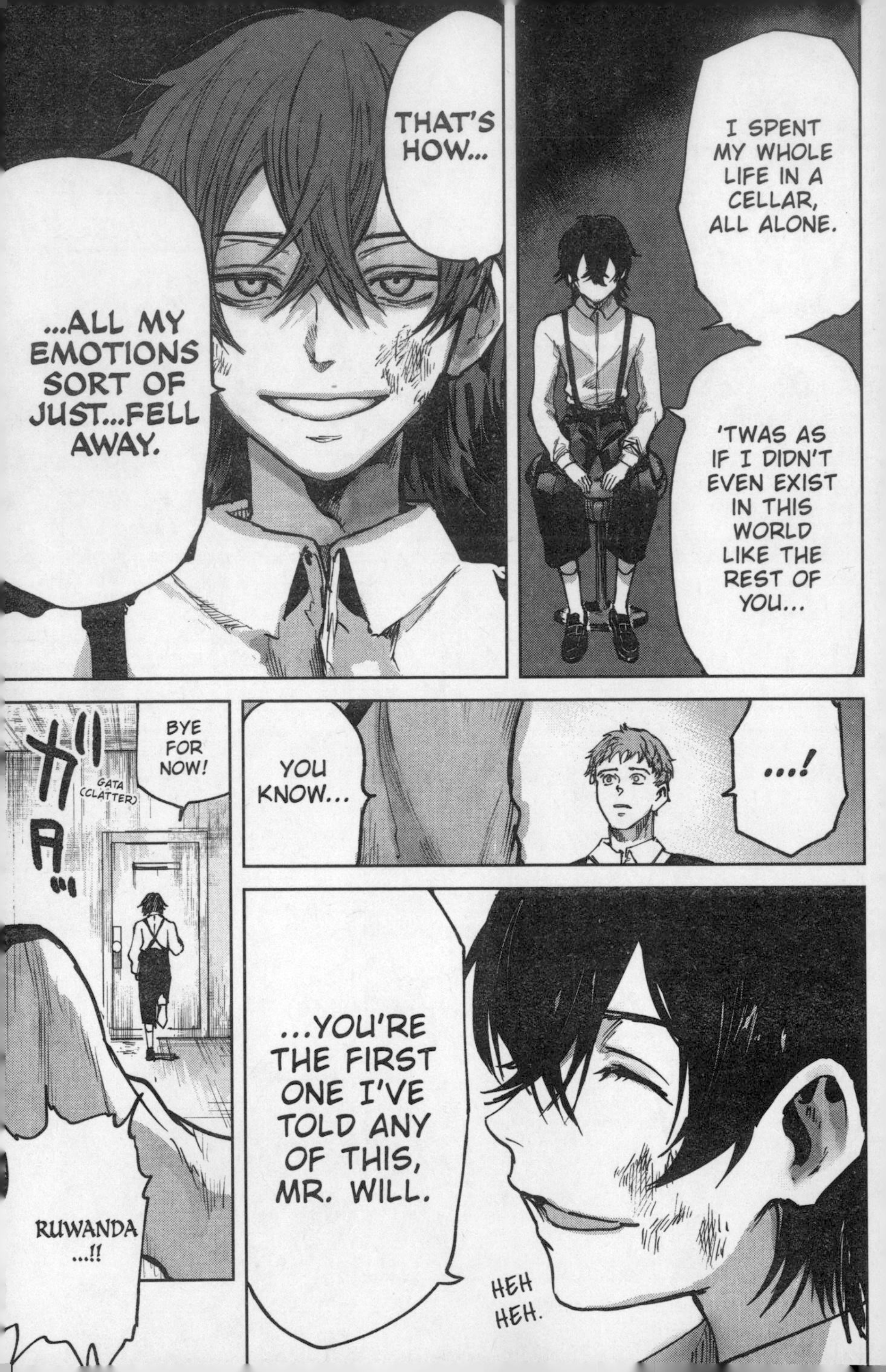
I SPENT MY WHOLE LIFE IN A CELLAR, ALL ALONE.
'TWAS AS IF I DIDN'T EVEN EXIST IN THIS WORLD LIKE THE REST OF YOU...
THAT'S HOW...
...ALL MY EMOTIONS SORT OF JUST...FELL AWAY.
...!
YOU KNOW...
...YOU'RE THE FIRST ONE I'VE TOLD ANY OF THIS, MR. WILL.
HEH HEH.
BYE FOR NOW!
GATA (CLATTER)
RUWANDA ...!!

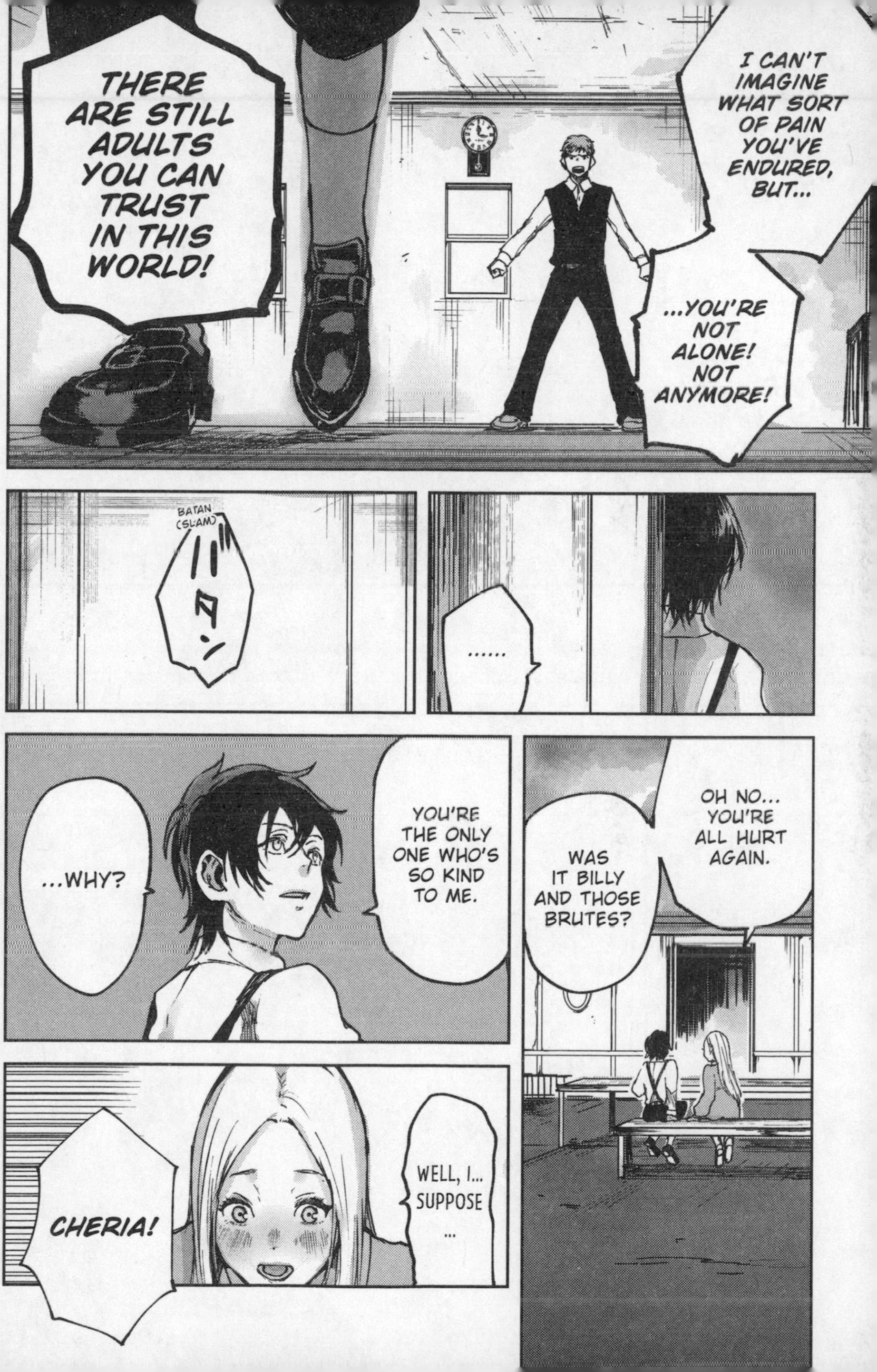
I CAN'T IMAGINE WHAT SORT OF PAIN YOU'VE ENDURED, BUT...
...YOU'RE NOT ALONE! NOT ANYMORE!
THERE ARE STILL ADULTS YOU CAN TRUST IN THIS WORLD!
......
BATAN (SLAM)
バタン
OH NO... YOU'RE ALL HURT AGAIN.
WAS IT BILLY AND THOSE BRUTES?
YOU'RE THE ONLY ONE WHO'S SO KIND TO ME.
...WHY?
WELL, I... SUPPOSE ...
CHERIA!

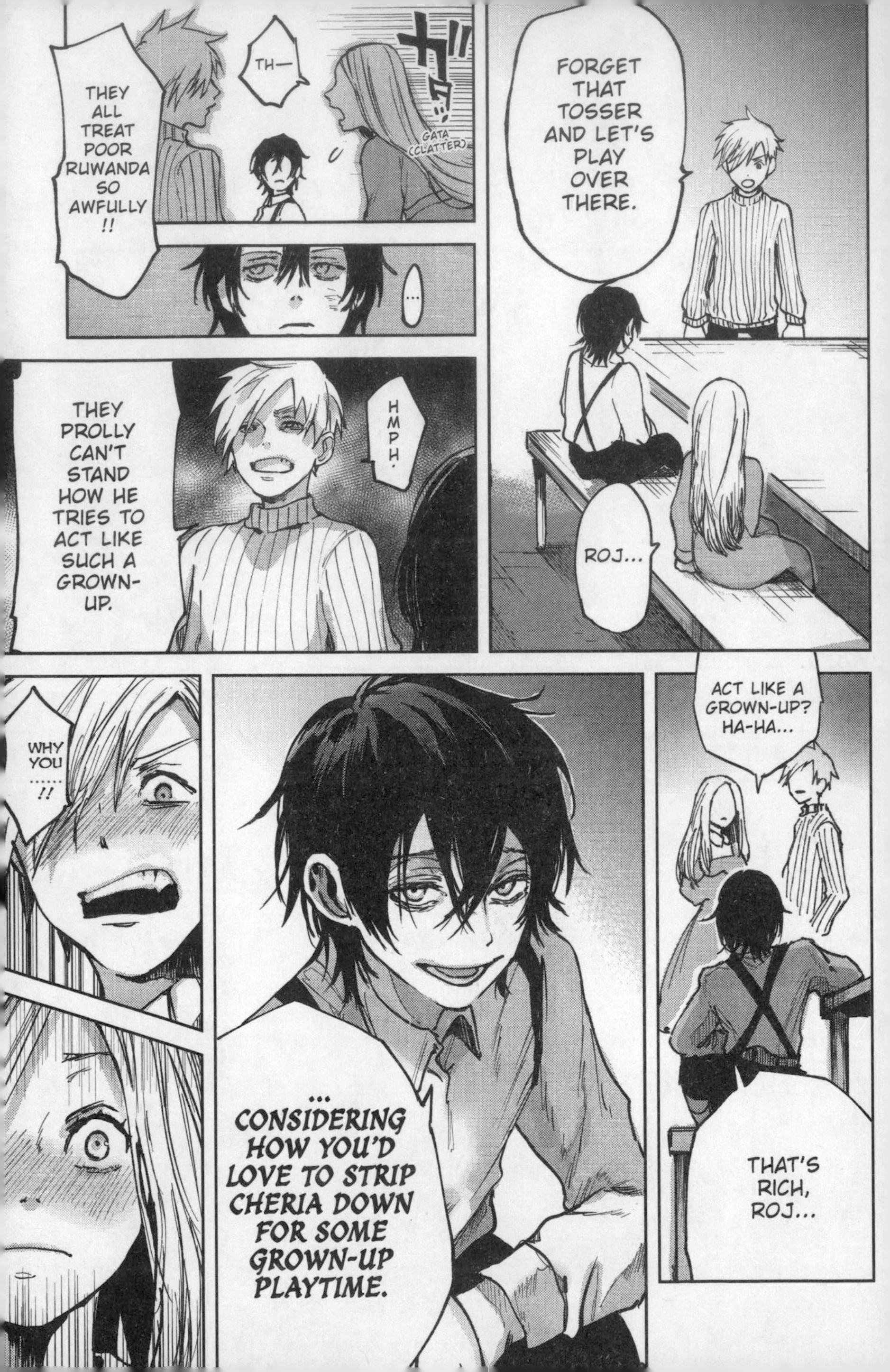
FORGET THAT TOSSER AND LET'S PLAY OVER THERE.
ROJ...
GATA (CLATTER)
TH—
THEY ALL TREAT POOR RUWANDA SO AWFULLY!!
...
HMPH.
THEY PROLLY CAN'T STAND HOW HE TRIES TO ACT LIKE SUCH A GROWN-UP.
ACT LIKE A GROWN-UP? HA-HA...
THAT'S RICH, ROJ...
...CONSIDERING HOW YOU'D LOVE TO STRIP CHERIA DOWN FOR SOME GROWN-UP PLAYTIME.
WHY YOU......!!

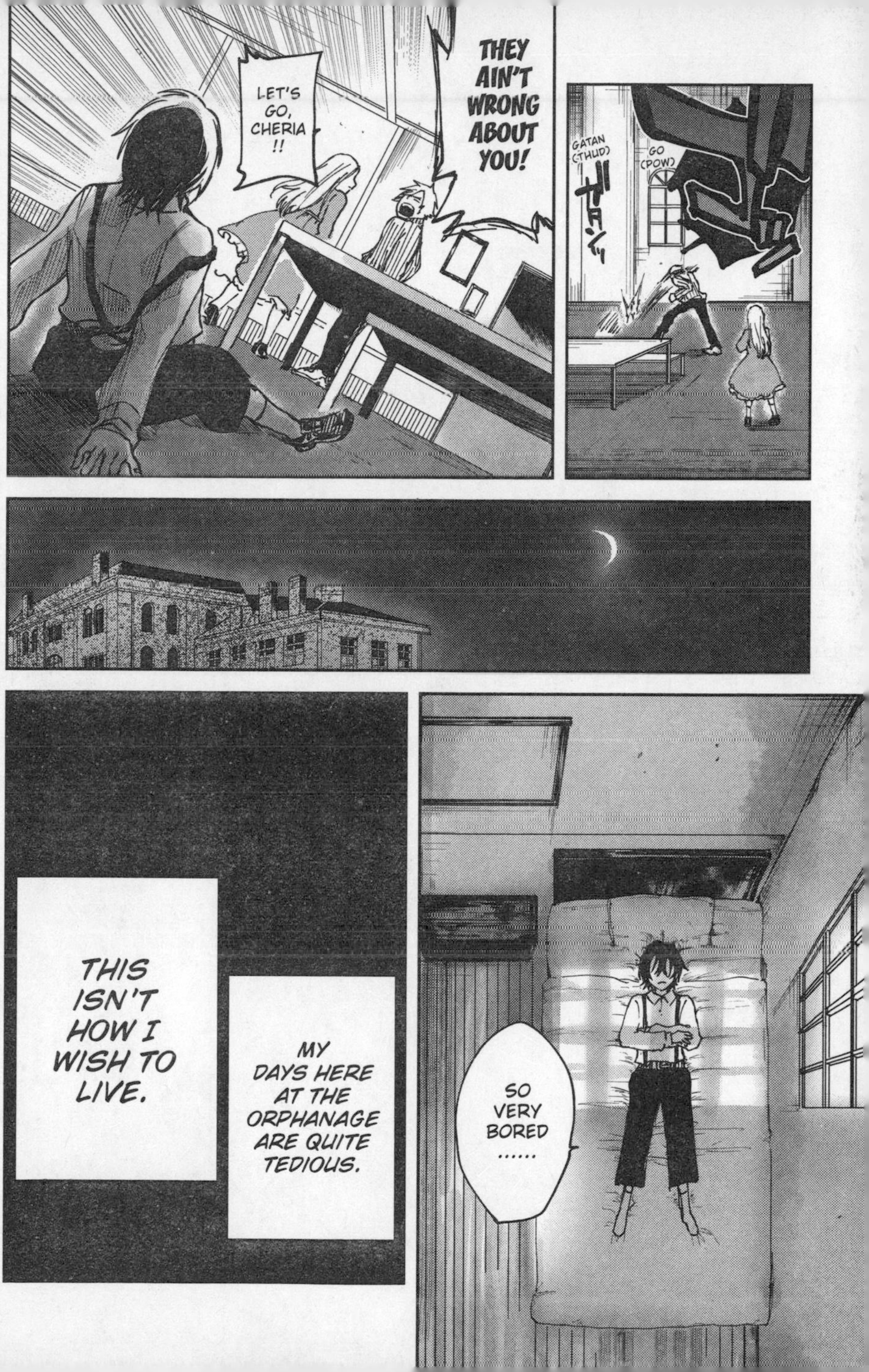
GATAN (THUD)
GO (POW)
THEY AIN'T WRONG ABOUT YOU!
LET'S GO, CHERIA!!
SO VERY BORED......
MY DAYS HERE AT THE ORPHANAGE ARE QUITE TEDIOUS.
THIS ISN'T HOW I WISH TO LIVE.

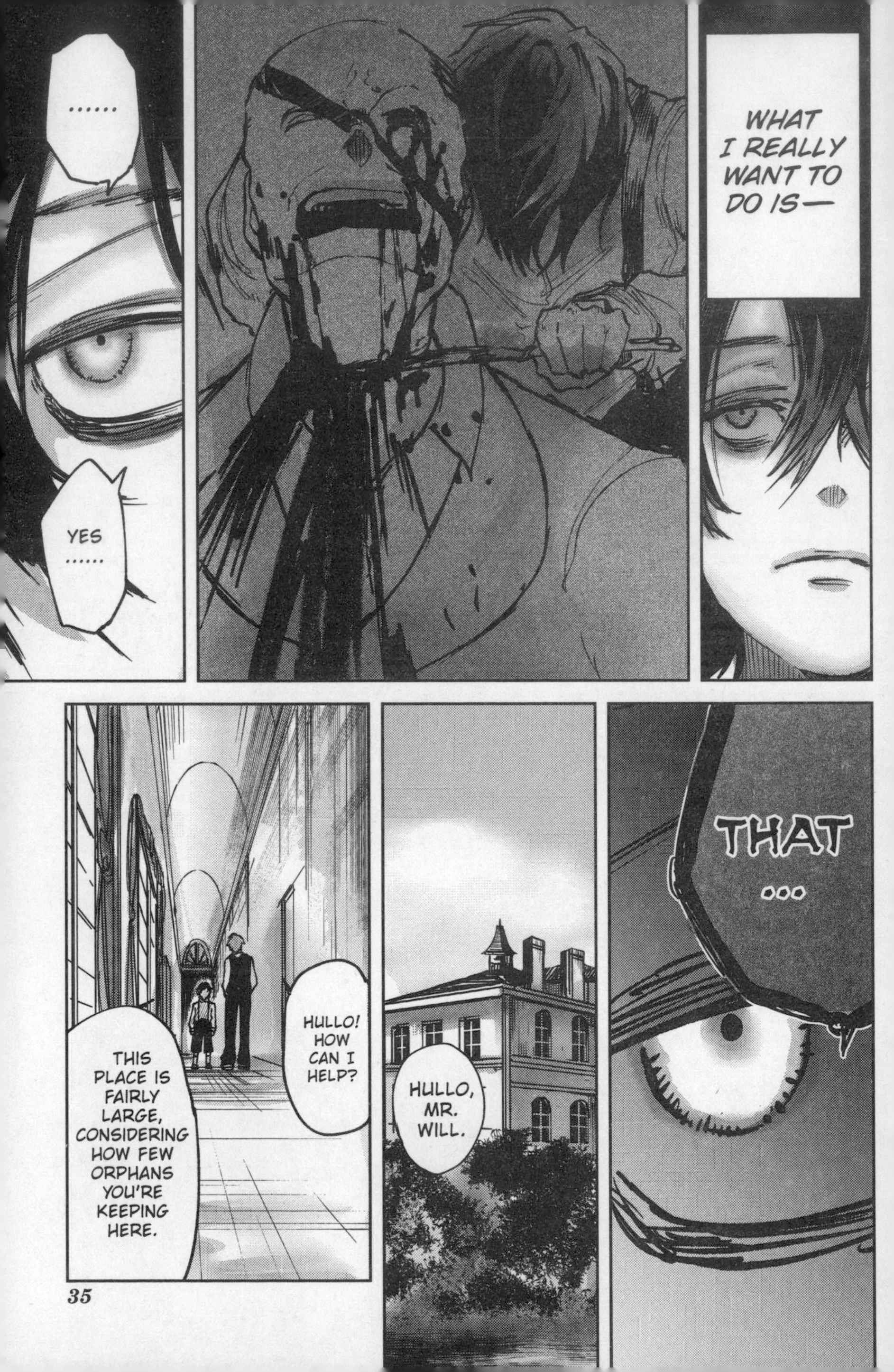
WHAT I REALLY WANT TO DO IS—
......
YES ......
THAT ...
HULLO, MR. WILL.
HULLO! HOW CAN I HELP?
THIS PLACE IS FAIRLY LARGE, CONSIDERING HOW FEW ORPHANS YOU'RE KEEPING HERE.

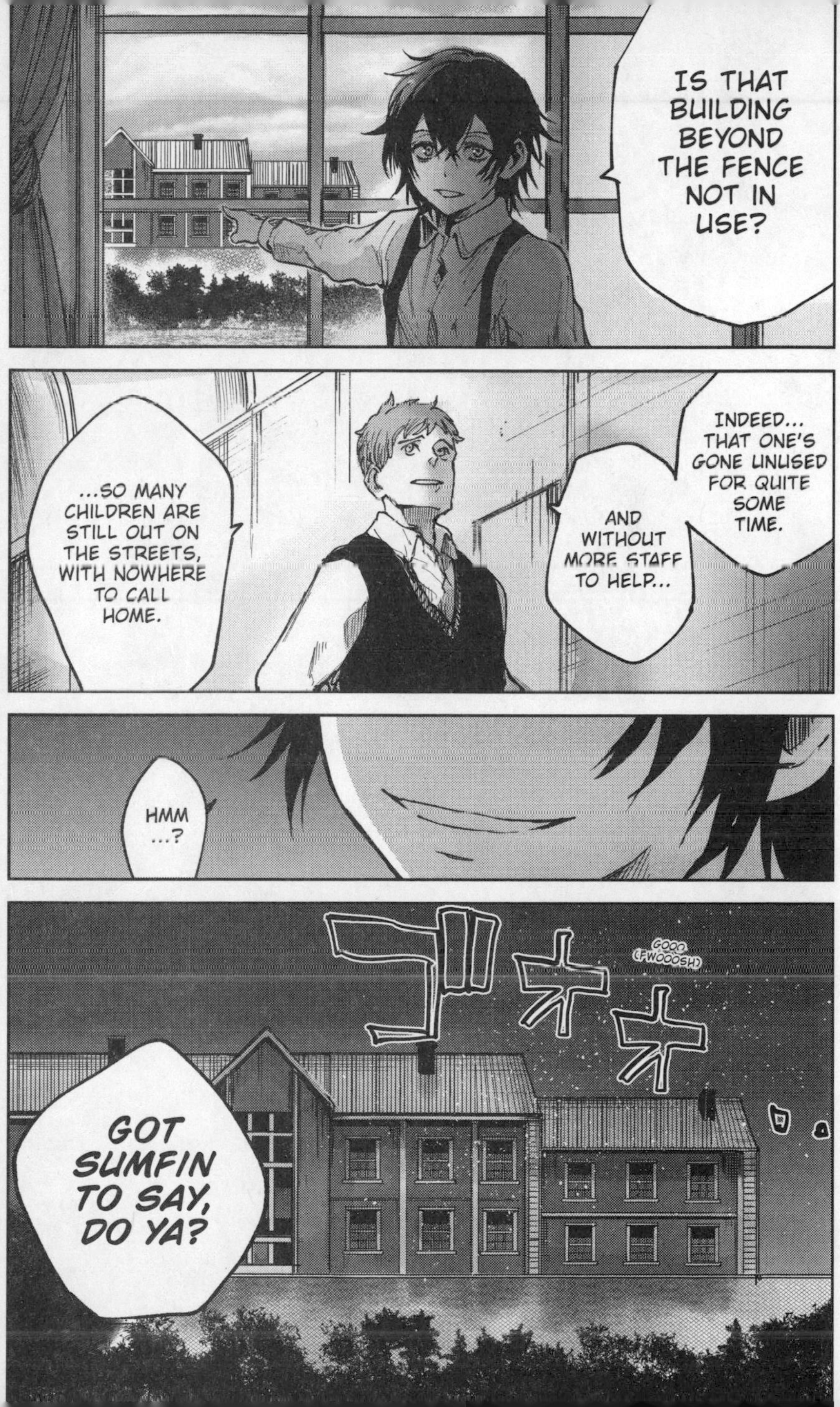
IS THAT BUILDING BEYOND THE FENCE NOT IN USE?
INDEED... THAT ONE'S GONE UNUSED FOR QUITE SOME TIME.
AND WITHOUT MORE STAFF TO HELP...
...SO MANY CHILDREN ARE STILL OUT ON THE STREETS, WITH NOWHERE TO CALL HOME.
HMM ...?
GOOO (FWOOOSH)
GOT SUMFIN TO SAY, DO YA?

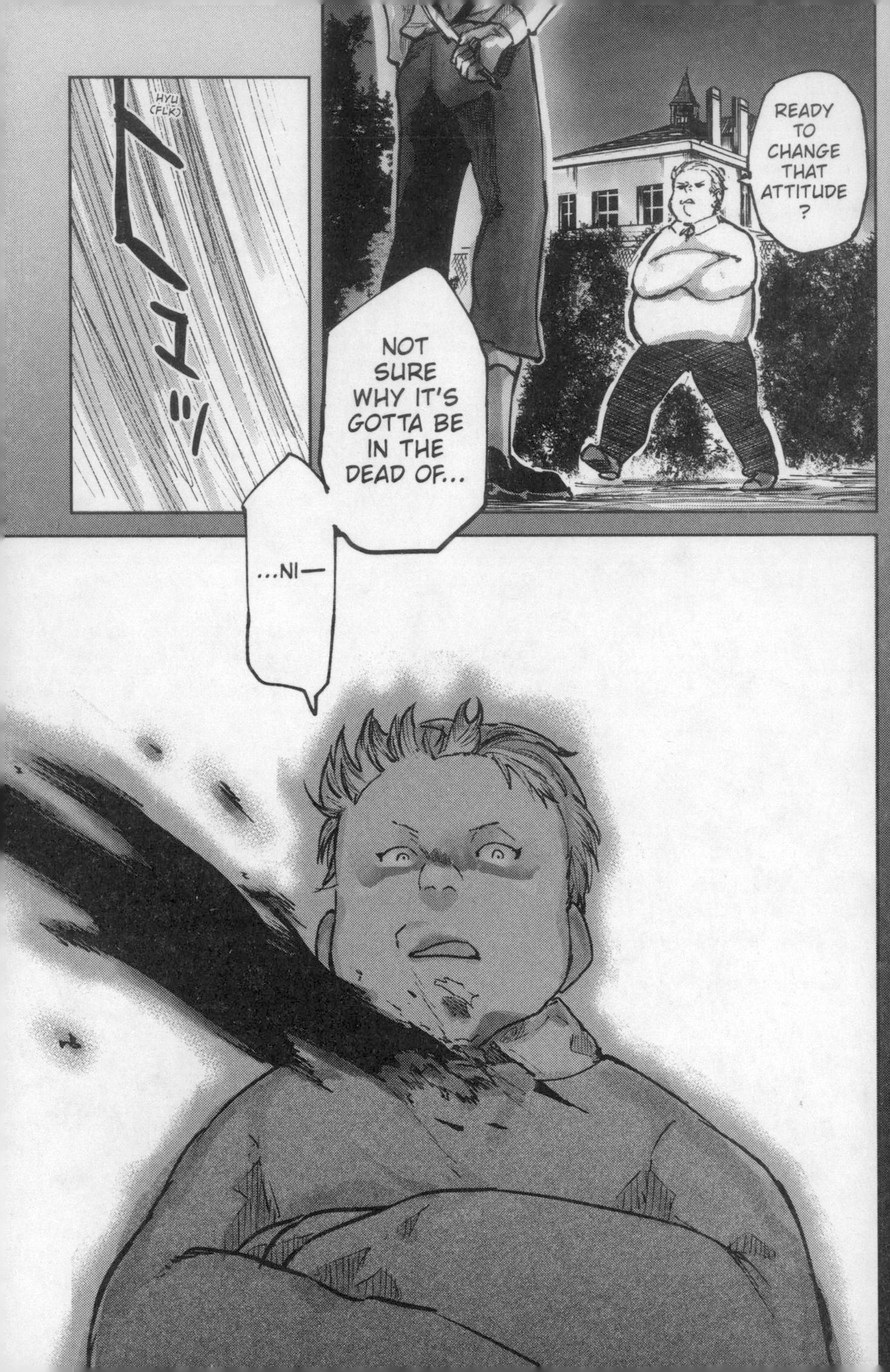
READY TO CHANGE THAT ATTITUDE ?
NOT SURE WHY IT'S GOTTA BE IN THE DEAD OF...
HYU (FLK)
...NI—

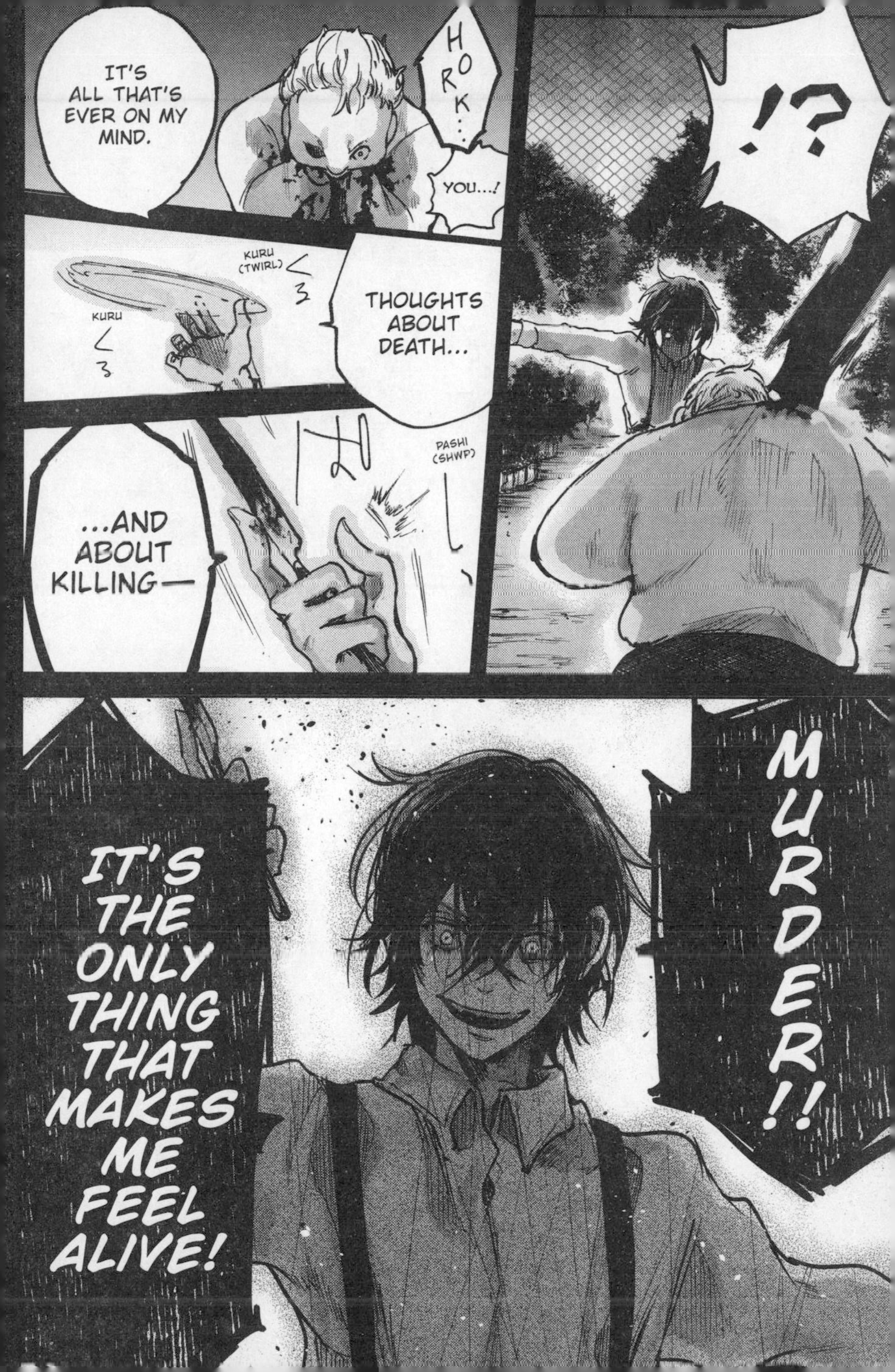
!?
HORK...
IT'S ALL THAT'S EVER ON MY MIND.
YOU...!
THOUGHTS ABOUT DEATH...
KURU (TWIRL)
KURU
PASHI (SHWP)
...AND ABOUT KILLING—
MURDER!!
IT'S THE ONLY THING THAT MAKES ME FEEL ALIVE!

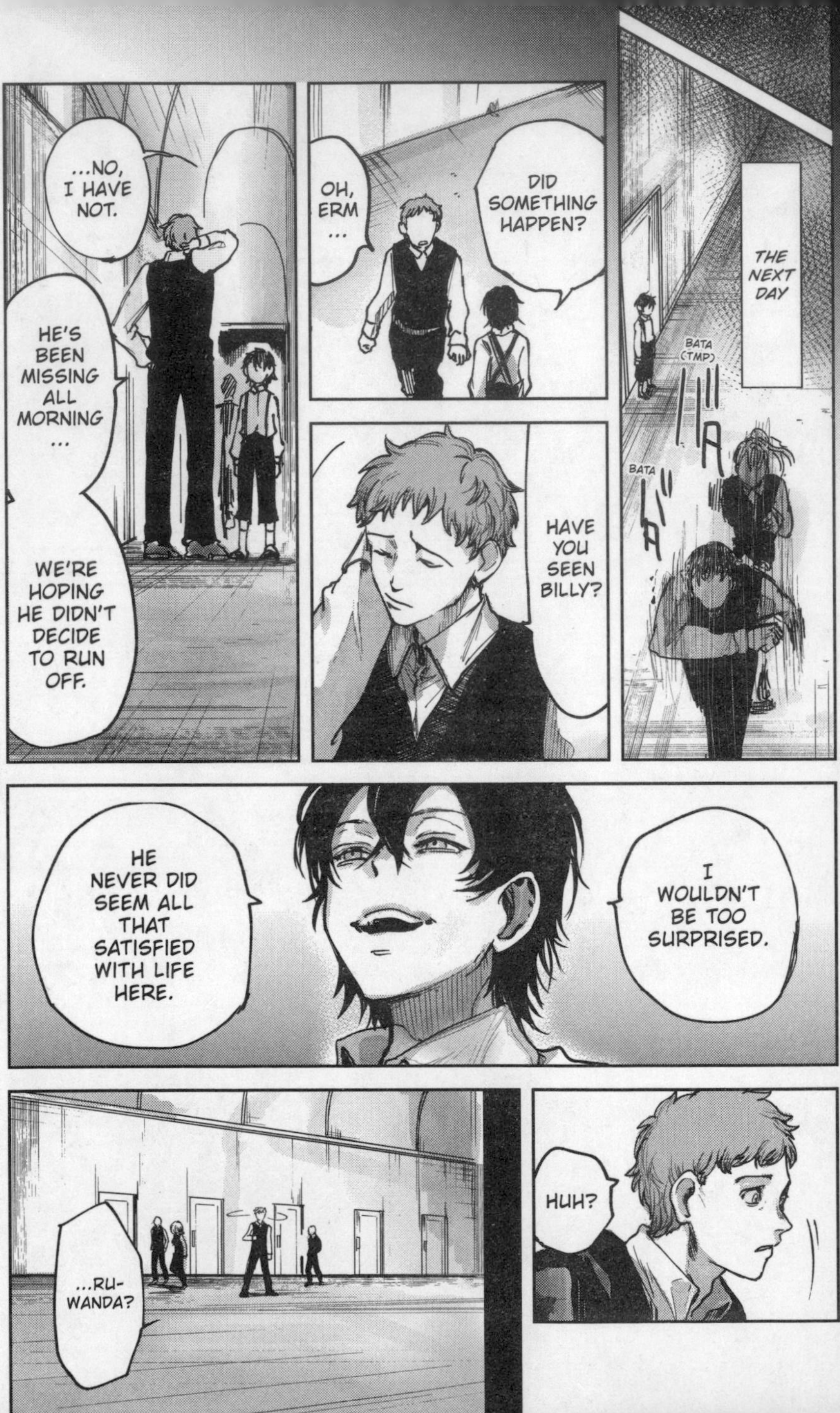
THE NEXT DAY
BATA (TMP)
BATA
DID SOMETHING HAPPEN?
OH, ERM...
HAVE YOU SEEN BILLY?
...NO, I HAVE NOT.
HE'S BEEN MISSING ALL MORNING...
WE'RE HOPING HE DIDN'T DECIDE TO RUN OFF.
I WOULDN'T BE TOO SURPRISED.
HE NEVER DID SEEM ALL THAT SATISFIED WITH LIFE HERE.
HUH?
...RU-WANDA?

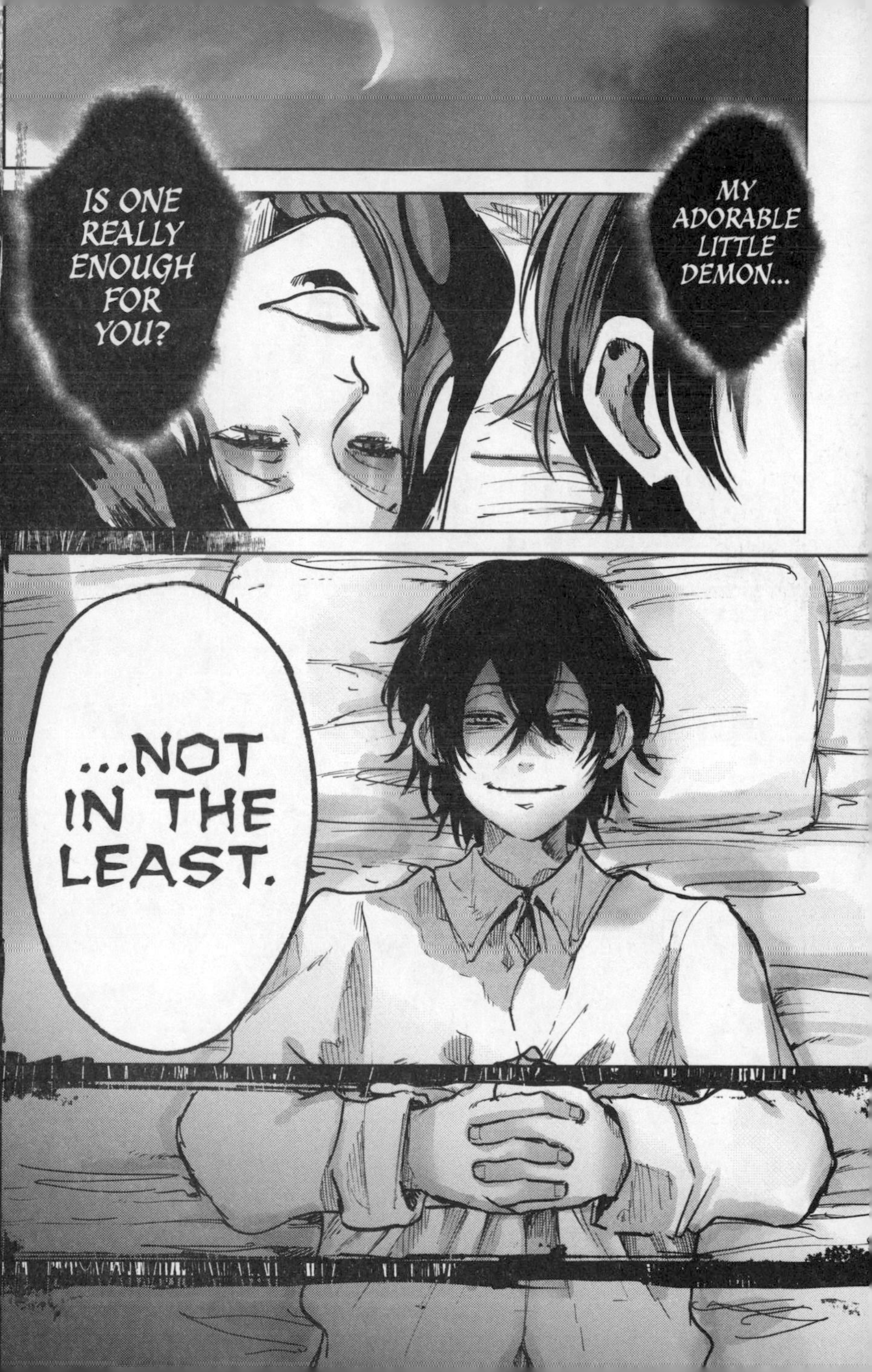
MY ADORABLE LITTLE DEMON...
IS ONE REALLY ENOUGH FOR YOU?
...NOT IN THE LEAST.

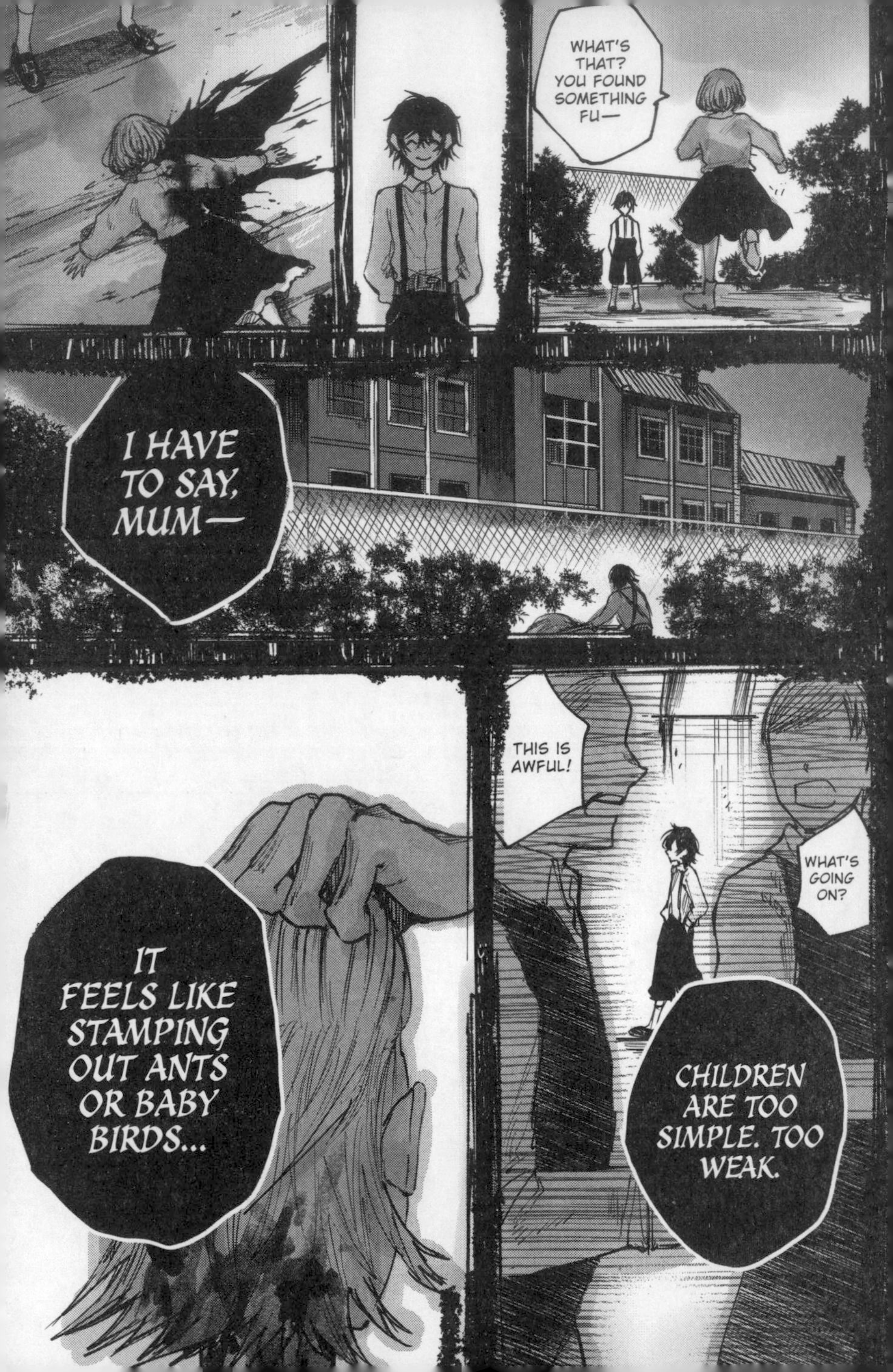
WHAT'S THAT? YOU FOUND SOMETHING FU—
I HAVE TO SAY, MUM—
WHAT'S GOING ON?
THIS IS AWFUL!
CHILDREN ARE TOO SIMPLE. TOO WEAK.
IT FEELS LIKE STAMPING OUT ANTS OR BABY BIRDS...

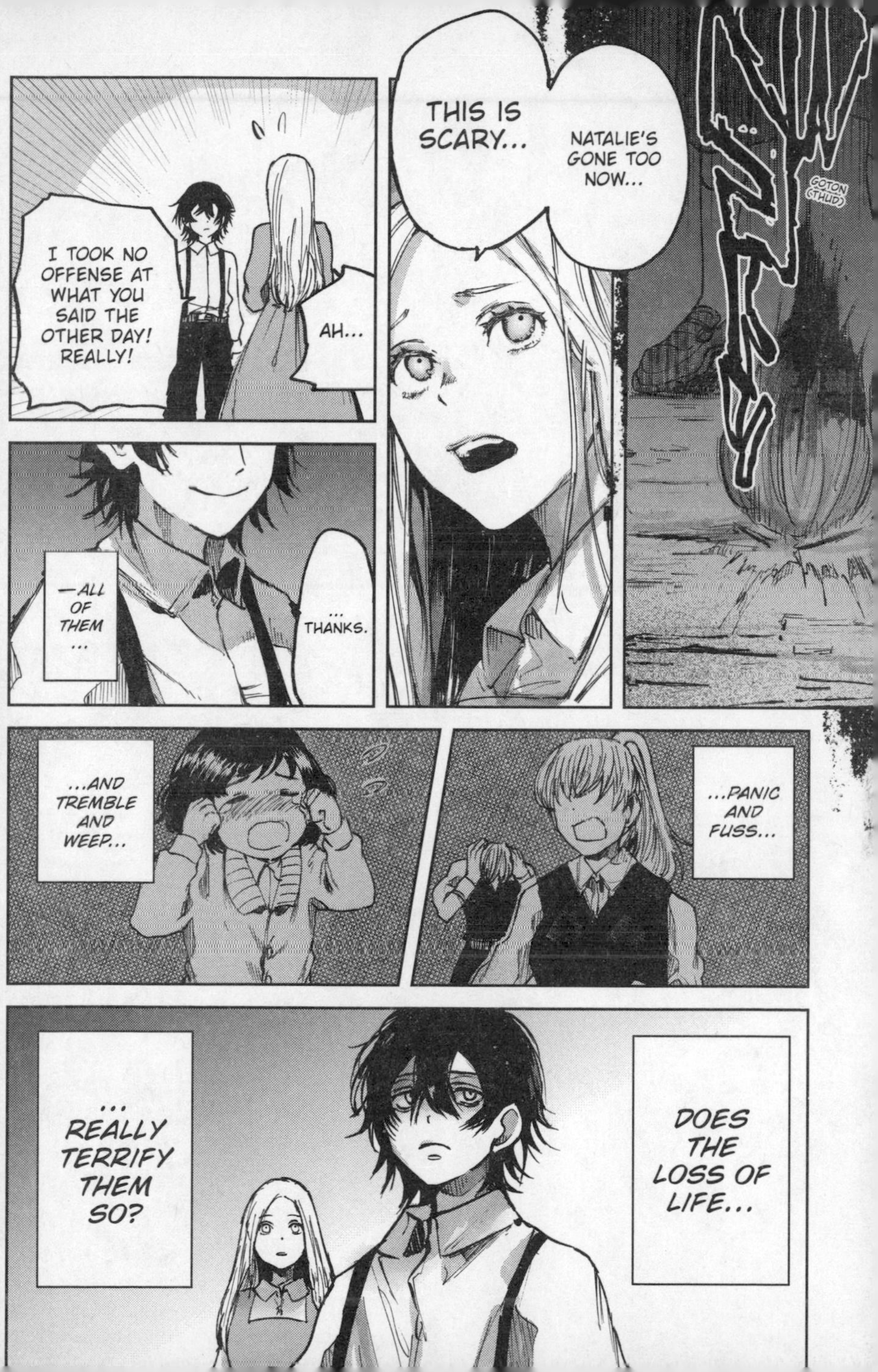
GOTON (THUD)
THIS IS SCARY...
NATALIE'S GONE TOO NOW...
AH...
I TOOK NO OFFENSE AT WHAT YOU SAID THE OTHER DAY! REALLY!
...THANKS.
—ALL OF THEM...
...PANIC AND FUSS...
...AND TREMBLE AND WEEP...
DOES THE LOSS OF LIFE...
...REALLY TERRIFY THEM SO?

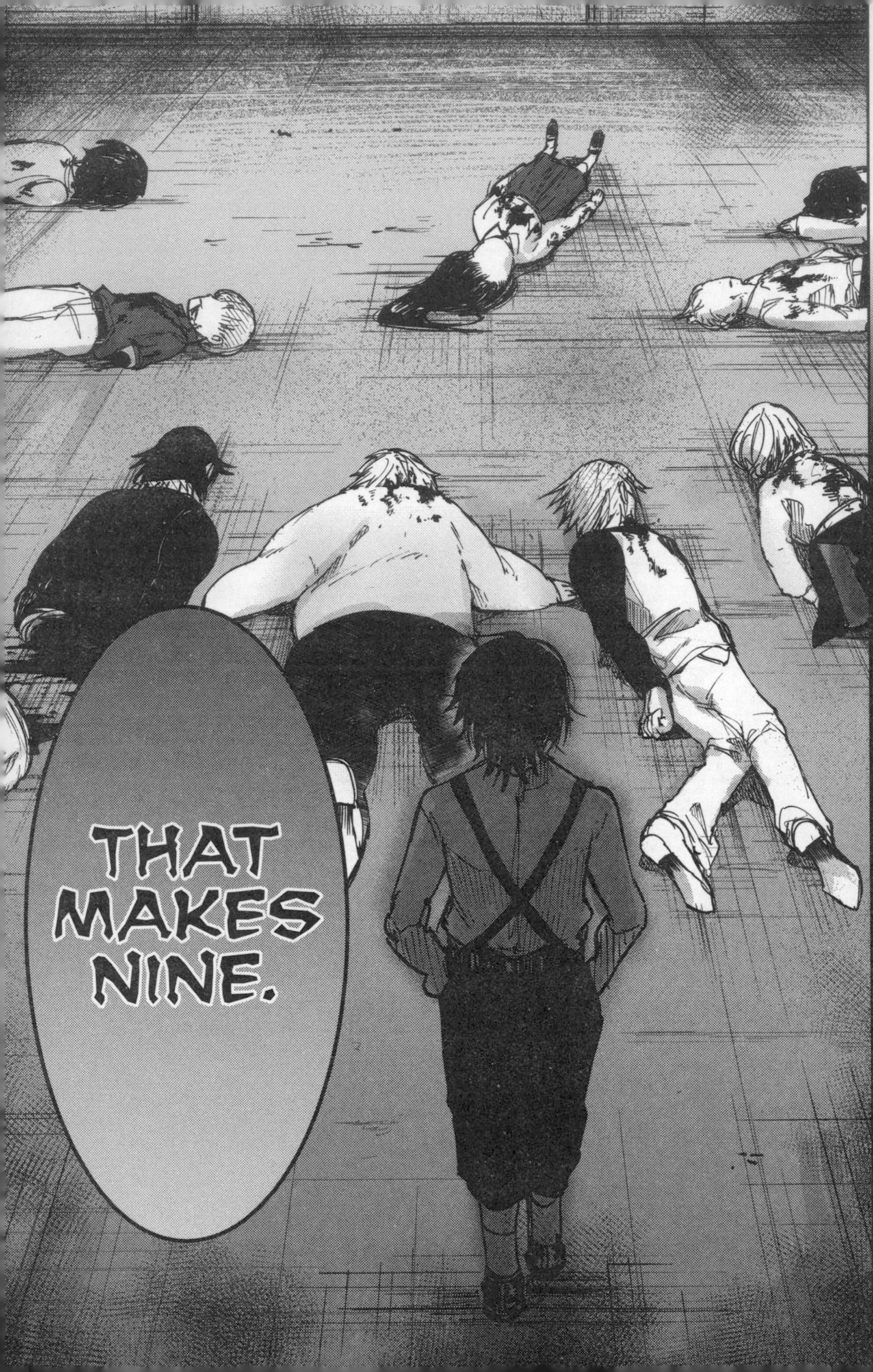
THAT MAKES NINE.

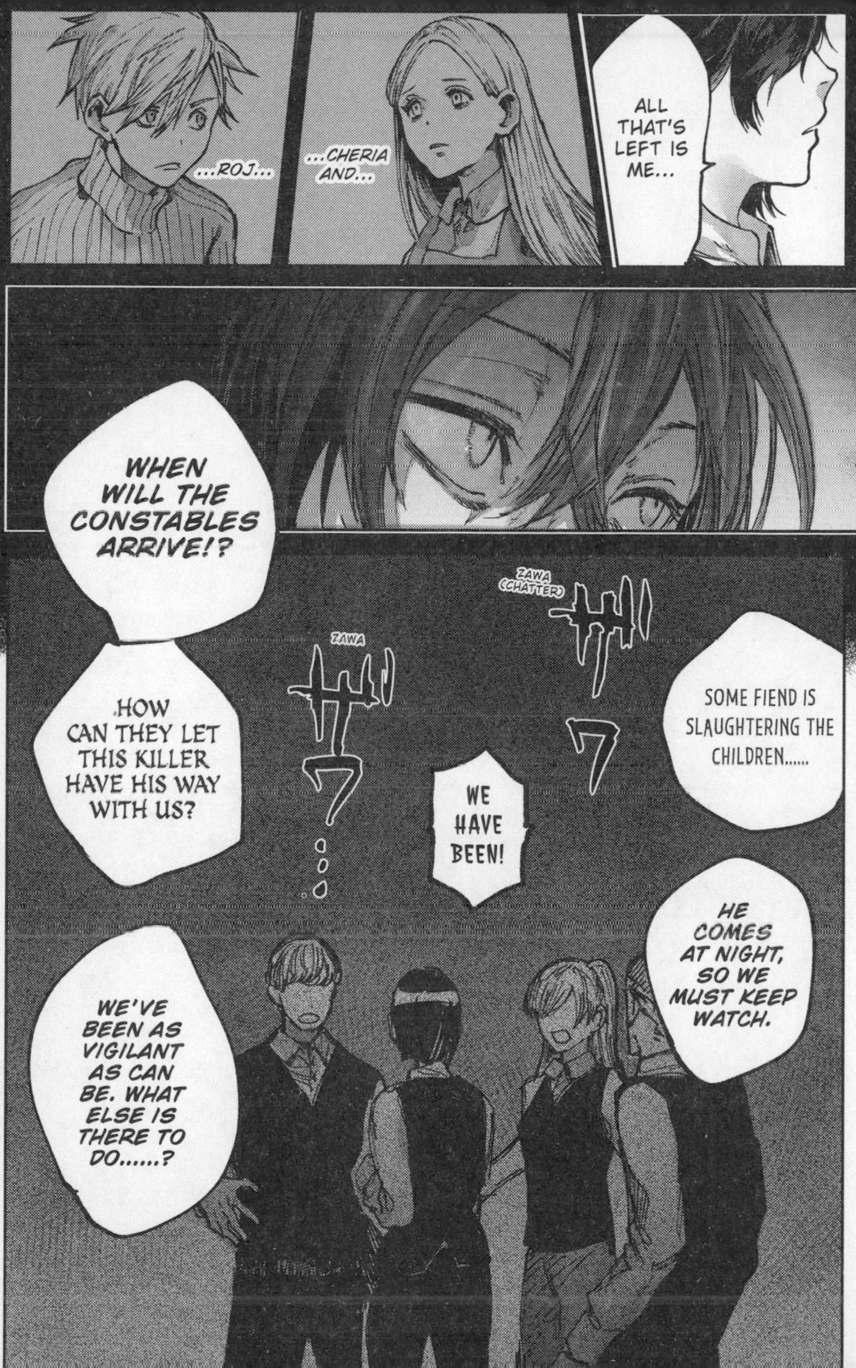
ALL THAT'S LEFT IS ME...
...CHERIA AND...
...ROJ...
WHEN WILL THE CONSTABLES ARRIVE!?
ZAWA (CHATTER)
SOME FIEND IS SLAUGHTERING THE CHILDREN......
ZAWA
WE HAVE BEEN!
HOW CAN THEY LET THIS KILLER HAVE HIS WAY WITH US?
HE COMES AT NIGHT, SO WE MUST KEEP WATCH.
WE'VE BEEN AS VIGILANT AS CAN BE. WHAT ELSE IS THERE TO DO......?

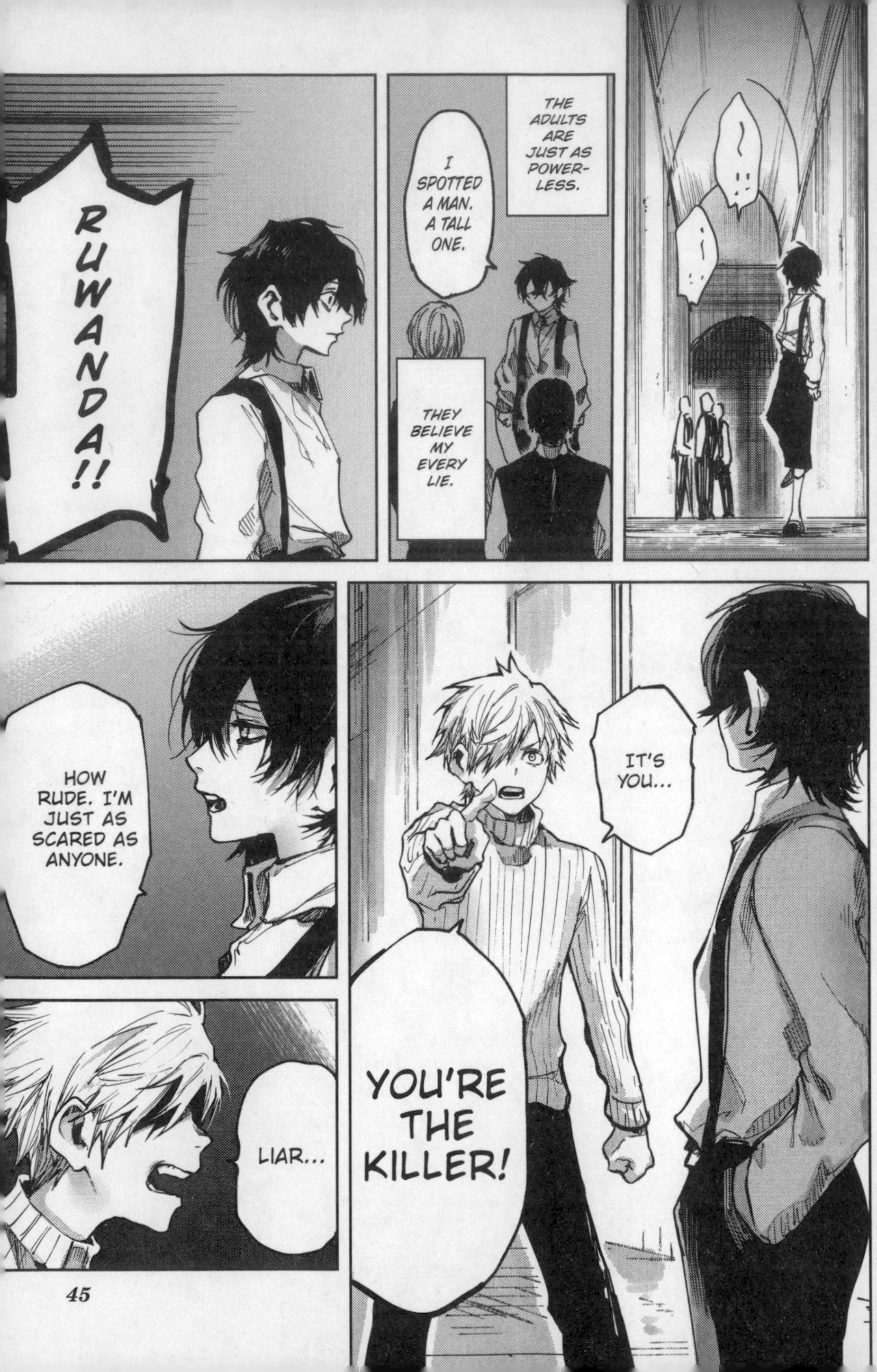
THE ADULTS ARE JUST AS POWERLESS.
I SPOTTED A MAN. A TALL ONE.
THEY BELIEVE MY EVERY LIE.
RUWANDA!!
IT'S YOU...
YOU'RE THE KILLER!
HOW RUDE. I'M JUST AS SCARED AS ANYONE.
LIAR...

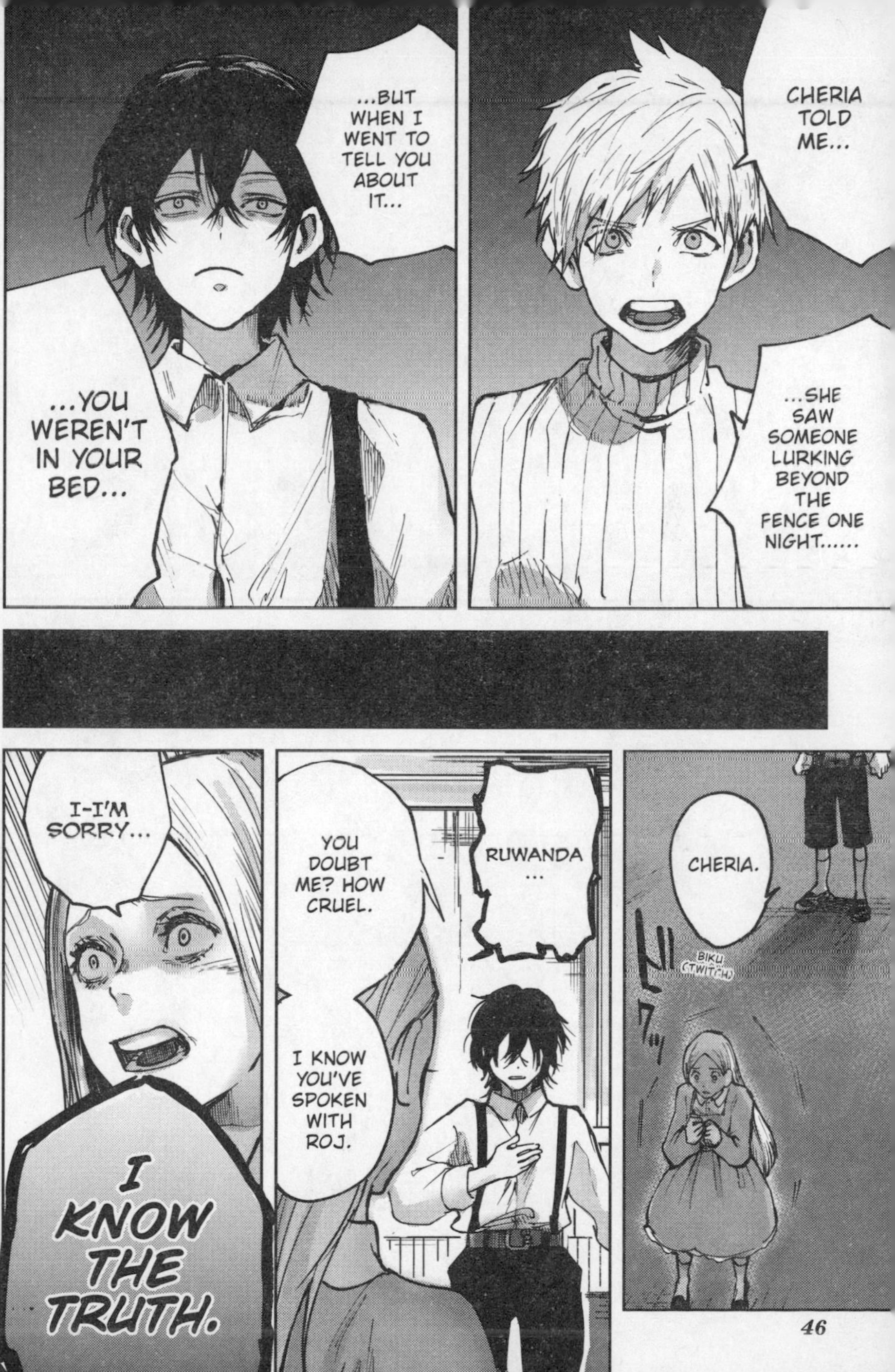
CHERIA TOLD ME...
...SHE SAW SOMEONE LURKING BEYOND THE FENCE ONE NIGHT......
...BUT WHEN I WENT TO TELL YOU ABOUT IT...
...YOU WEREN'T IN YOUR BED...
CHERIA.
BIKU (TWITCH)
RUWANDA ...
YOU DOUBT ME? HOW CRUEL.
I KNOW YOU'VE SPOKEN WITH ROJ.
I-I'M SORRY...
I KNOW THE TRUTH.

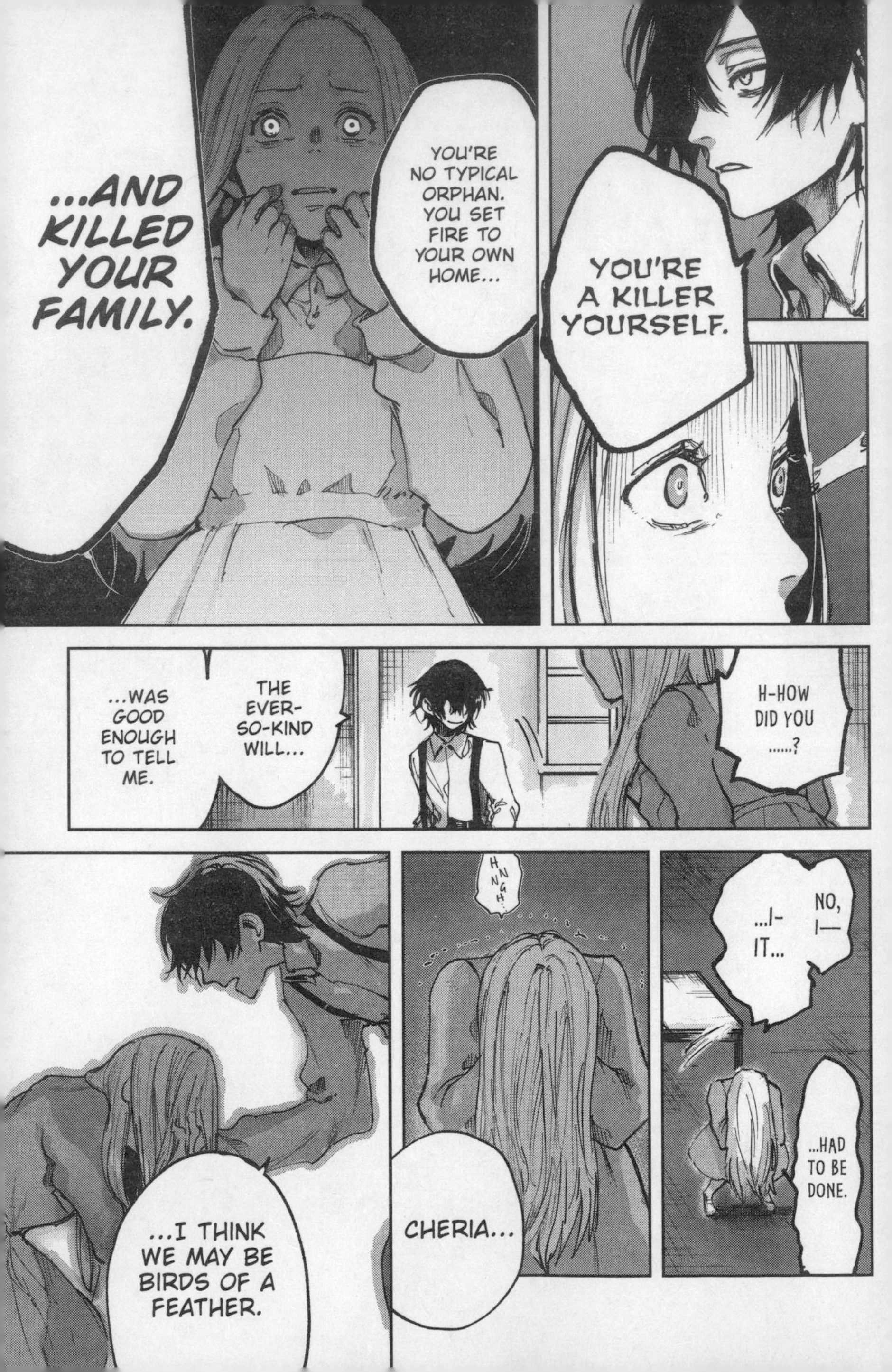
YOU'RE A KILLER YOURSELF.
YOU'RE NO TYPICAL ORPHAN. YOU SET FIRE TO YOUR OWN HOME...
...AND KILLED YOUR FAMILY.
H-HOW DID YOU ......?
THE EVER-SO-KIND WILL...
...WAS GOOD ENOUGH TO TELL ME.
NO, I—
...I- IT...
...HAD TO BE DONE.
HNGH...
CHERIA...
...I THINK WE MAY BE BIRDS OF A FEATHER.

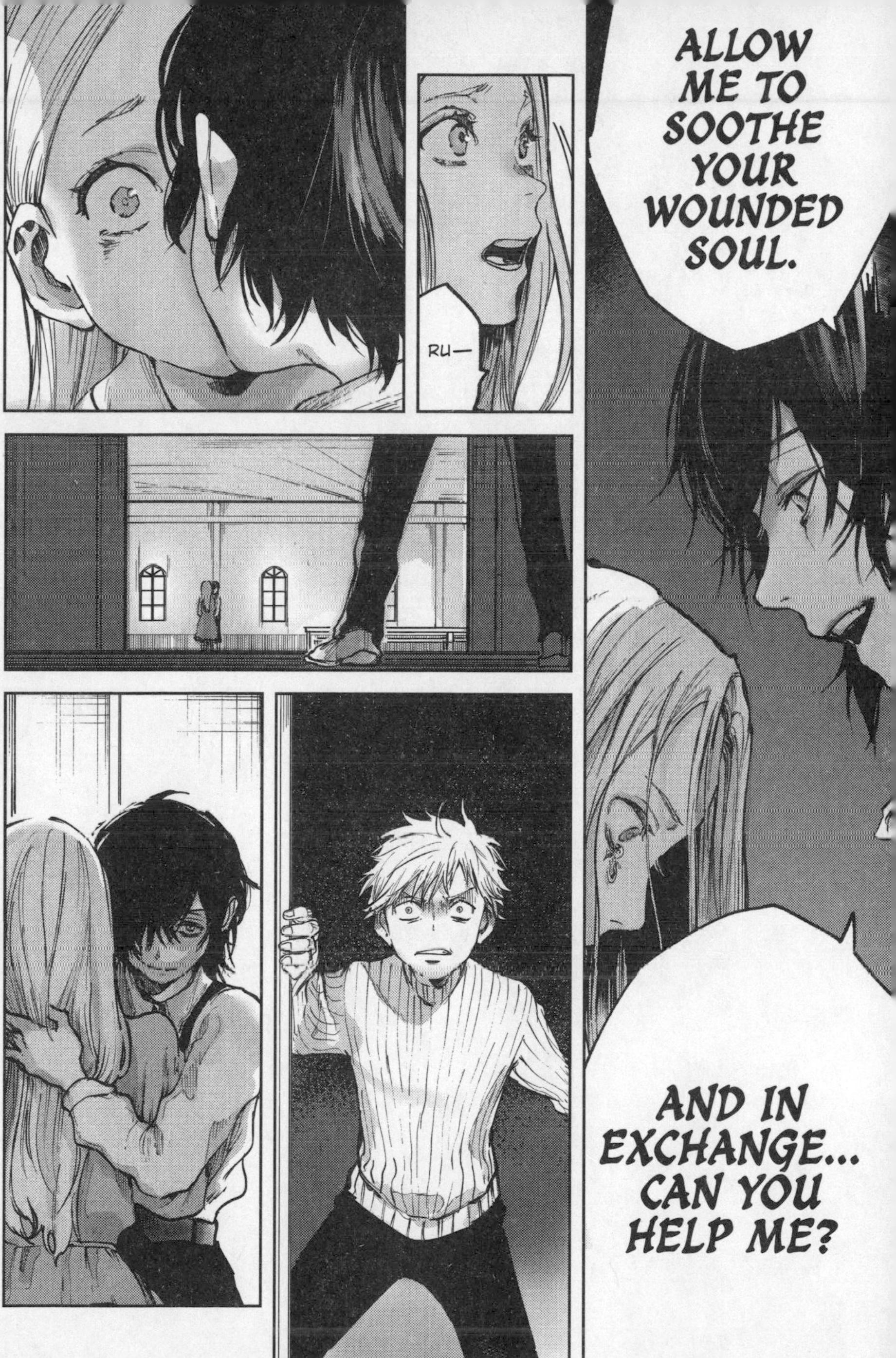
ALLOW ME TO SOOTHE YOUR WOUNDED SOUL.
AND IN EXCHANGE... CAN YOU HELP ME?
RU—

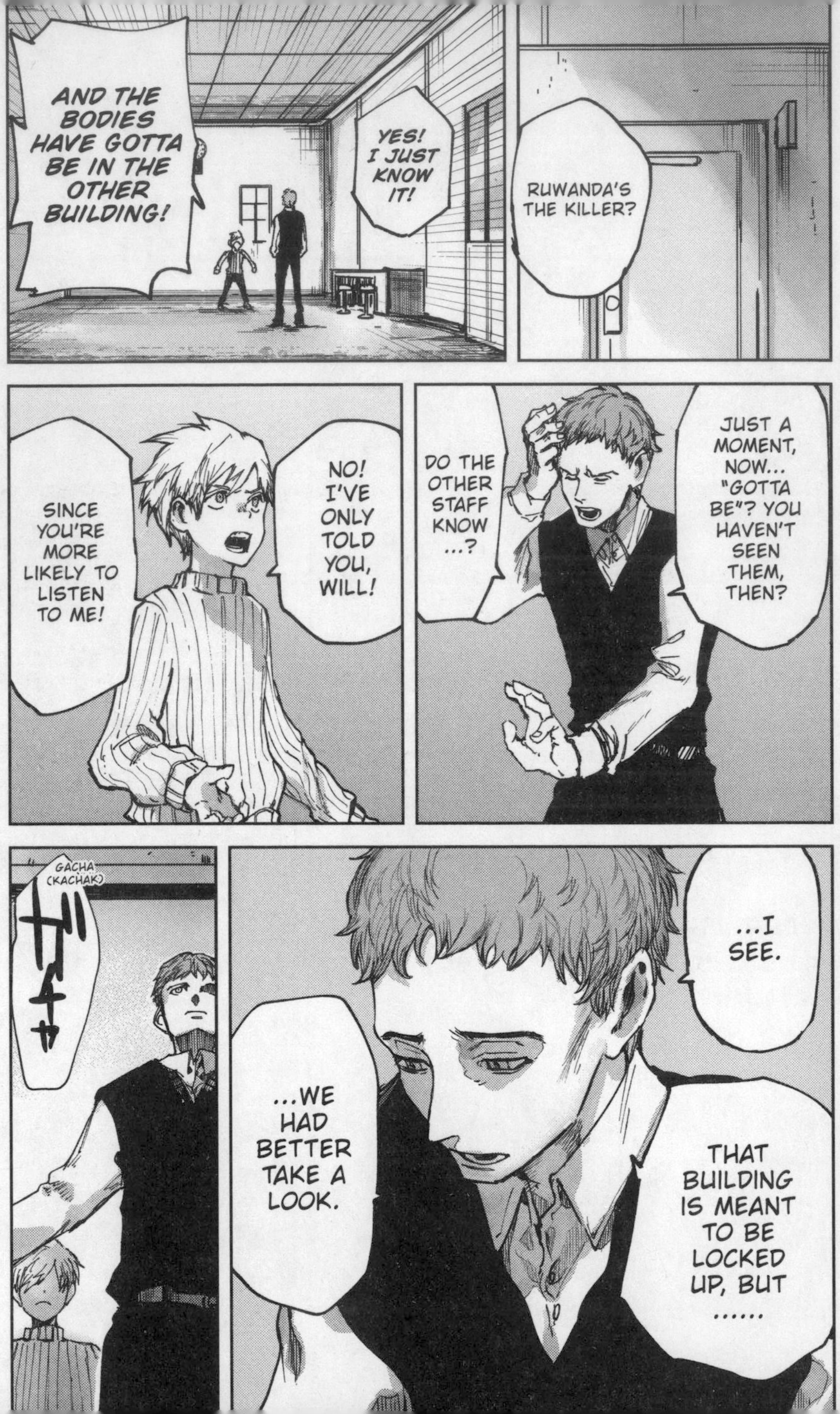
RUWANDA'S THE KILLER?
YES! I JUST KNOW IT!
AND THE BODIES HAVE GOTTA BE IN THE OTHER BUILDING!
JUST A MOMENT, NOW... "GOTTA BE"? YOU HAVEN'T SEEN THEM, THEN?
DO THE OTHER STAFF KNOW ...?
NO! I'VE ONLY TOLD YOU, WILL!
SINCE YOU'RE MORE LIKELY TO LISTEN TO ME!
...I SEE.
THAT BUILDING IS MEANT TO BE LOCKED UP, BUT ......
...WE HAD BETTER TAKE A LOOK.
GACHA (KACHAK)
ガチャ

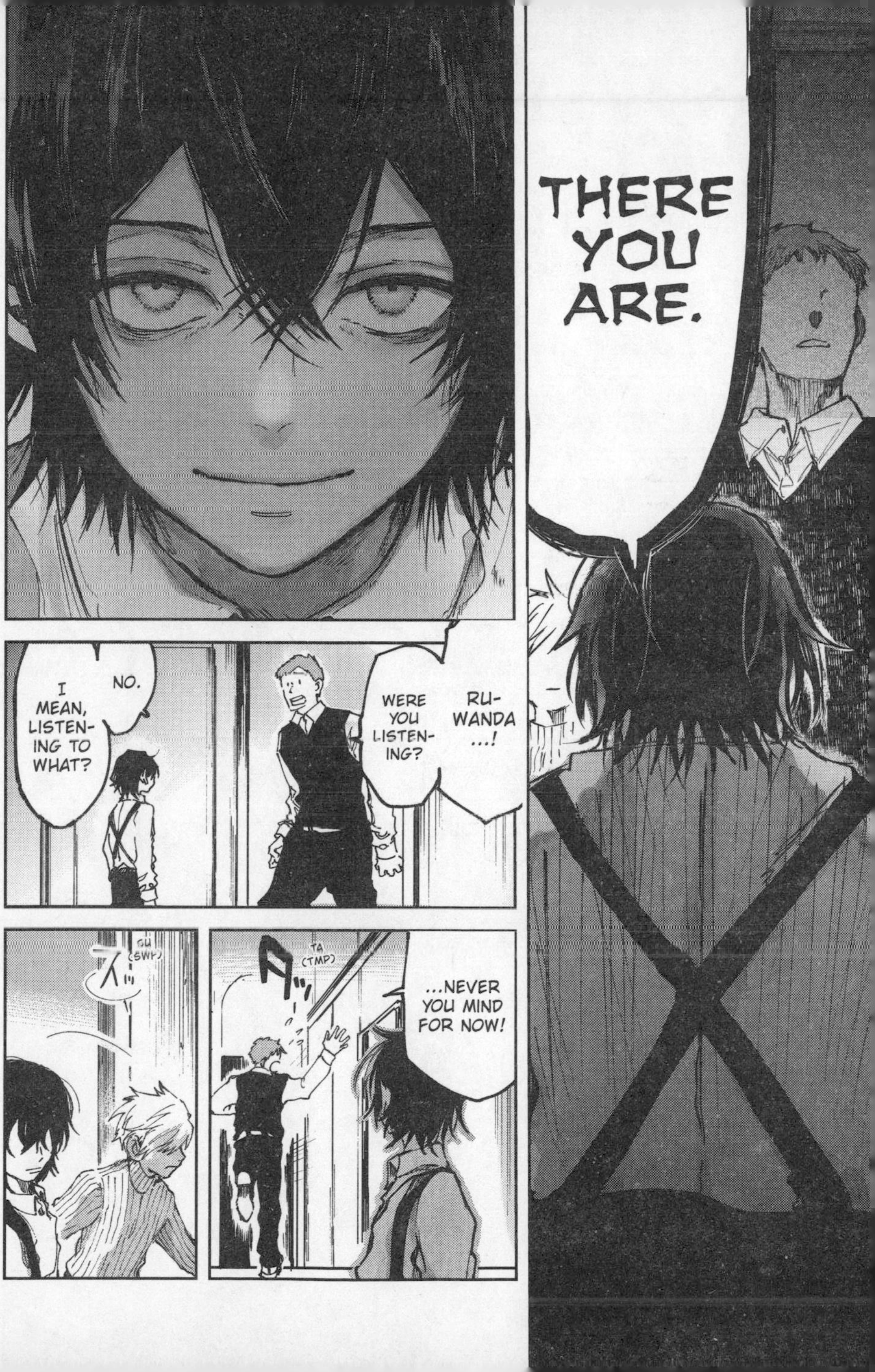
THERE YOU ARE.
RU-WANDA...!
WERE YOU LISTENING?
NO.
I MEAN, LISTENING TO WHAT?
TA (TMP)
...NEVER YOU MIND FOR NOW!
SU (SWP)

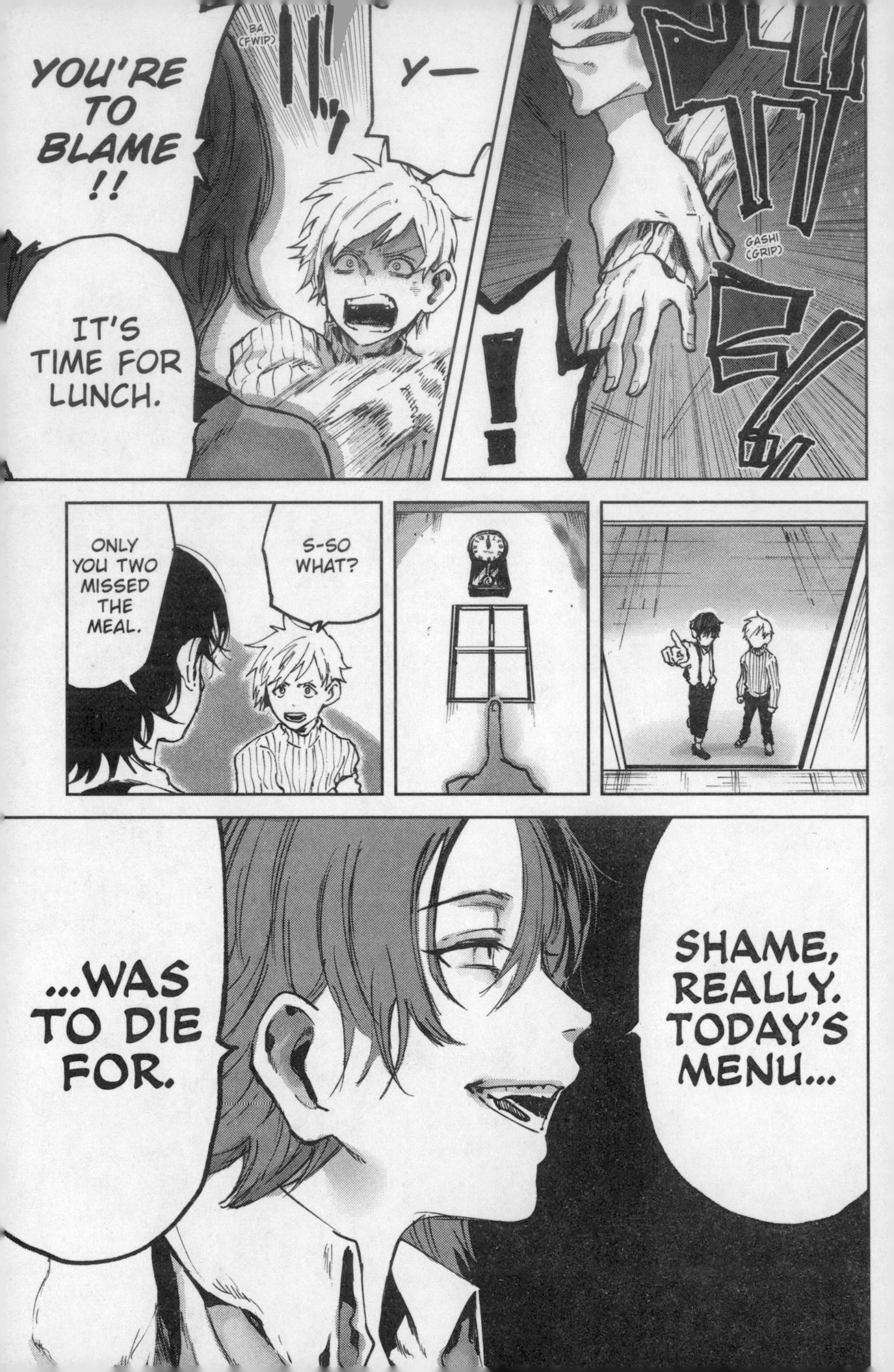
GASHI (GRIP)
!
Y—
BA (FWIP)
YOU'RE TO BLAME!!
IT'S TIME FOR LUNCH.
ONLY YOU TWO MISSED THE MEAL.
S-SO WHAT?
SHAME, REALLY. TODAY'S MENU...
...WAS TO DIE FOR.

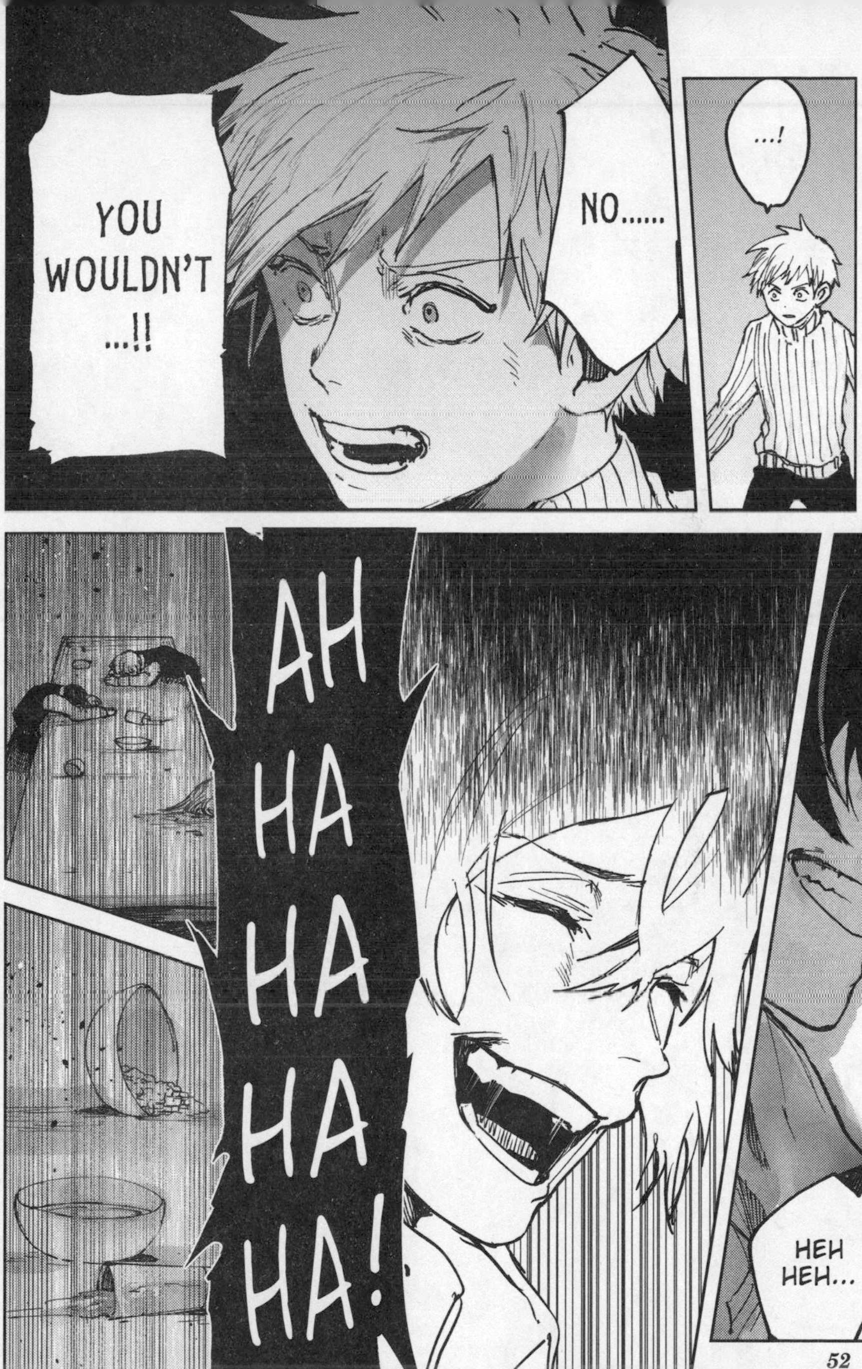
...!
NO......
YOU WOULDN'T ...!!
HEH HEH...
AH HA HA HA HA HA!

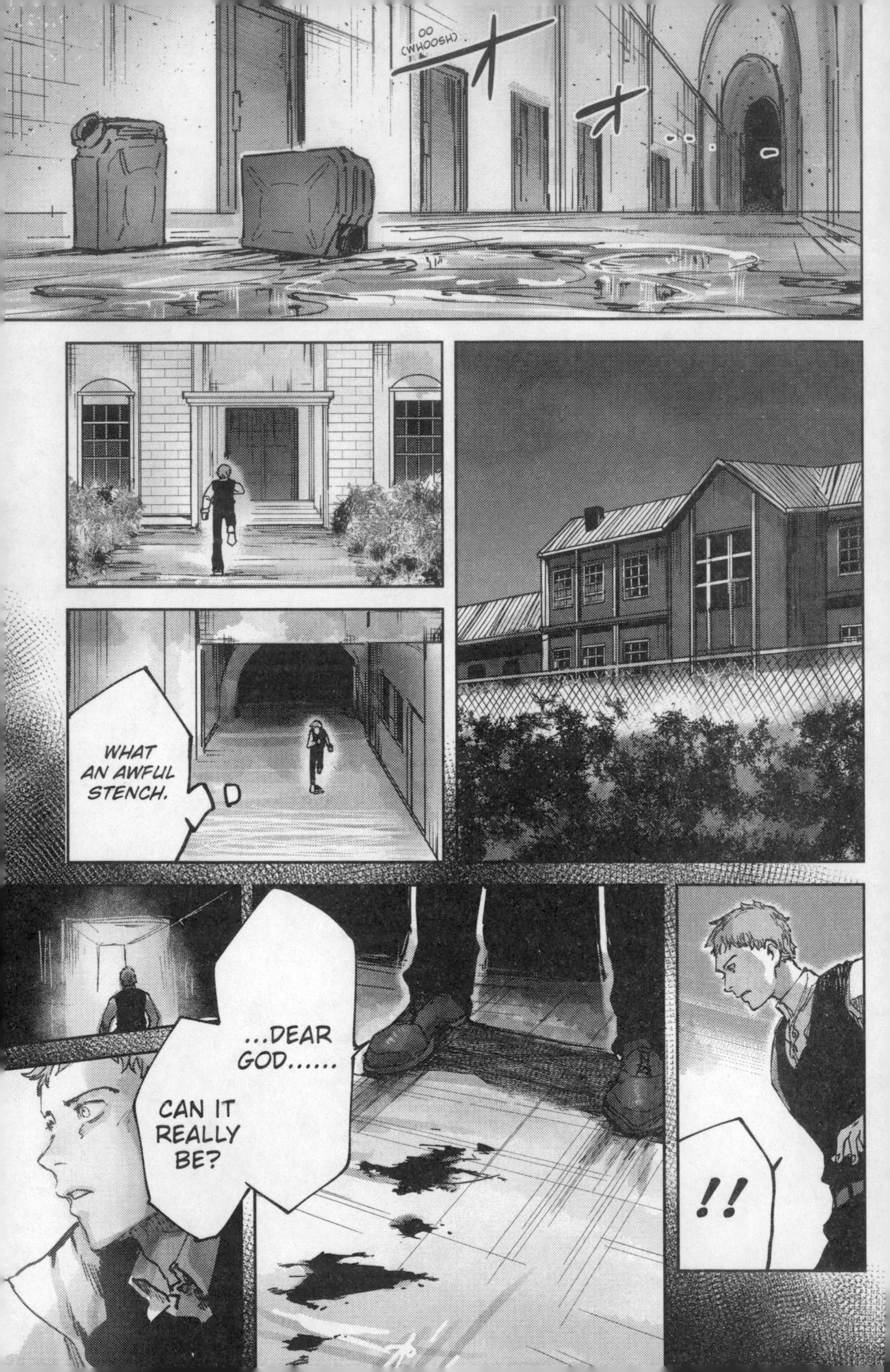
OO (WHOOSH)
WHAT AN AWFUL STENCH.
!!
...DEAR GOD......
CAN IT REALLY BE?

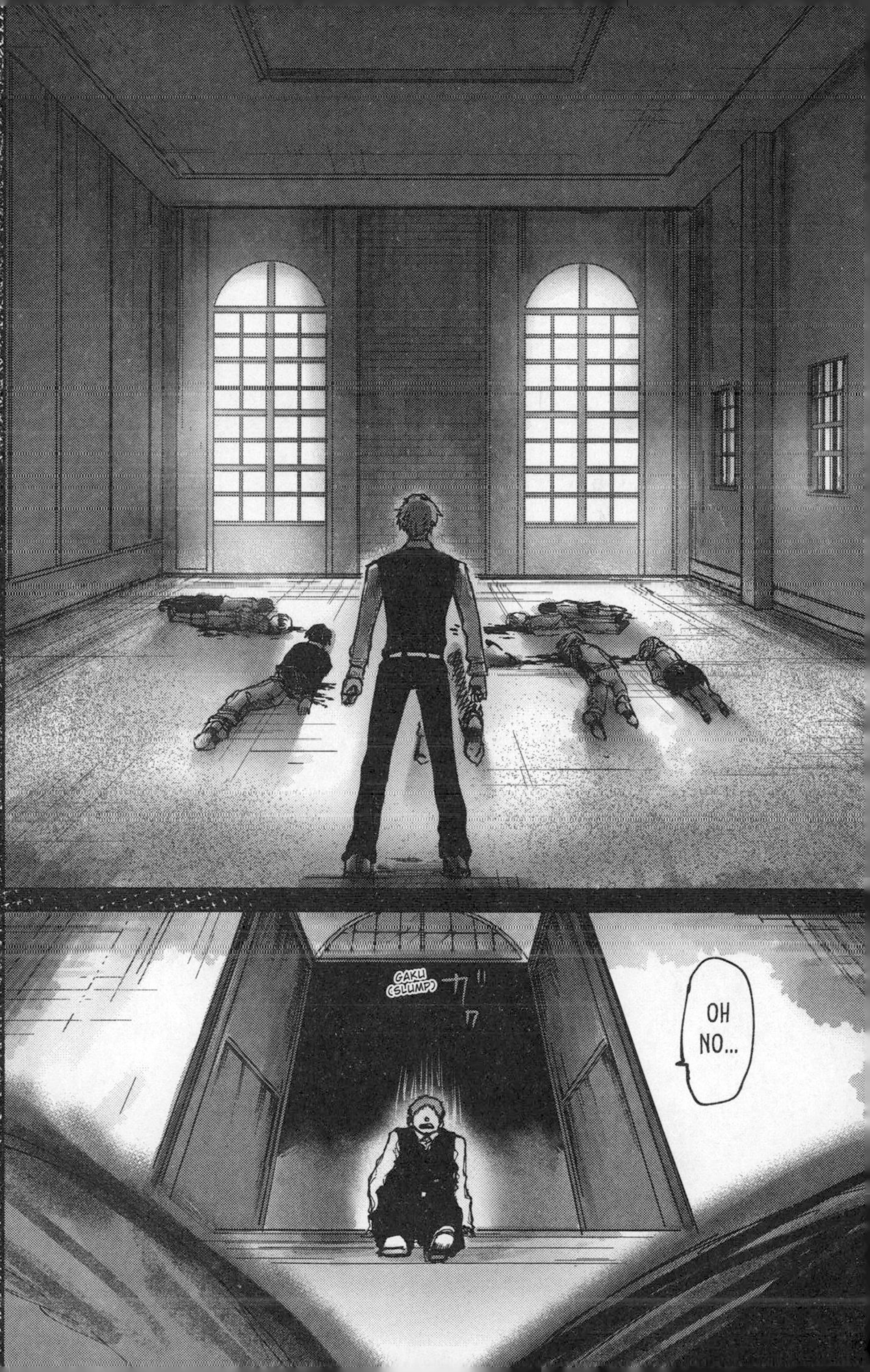
OH NO...
GAKU (SLUMP)

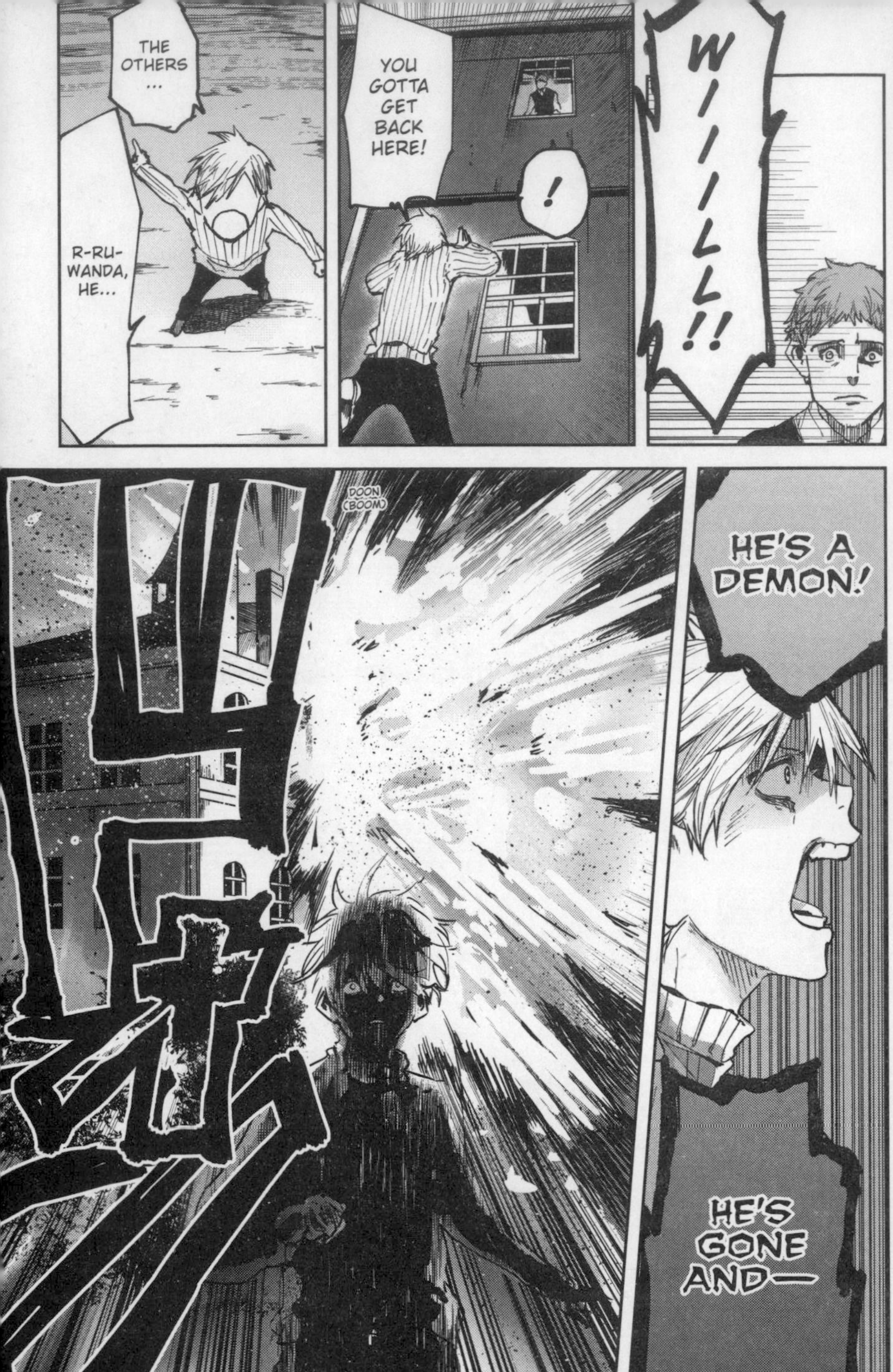
W-I-I-I-L-L-L!!
YOU GOTTA GET BACK HERE!
!
THE OTHERS...
R-RU-WANDA, HE...
HE'S A DEMON!
HE'S GONE AND—
DOON (BOOM)

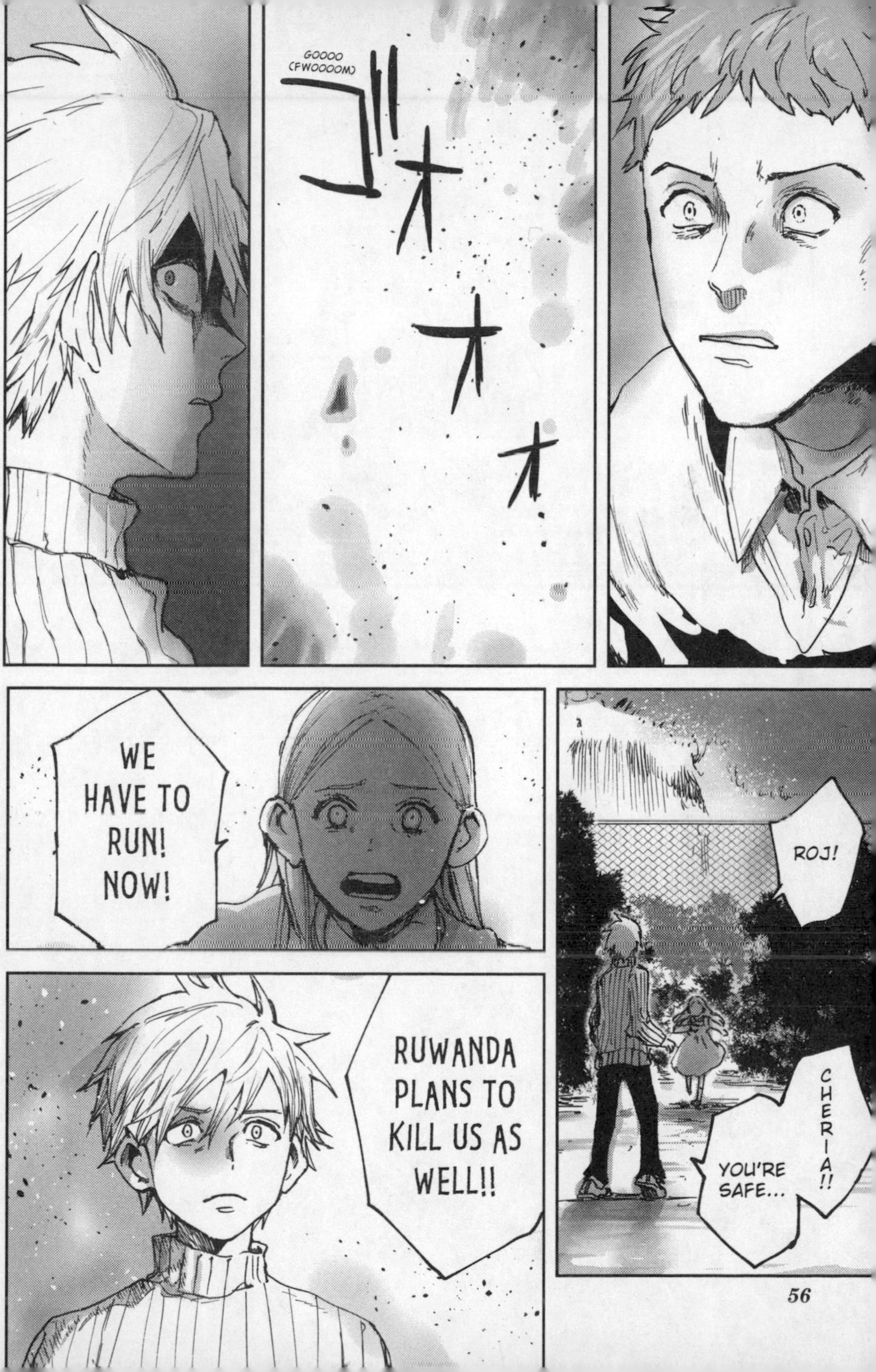
ゴオオオ
GOOOO (FWOOOOM)
ROJ!
CHERIA!!
YOU'RE SAFE...
WE HAVE TO RUN! NOW!
RUWANDA PLANS TO KILL US AS WELL!!

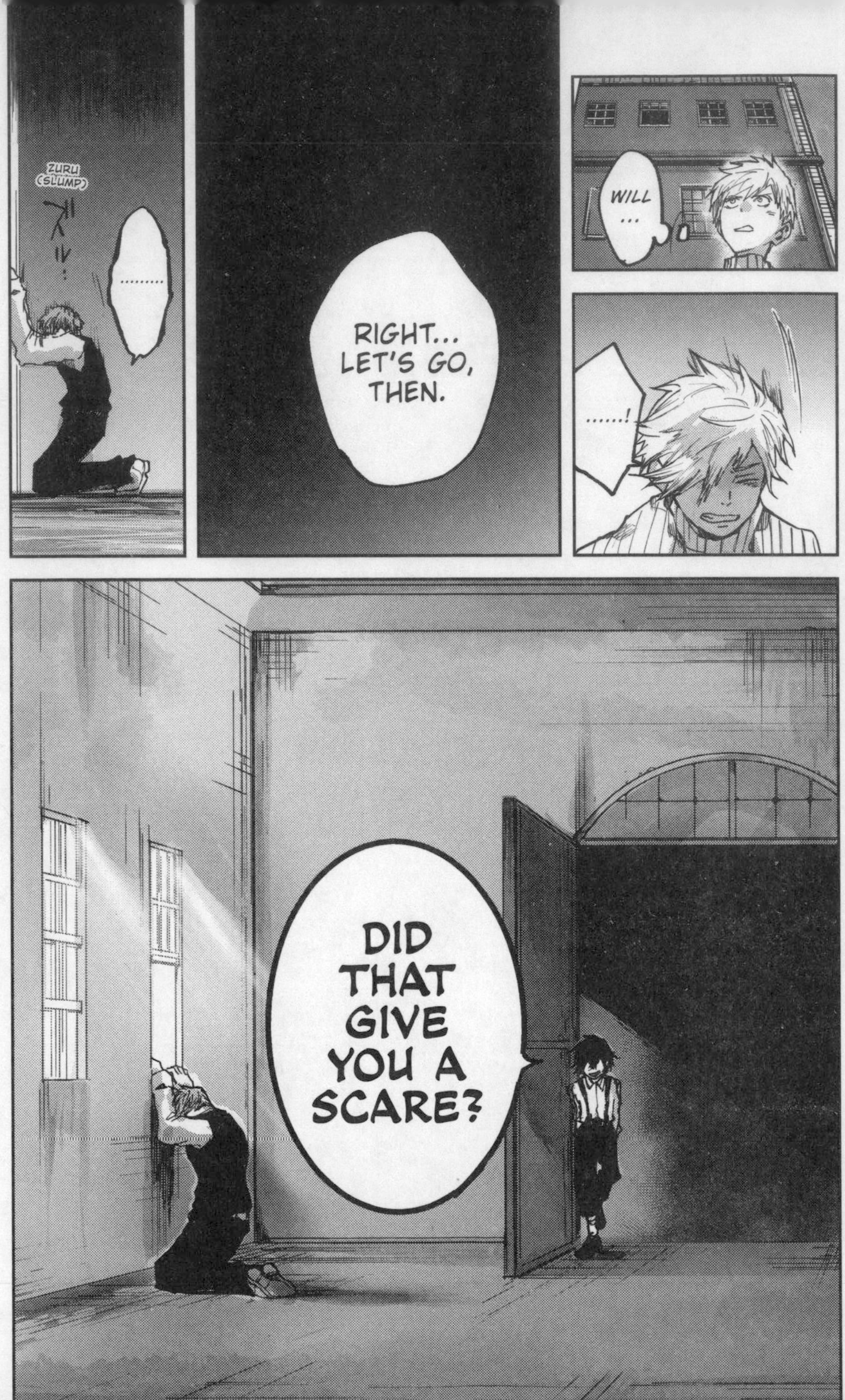

WILL
...
......!
RIGHT... LET'S GO, THEN.
ZURU (SLUMP)
....
DID THAT GIVE YOU A SCARE?

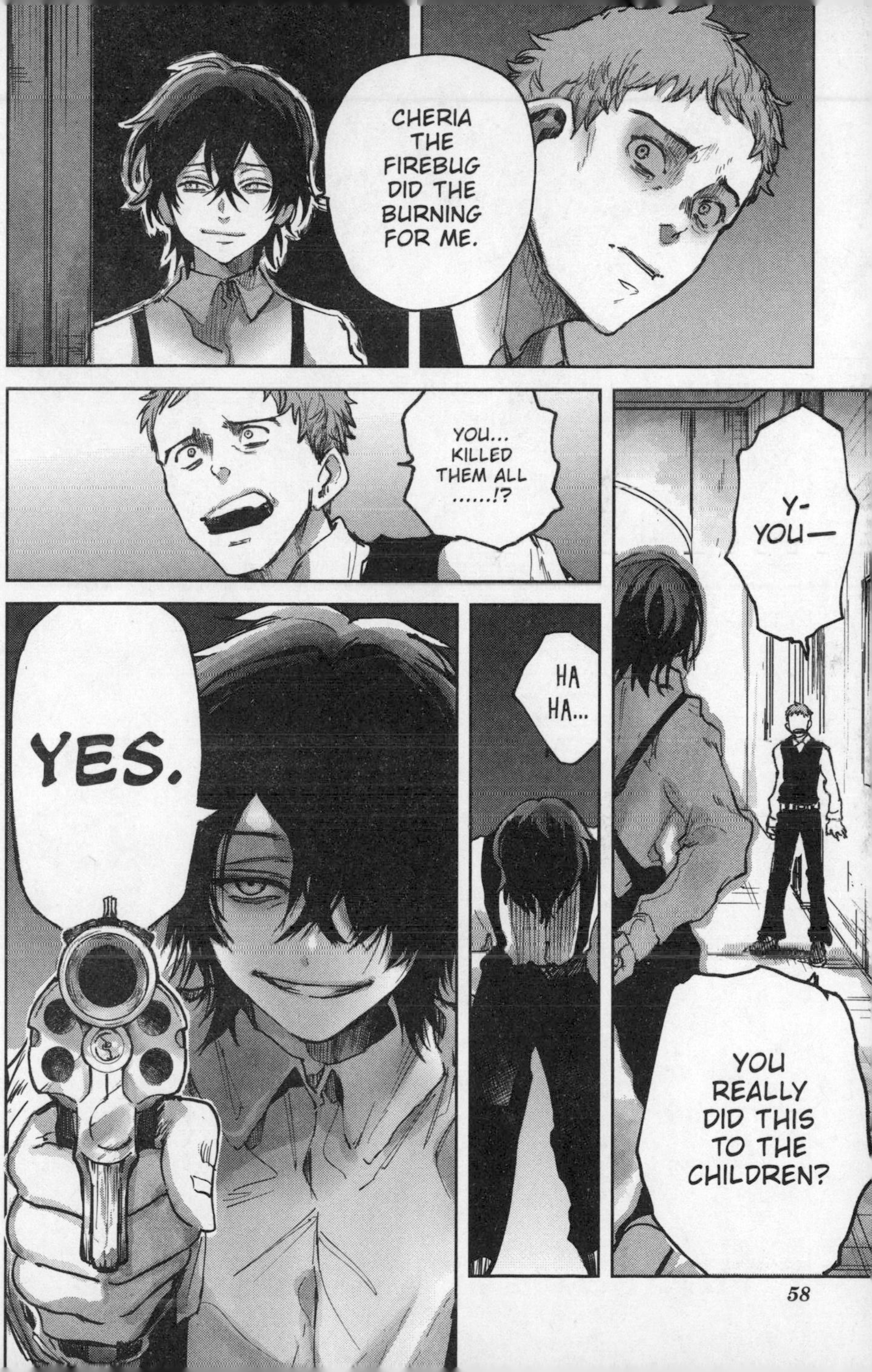
CHERIA THE FIREBUG DID THE BURNING FOR ME.
Y-YOU—
YOU REALLY DID THIS TO THE CHILDREN?
YOU... KILLED THEM ALL ......!?
HA HA...
YES.

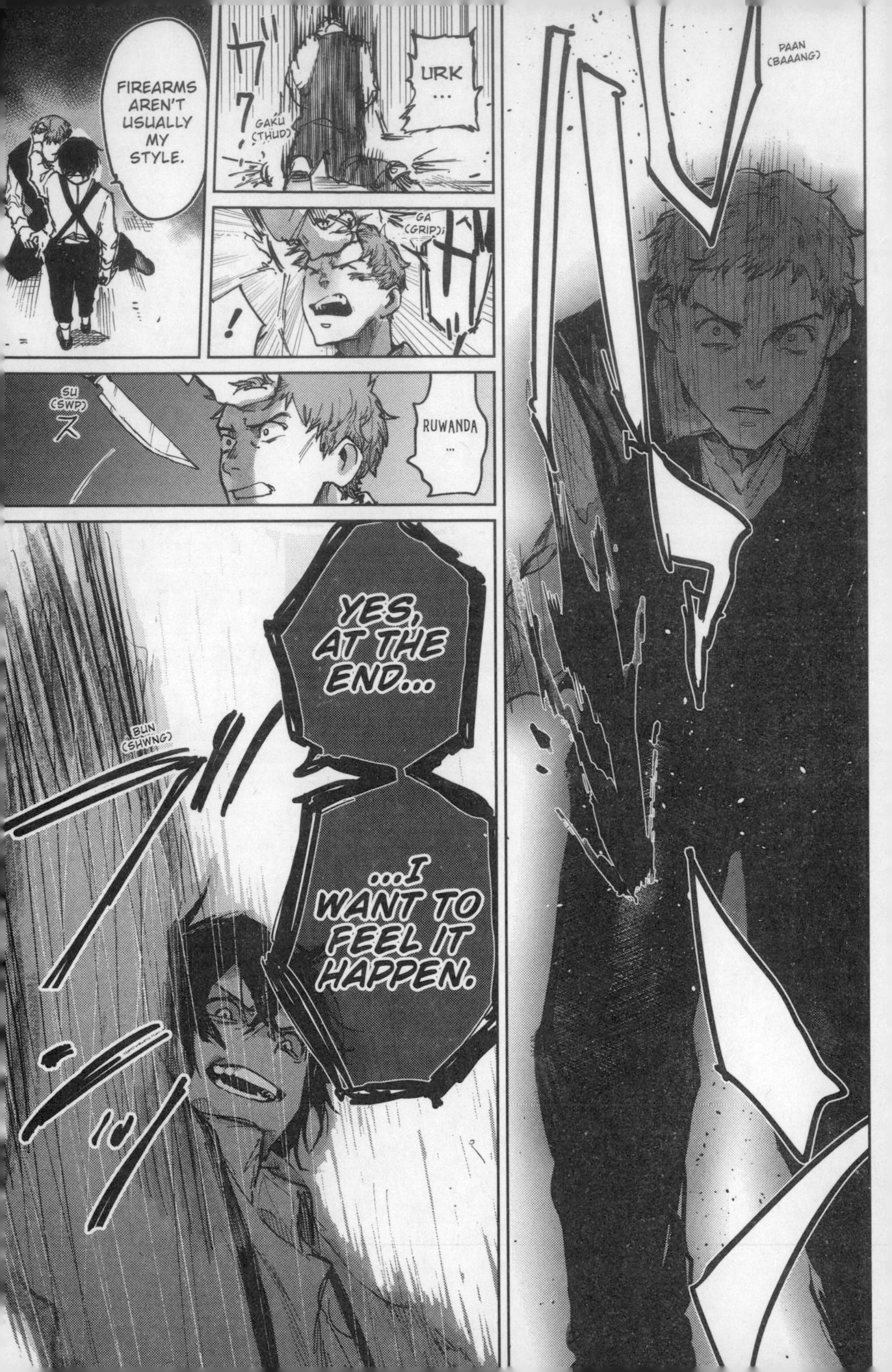
PAAN (BAAANG)
URK...
GAKU (THUD)
GA (GRIP)!
FIREARMS AREN'T USUALLY MY STYLE.
RUWANDA...
SU (SWP)
YES, AT THE END...
BUN (SHWNG)
...I WANT TO FEEL IT HAPPEN.

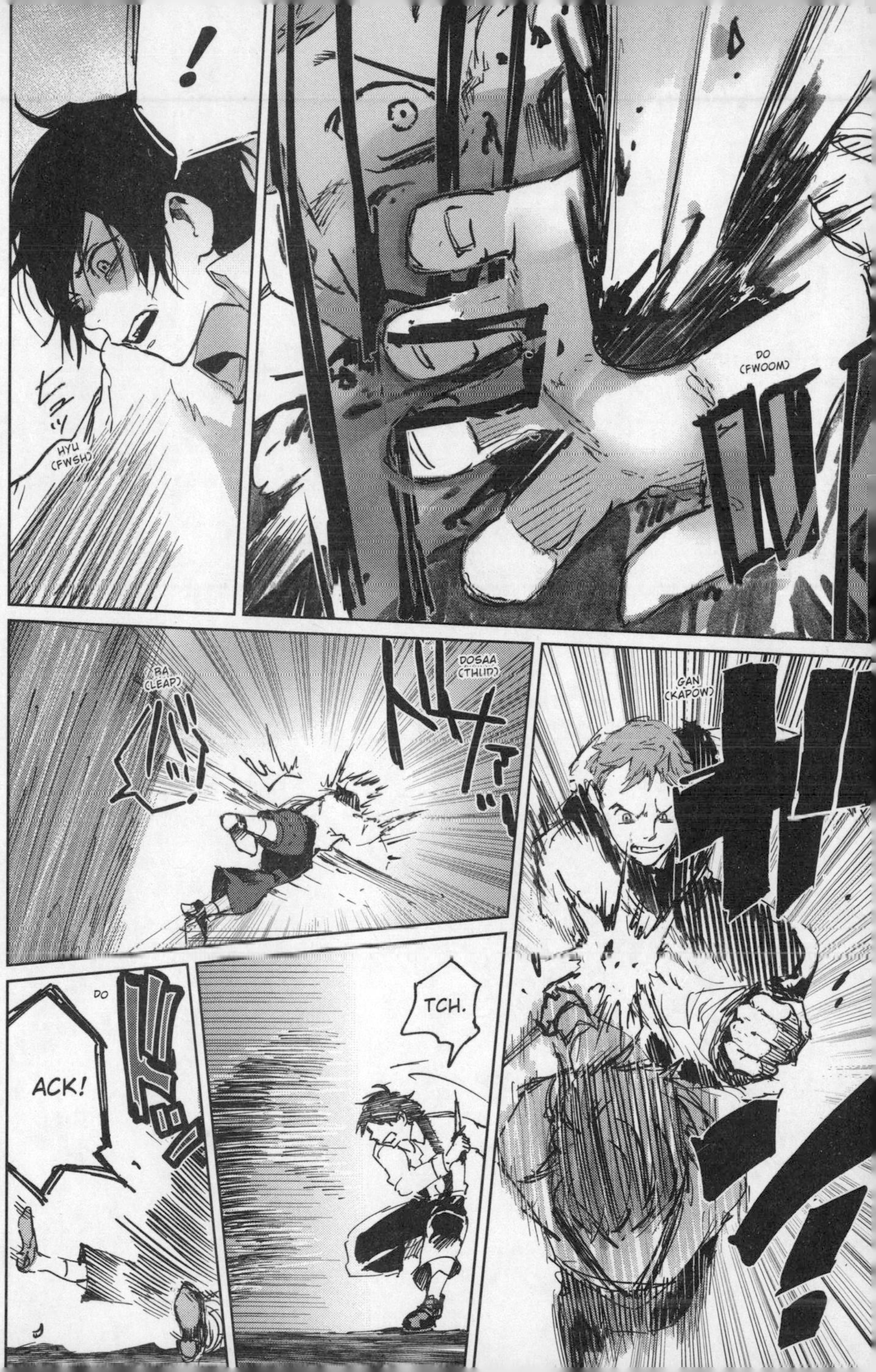
DO
(FWOOM)
!
HYU
(FWSH)
GAN
(KAPOW)
DOSAA
(THUD)
BA
(LEAP)
TCH.
DO
ACK!

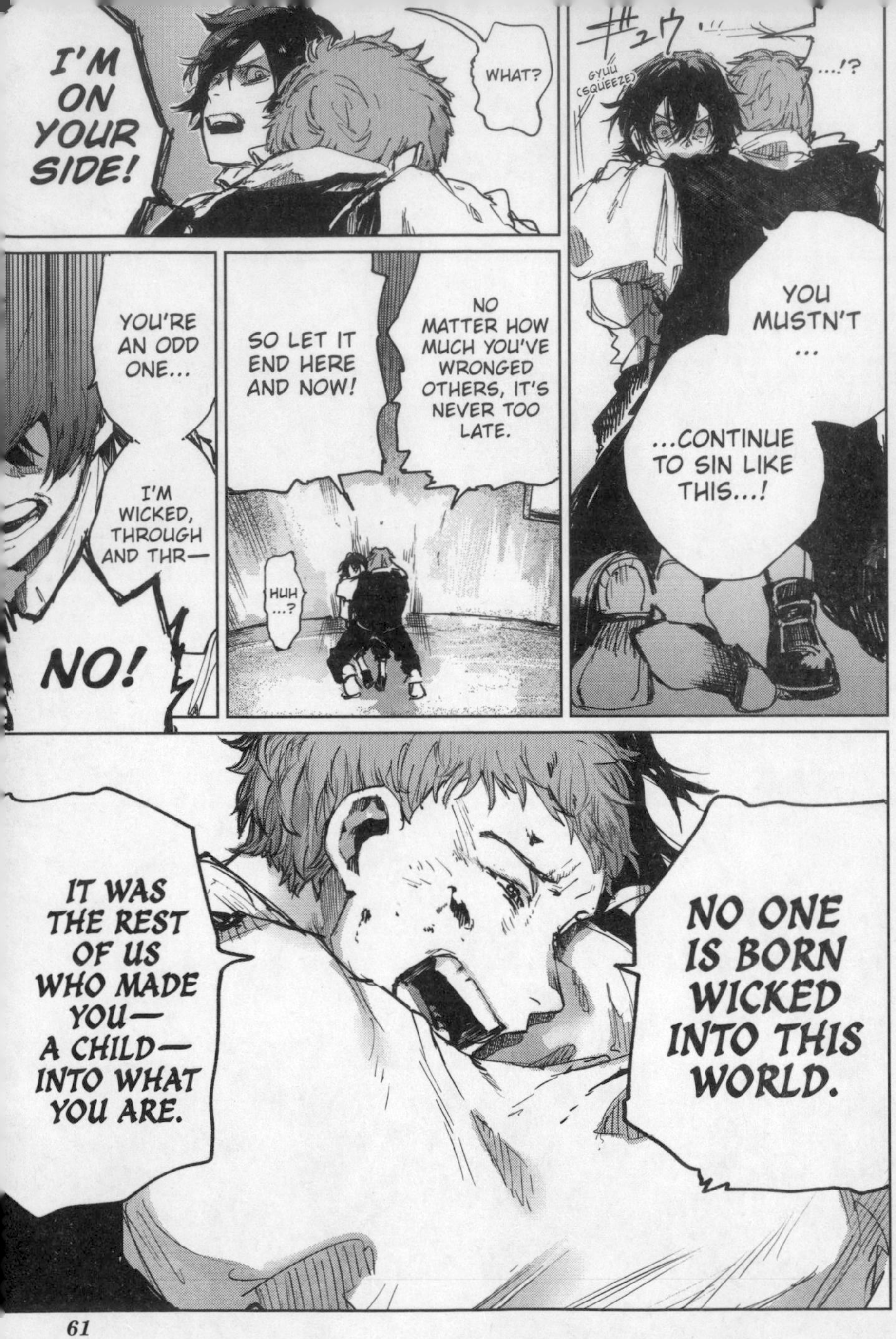
GYUU (SQUEEZE)
...!?
YOU MUSTN'T ...
...CONTINUE TO SIN LIKE THIS...!
WHAT?
I'M ON YOUR SIDE!
NO MATTER HOW MUCH YOU'VE WRONGED OTHERS, IT'S NEVER TOO LATE.
SO LET IT END HERE AND NOW!
HUH ...?
YOU'RE AN ODD ONE...
I'M WICKED, THROUGH AND THR—
NO!
NO ONE IS BORN WICKED INTO THIS WORLD.
IT WAS THE REST OF US WHO MADE YOU—A CHILD—INTO WHAT YOU ARE.

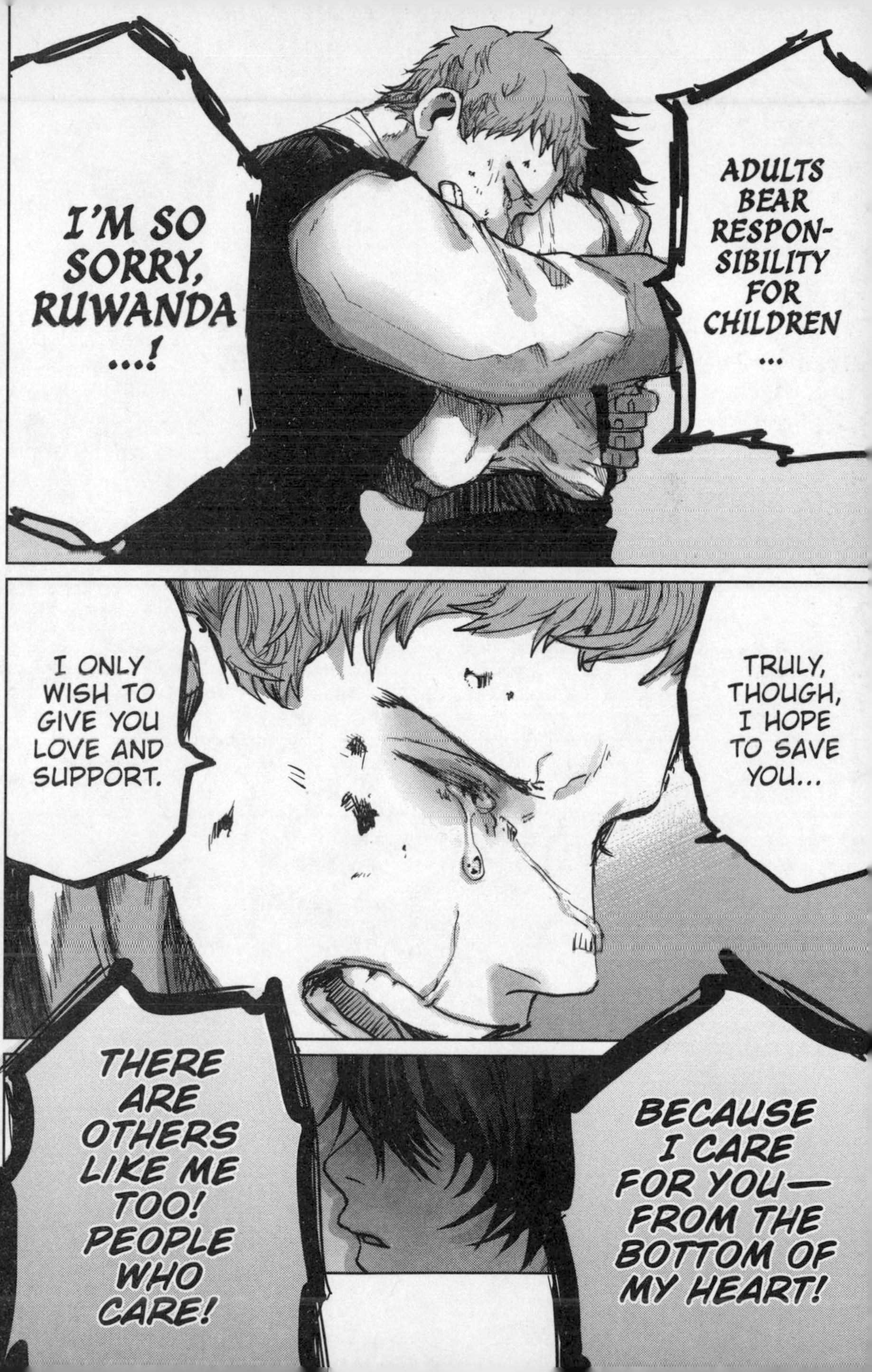
ADULTS BEAR RESPON-SIBILITY FOR CHILDREN...
I'M SO SORRY, RUWANDA...!
TRULY, THOUGH, I HOPE TO SAVE YOU...
I ONLY WISH TO GIVE YOU LOVE AND SUPPORT.
BECAUSE I CARE FOR YOU— FROM THE BOTTOM OF MY HEART!
THERE ARE OTHERS LIKE ME TOO! PEOPLE WHO CARE!

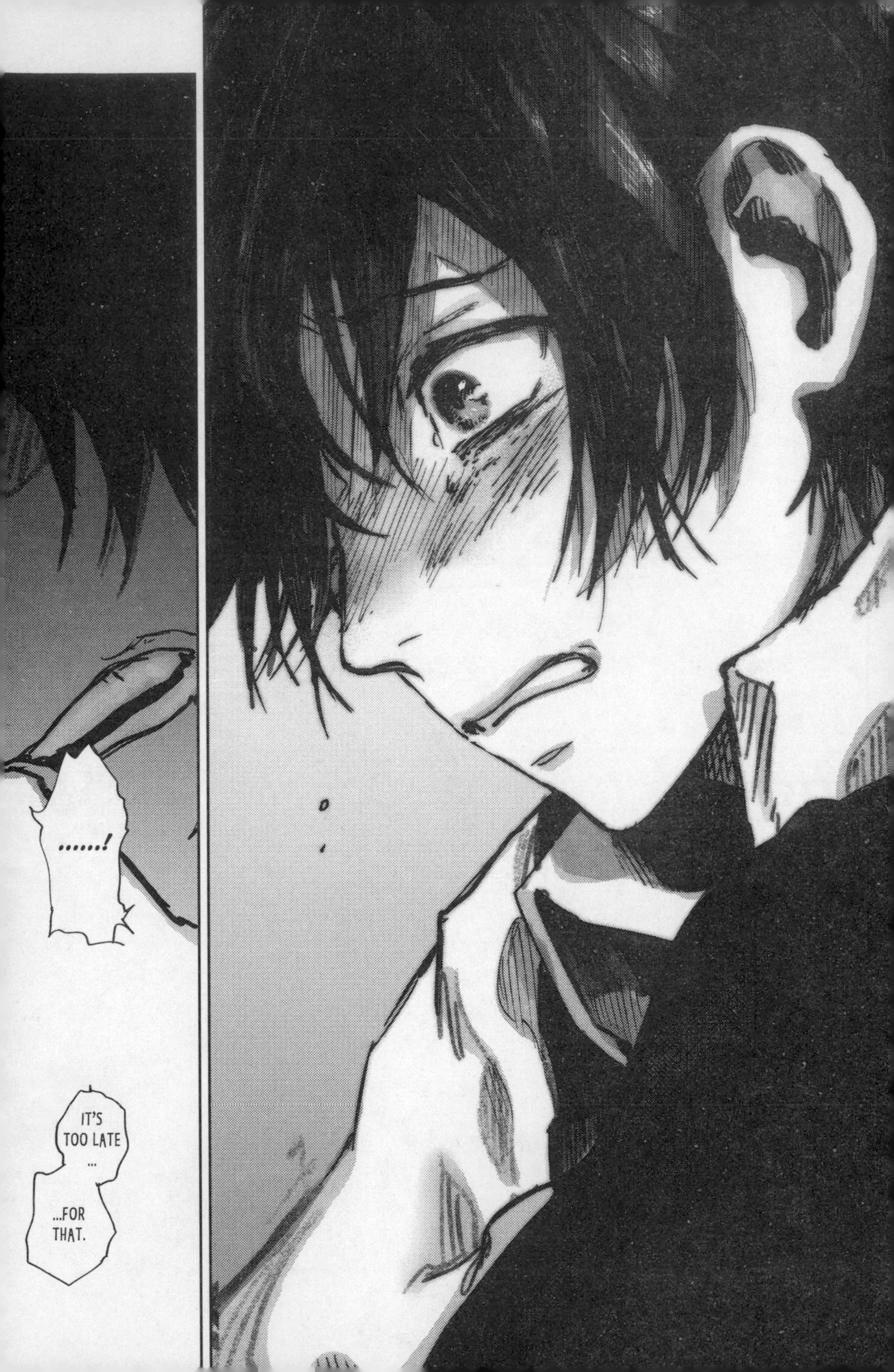
……!
IT'S TOO LATE ... ...FOR THAT.

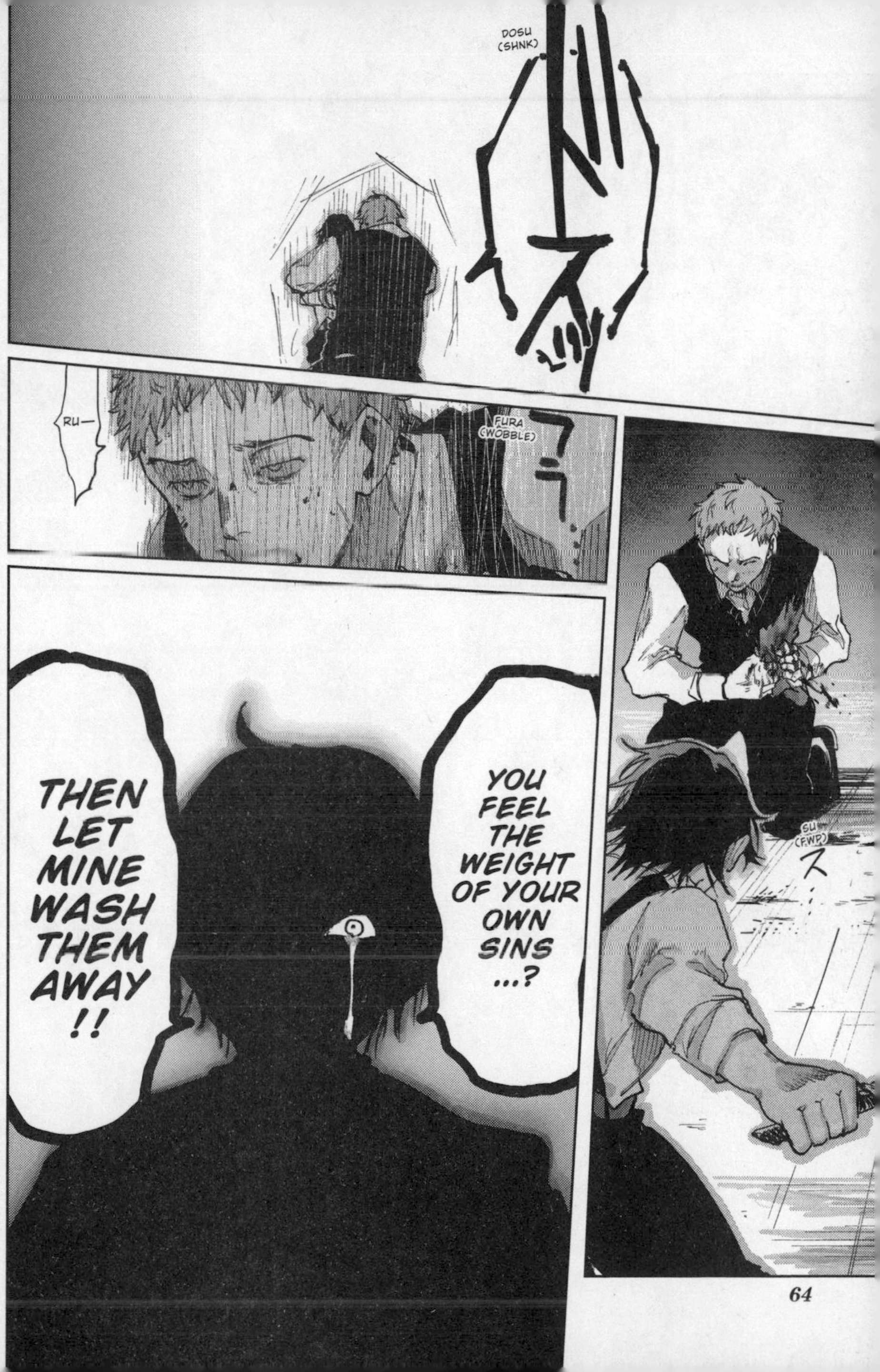
DOSU (SHNK)
SU (FWP)
FURA (WOBBLE)
RU—
YOU FEEL THE WEIGHT OF YOUR OWN SINS ...?
THEN LET MINE WASH THEM AWAY !!

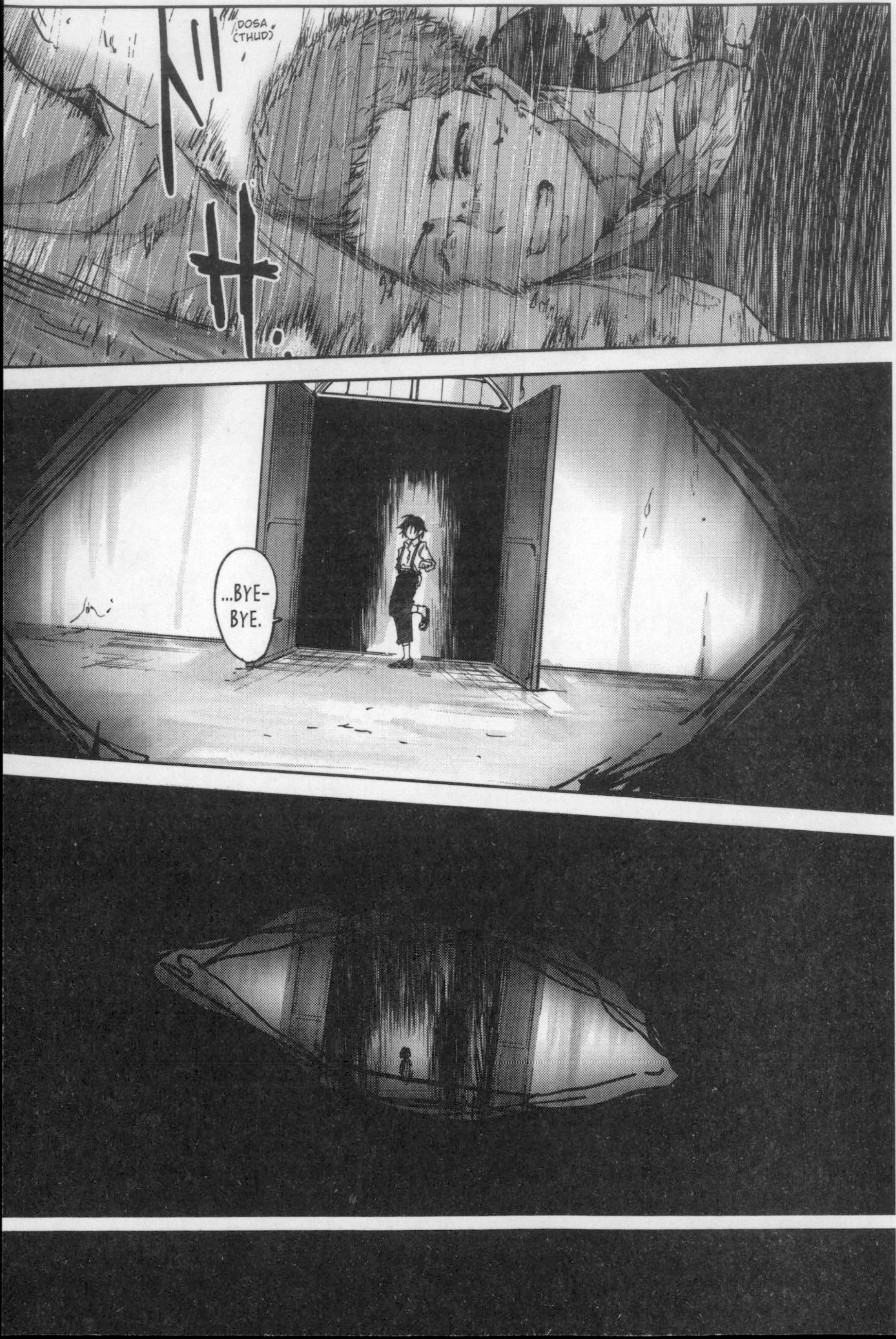
DOSA (THUD)
...BYE-BYE.

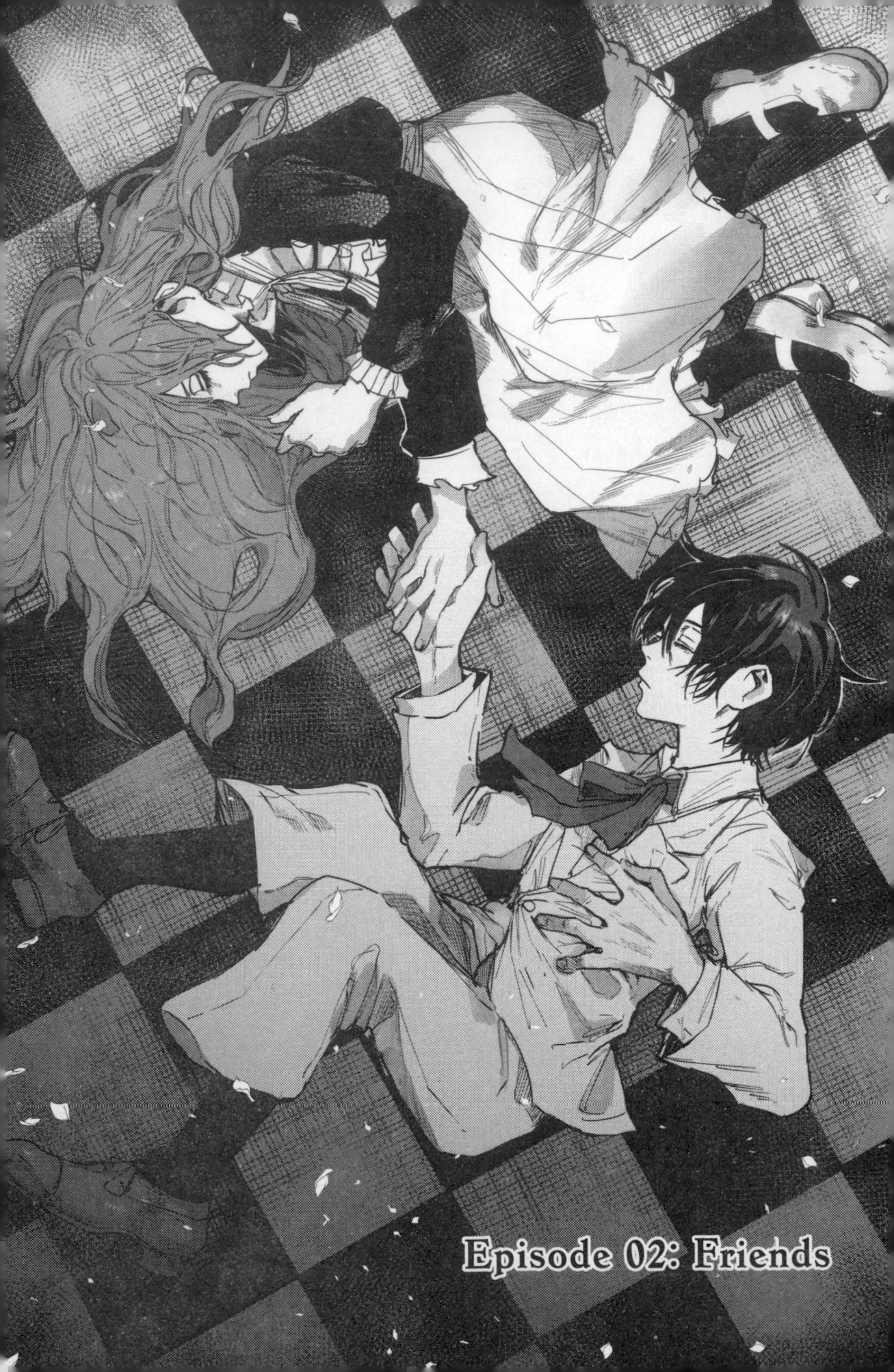
Episode 02: Friends

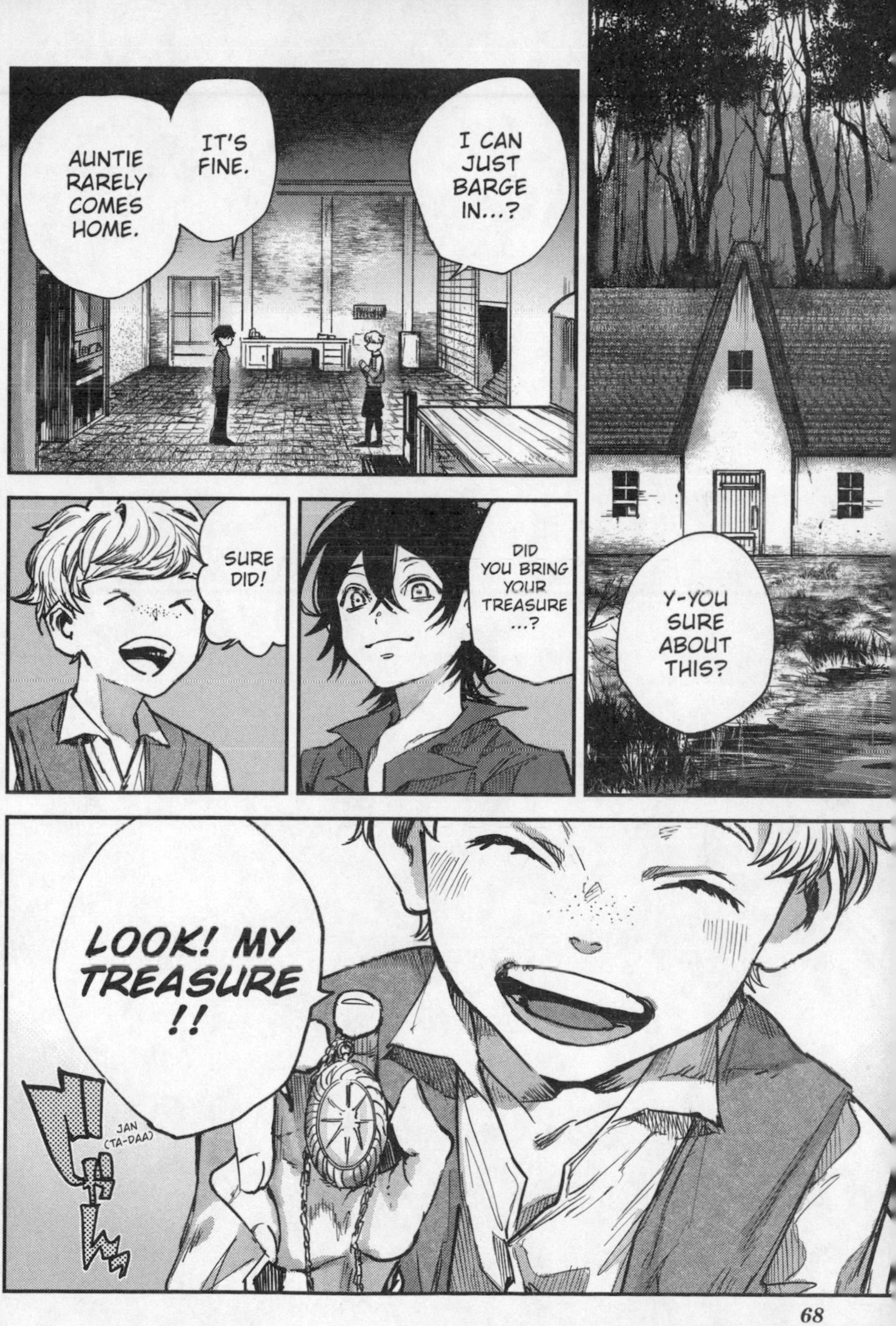
Y-YOU SURE ABOUT THIS?
I CAN JUST BARGE IN...?
IT'S FINE.
AUNTIE RARELY COMES HOME.
DID YOU BRING YOUR TREASURE ...?
SURE DID!
LOOK! MY TREASURE !!
JAN (TA-DAA)

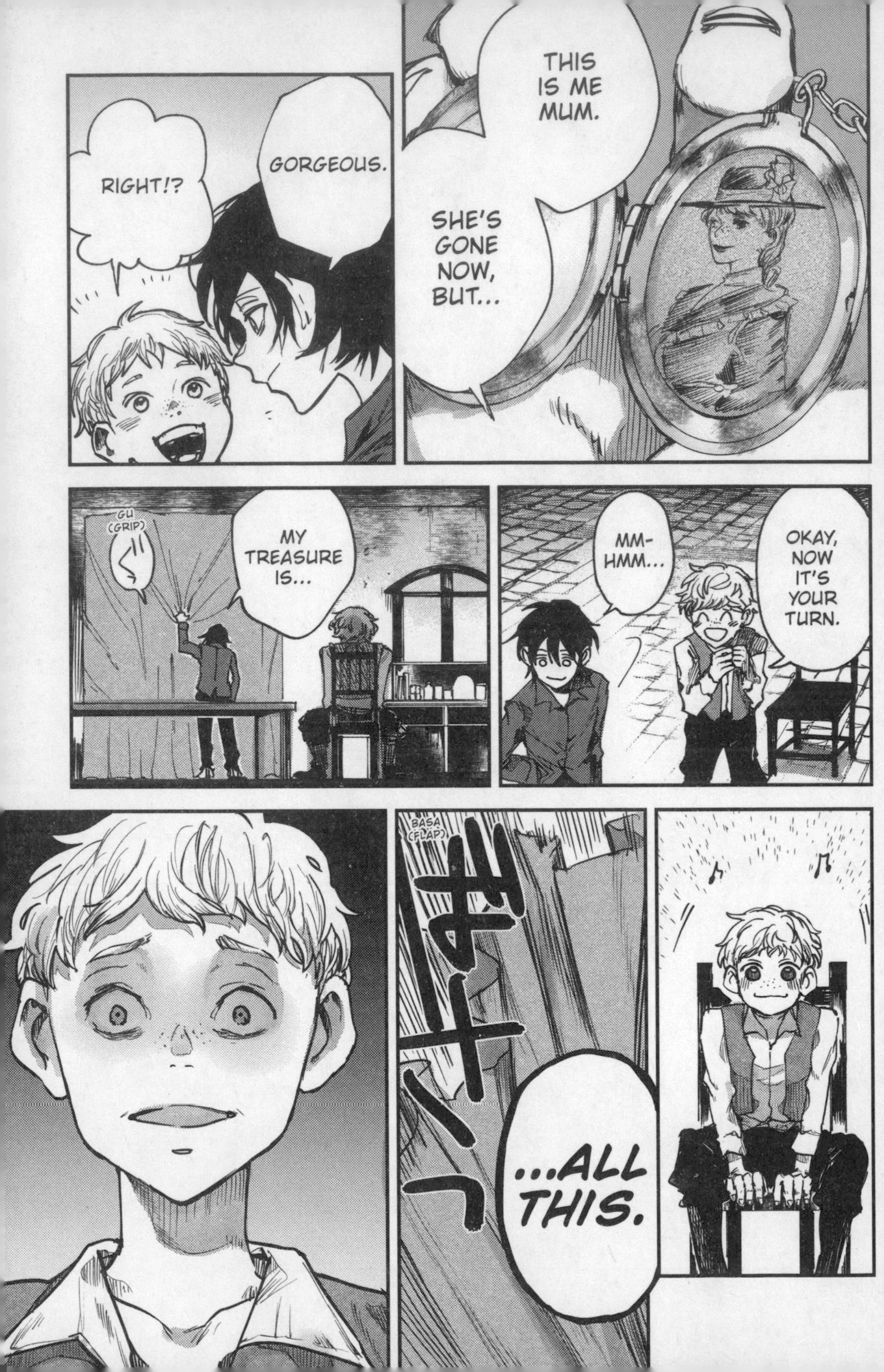
THIS IS ME MUM.
SHE'S GONE NOW, BUT...
GORGEOUS.
RIGHT!?
OKAY, NOW IT'S YOUR TURN.
MM-HMM...
MY TREASURE IS...
GU (GRIP)
BASA (FLAP)
...ALL THIS.

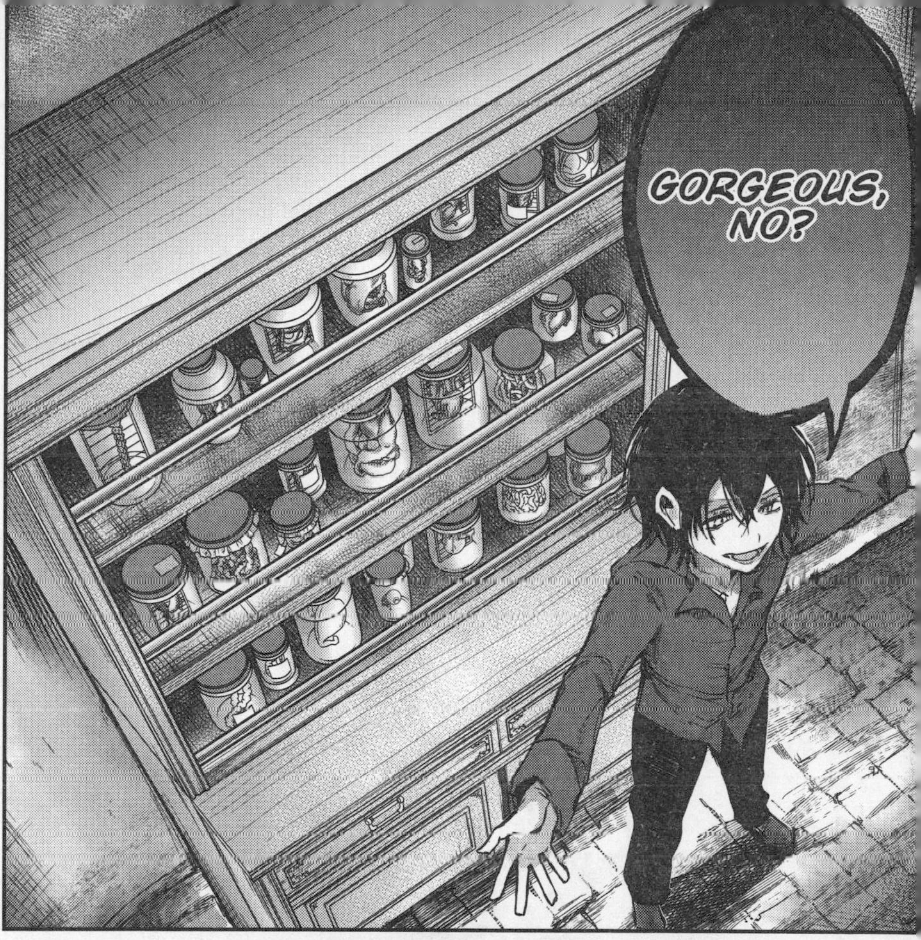
GORGEOUS, NO?
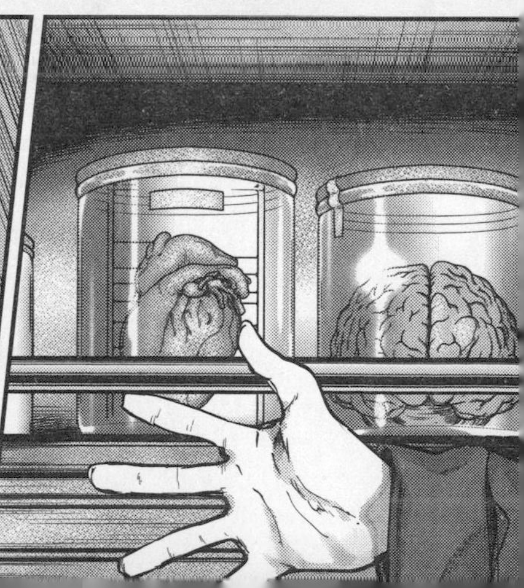
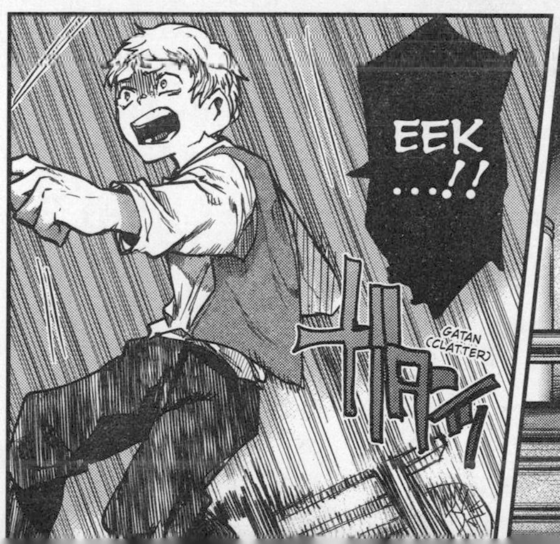
EEK ...!!
GATAN (CLATTER)

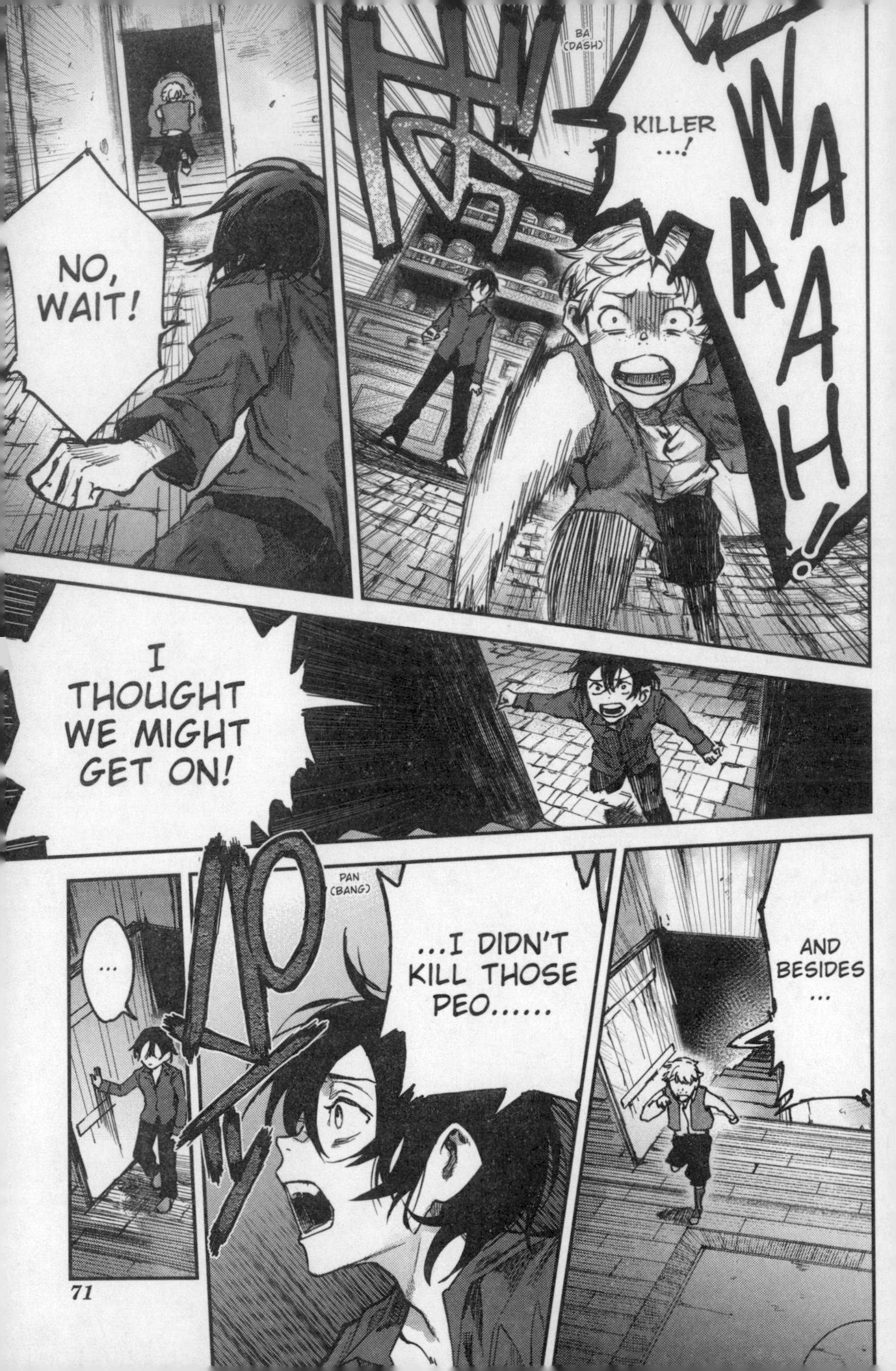
BA (DASH)
KILLER ...!
WAAAH!
NO, WAIT!
I THOUGHT WE MIGHT GET ON!
AND BESIDES ...
PAN (BANG)
...I DIDN'T KILL THOSE PEO......
...

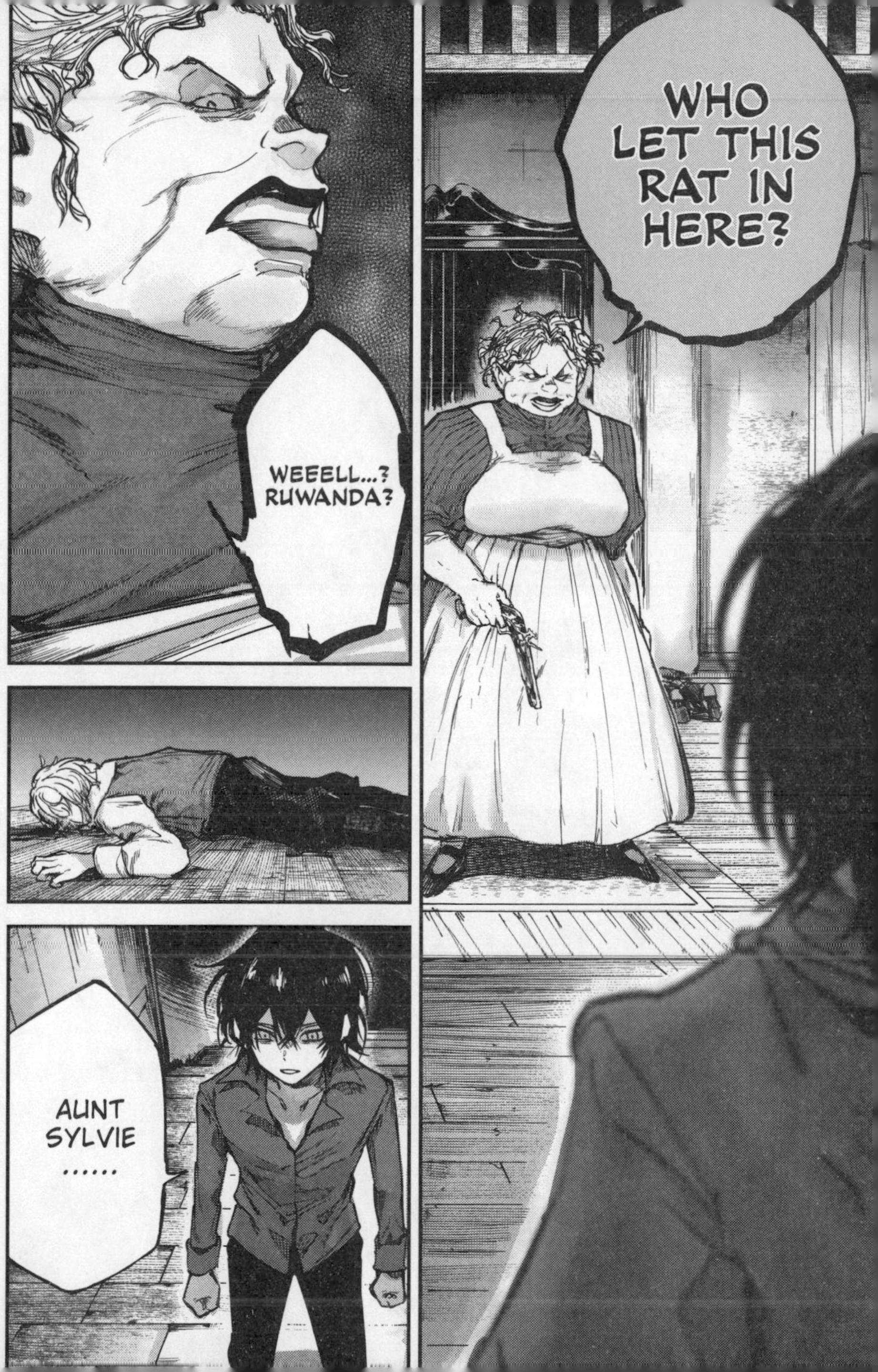
WHO LET THIS RAT IN HERE?
WEEELL...? RUWANDA?
AUNT SYLVIE ......

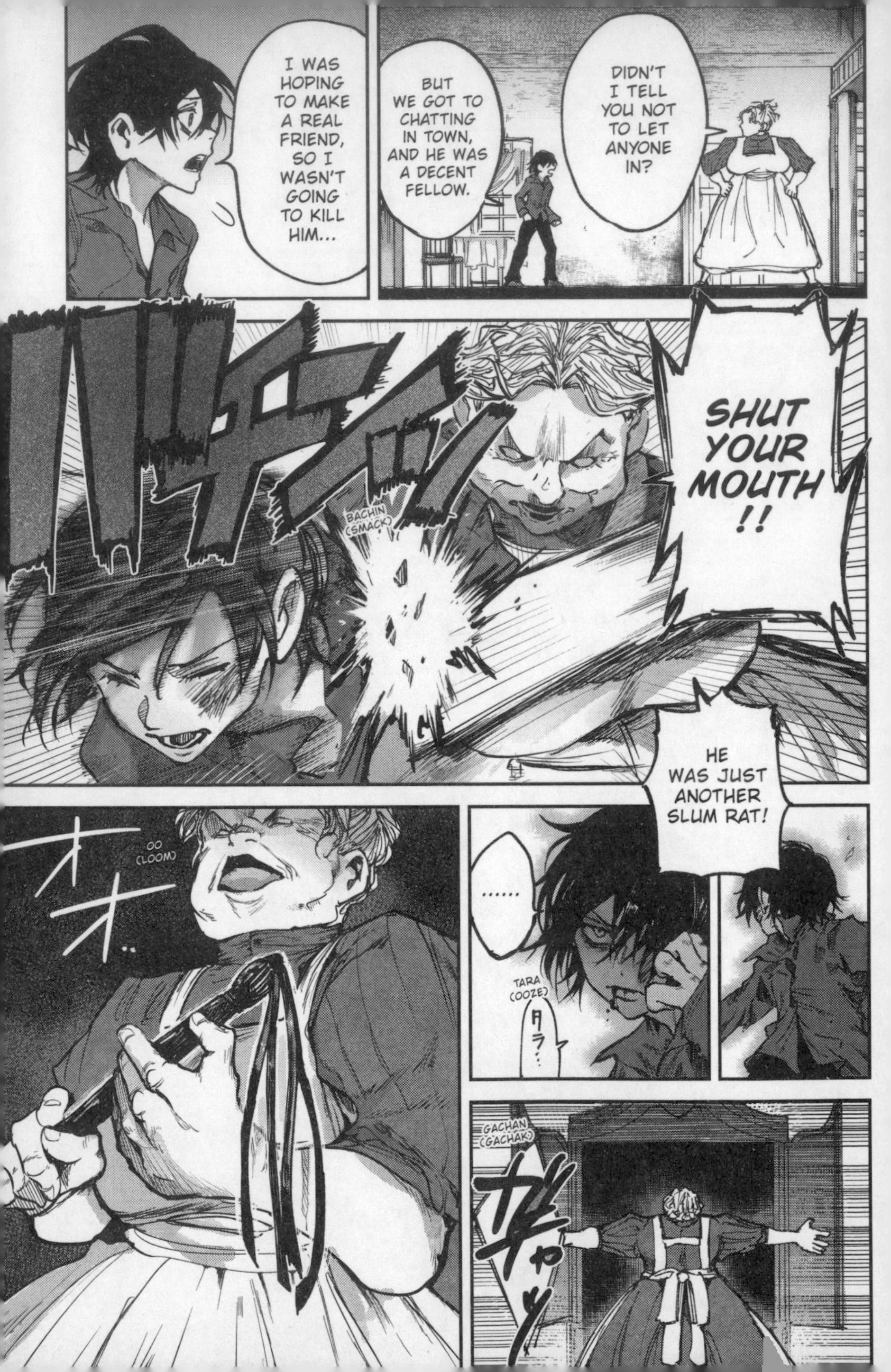
DIDN'T I TELL YOU NOT TO LET ANYONE IN?
BUT WE GOT TO CHATTING IN TOWN, AND HE WAS A DECENT FELLOW.
I WAS HOPING TO MAKE A REAL FRIEND, SO I WASN'T GOING TO KILL HIM...
SHUT YOUR MOUTH!!
BACHIN (SMACK)
HE WAS JUST ANOTHER SLUM RAT!
......
TARA (OOZE)
GACHAN (GACHAK)
OO (LOOM)

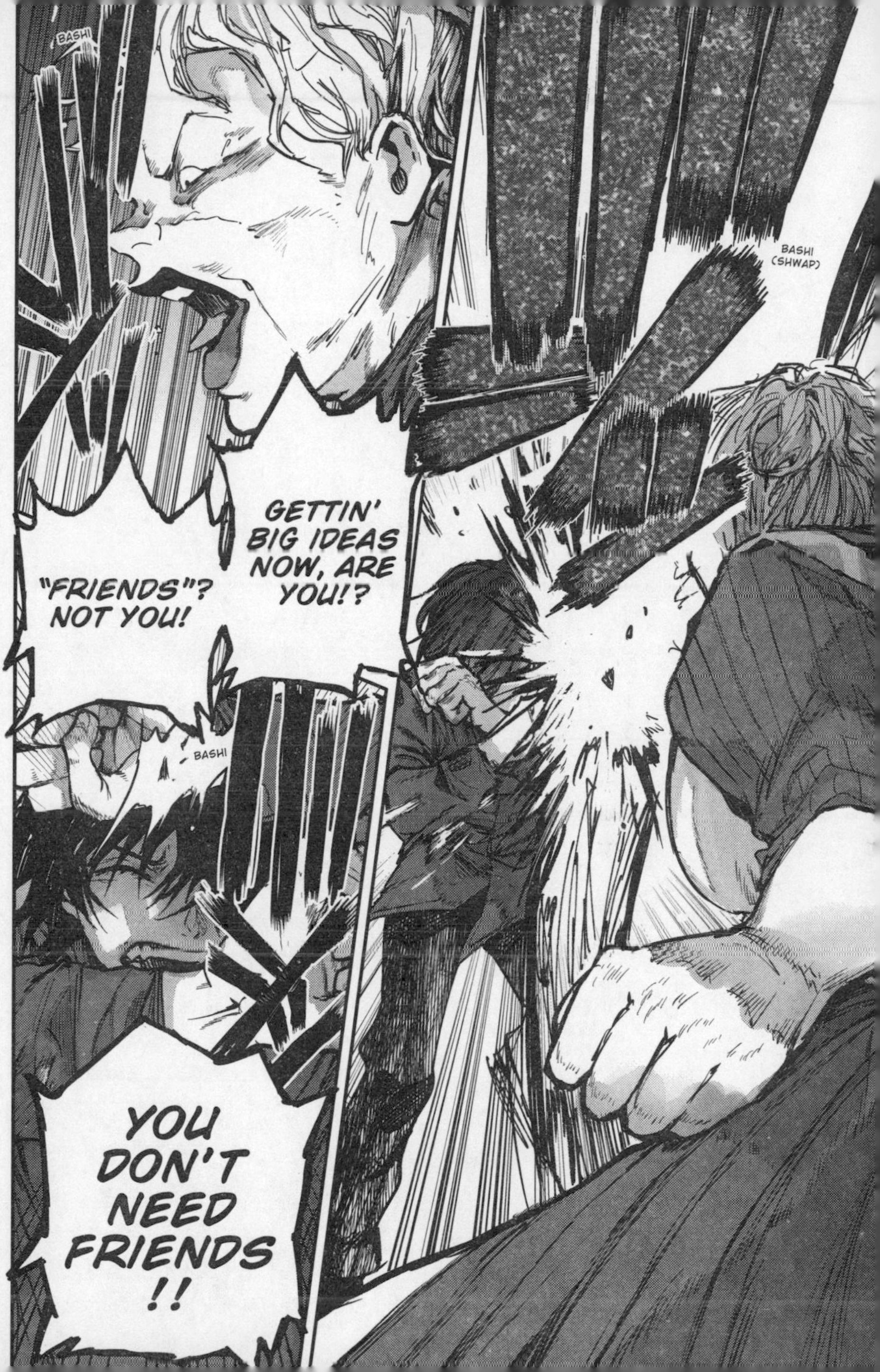
BASHI (SHWAP)
BASHI
GETTIN' BIG IDEAS NOW, ARE YOU!?
"FRIENDS"? NOT YOU!
BASHI
YOU DON'T NEED FRIENDS !!

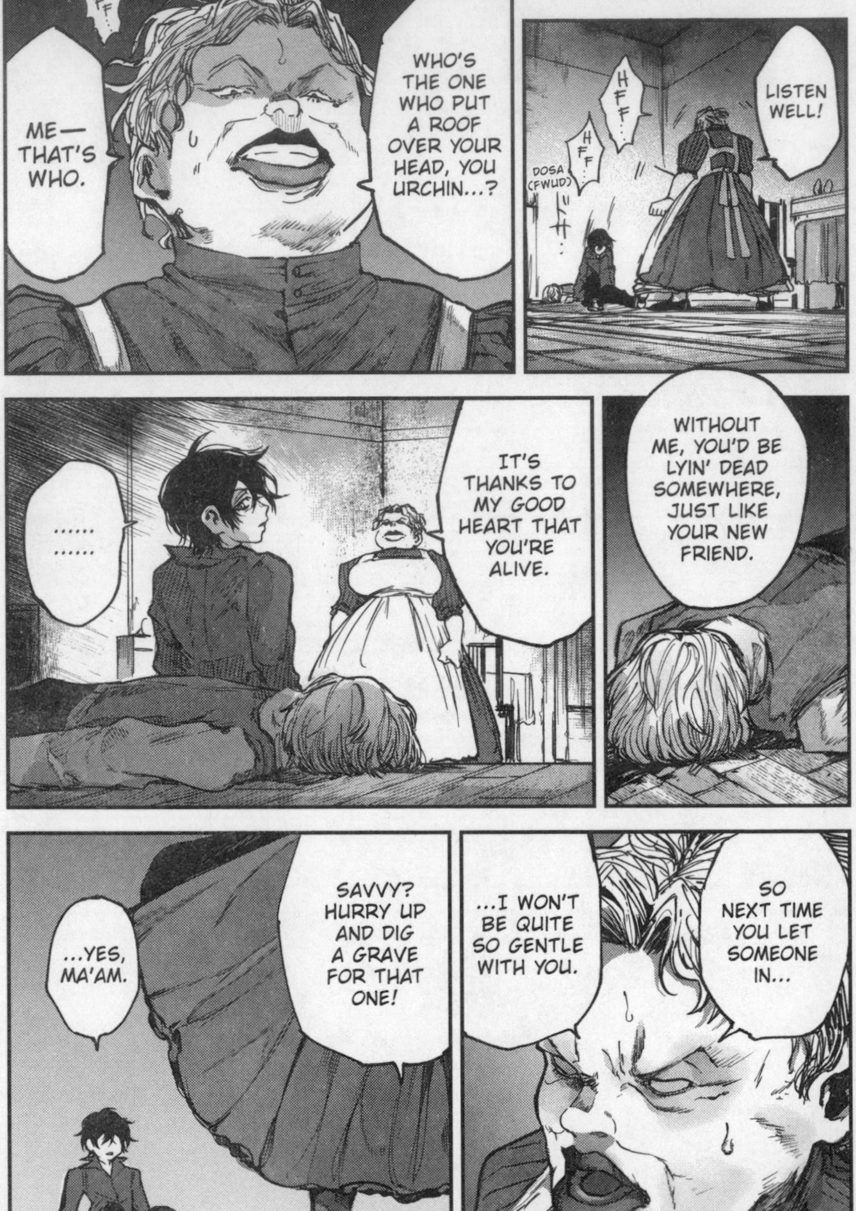
LISTEN WELL!
HFF...
HFF...
DOSA (FWUD)
HFF...
WHO'S THE ONE WHO PUT A ROOF OVER YOUR HEAD, YOU URCHIN...?
ME—THAT'S WHO.
WITHOUT ME, YOU'D BE LYIN' DEAD SOMEWHERE, JUST LIKE YOUR NEW FRIEND.
IT'S THANKS TO MY GOOD HEART THAT YOU'RE ALIVE.
....
SO NEXT TIME YOU LET SOMEONE IN...
...I WON'T BE QUITE SO GENTLE WITH YOU.
SAVVY? HURRY UP AND DIG A GRAVE FOR THAT ONE!
...YES, MA'AM.

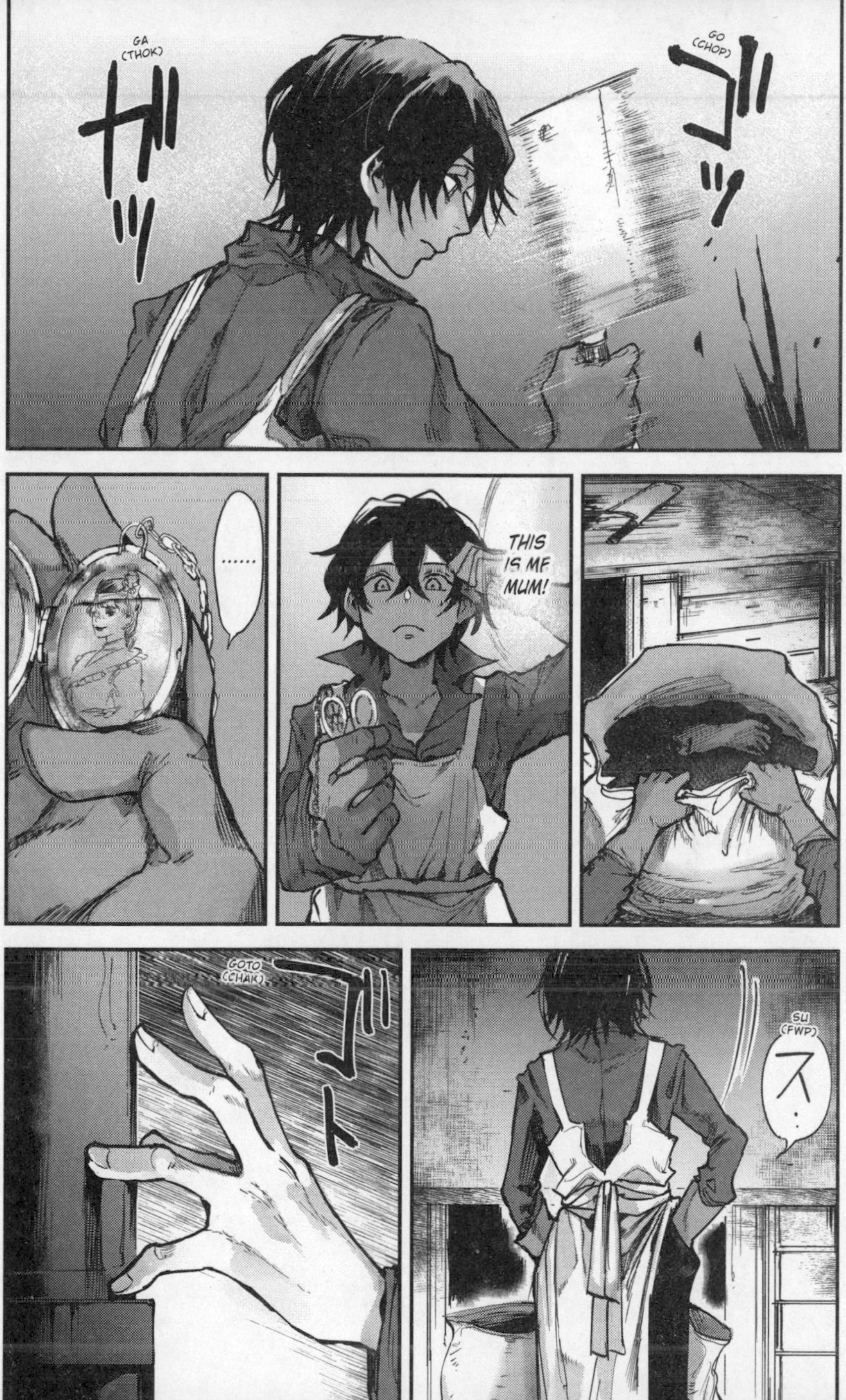
GO (CHOP)
ゴッ
GA (THOK)
THIS IS ME MUM!
......
SU (FWP)
ス
GOTO (CHAK)
ゴトッ

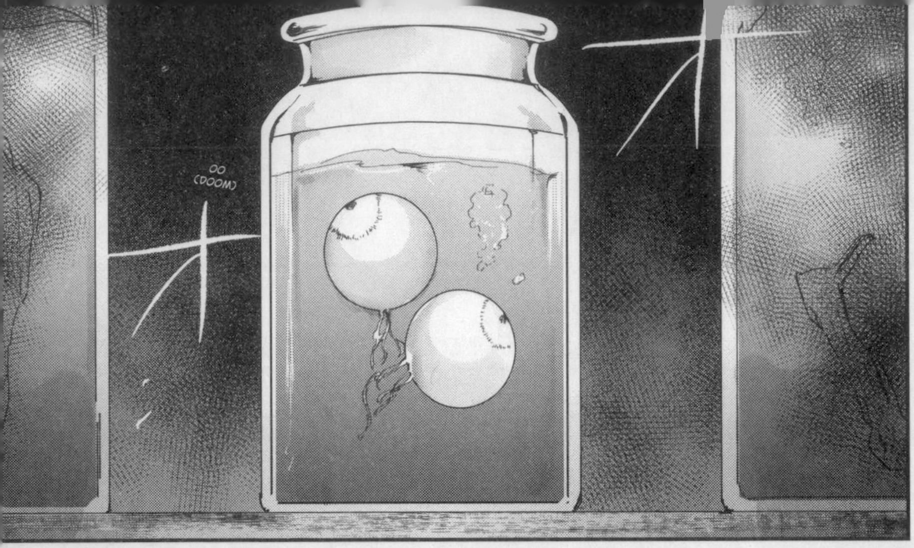
OO
(DOOM)

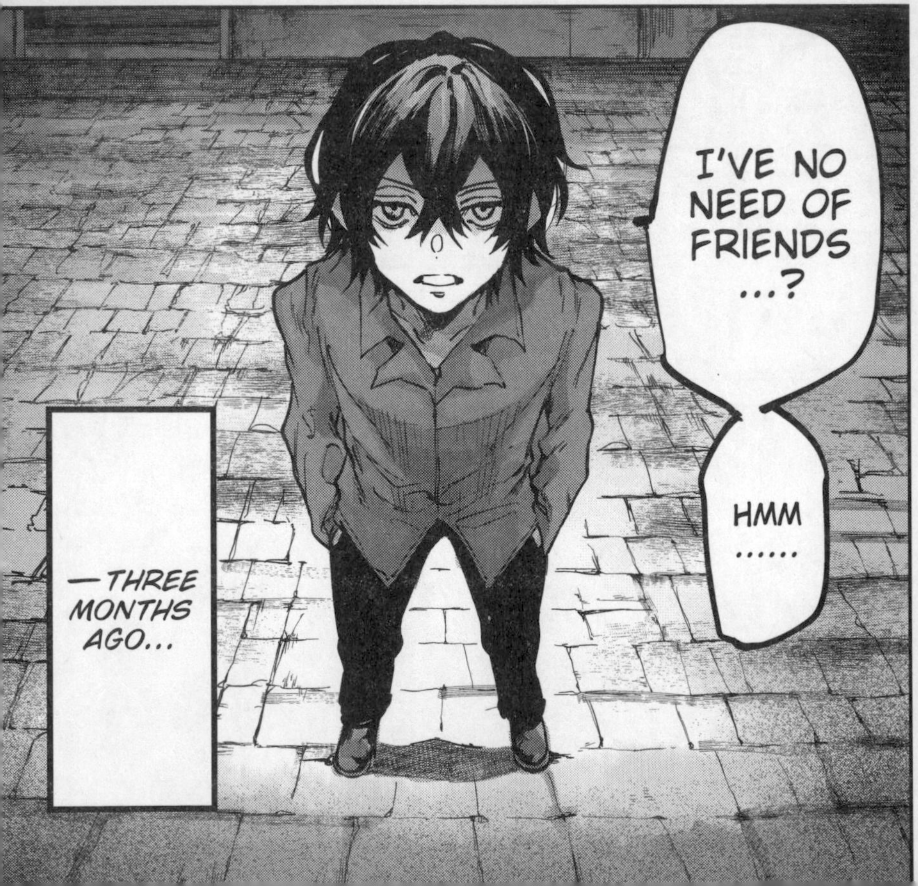
I'VE NO NEED OF FRIENDS ...?
HMM ......
—THREE MONTHS AGO...

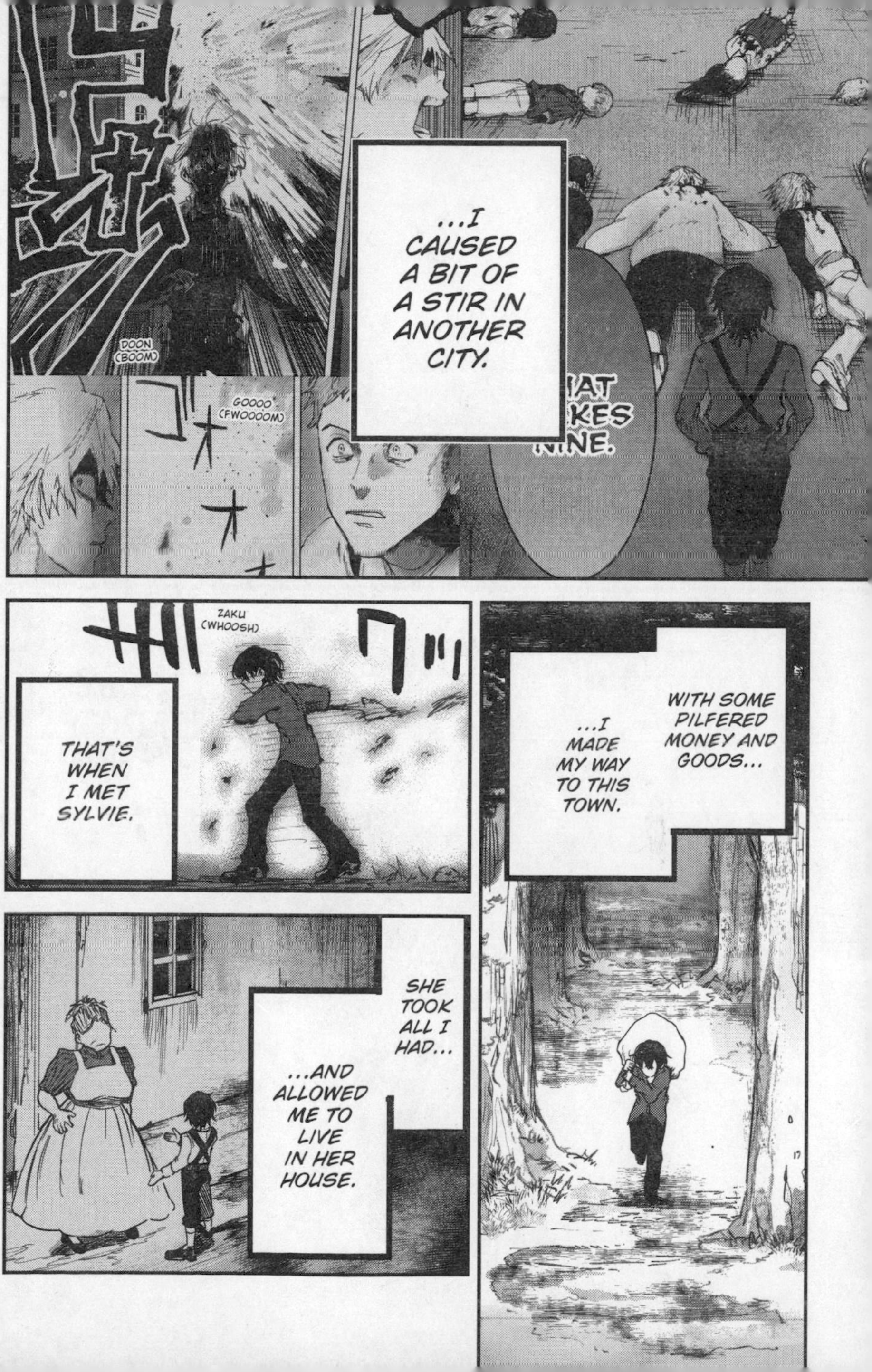
...I CAUSED A BIT OF A STIR IN ANOTHER CITY.
DOON (BOOM)
GOOOO (FWOOOOM)
WITH SOME PILFERED MONEY AND GOODS...
...I MADE MY WAY TO THIS TOWN.
ZAKU (WHOOSH)
THAT'S WHEN I MET SYLVIE.
SHE TOOK ALL I HAD...
...AND ALLOWED ME TO LIVE IN HER HOUSE.

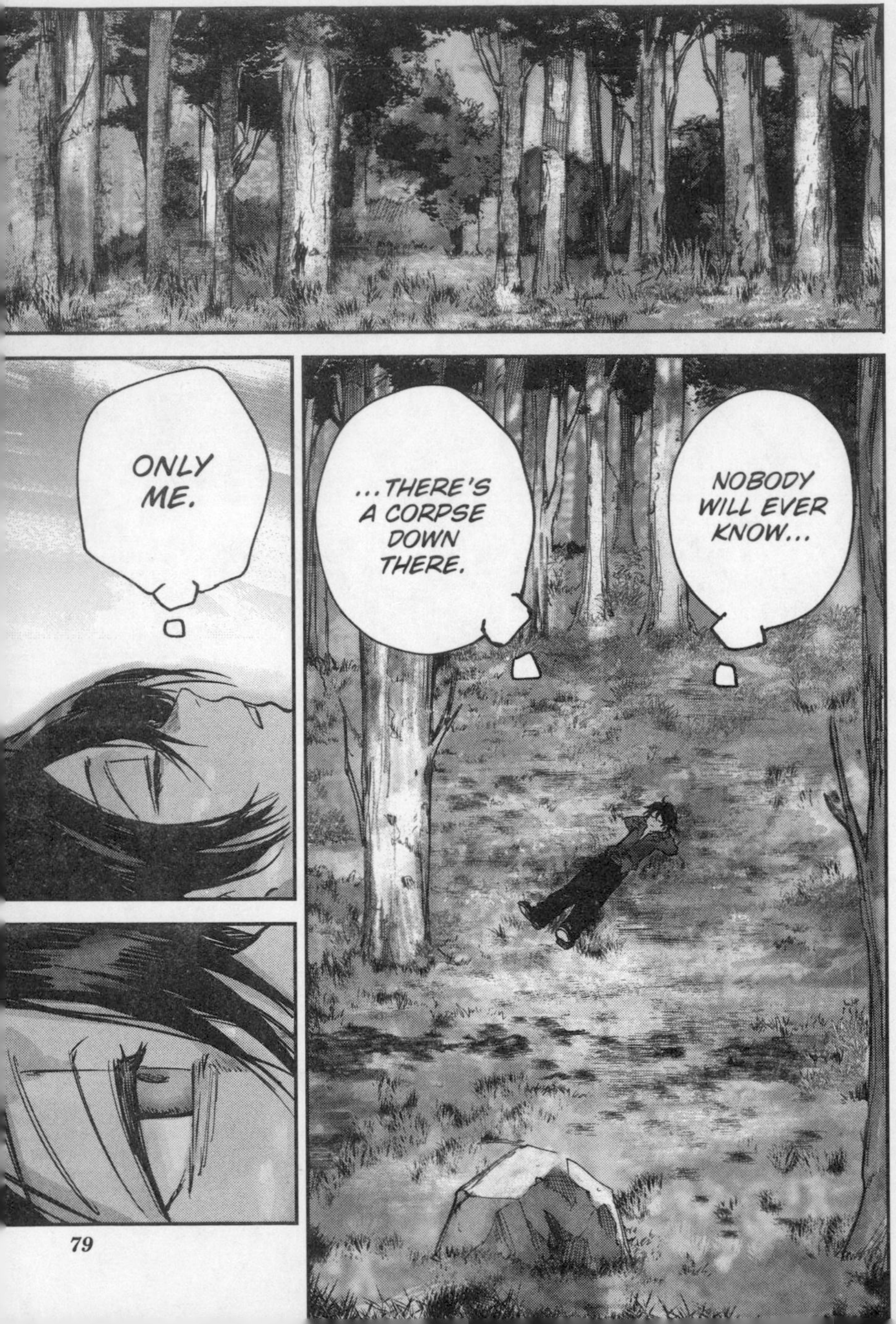
NOBODY WILL EVER KNOW...
...THERE'S A CORPSE DOWN THERE.
ONLY ME.

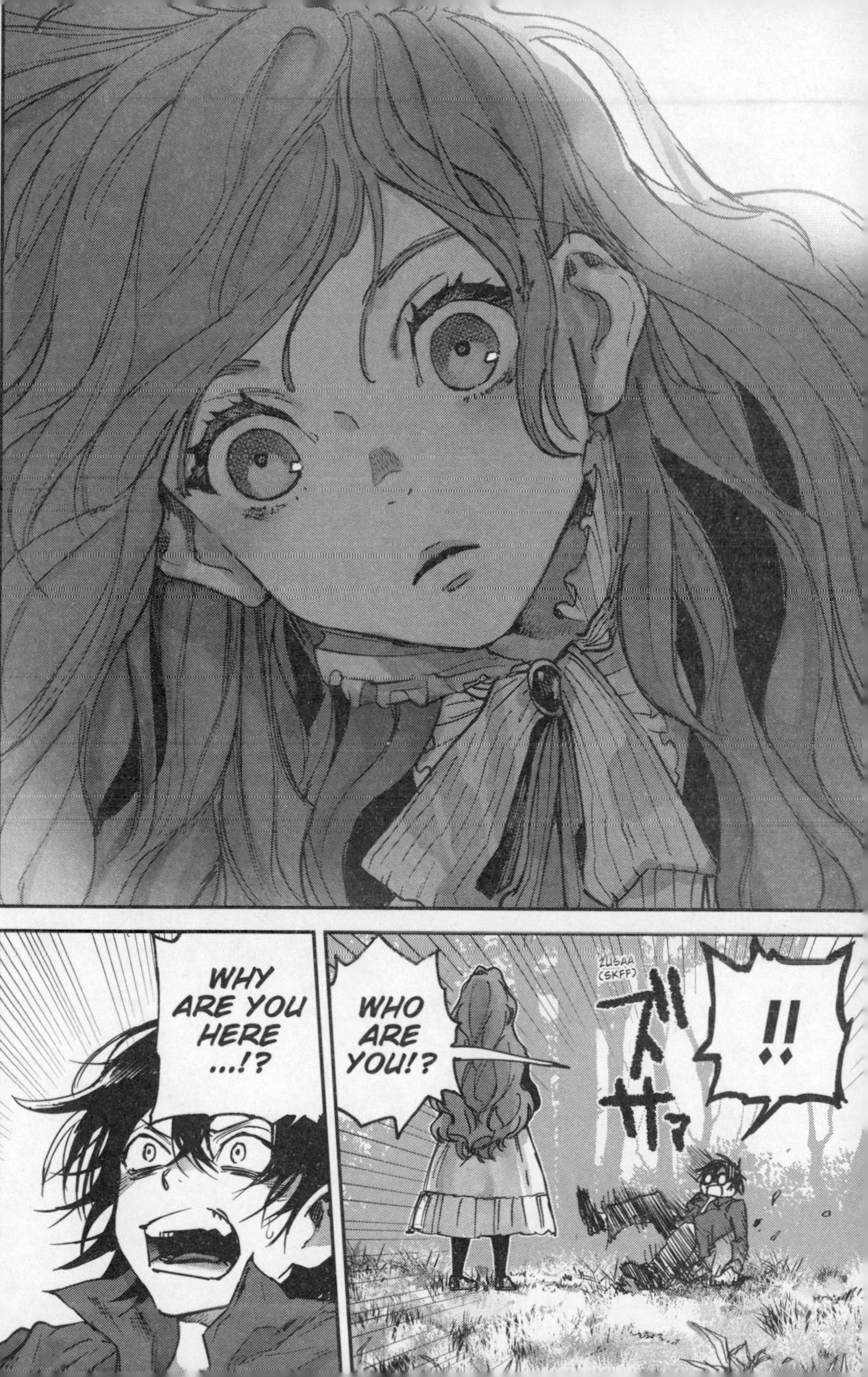
ZUSAA (SKFF)
!!
WHO ARE YOU!?
WHY ARE YOU HERE ...!?

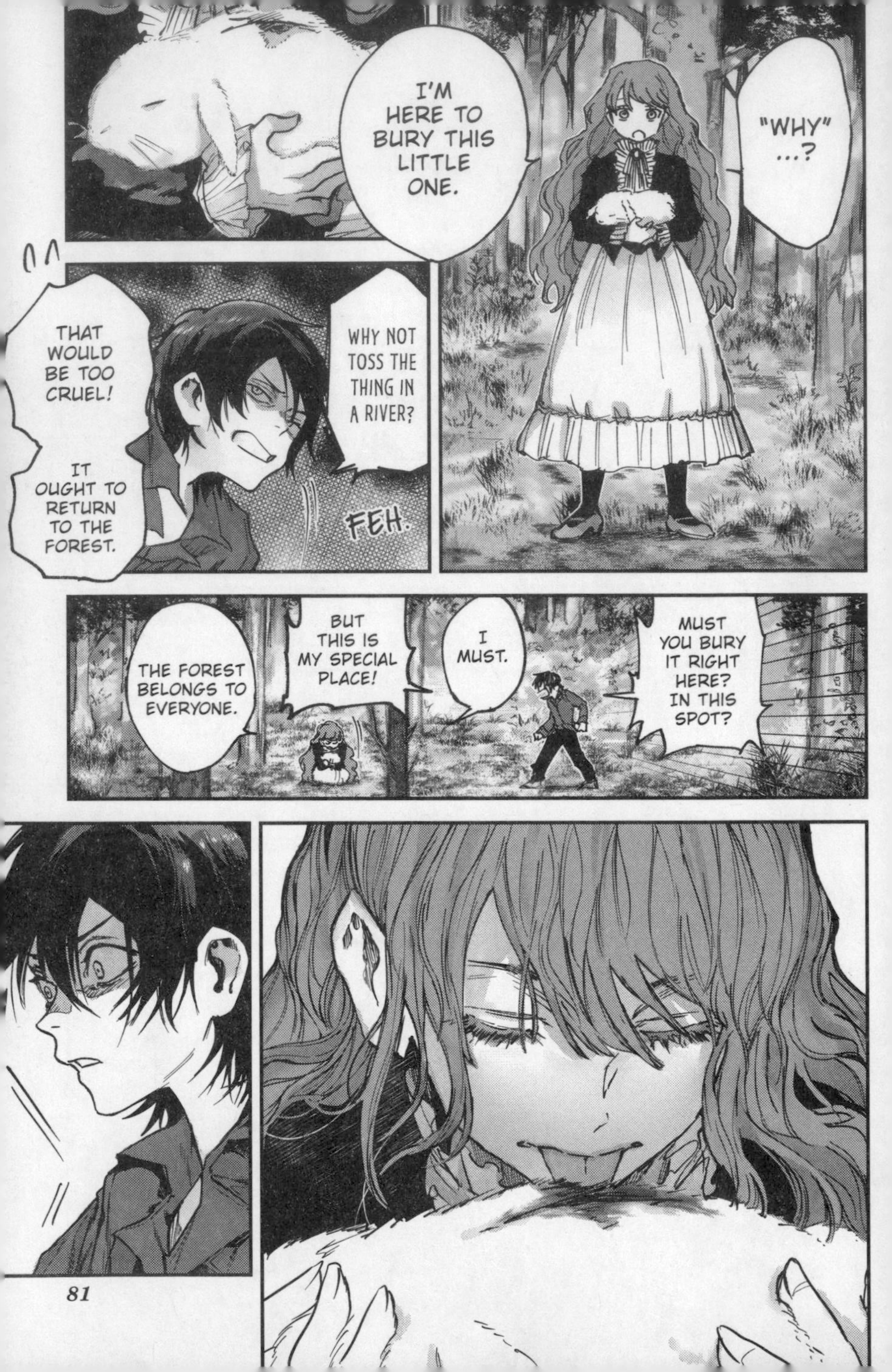
"WHY" ...?
I'M HERE TO BURY THIS LITTLE ONE.
WHY NOT TOSS THE THING IN A RIVER?
FEH.
THAT WOULD BE TOO CRUEL!
IT OUGHT TO RETURN TO THE FOREST.
MUST YOU BURY IT RIGHT HERE? IN THIS SPOT?
I MUST.
BUT THIS IS MY SPECIAL PLACE!
THE FOREST BELONGS TO EVERYONE.

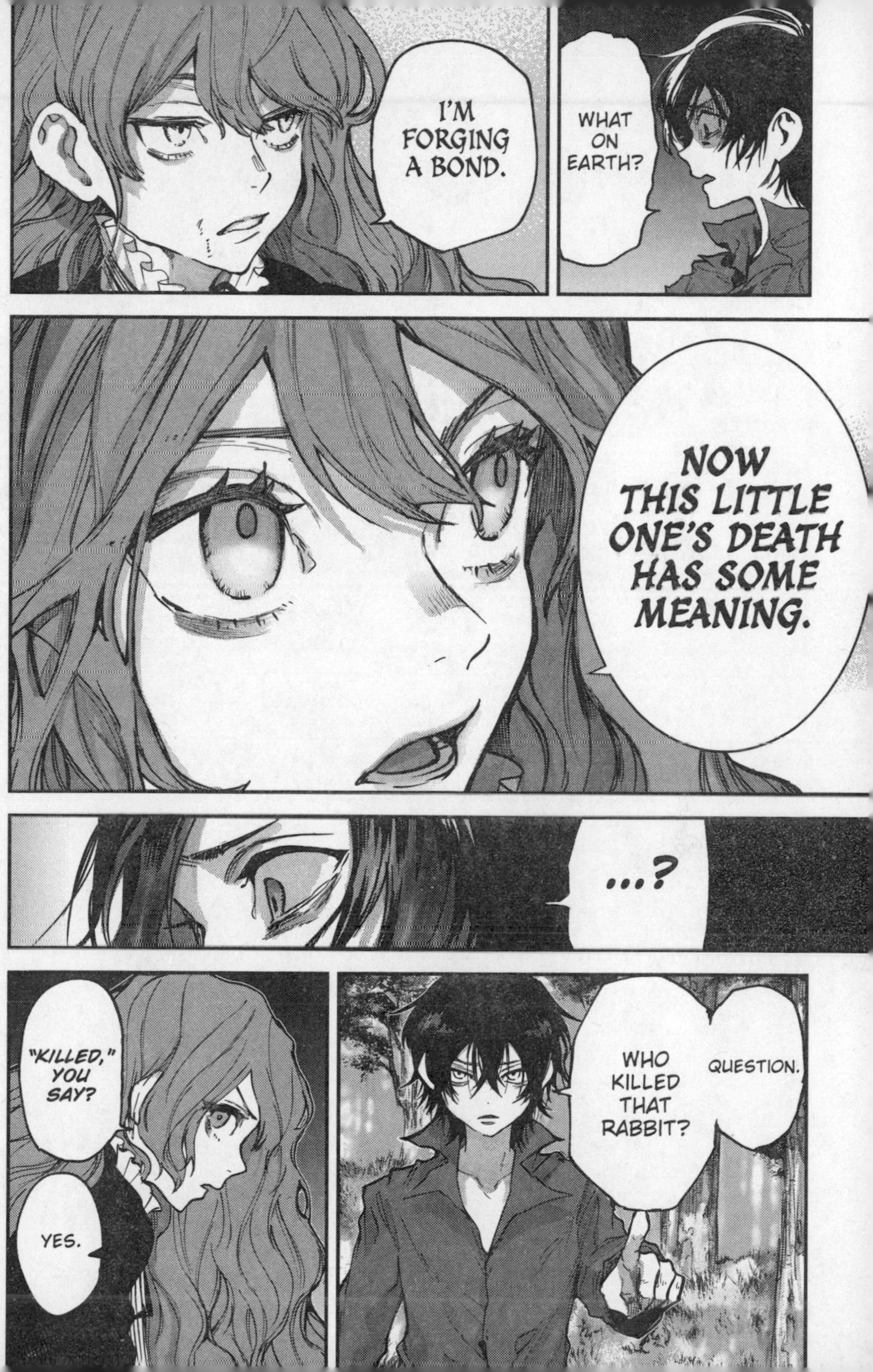
WHAT ON EARTH?
I'M FORGING A BOND.
NOW THIS LITTLE ONE'S DEATH HAS SOME MEANING.
...?
QUESTION.
WHO KILLED THAT RABBIT?
"KILLED," YOU SAY?
YES.

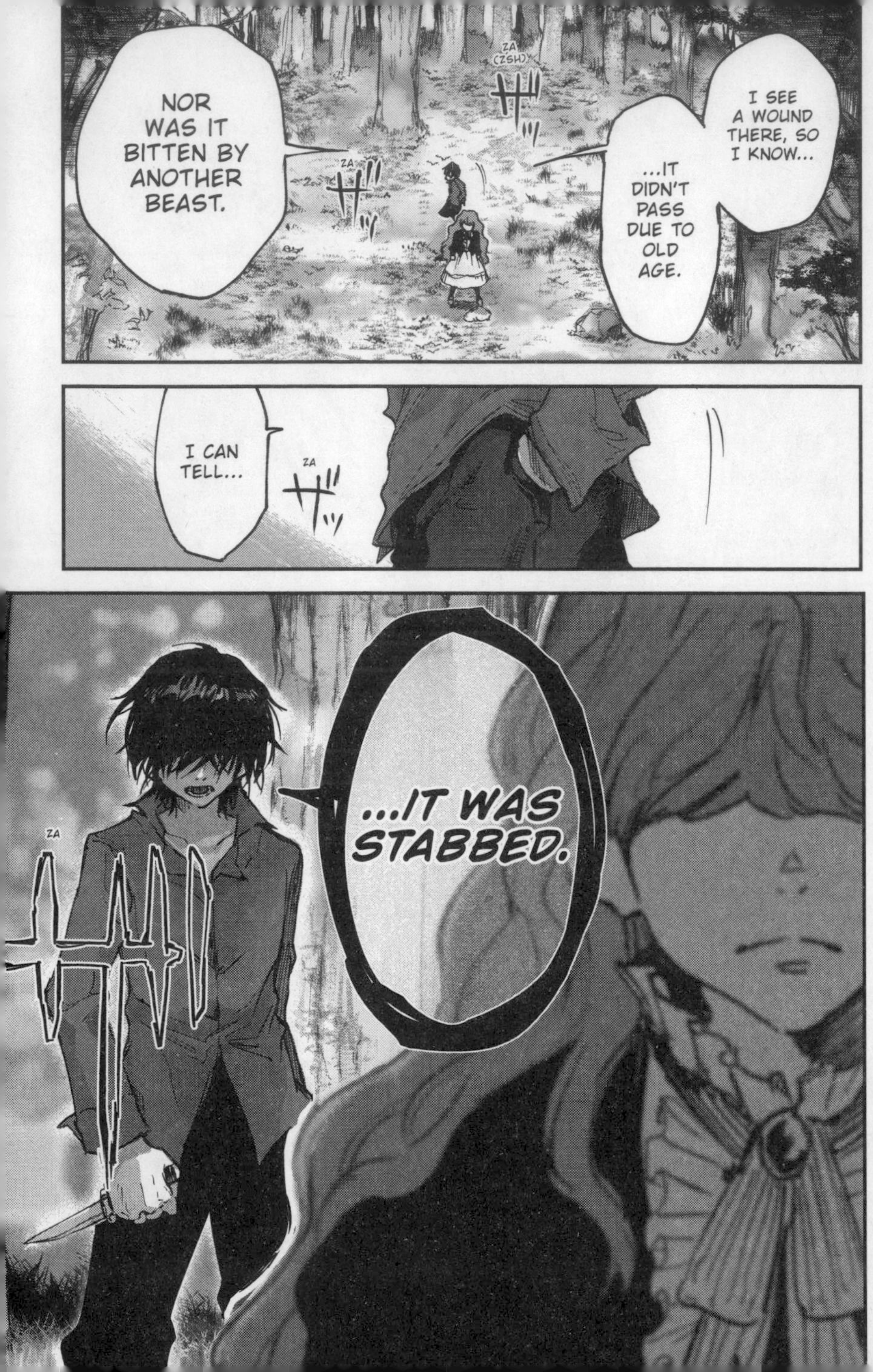
I SEE A WOUND THERE, SO I KNOW...
...IT DIDN'T PASS DUE TO OLD AGE.
ZA (ZSH)
ZA
NOR WAS IT BITTEN BY ANOTHER BEAST.
ZA
I CAN TELL...
...IT WAS STABBED.
ZA

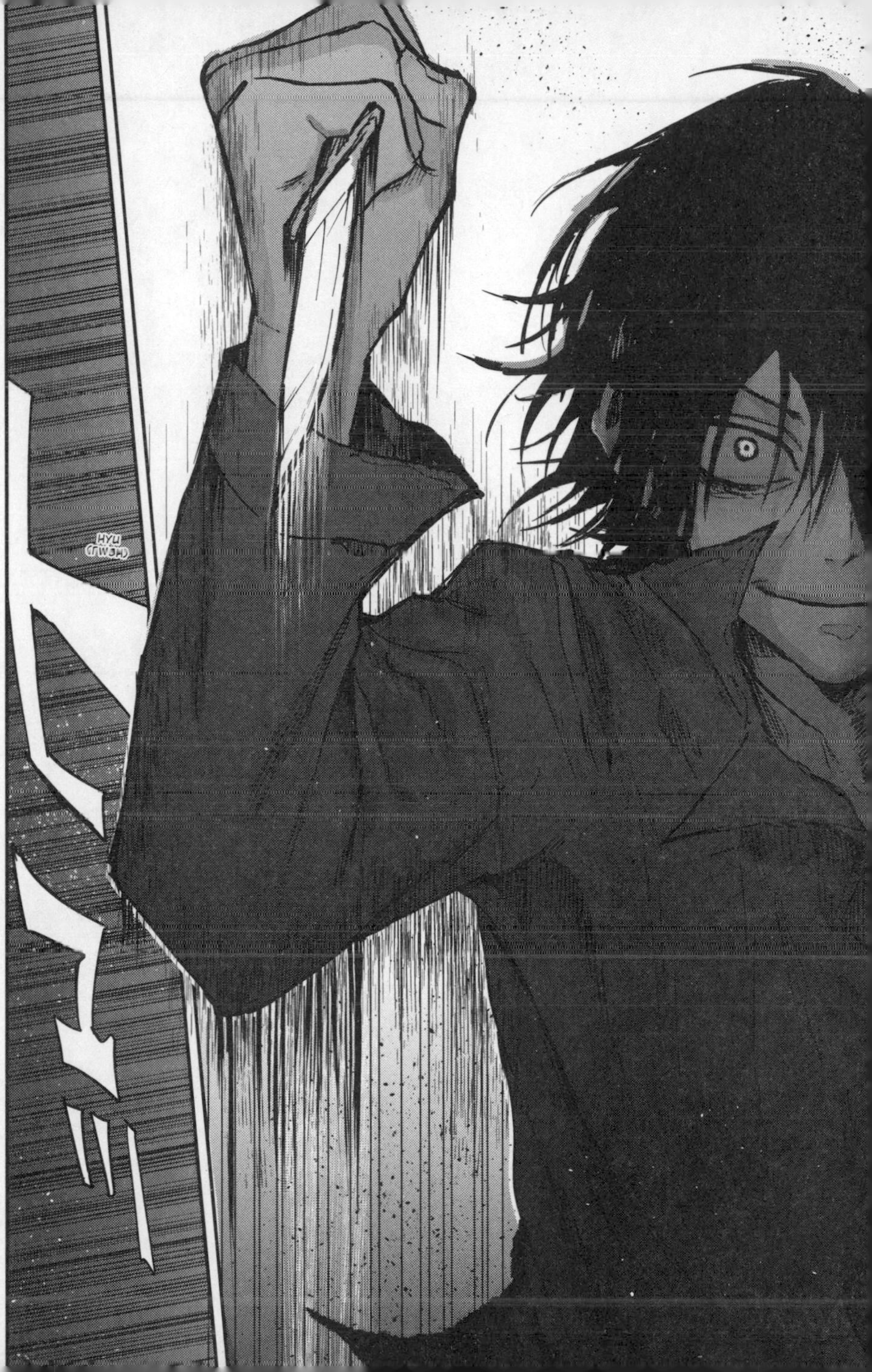
HYU
(FWSH)

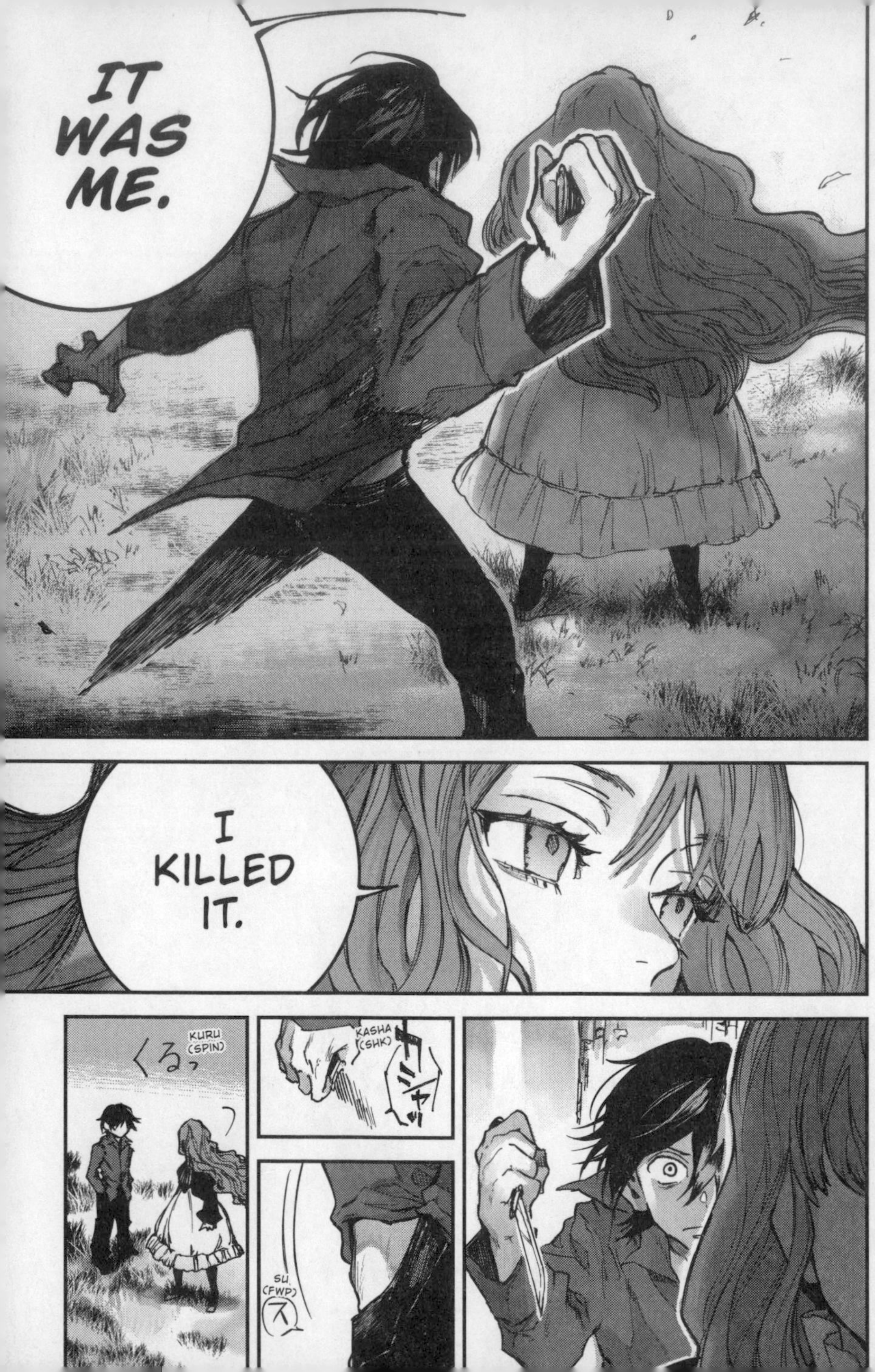
IT WAS ME.
I KILLED IT.
KASHA (SHK)
シャッ
SU (FWP)
ス
KURU (SPIN)
くるっ

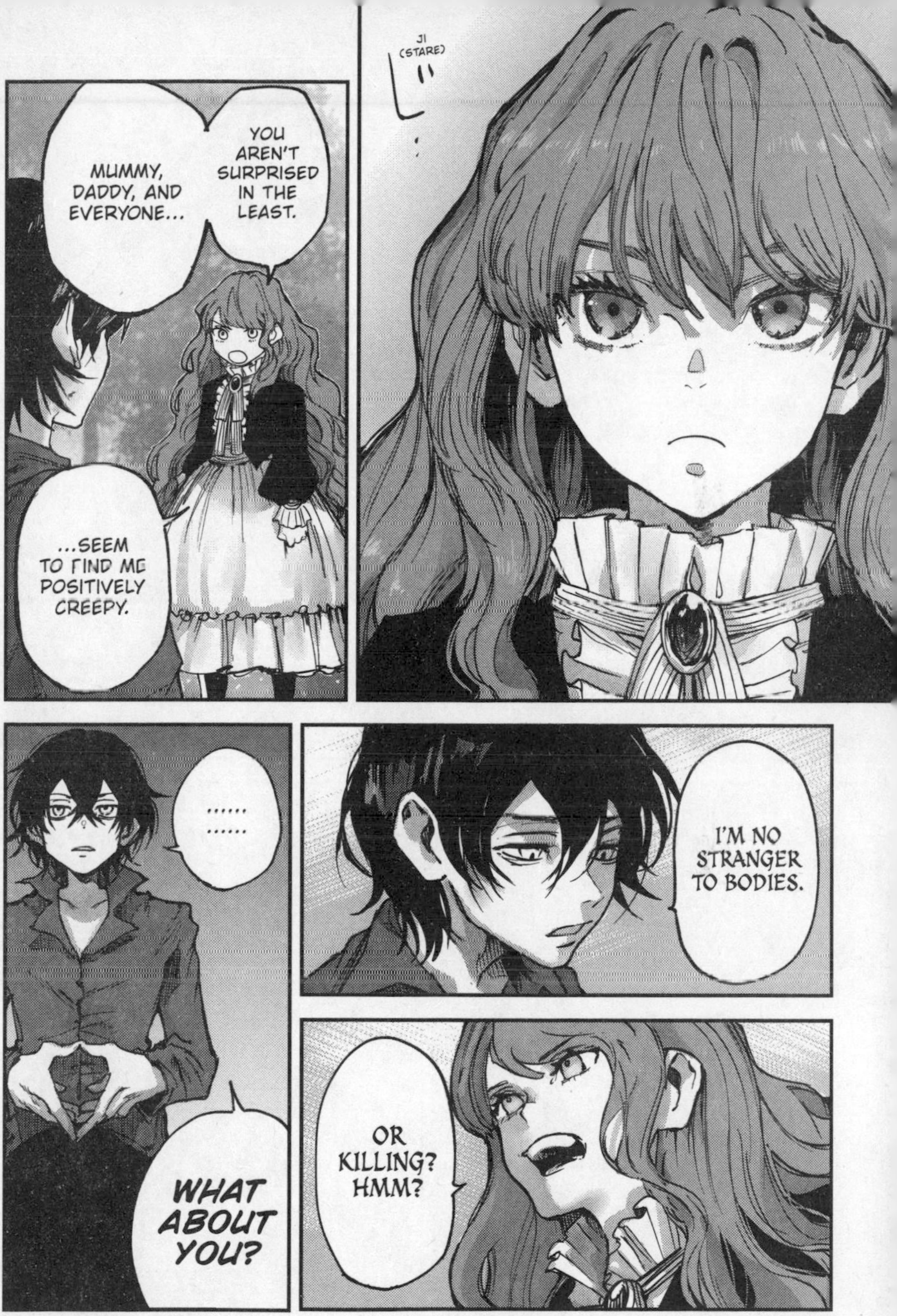
JI (STARE)
YOU AREN'T SURPRISED IN THE LEAST.
MUMMY, DADDY, AND EVERYONE...
...SEEM TO FIND ME POSITIVELY CREEPY.
I'M NO STRANGER TO BODIES.
OR KILLING? HMM?
......
......
WHAT ABOUT YOU?

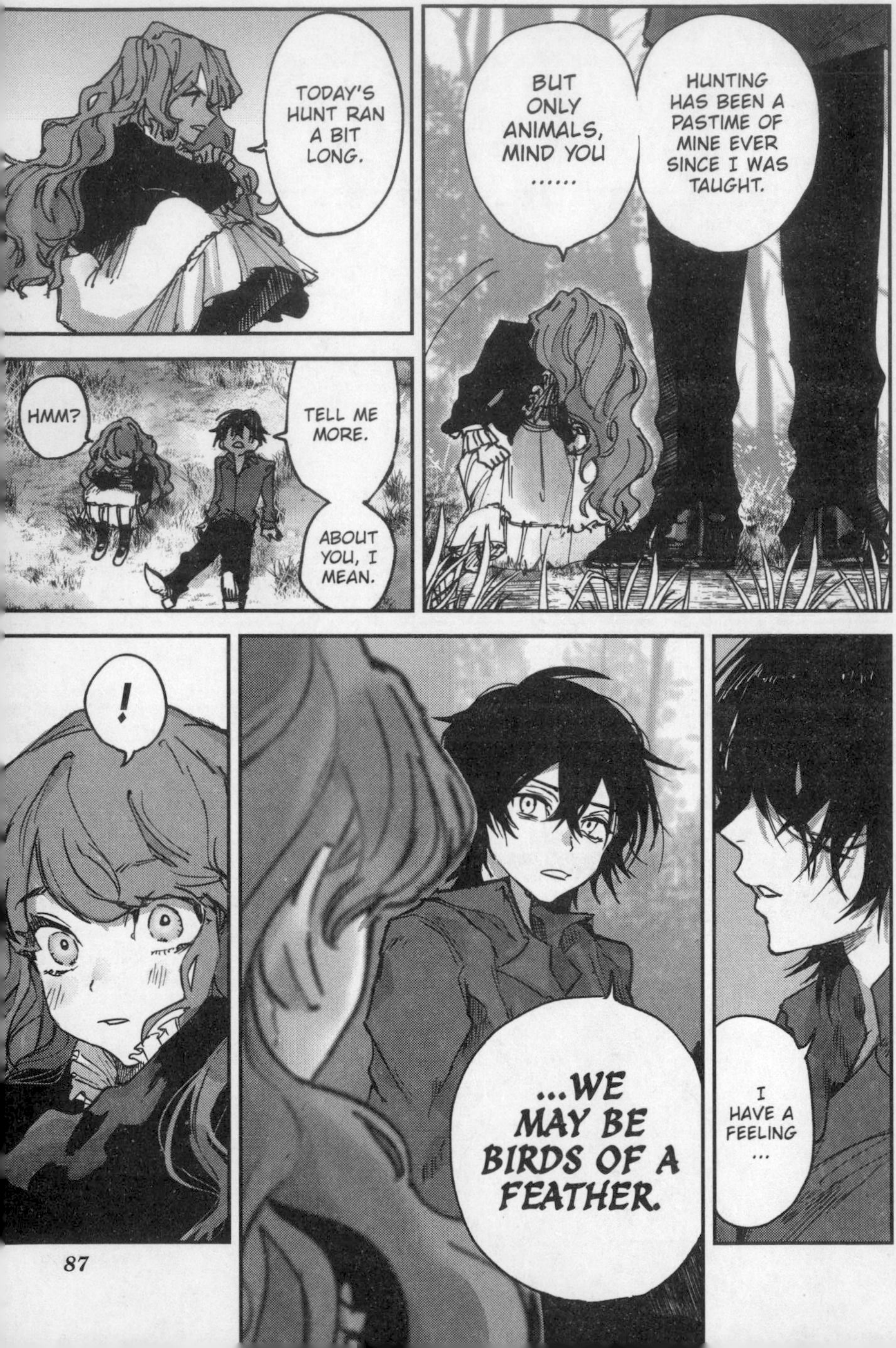
HUNTING HAS BEEN A PASTIME OF MINE EVER SINCE I WAS TAUGHT.
BUT ONLY ANIMALS, MIND YOU ......
TODAY'S HUNT RAN A BIT LONG.
TELL ME MORE.
ABOUT YOU, I MEAN.
HMM?
I HAVE A FEELING ...
...WE MAY BE BIRDS OF A FEATHER.
!

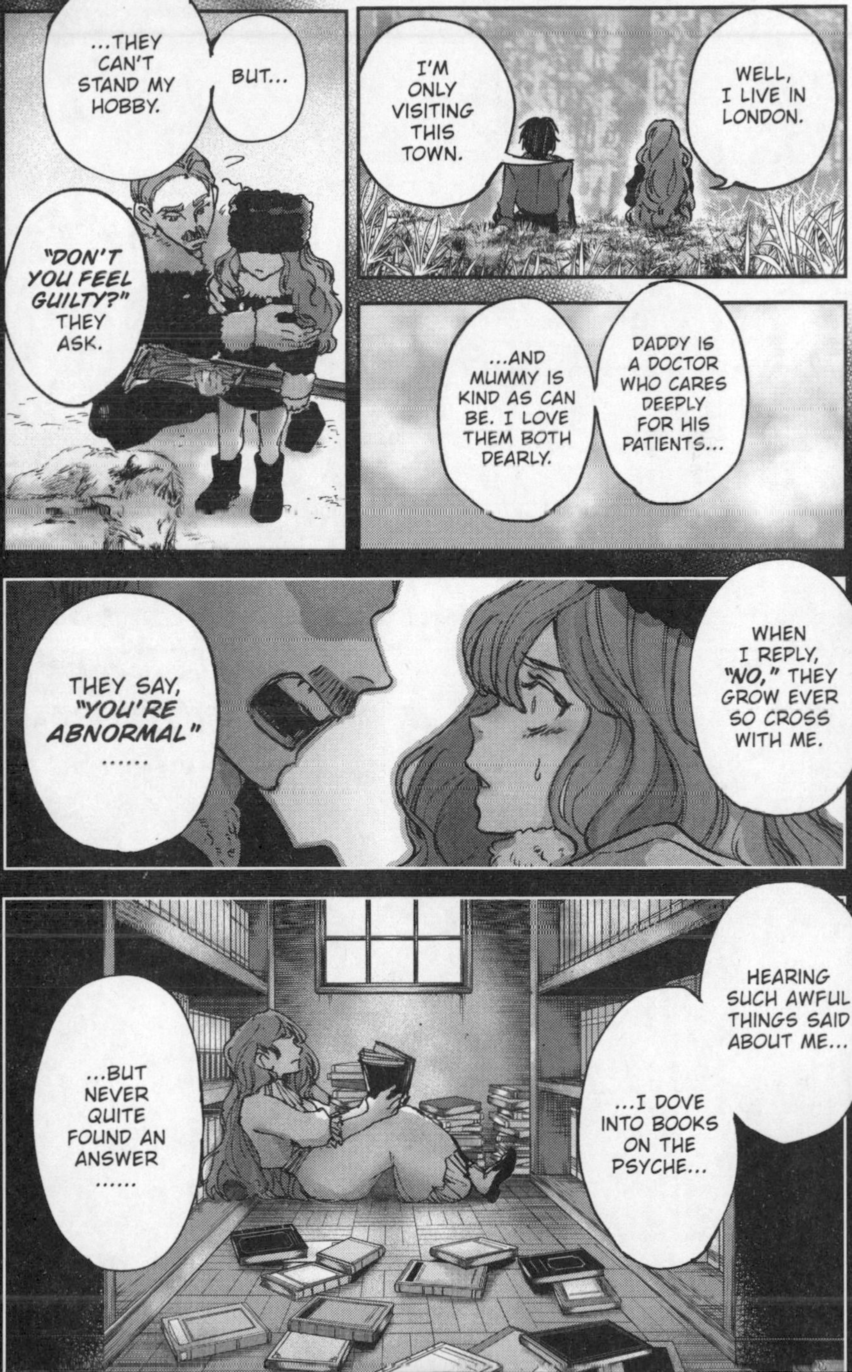
WELL, I LIVE IN LONDON.
I'M ONLY VISITING THIS TOWN.
DADDY IS A DOCTOR WHO CARES DEEPLY FOR HIS PATIENTS...
...AND MUMMY IS KIND AS CAN BE. I LOVE THEM BOTH DEARLY.
BUT...
...THEY CAN'T STAND MY HOBBY.
"DON'T YOU FEEL GUILTY?" THEY ASK.
WHEN I REPLY, *"NO,"* THEY GROW EVER SO CROSS WITH ME.
THEY SAY, *"YOU'RE ABNORMAL"* ......
HEARING SUCH AWFUL THINGS SAID ABOUT ME...
...I DOVE INTO BOOKS ON THE PSYCHE...
...BUT NEVER QUITE FOUND AN ANSWER ......

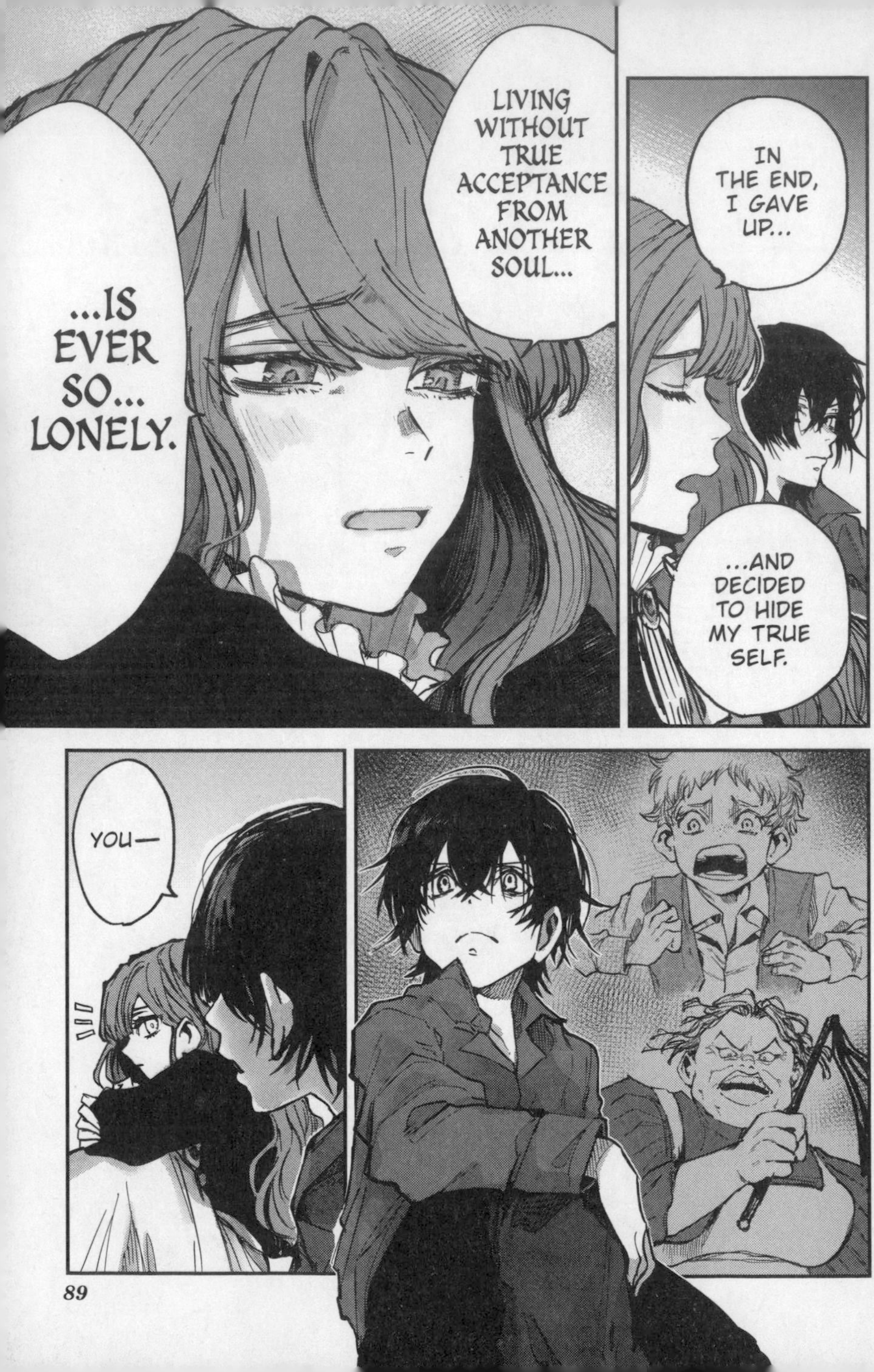
IN THE END, I GAVE UP...
...AND DECIDED TO HIDE MY TRUE SELF.
LIVING WITHOUT TRUE ACCEPTANCE FROM ANOTHER SOUL...
...IS EVER SO... LONELY.
YOU—

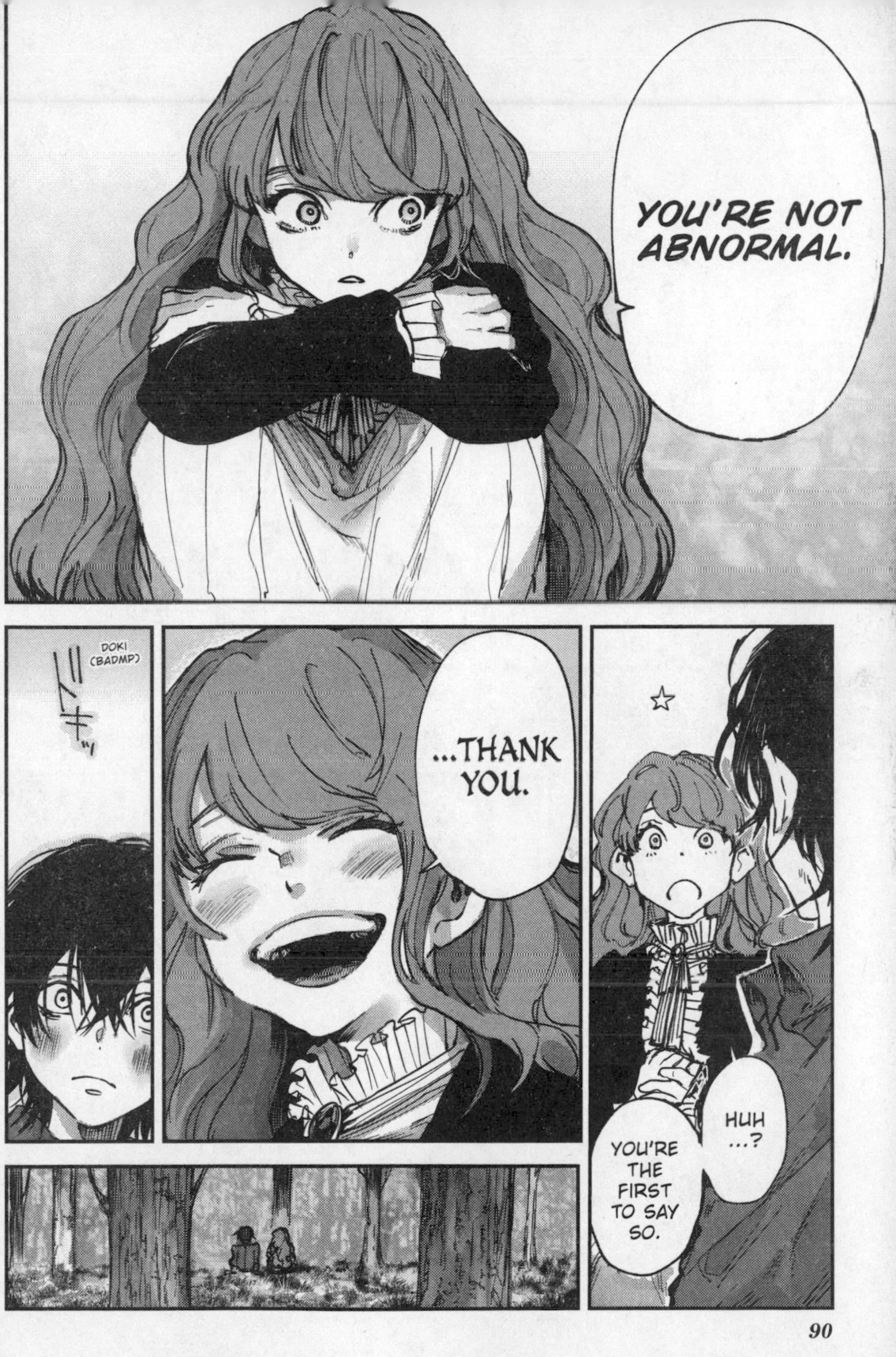
YOU'RE NOT ABNORMAL.
HUH ...?
YOU'RE THE FIRST TO SAY SO.
...THANK YOU.
ドキッ
DOKI (BADMP)

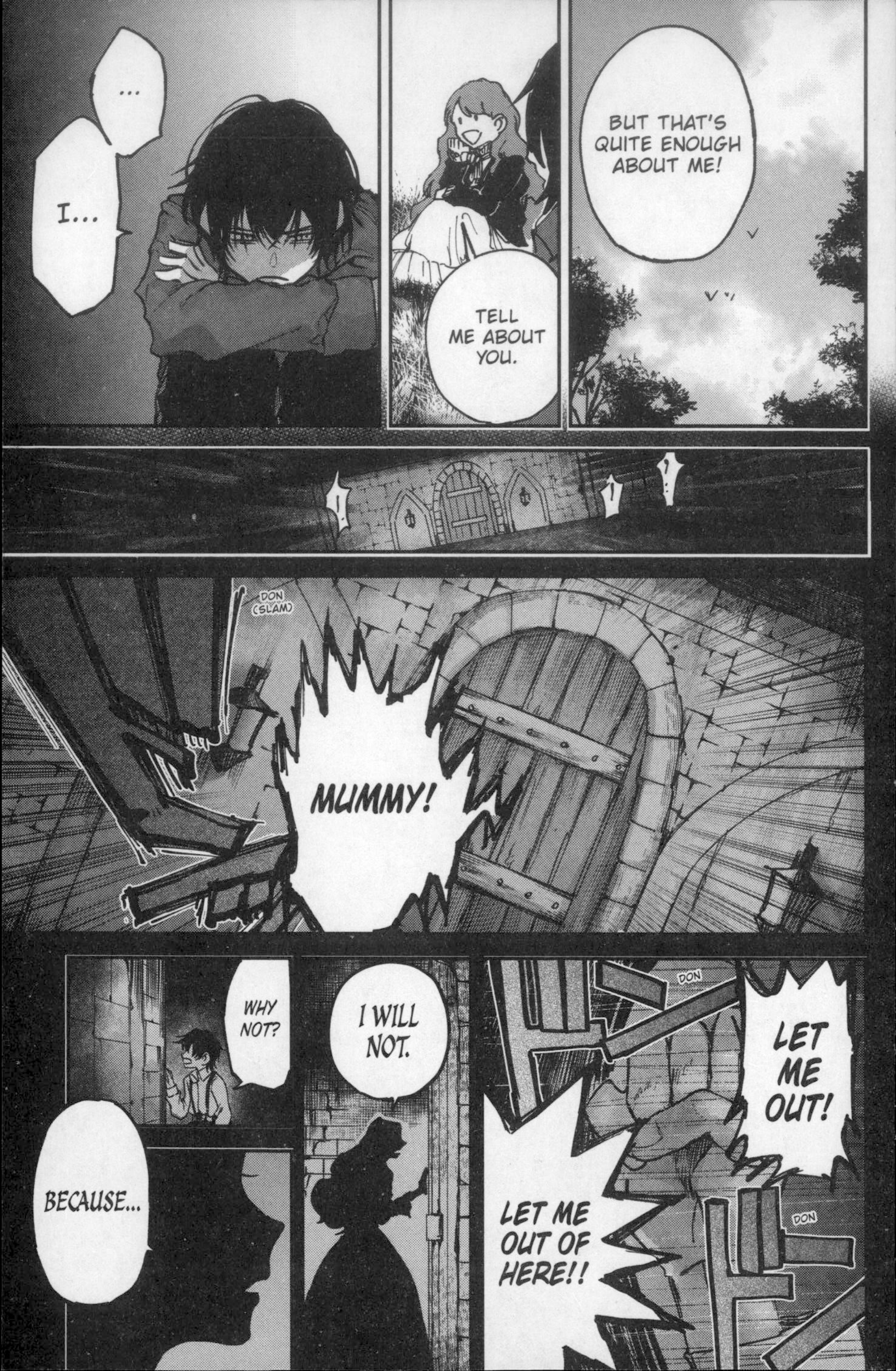
BUT THAT'S QUITE ENOUGH ABOUT ME!
TELL ME ABOUT YOU.
...
I...
DON (SLAM)
MUMMY!
DON
LET ME OUT!
LET ME OUT OF HERE!!
DON
I WILL NOT.
WHY NOT?
BECAUSE...

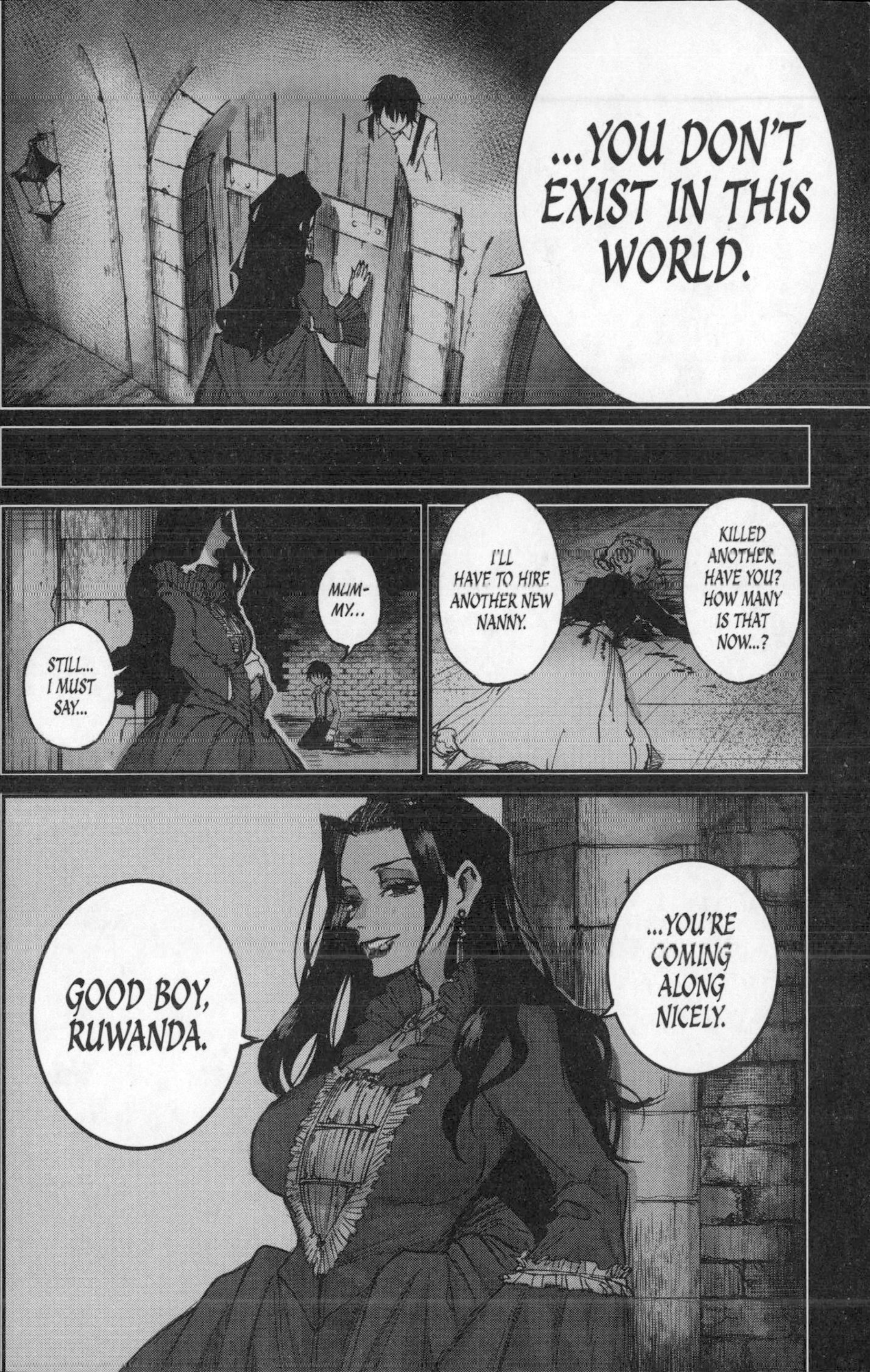
...YOU DON'T EXIST IN THIS WORLD.
KILLED ANOTHER HAVE YOU? HOW MANY IS THAT NOW...?
I'LL HAVE TO HIRE ANOTHER NEW NANNY.
MUMMY...
STILL... I MUST SAY...
...YOU'RE COMING ALONG NICELY.
GOOD BOY, RUWANDA.

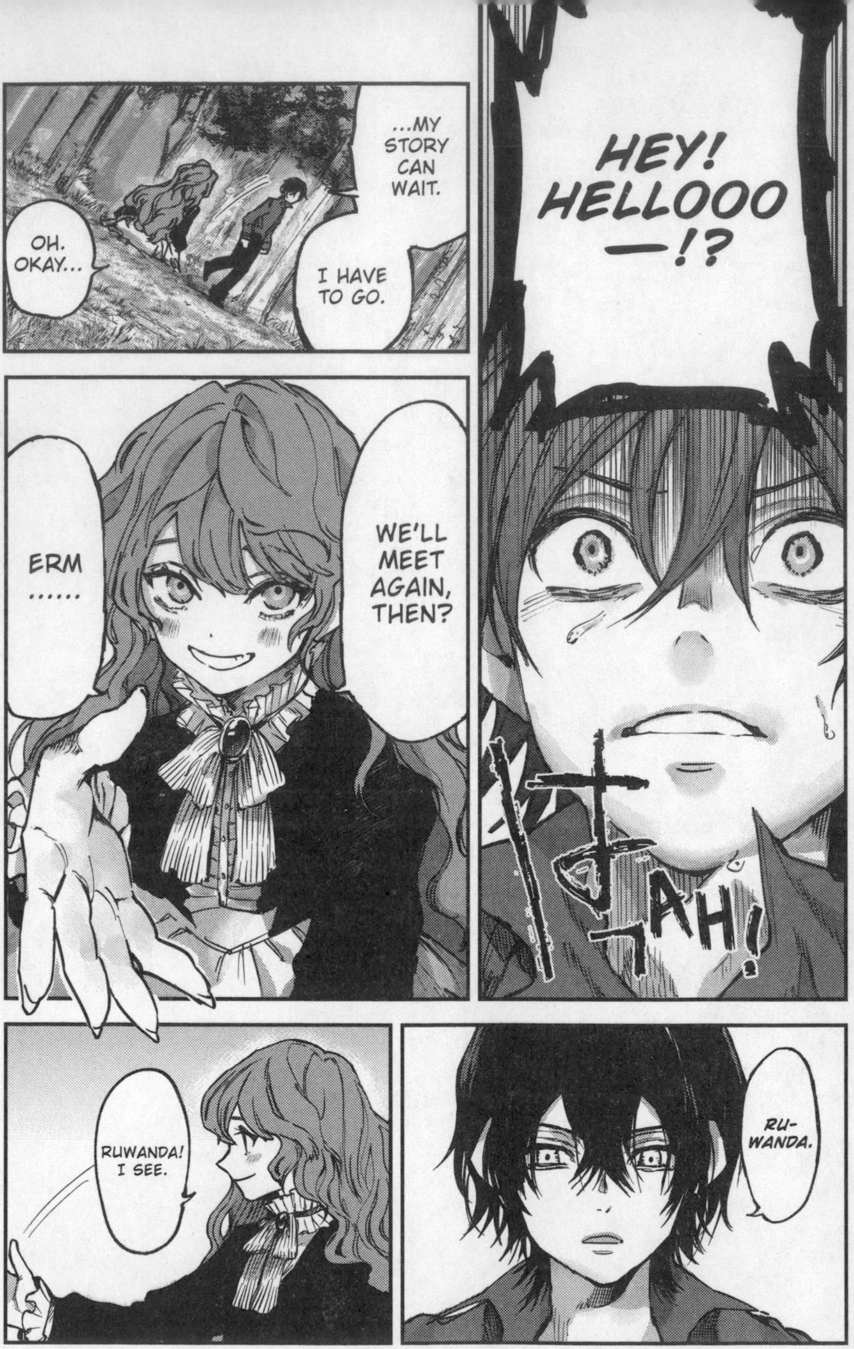
HEY! HELLOOO—!?
AH!
...MY STORY CAN WAIT.
I HAVE TO GO.
OH. OKAY...
WE'LL MEET AGAIN, THEN?
ERM ......
RU-WANDA.
RUWANDA! I SEE.

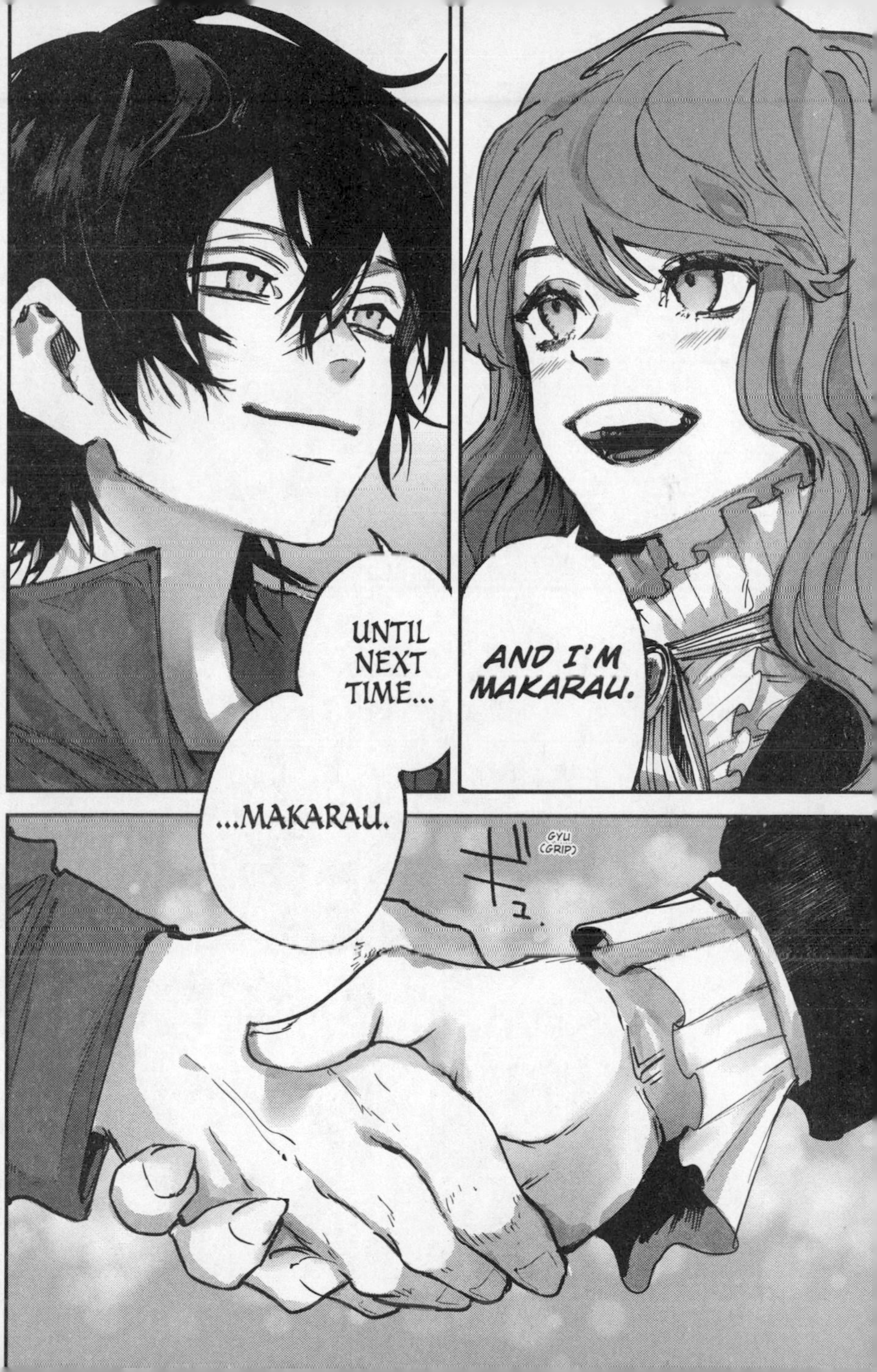
AND I'M MAKARAU.
UNTIL NEXT TIME...
...MAKARAU.
GYU (GRIP)

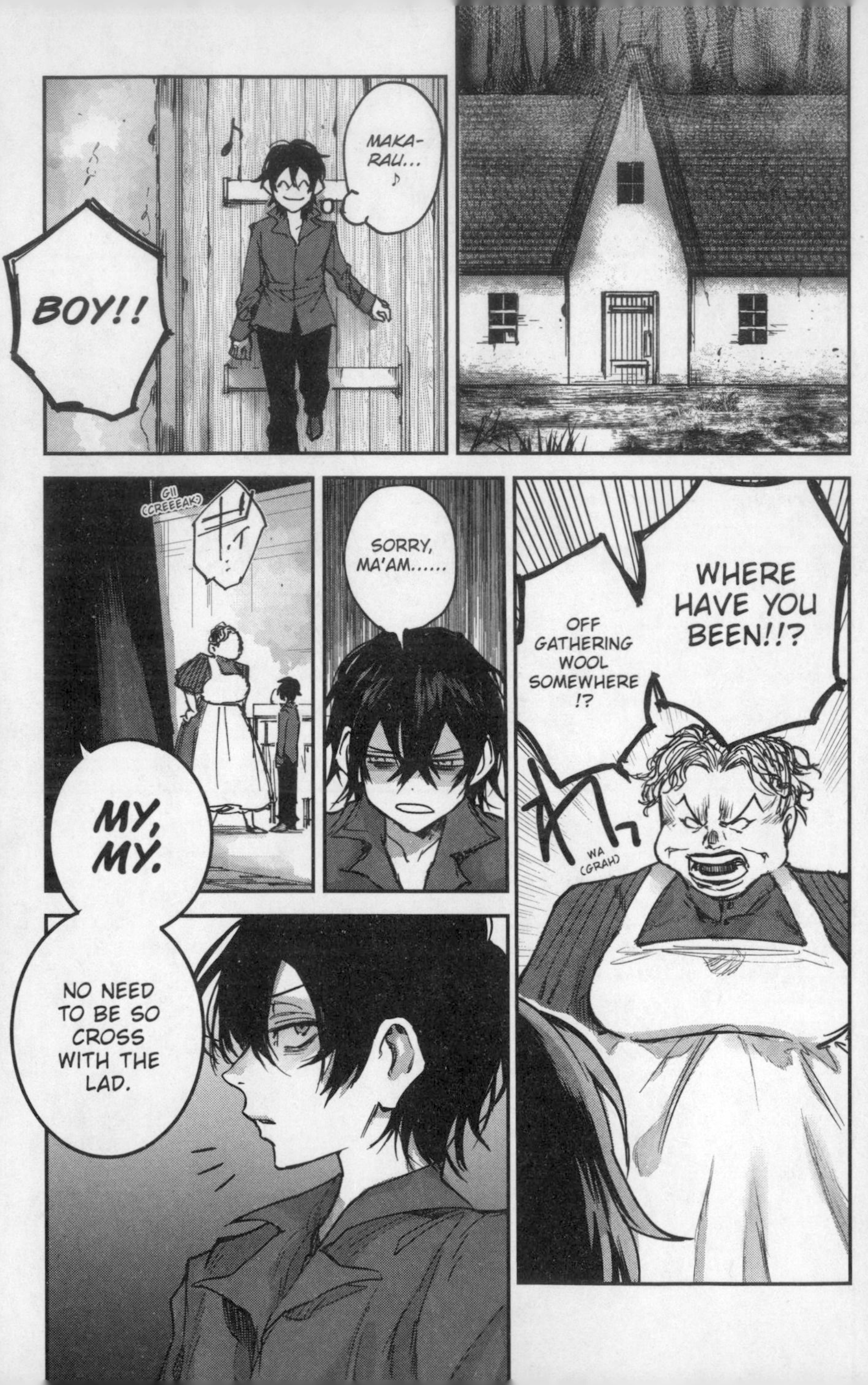
MAKA-RAU... ♪
BOY!!
WHERE HAVE YOU BEEN!!?
OFF GATHERING WOOL SOMEWHERE!?
WA (GRAH)
SORRY, MA'AM......
GII (CREEEAK)
MY, MY.
NO NEED TO BE SO CROSS WITH THE LAD.

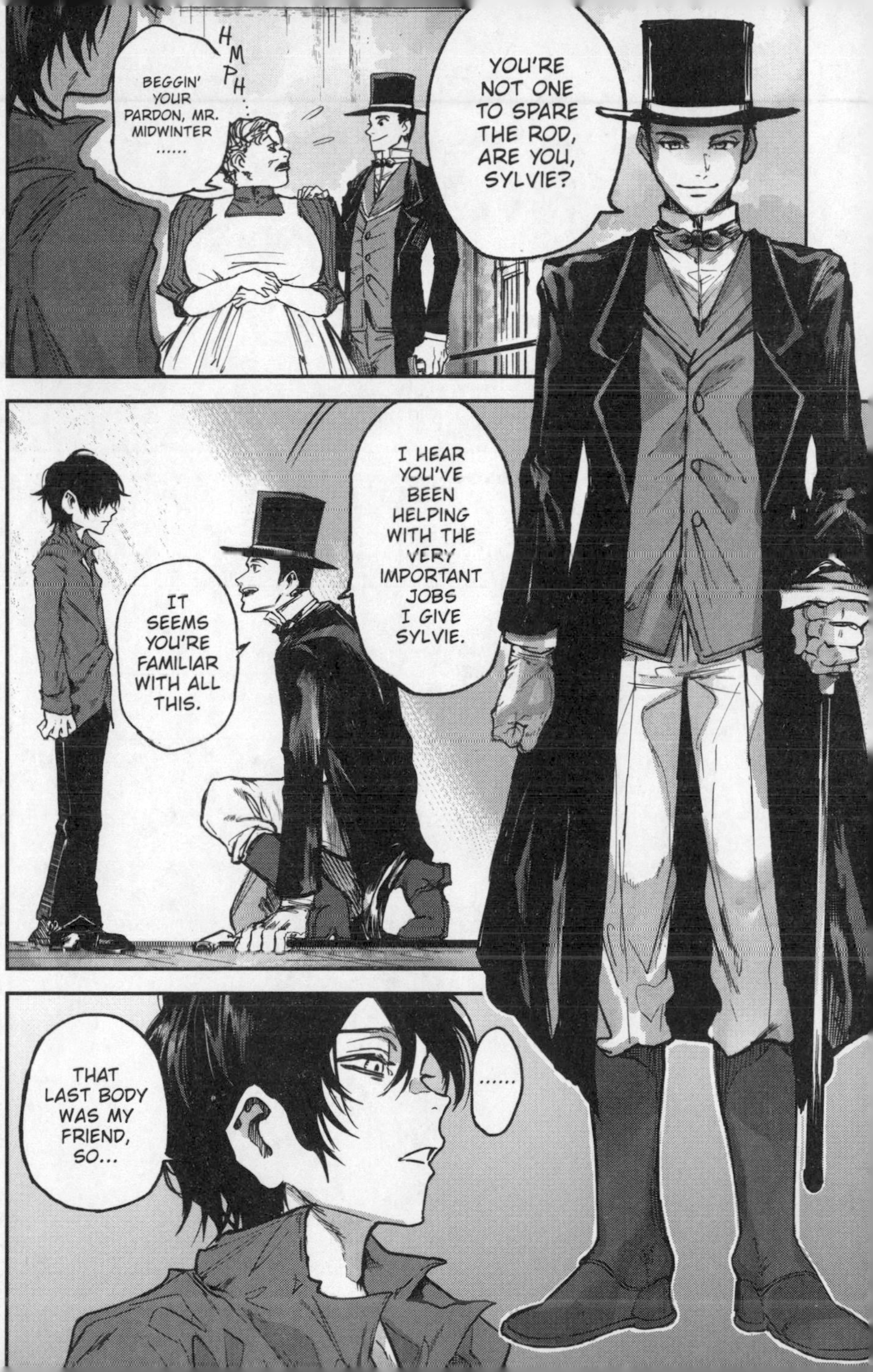

YOU'RE NOT ONE TO SPARE THE ROD, ARE YOU, SYLVIE?
HMPH...
BEGGIN' YOUR PARDON, MR. MIDWINTER ......
I HEAR YOU'VE BEEN HELPING WITH THE VERY IMPORTANT JOBS I GIVE SYLVIE.
IT SEEMS YOU'RE FAMILIAR WITH ALL THIS.
......
THAT LAST BODY WAS MY FRIEND, SO...

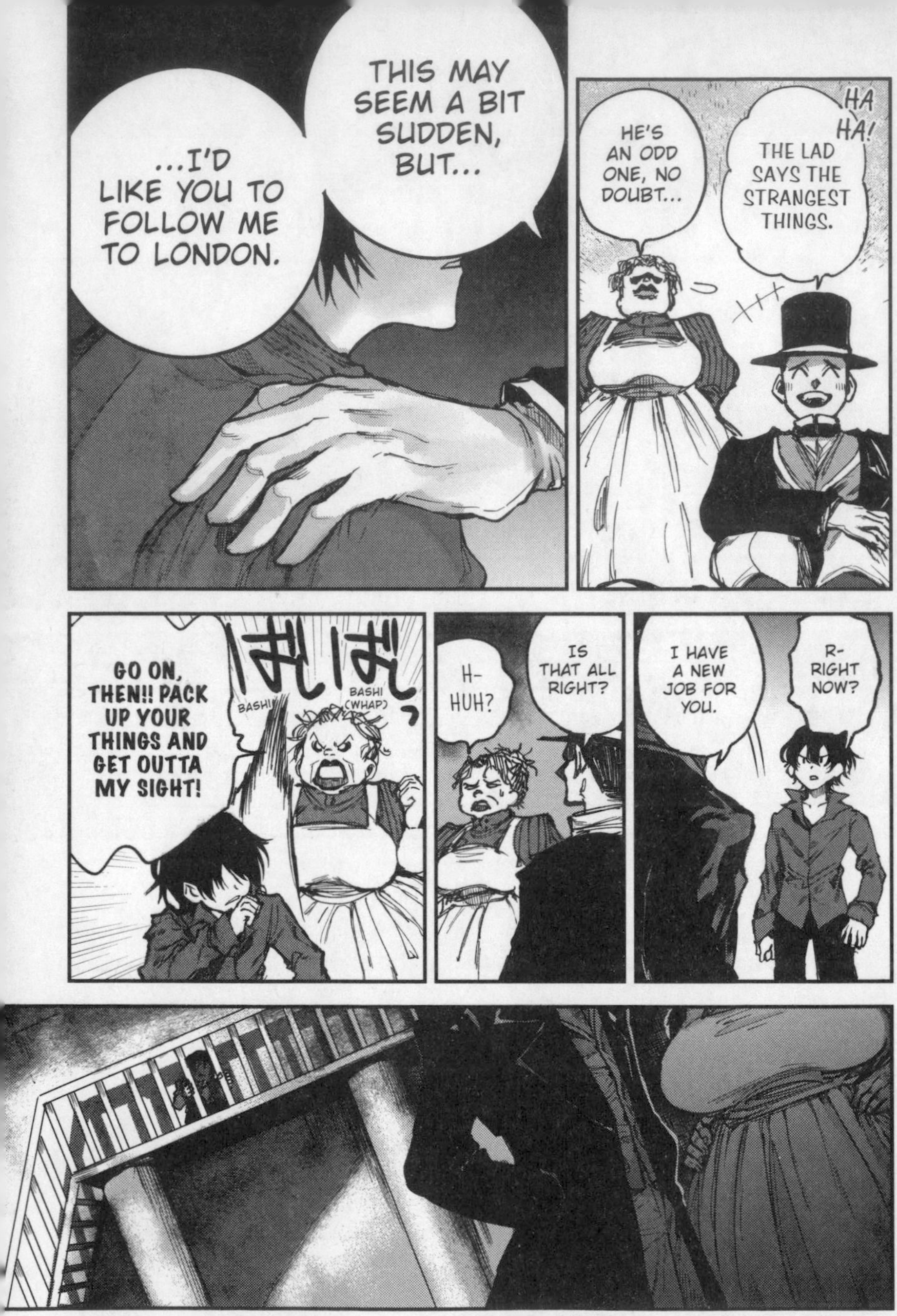
HA HA!
THE LAD SAYS THE STRANGEST THINGS.
HE'S AN ODD ONE, NO DOUBT...
THIS MAY SEEM A BIT SUDDEN, BUT...
...I'D LIKE YOU TO FOLLOW ME TO LONDON.
R-RIGHT NOW?
I HAVE A NEW JOB FOR YOU.
IS THAT ALL RIGHT?
H-HUH?
ばしばし
BASHI (WHAP)
BASHI
GO ON, THEN!! PACK UP YOUR THINGS AND GET OUTTA MY SIGHT!

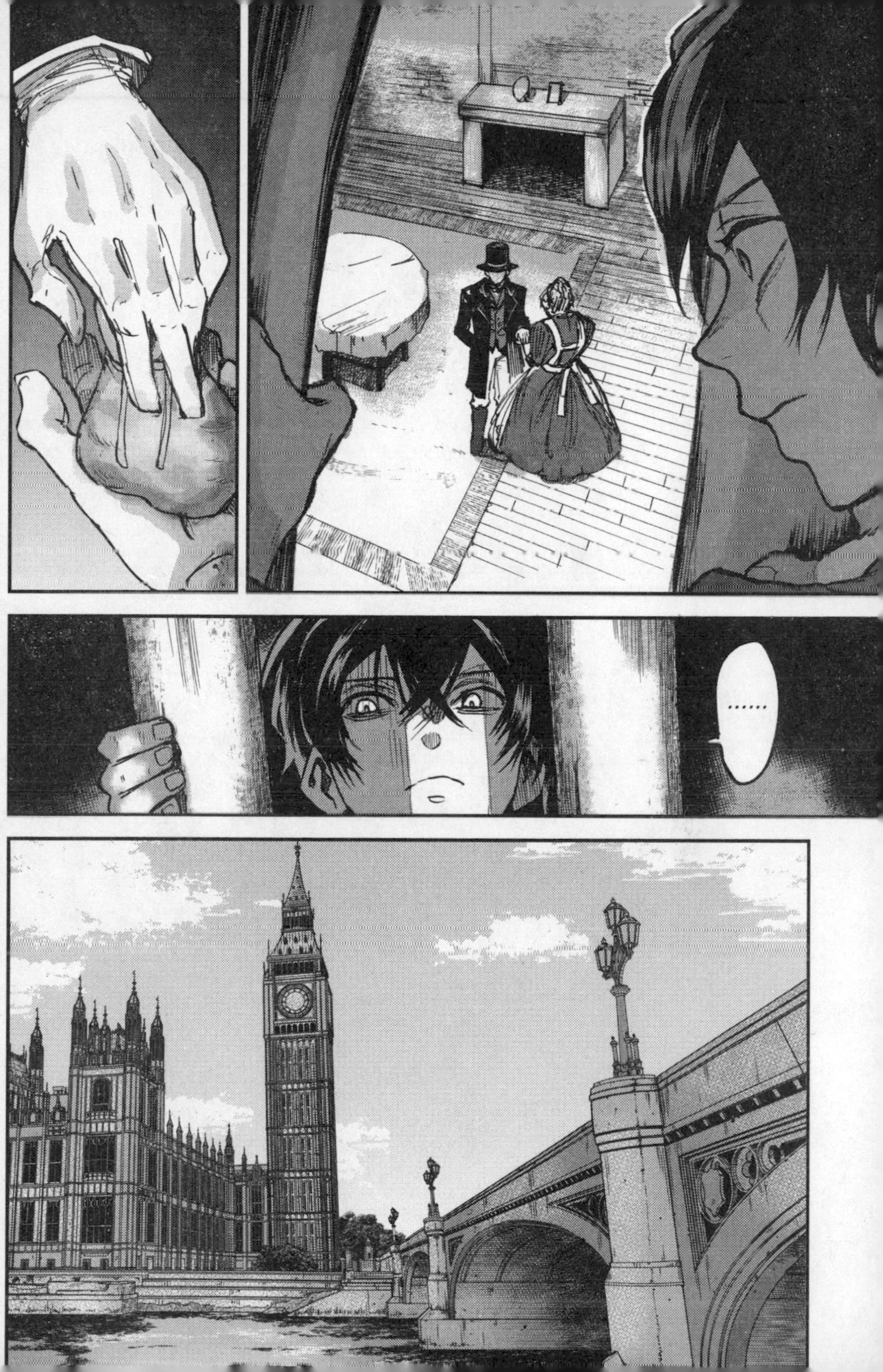
......

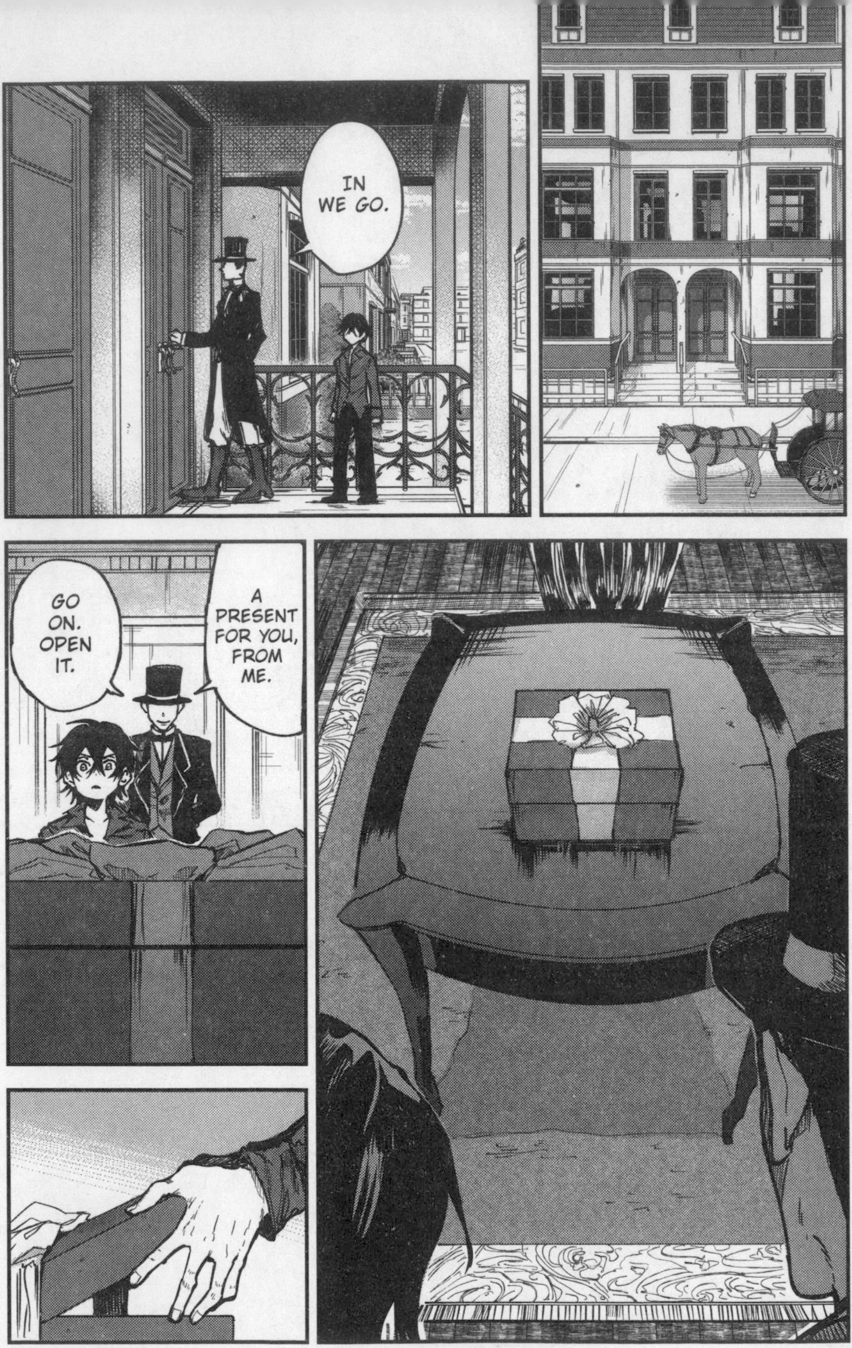
IN WE GO.
A PRESENT FOR YOU, FROM ME.
GO ON. OPEN IT.

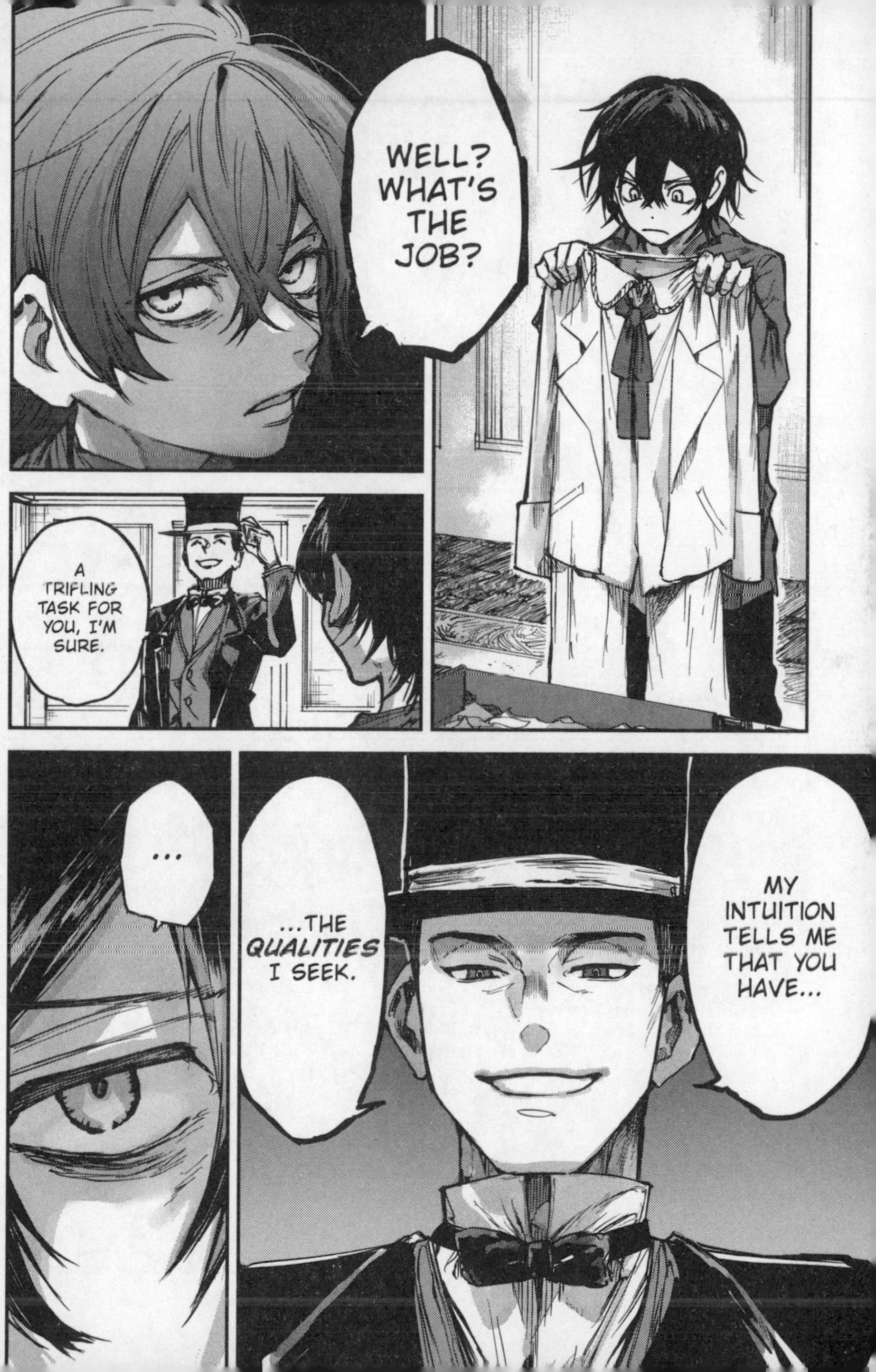
WELL? WHAT'S THE JOB?
A TRIFLING TASK FOR YOU, I'M SURE.
MY INTUITION TELLS ME THAT YOU HAVE...
...THE *QUALITIES* I SEEK.
...

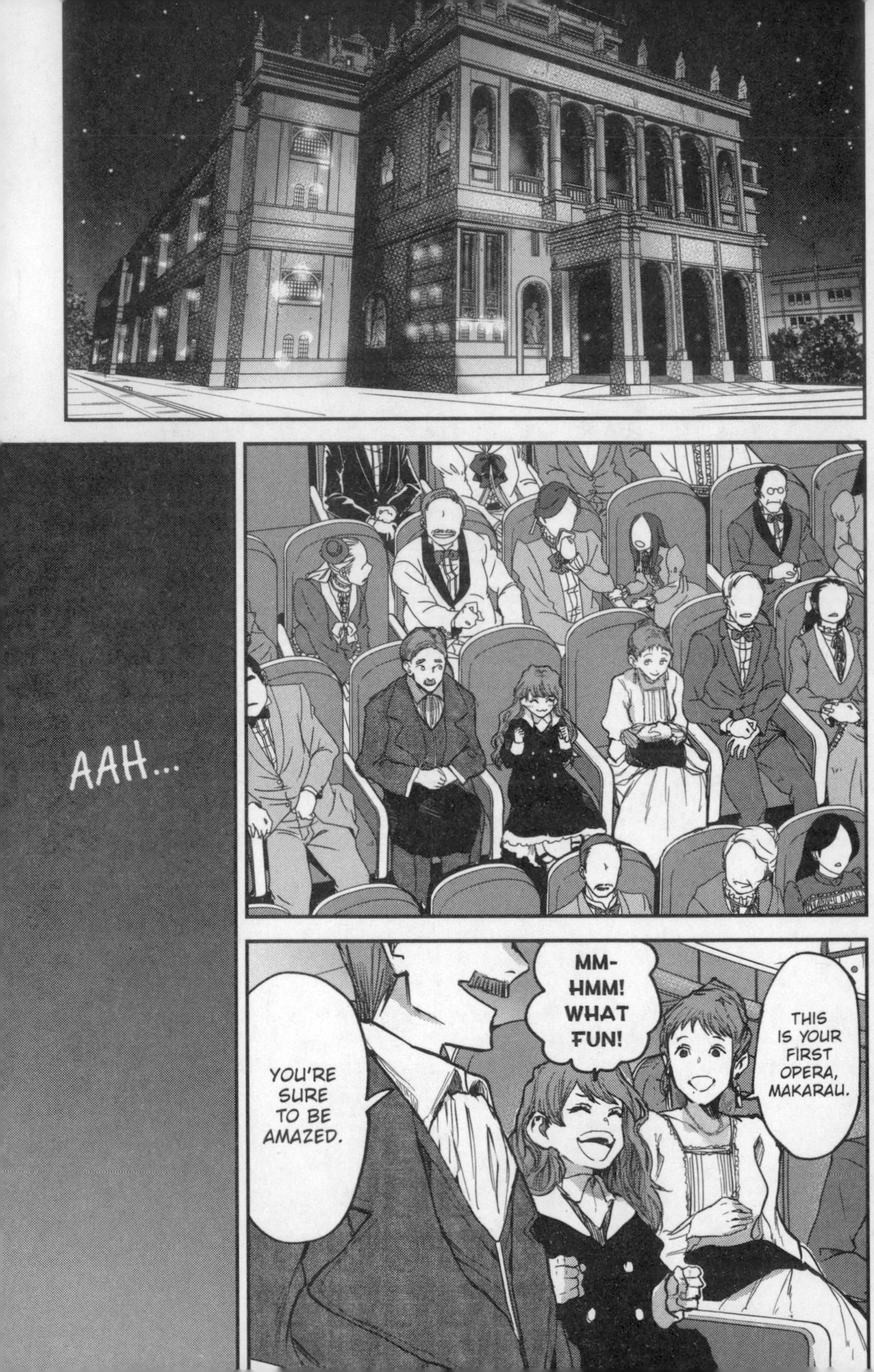
THIS IS YOUR FIRST OPERA, MAKARAU.
MM-HMM! WHAT FUN!
YOU'RE SURE TO BE AMAZED.
AAH...

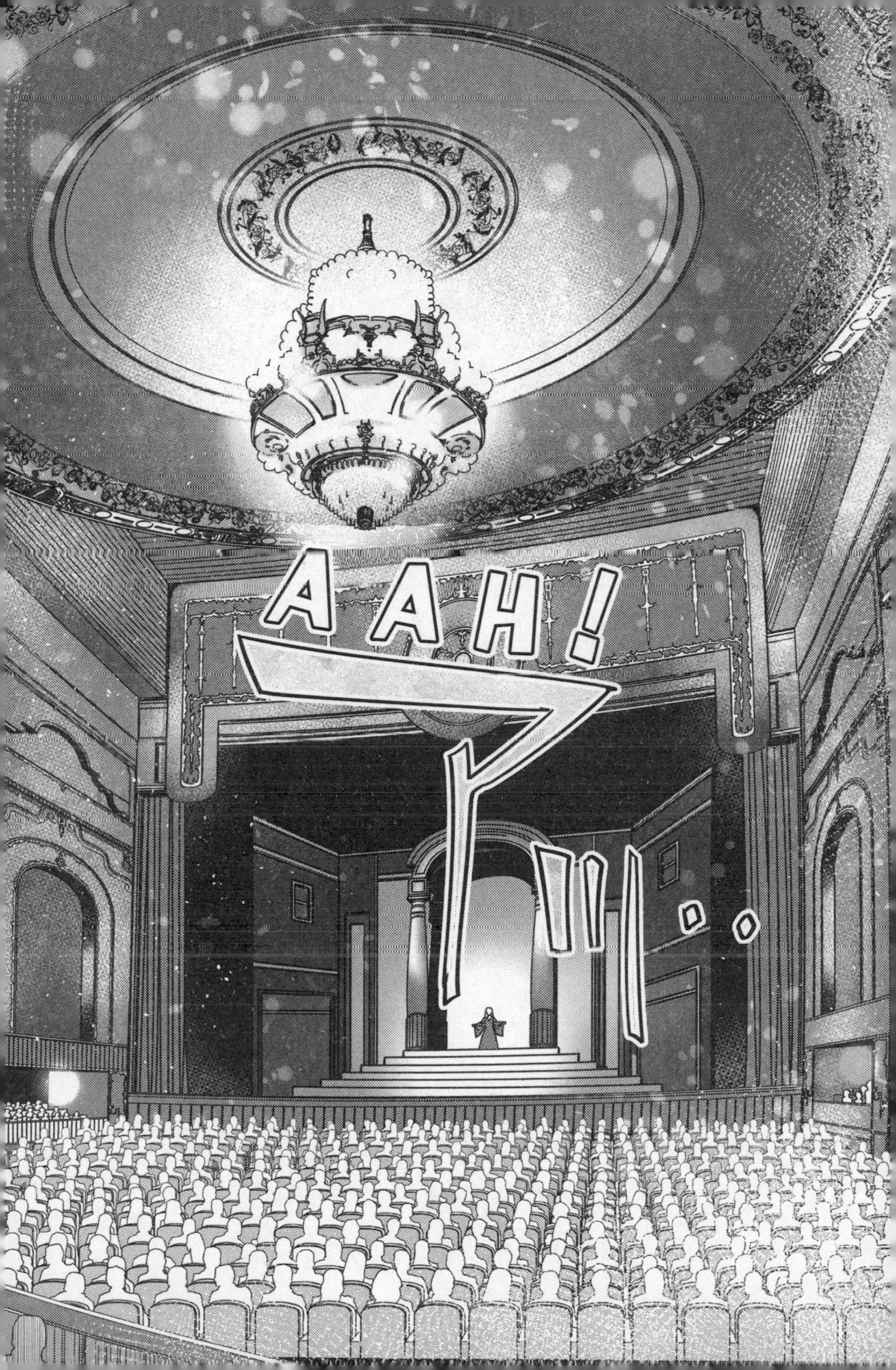
AAH!
ア!!..

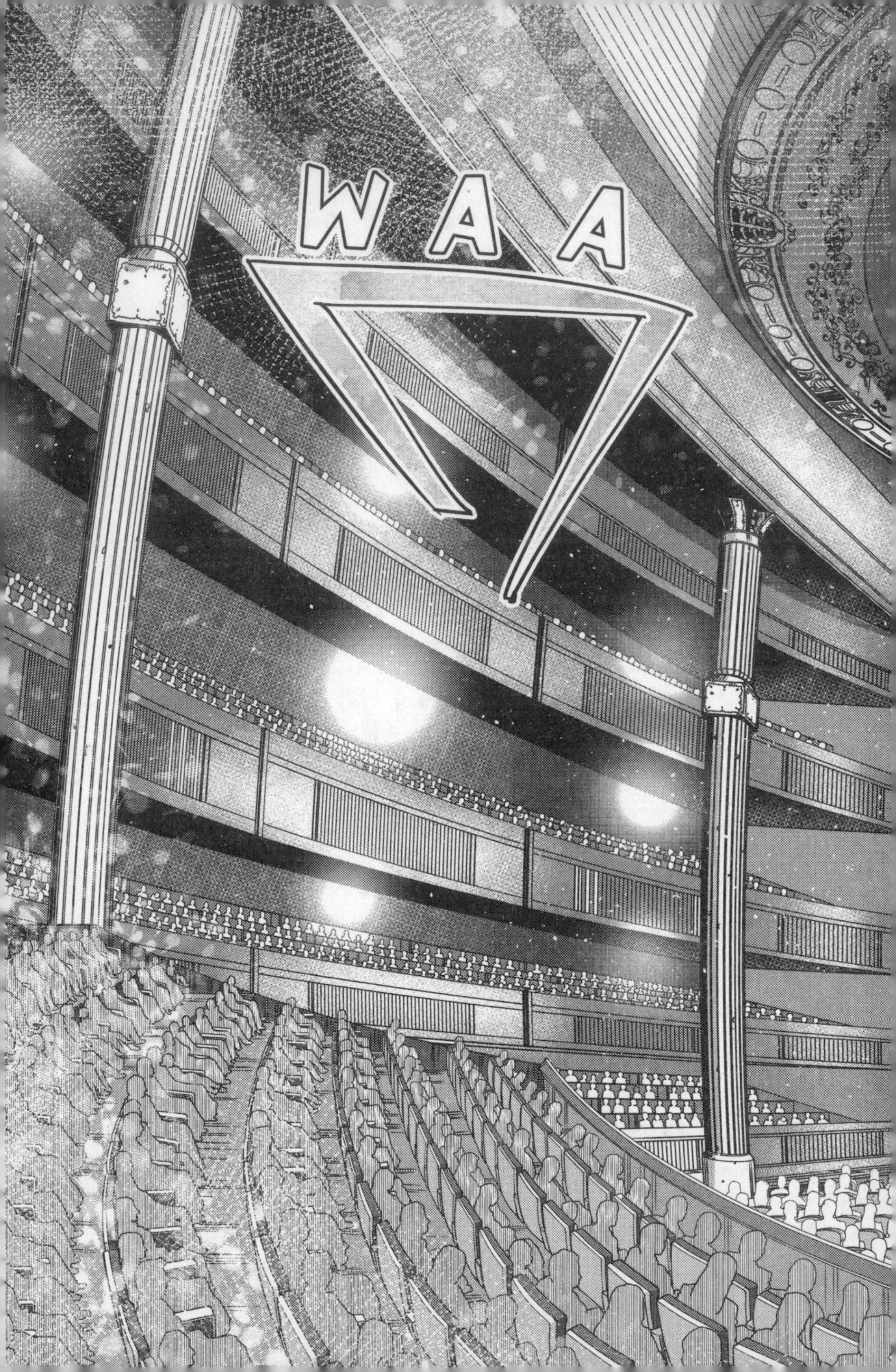
WAA

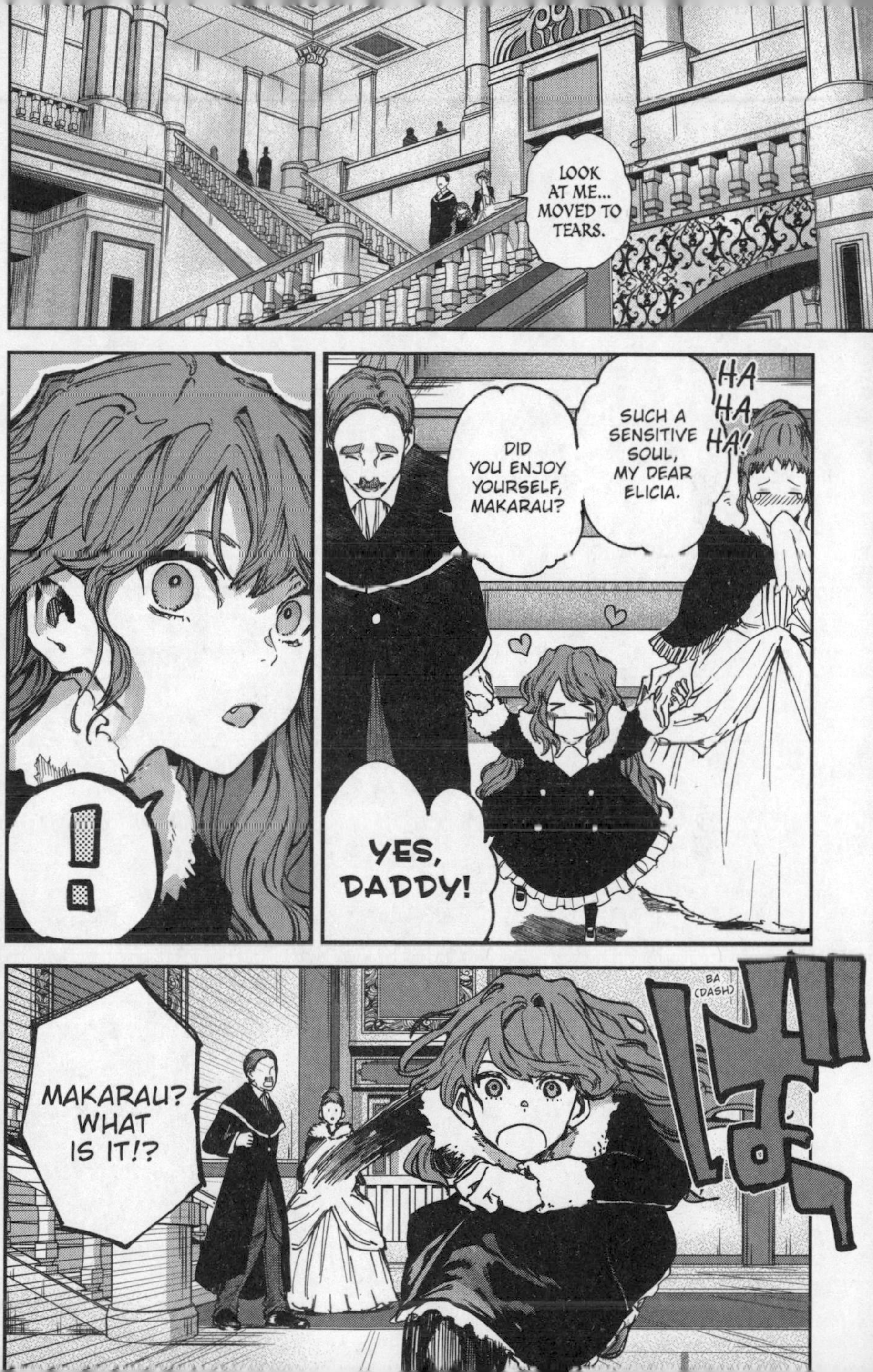
LOOK AT ME... MOVED TO TEARS.
HA HA HA!
SUCH A SENSITIVE SOUL, MY DEAR ELICIA.
DID YOU ENJOY YOURSELF, MAKARAU?
YES, DADDY!
!!
BA (DASH)
ばっ
MAKARAU? WHAT IS IT!?

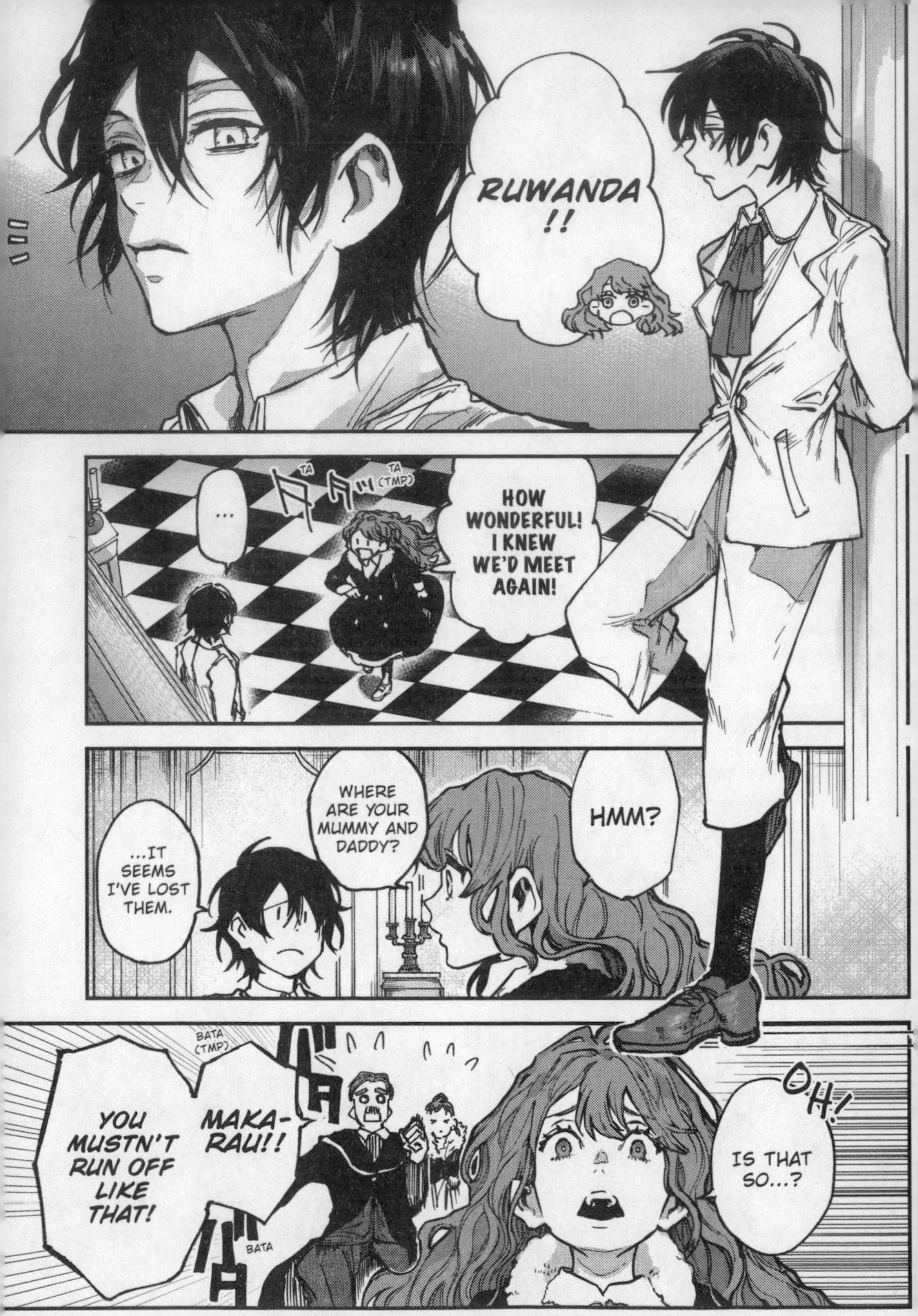
RUWANDA !!
TA TA (TMP)
HOW WONDERFUL! I KNEW WE'D MEET AGAIN!
...
HMM?
WHERE ARE YOUR MUMMY AND DADDY?
...IT SEEMS I'VE LOST THEM.
OH!
IS THAT SO...?
BATA (TMP)
MAKA-RAU!!
YOU MUSTN'T RUN OFF LIKE THAT!
BATA

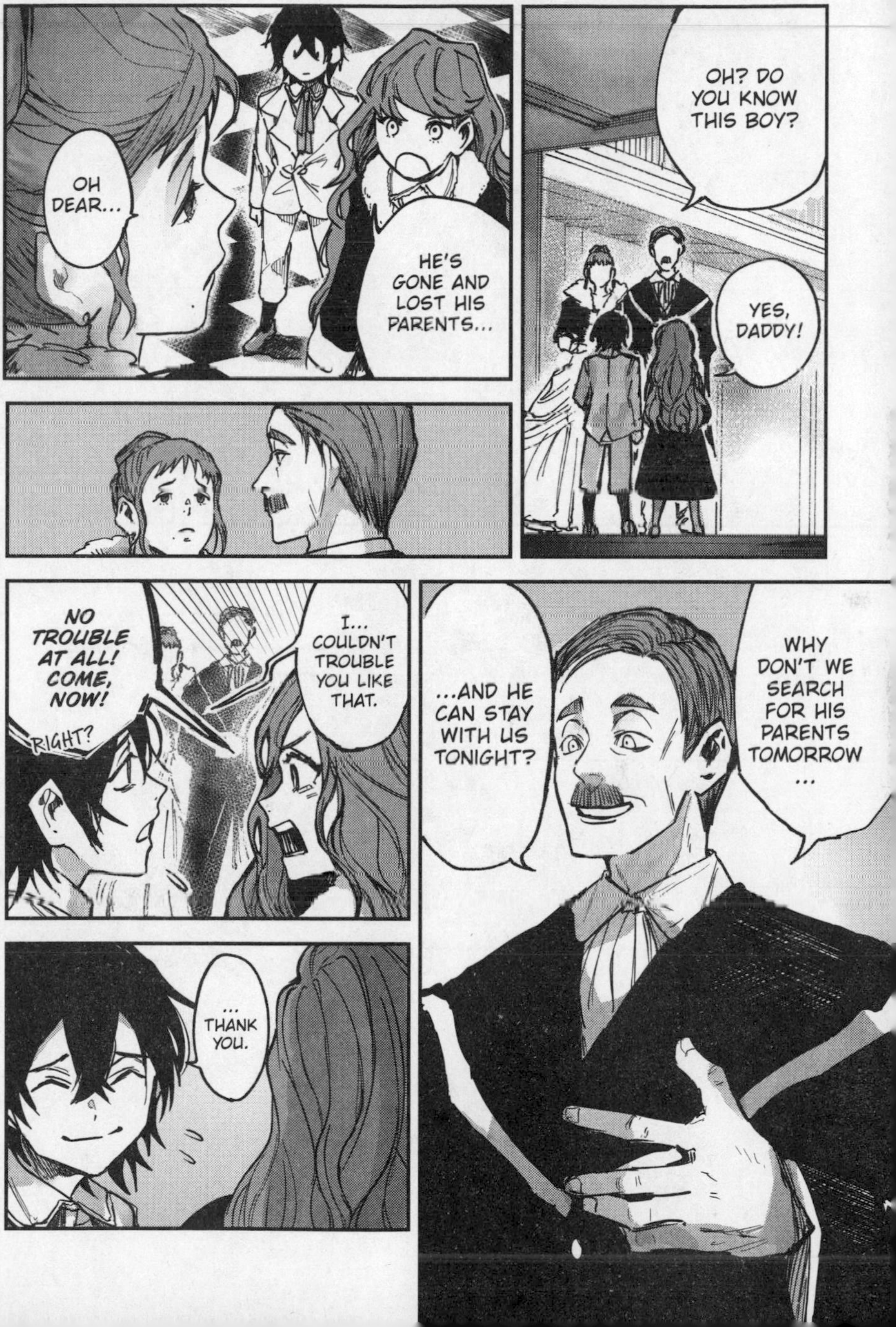
OH? DO YOU KNOW THIS BOY?
YES, DADDY!
HE'S GONE AND LOST HIS PARENTS...
OH DEAR...
WHY DON'T WE SEARCH FOR HIS PARENTS TOMORROW ...
...AND HE CAN STAY WITH US TONIGHT?
I... COULDN'T TROUBLE YOU LIKE THAT.
NO TROUBLE AT ALL! COME, NOW!
RIGHT?
... THANK YOU.

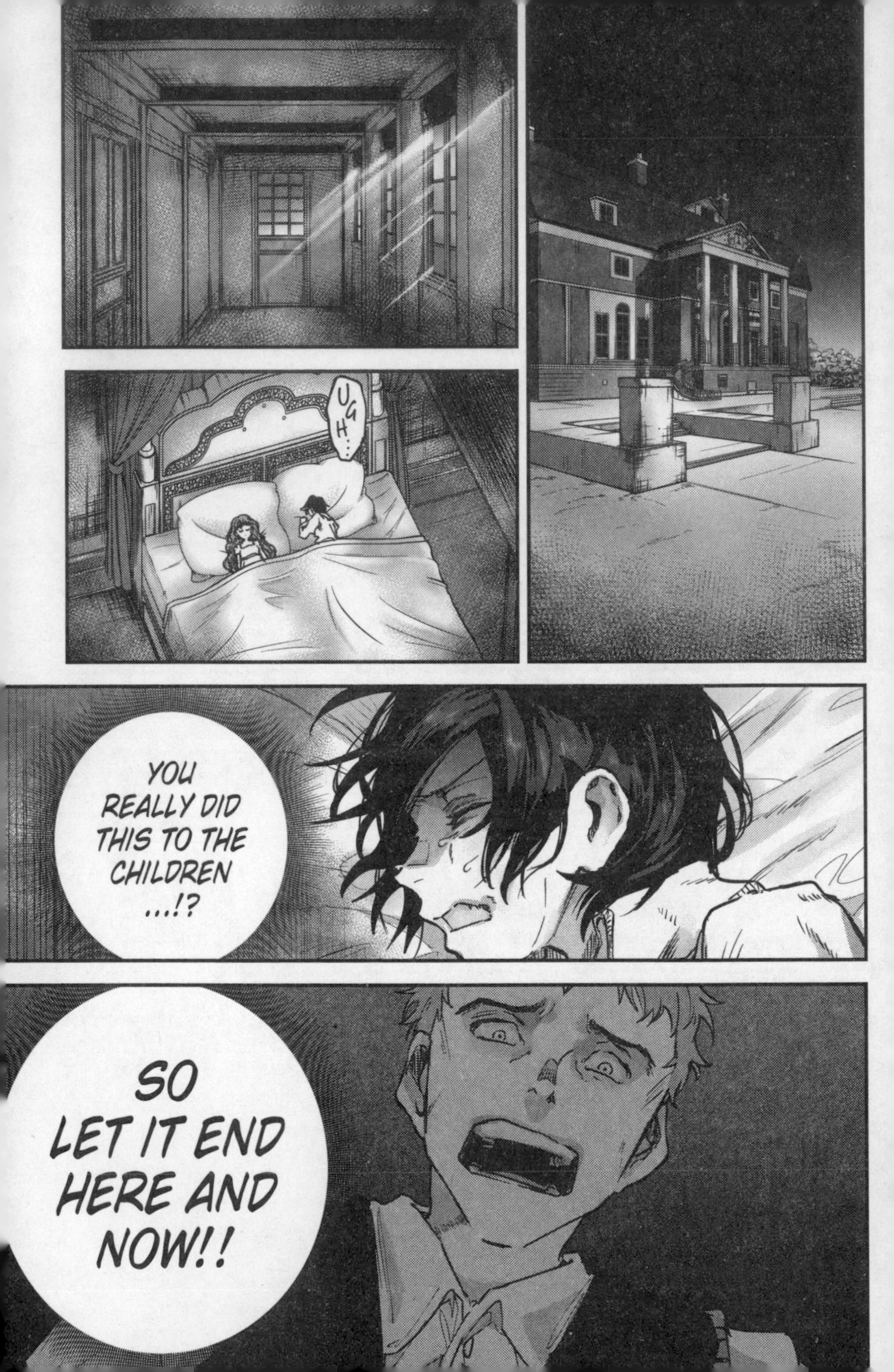
UGH...
YOU REALLY DID THIS TO THE CHILDREN ...!?
SO LET IT END HERE AND NOW!!

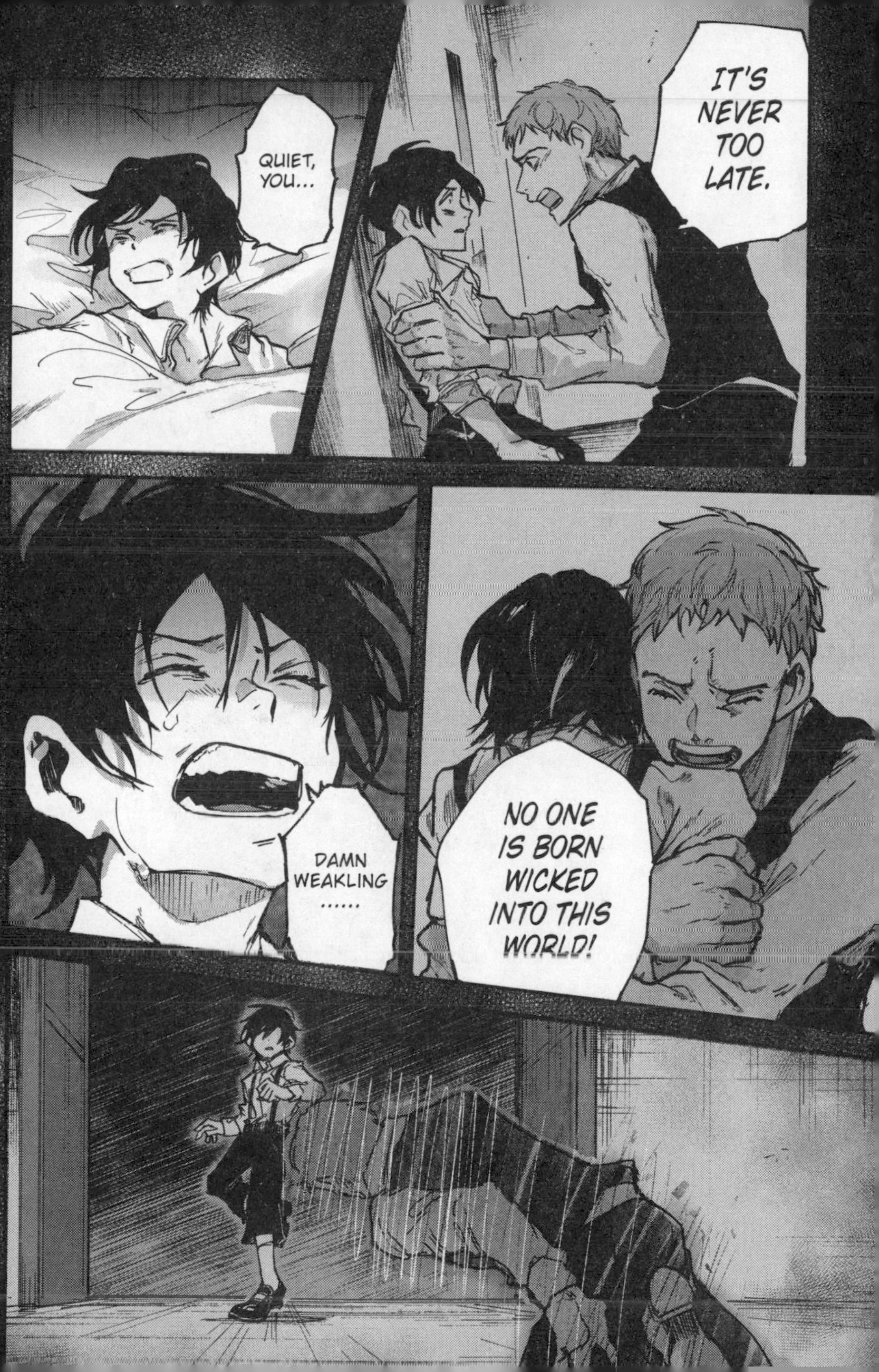
IT'S NEVER TOO LATE.
QUIET, YOU...
NO ONE IS BORN WICKED INTO THIS WORLD!
DAMN WEAKLING ......

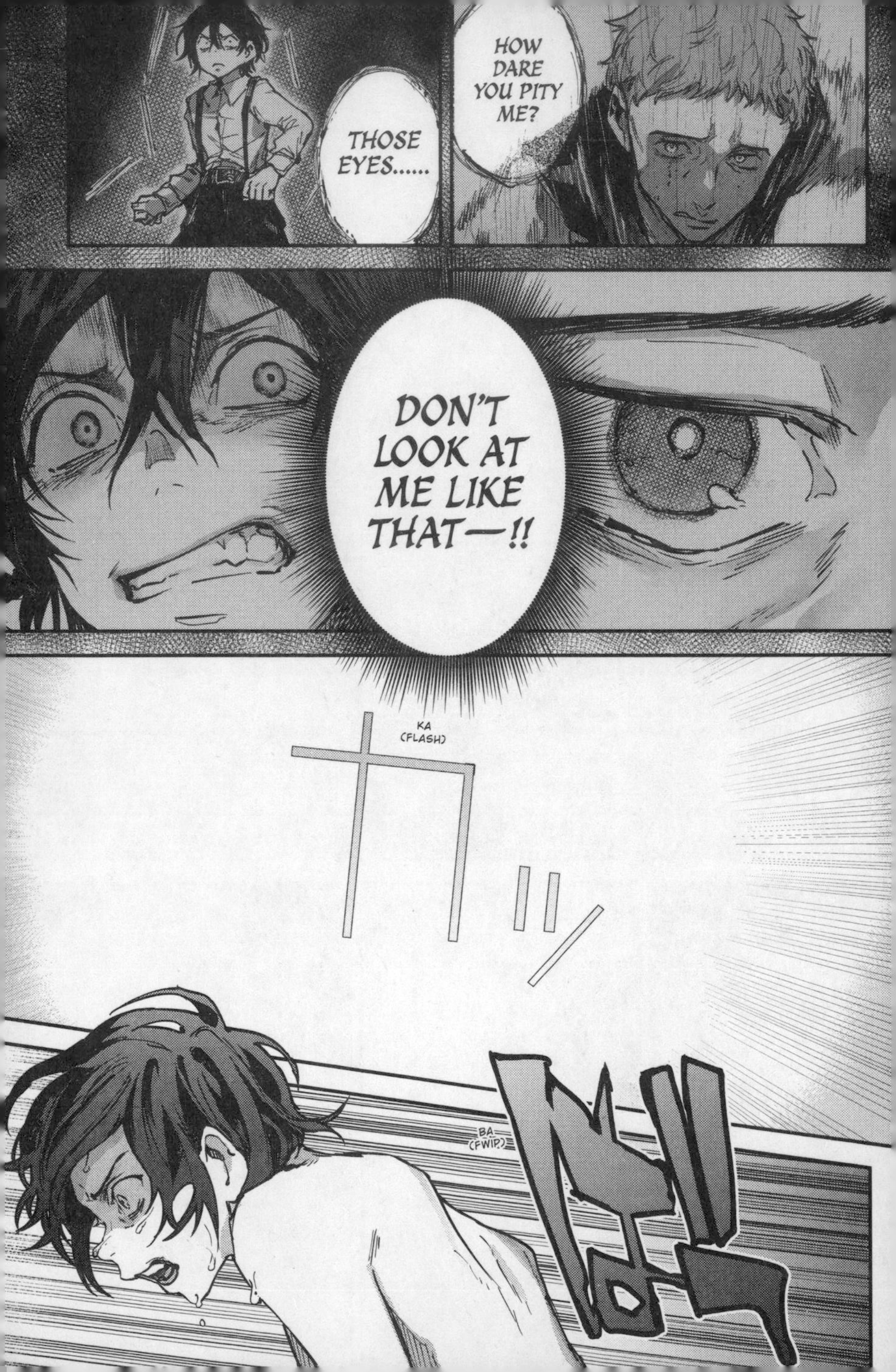
HOW DARE YOU PITY ME?
THOSE EYES......
DON'T LOOK AT ME LIKE THAT—!!
KA (FLASH)
BA (FWIP)

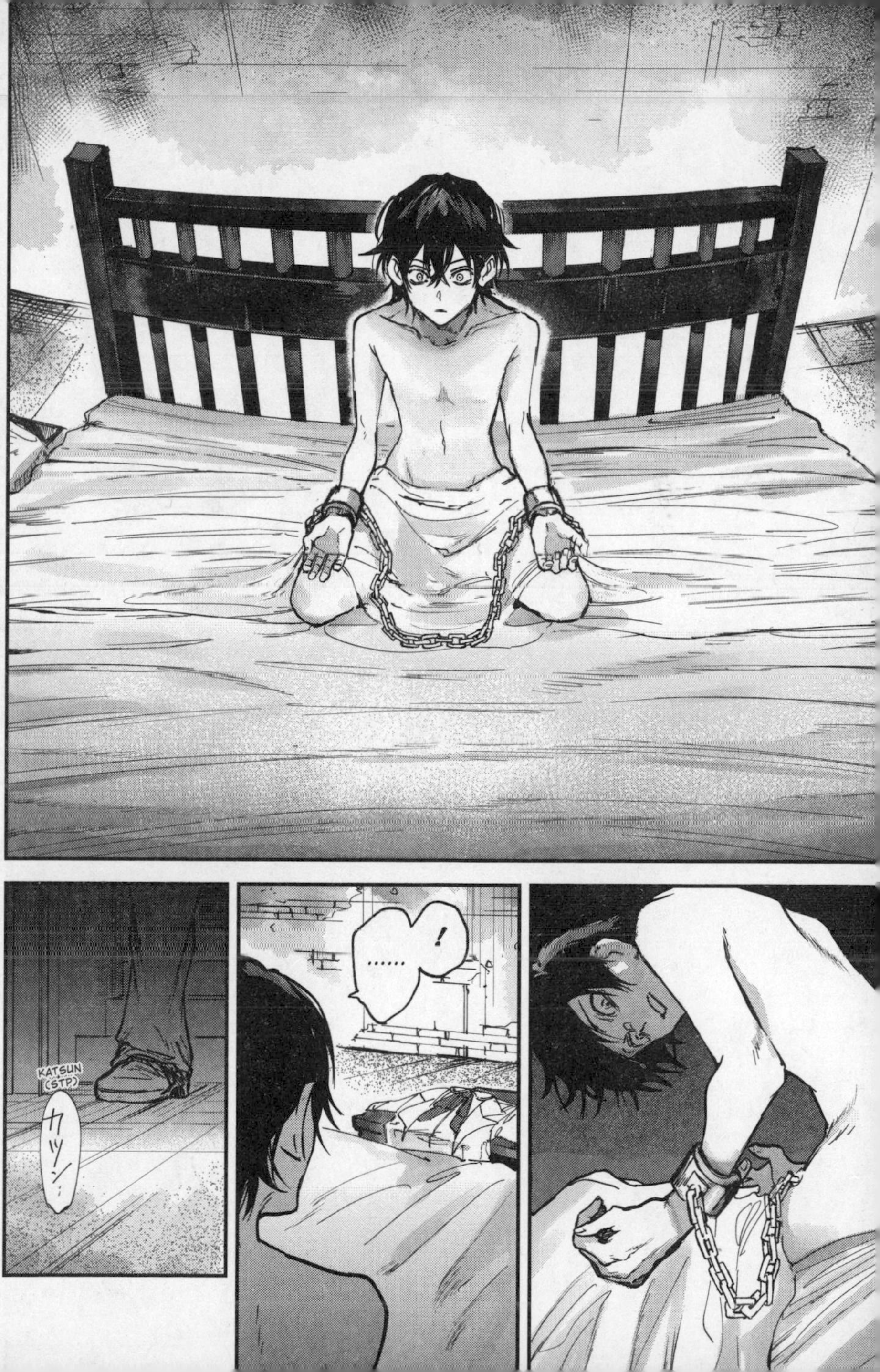
......!
カツン
KATSUN (STP)

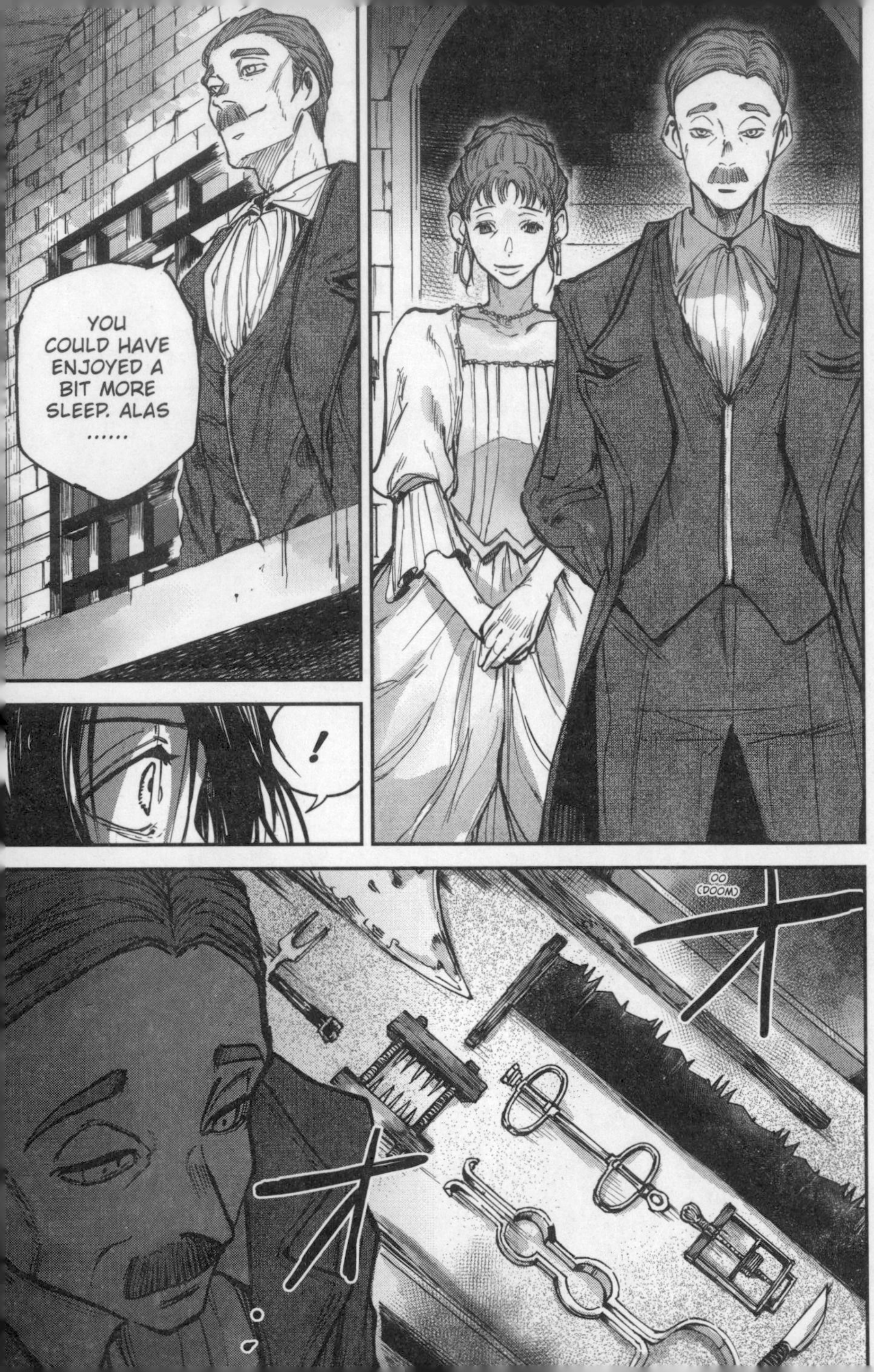
YOU COULD HAVE ENJOYED A BIT MORE SLEEP. ALAS ......
!
OO (DOOM)

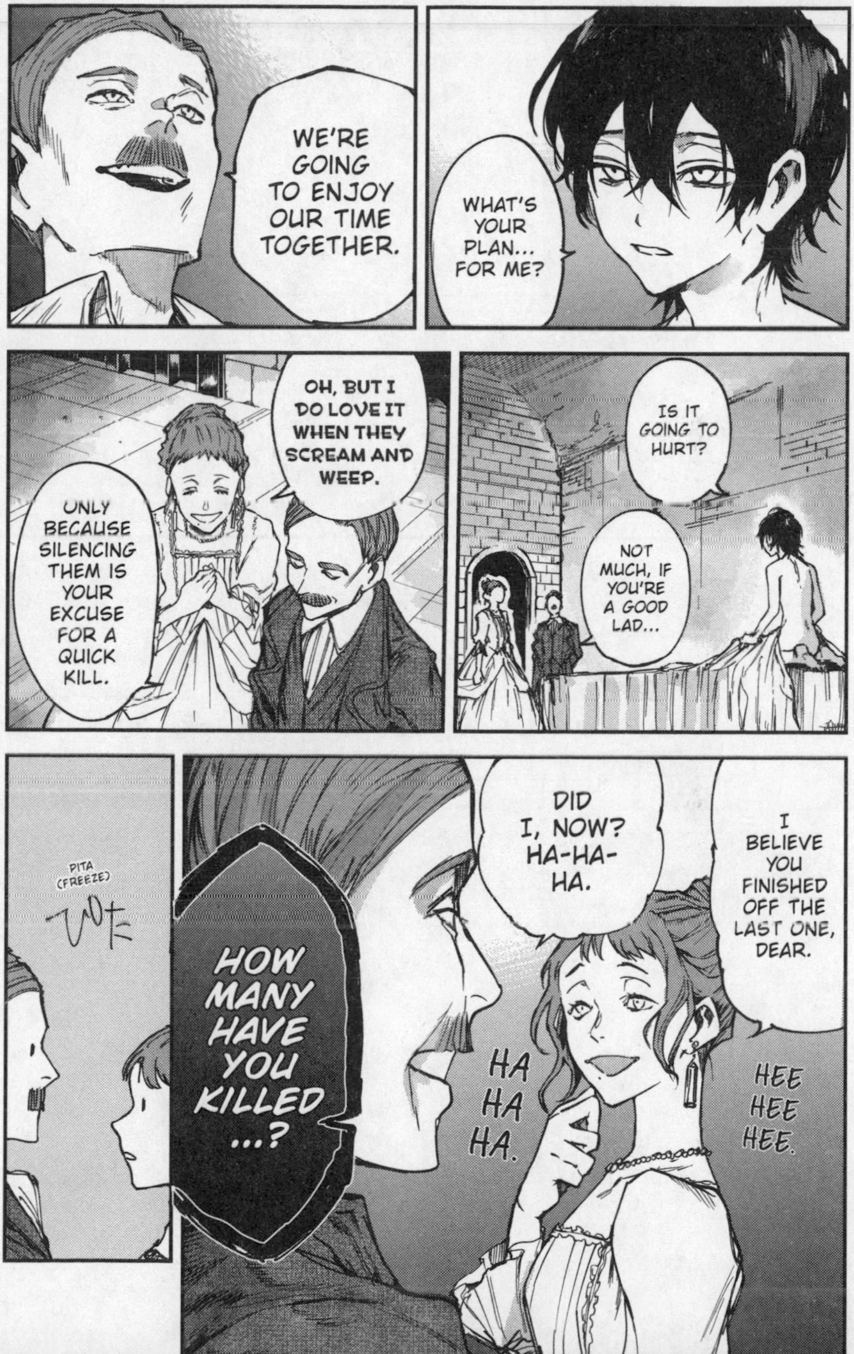
WHAT'S YOUR PLAN... FOR ME?
WE'RE GOING TO ENJOY OUR TIME TOGETHER.
IS IT GOING TO HURT?
NOT MUCH, IF YOU'RE A GOOD LAD...
OH, BUT I DO LOVE IT WHEN THEY SCREAM AND WEEP.
ONLY BECAUSE SILENCING THEM IS YOUR EXCUSE FOR A QUICK KILL.
I BELIEVE YOU FINISHED OFF THE LAST ONE, DEAR.
HEE HEE HEE.
DID I, NOW? HA-HA-HA.
HA HA HA.
HOW MANY HAVE YOU KILLED ...?
PITA (FREEZE)

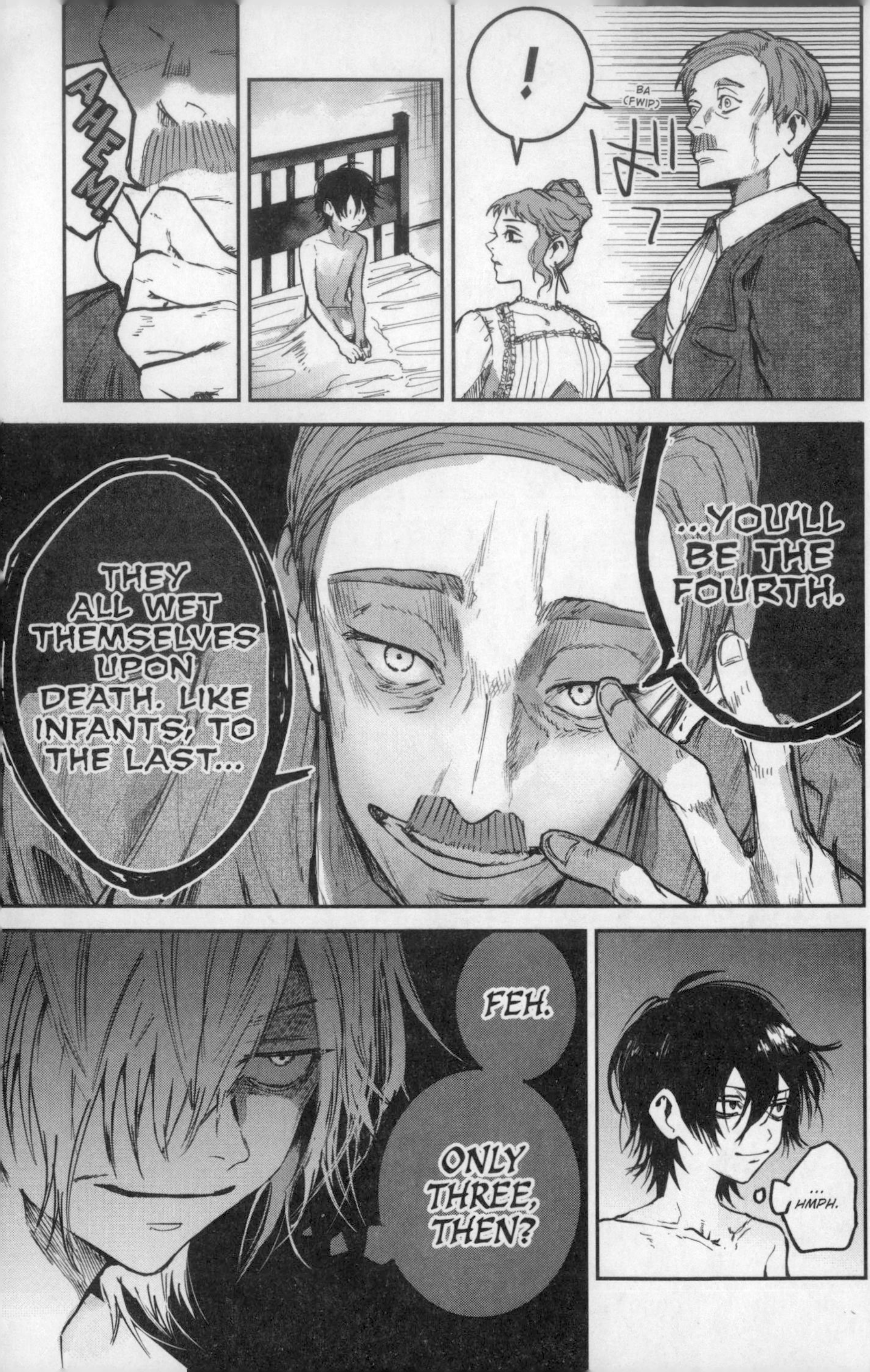
!
BA (FWIP)
AHEM!
...YOU'LL BE THE FOURTH.
THEY ALL WET THEMSELVES UPON DEATH. LIKE INFANTS, TO THE LAST...
...HMPH.
FEH.
ONLY THREE, THEN?

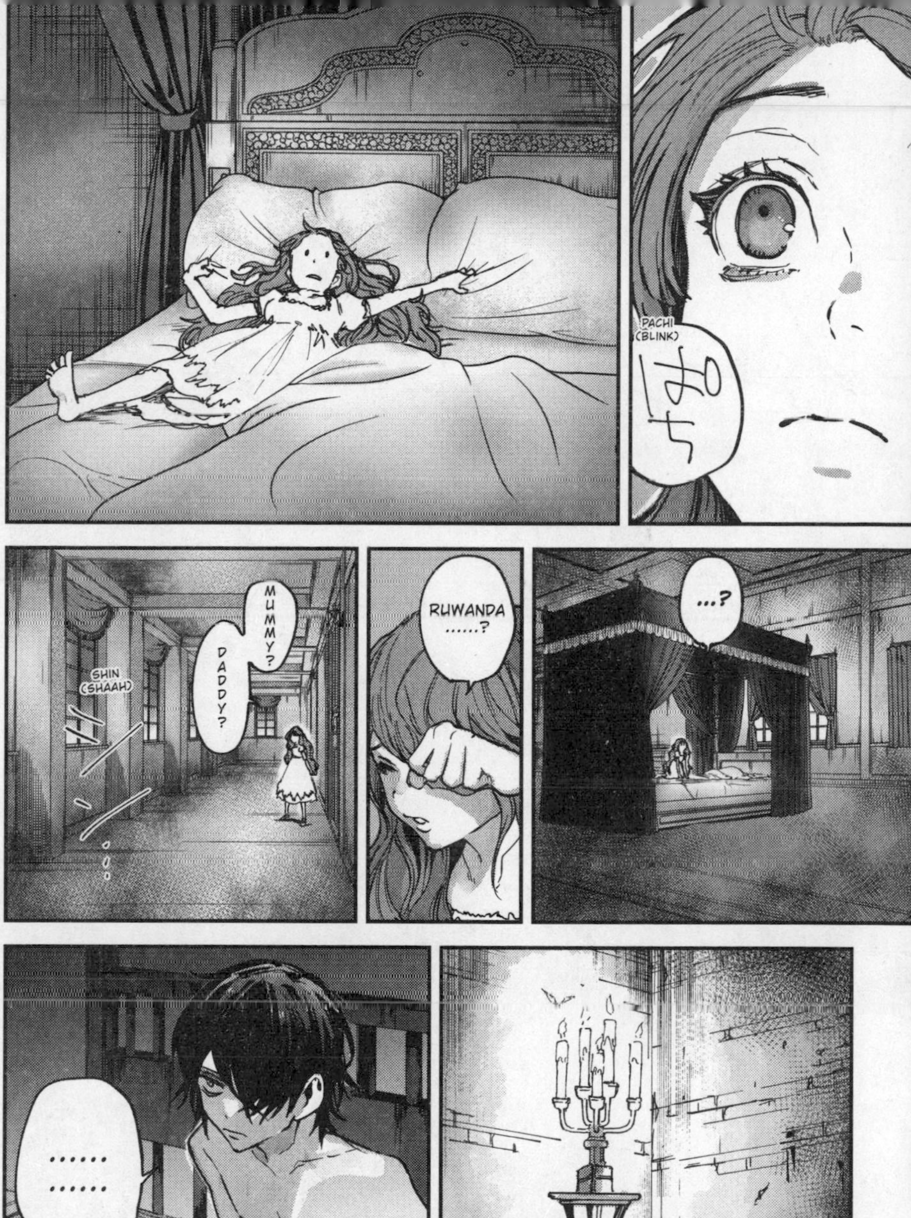
PACHI (BLINK)
ぱち
...?
RUWANDA ......?
MUMMY? DADDY?
SHIN (SHAAH)
......
......

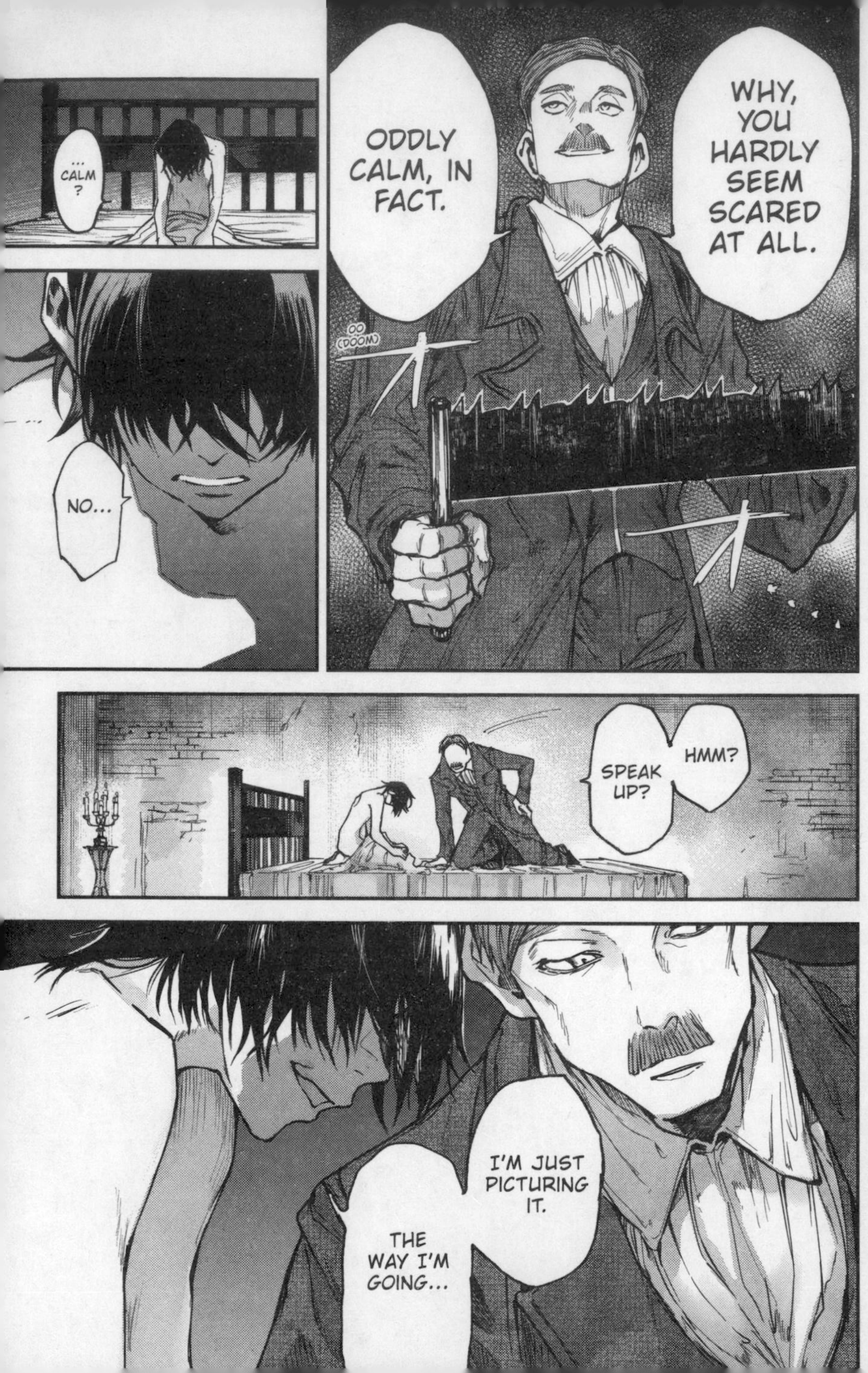
WHY, YOU HARDLY SEEM SCARED AT ALL.
ODDLY CALM, IN FACT.
OO (DOOM)
...CALM?
NO...
HMM?
SPEAK UP?
I'M JUST PICTURING IT.
THE WAY I'M GOING...

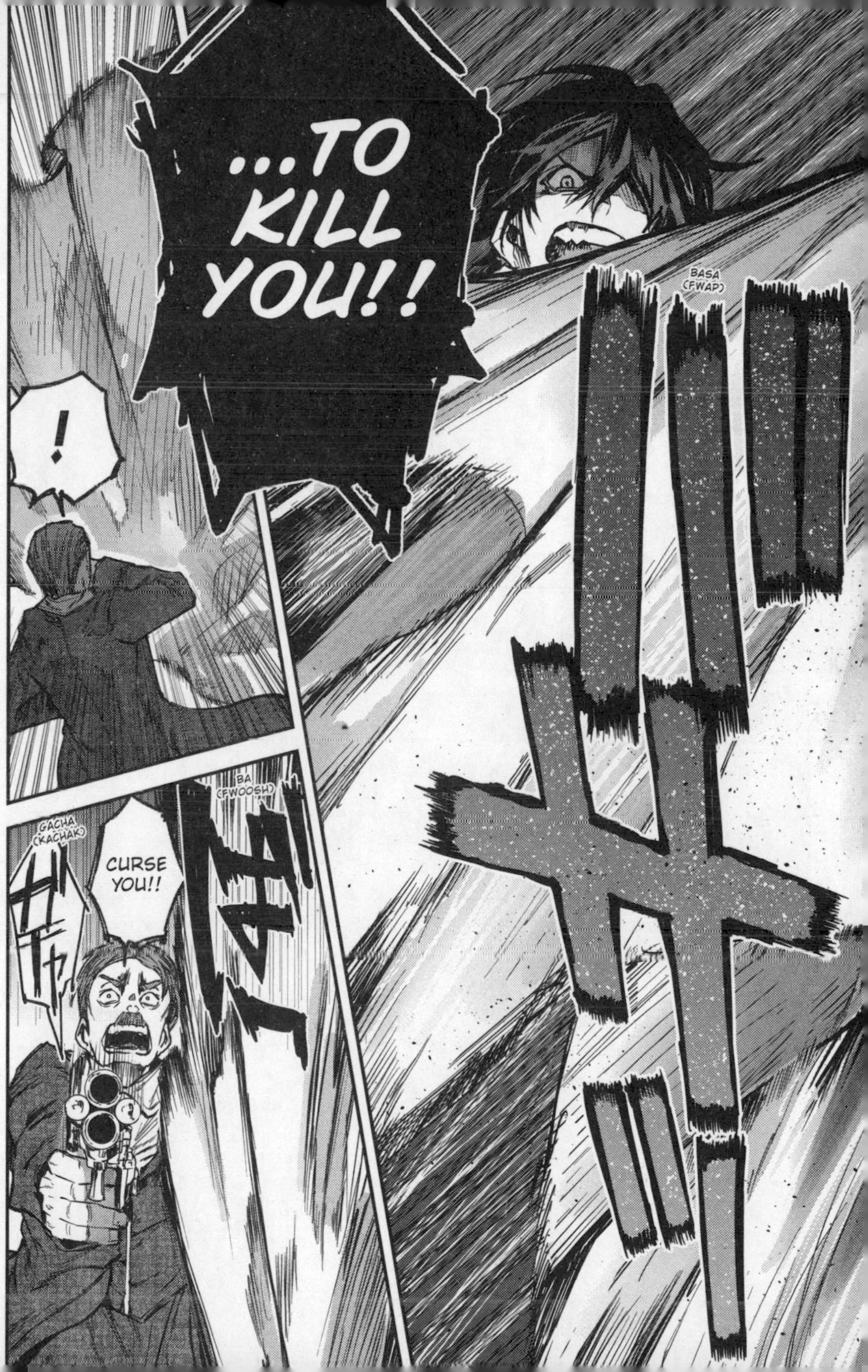
...TO KILL YOU!!
BASA (FWAP)
!
BA (FWOOSH)
CURSE YOU!!
GACHA (KACHAK)

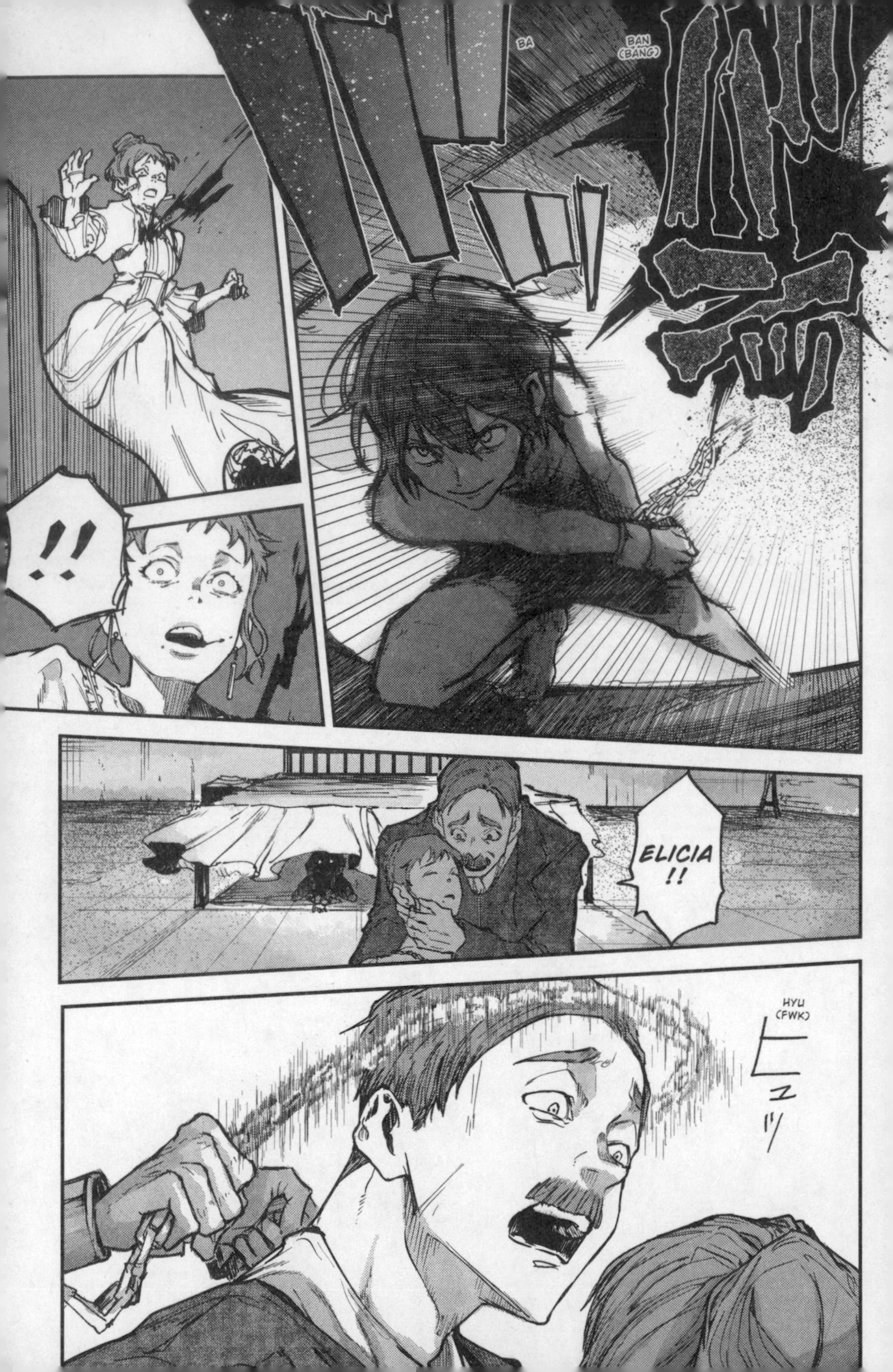
BA
BAN (BANG)
!!
ELICIA !!
HYU (FWK)

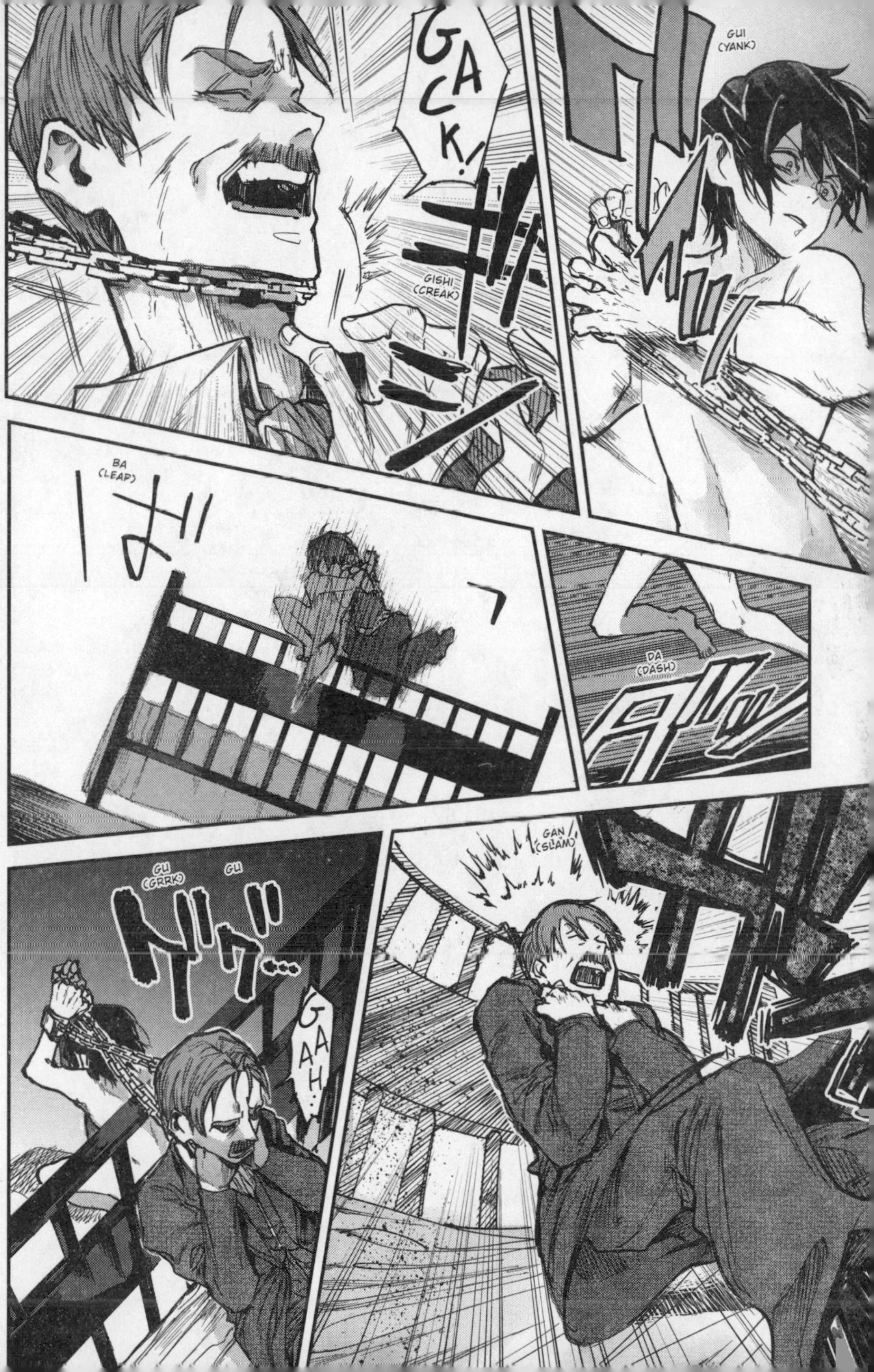
GUI
(YANK)
GACK!
GISHI
(CREAK)
DA
(DASH)
BA
(LEAP)
GAN
(SLAM)
GU
(GRRK)
GU
GAAH...

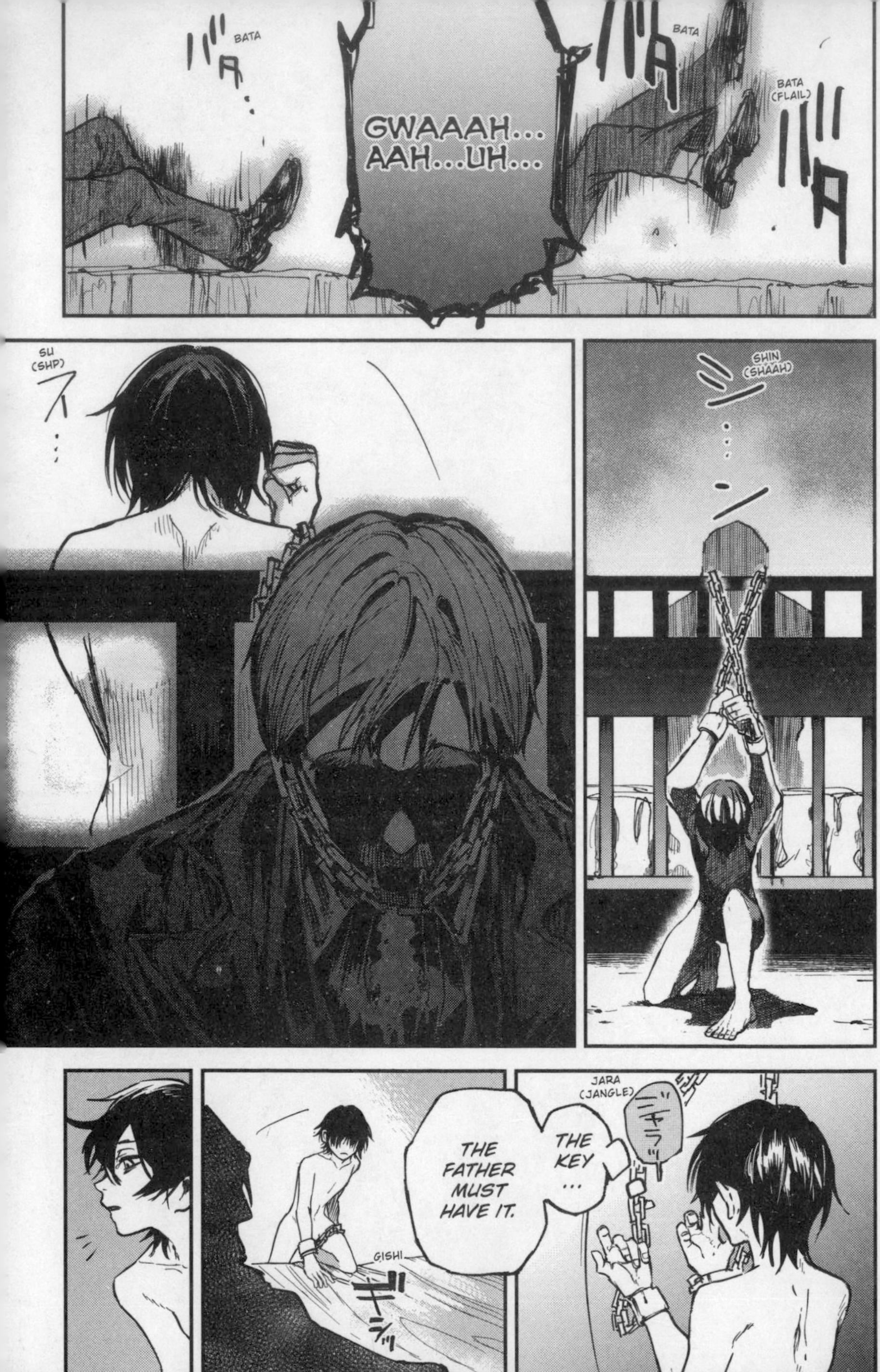
BATA (FLAIL)
BATA
GWAAAH... AAH...UH...
BATA
SHIN (SHAAH)
SU (SHP)
JARA (JANGLE)
THE KEY ...
THE FATHER MUST HAVE IT.
GISHI

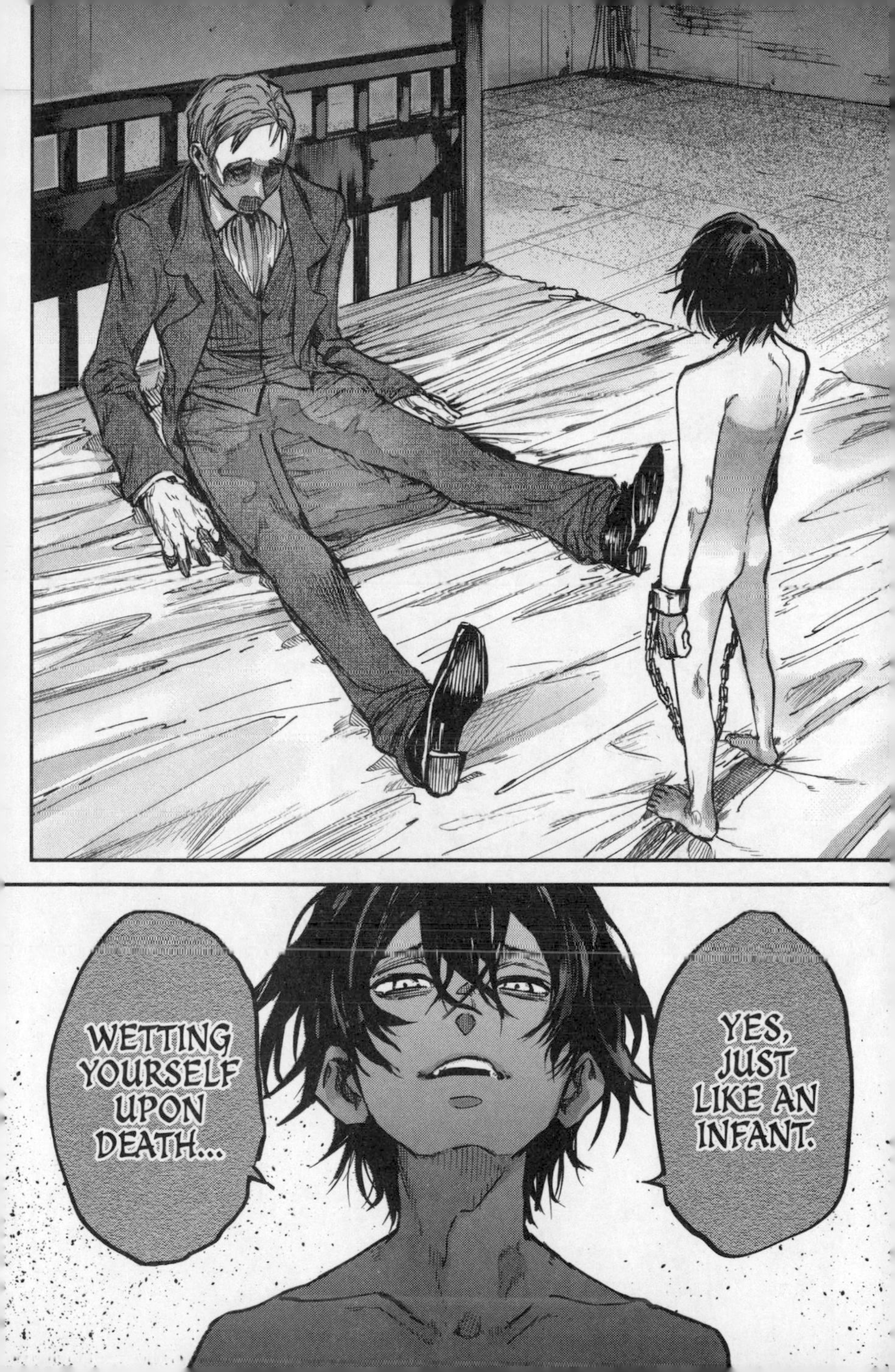
WETTING YOURSELF UPON DEATH...
YES, JUST LIKE AN INFANT.

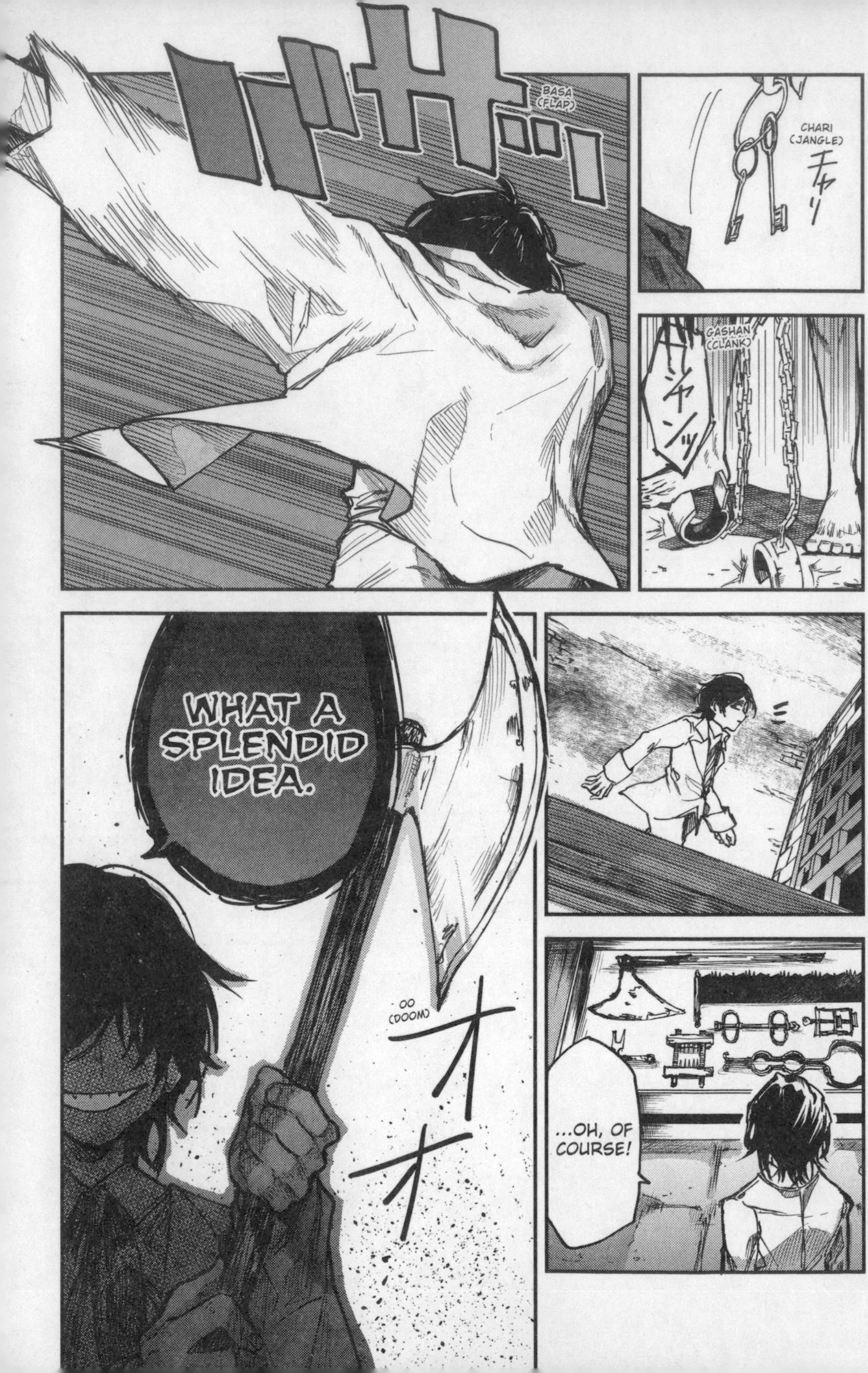
CHARI (JANGLE)
GASHAN (CLANK)
BASA (FLAP)
...OH, OF COURSE!
WHAT A SPLENDID IDEA.
OO (DOOM)

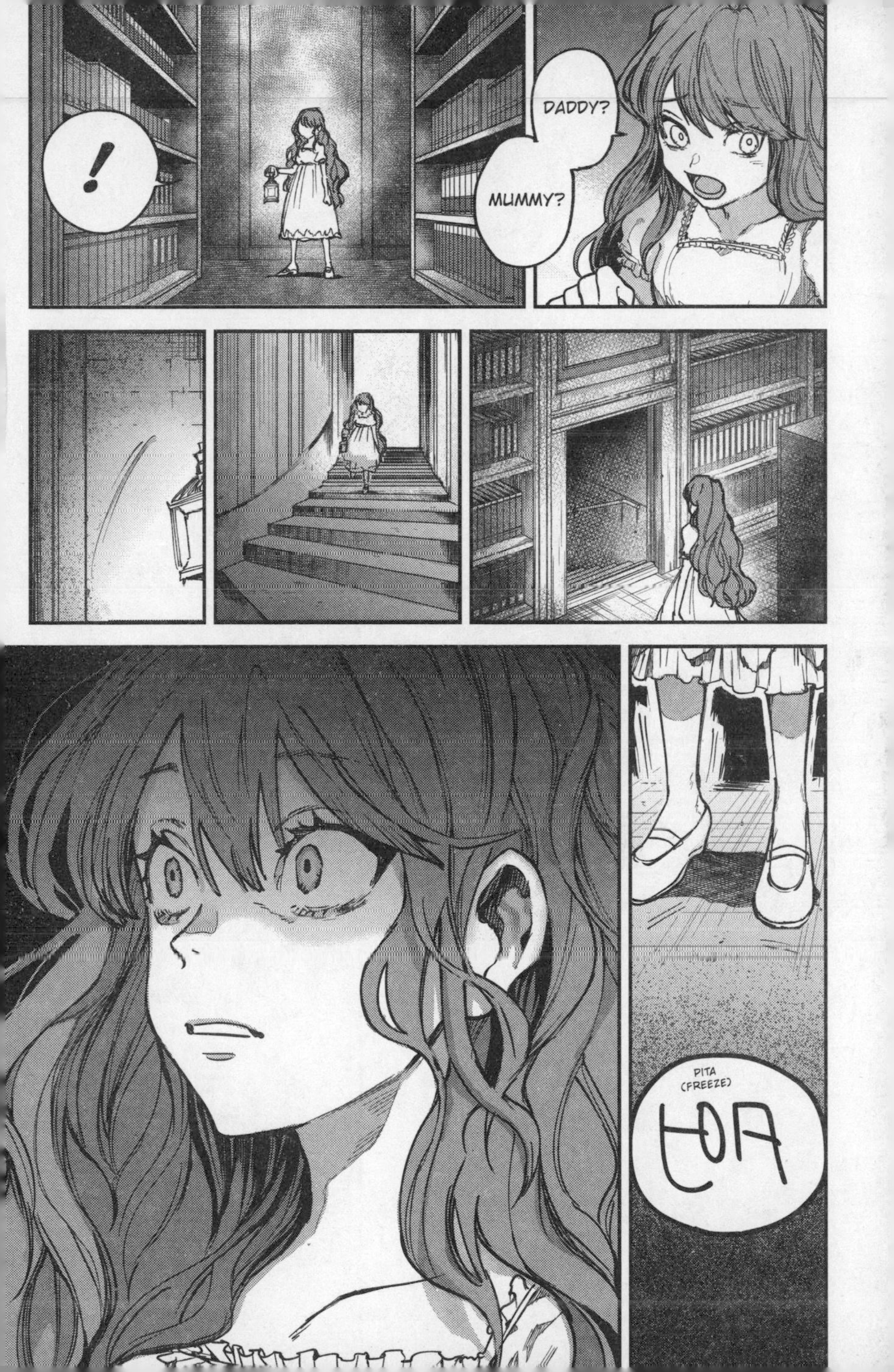
DADDY?
MUMMY?
!
PITA
(FREEZE)

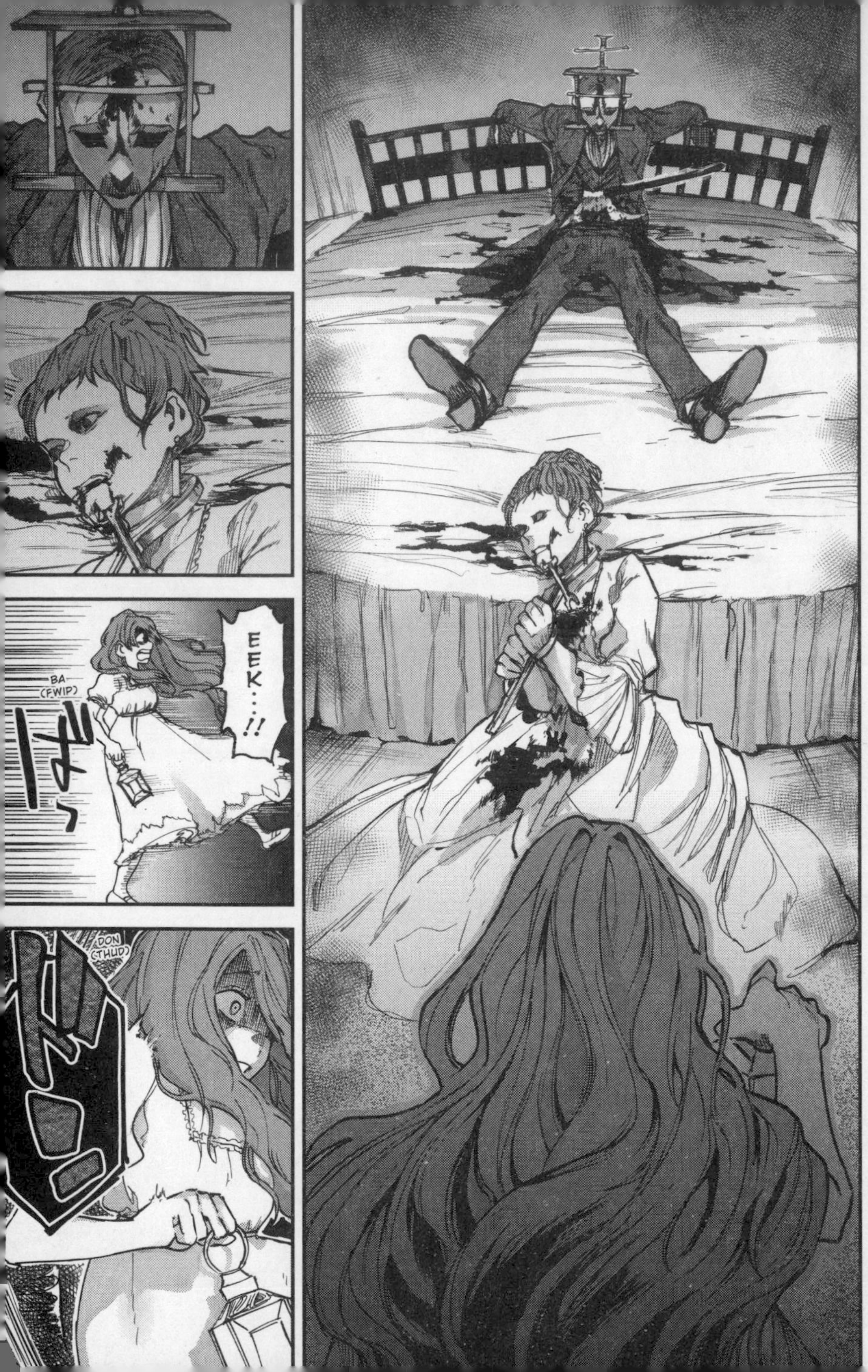
EEK...!!
BA (FWIP)
DON (THUD)

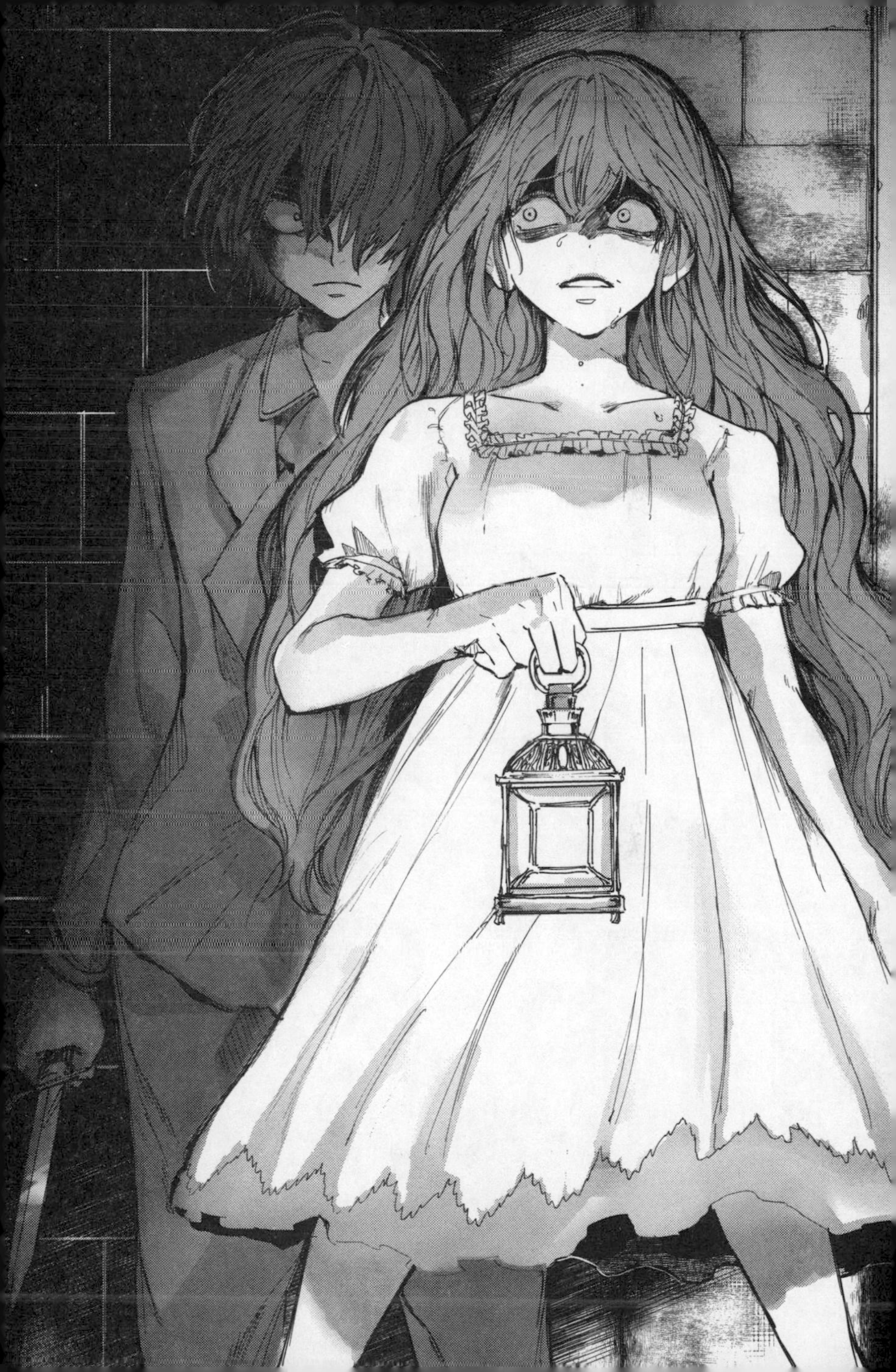

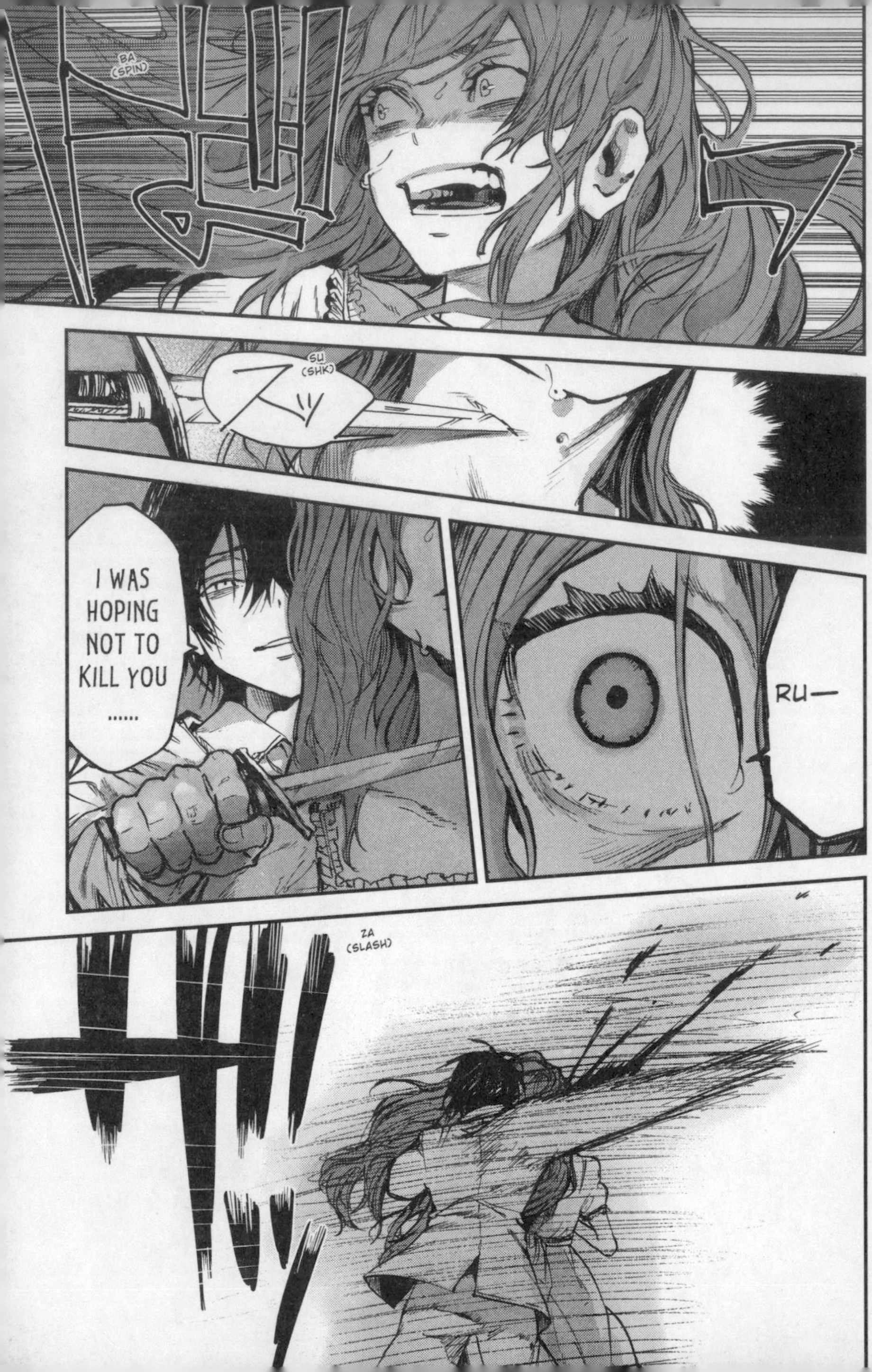
BA (SPIN)
SU (SHK)
RU—
I WAS HOPING NOT TO KILL YOU ......
ZA (SLASH)

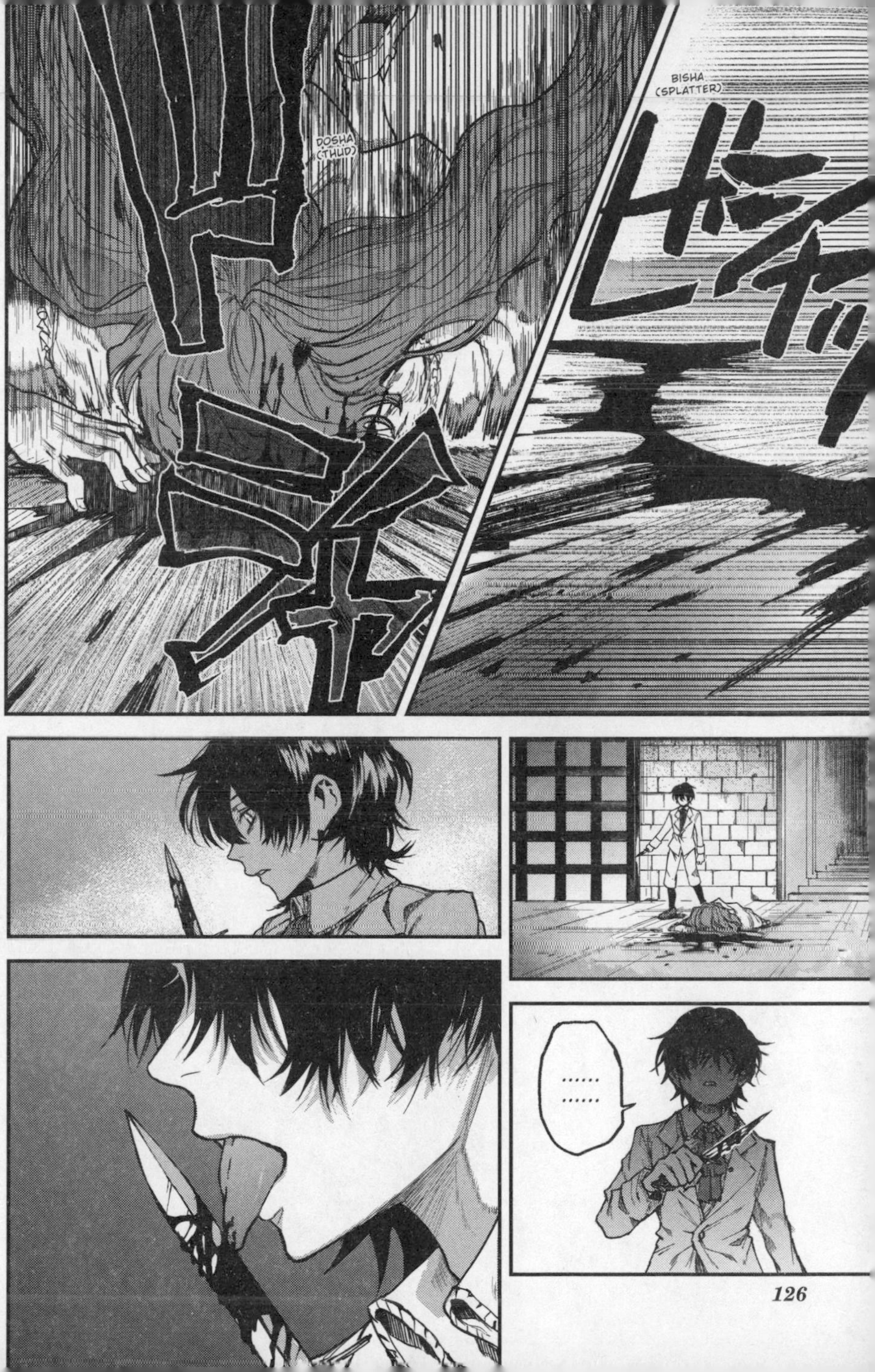
BISHA
(SPLATTER)
DOSHA
(THUD)
……
……

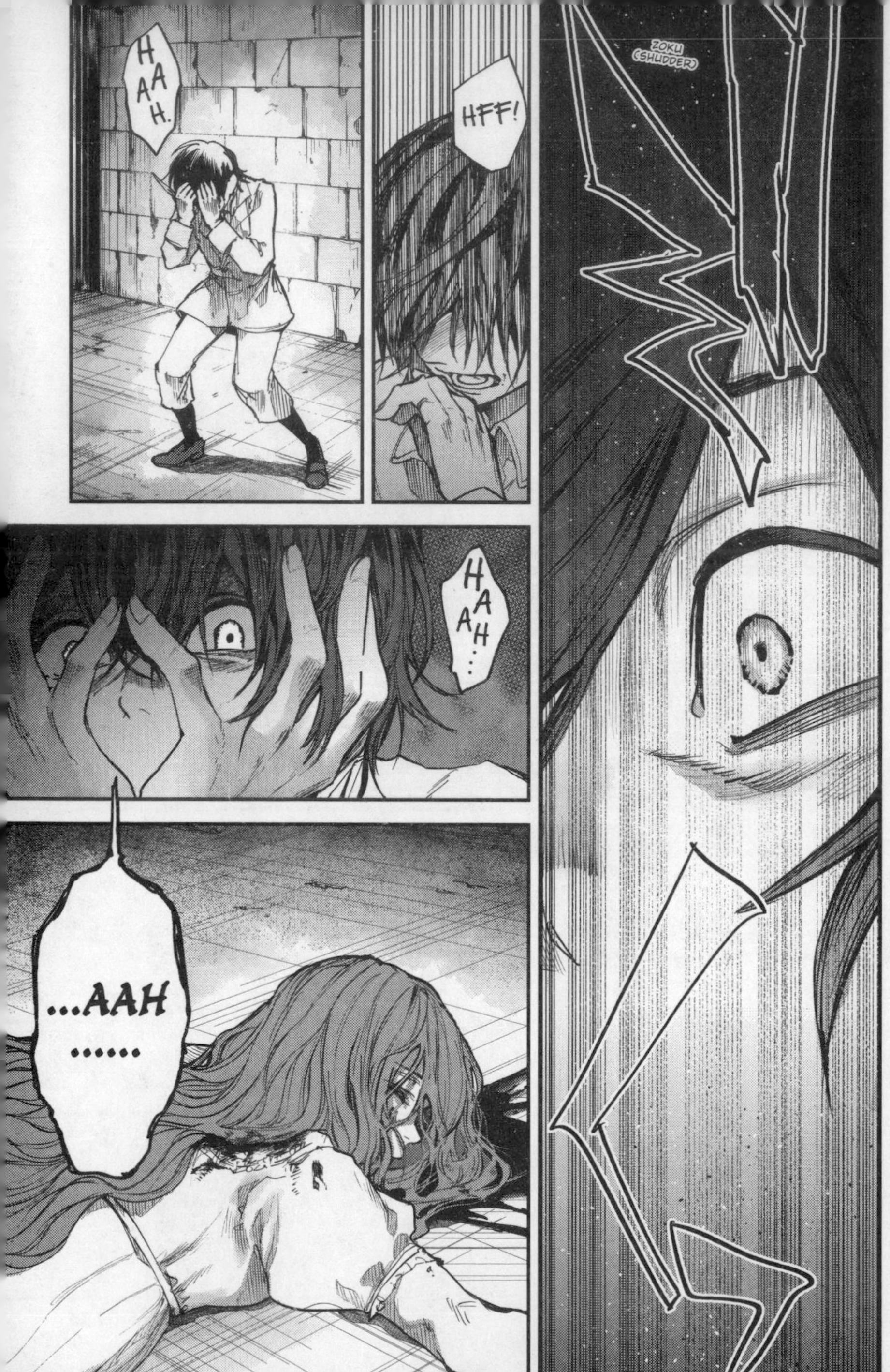
ZOKU
(SHUDDER)
HFF!
HAAH.
HAAH...
...AAH
......

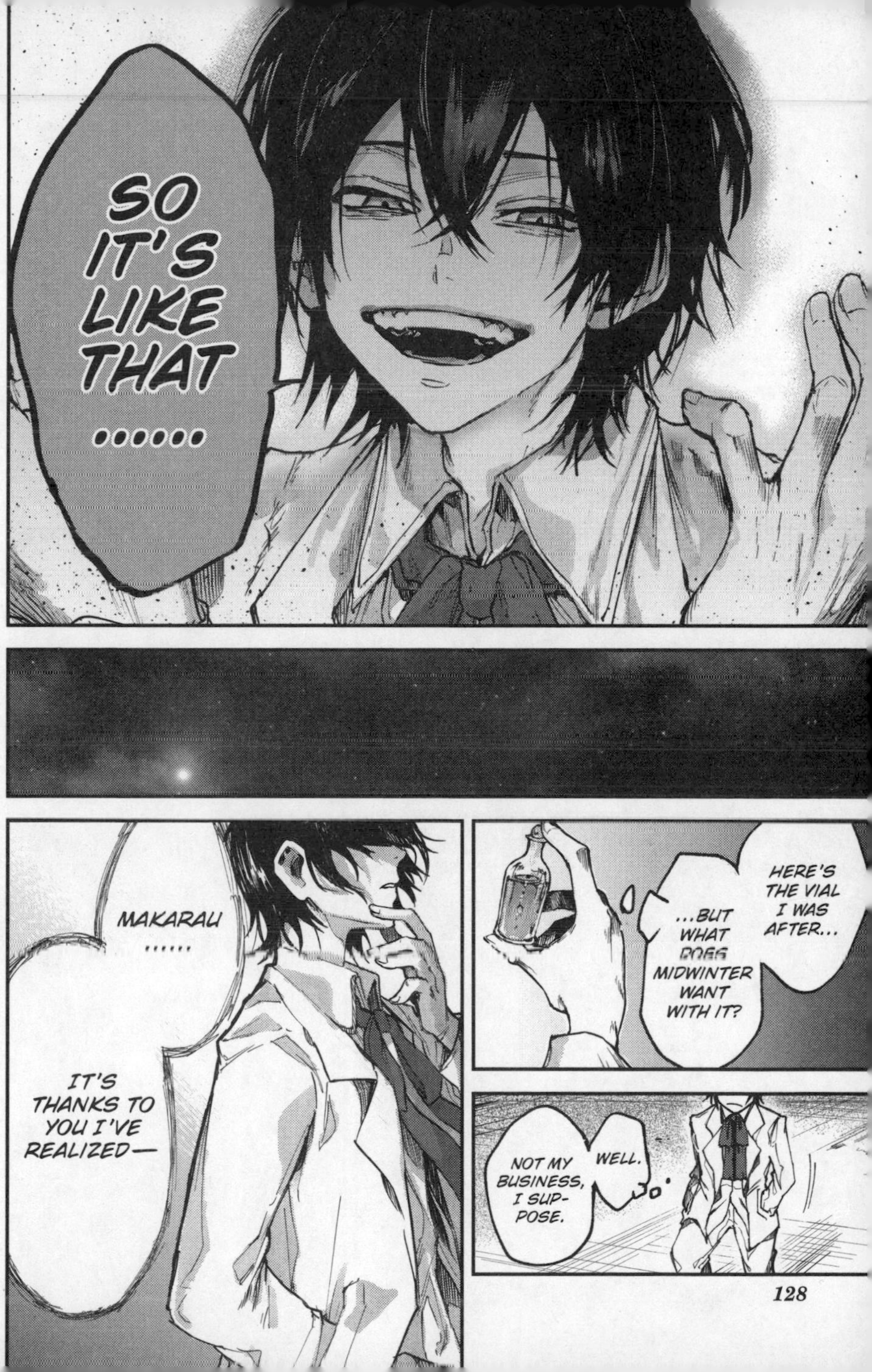
SO IT'S LIKE THAT ......
HERE'S THE VIAL I WAS AFTER...
...BUT WHAT DOES MIDWINTER WANT WITH IT?
WELL.
NOT MY BUSINESS, I SUP-POSE.
MAKARAU ......
IT'S THANKS TO YOU I'VE REALIZED—

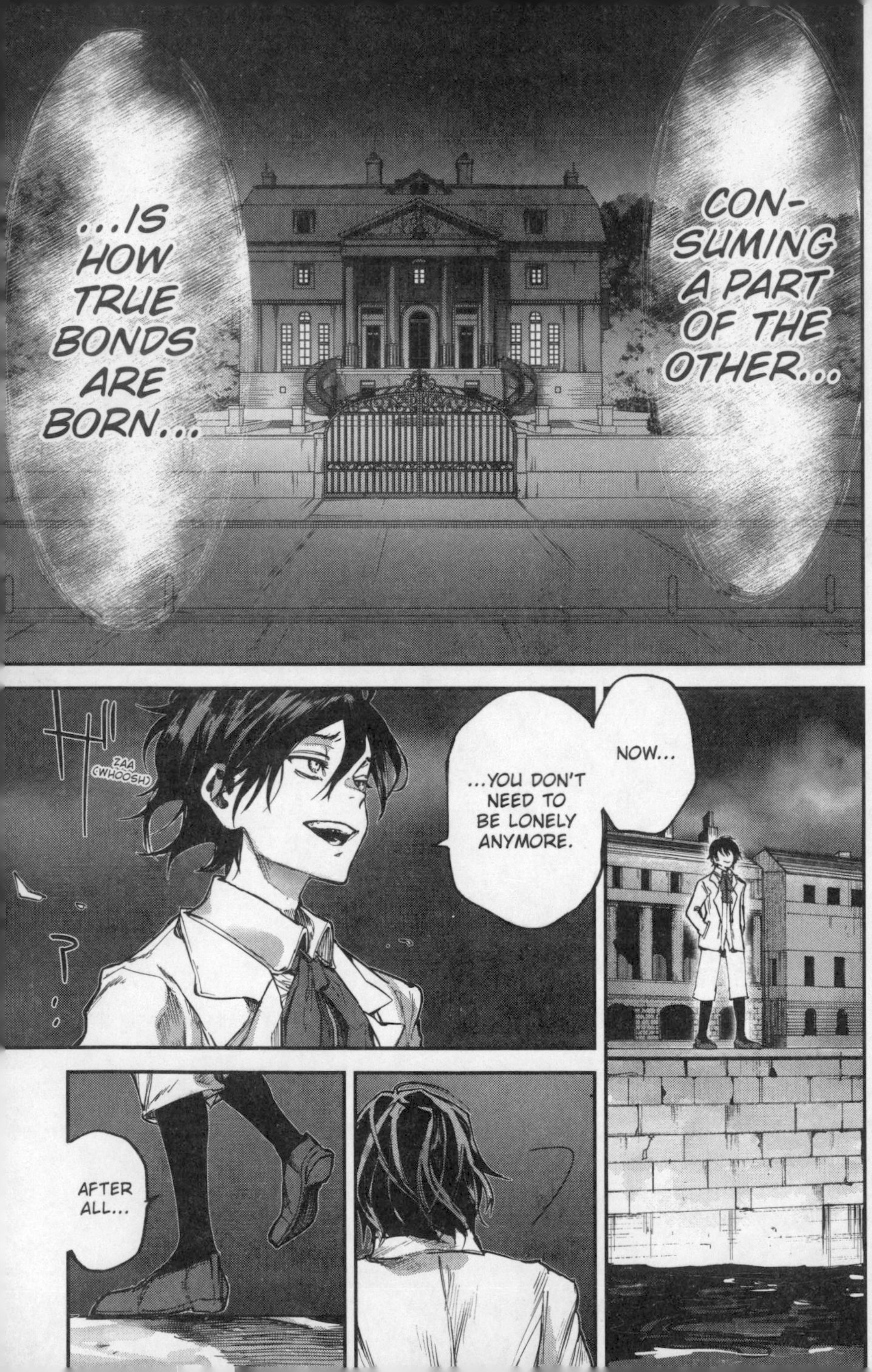
CON-SUMING A PART OF THE OTHER...
...IS HOW TRUE BONDS ARE BORN...
NOW...
...YOU DON'T NEED TO BE LONELY ANYMORE.
ZAA (WHOOSH)
AFTER ALL...

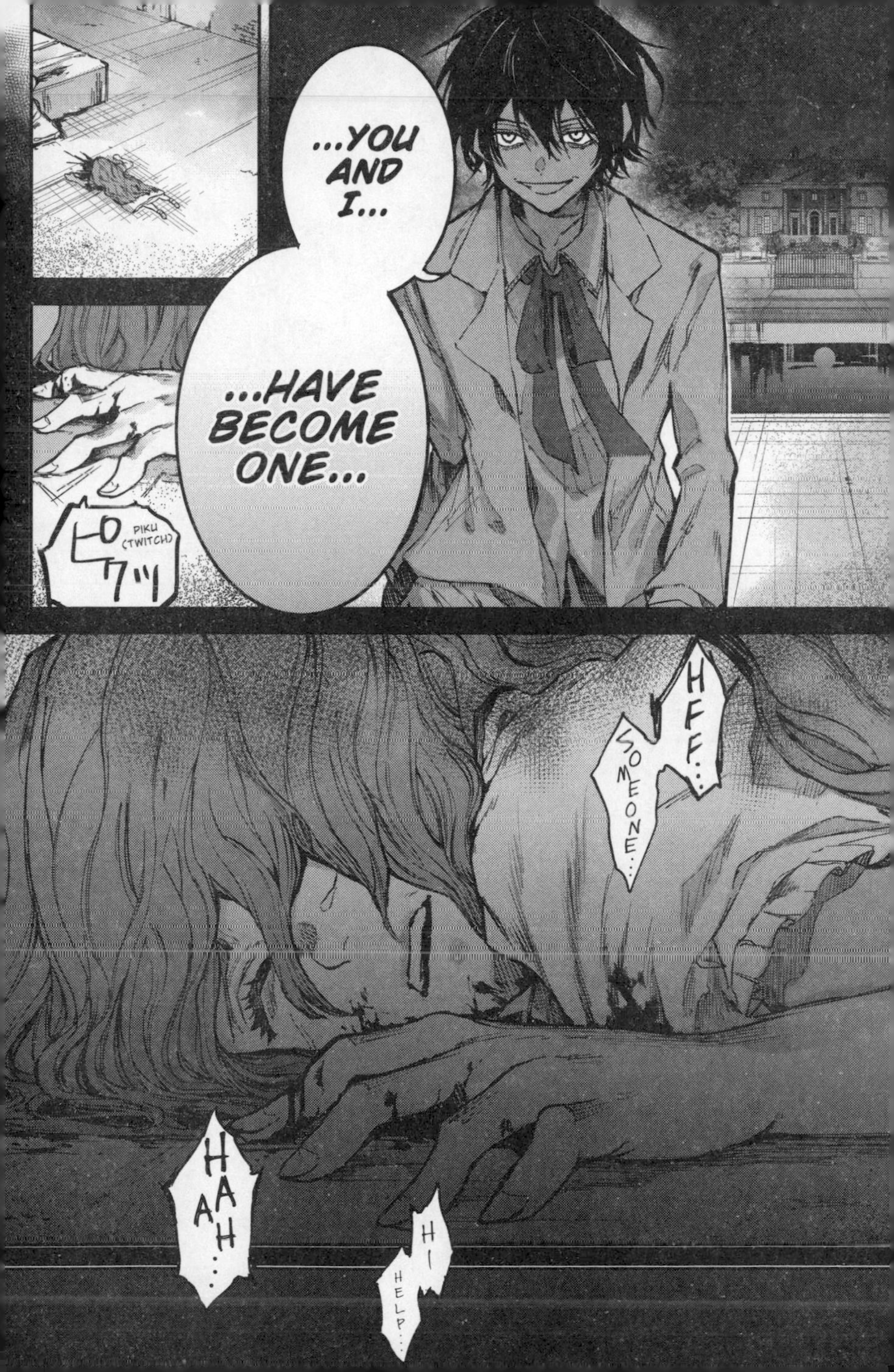

...YOU AND I...
...HAVE BECOME ONE...
ピクッ
PIKU (TWITCH)
HFF...
SOMEONE...
HAAH...
HI
HELP...

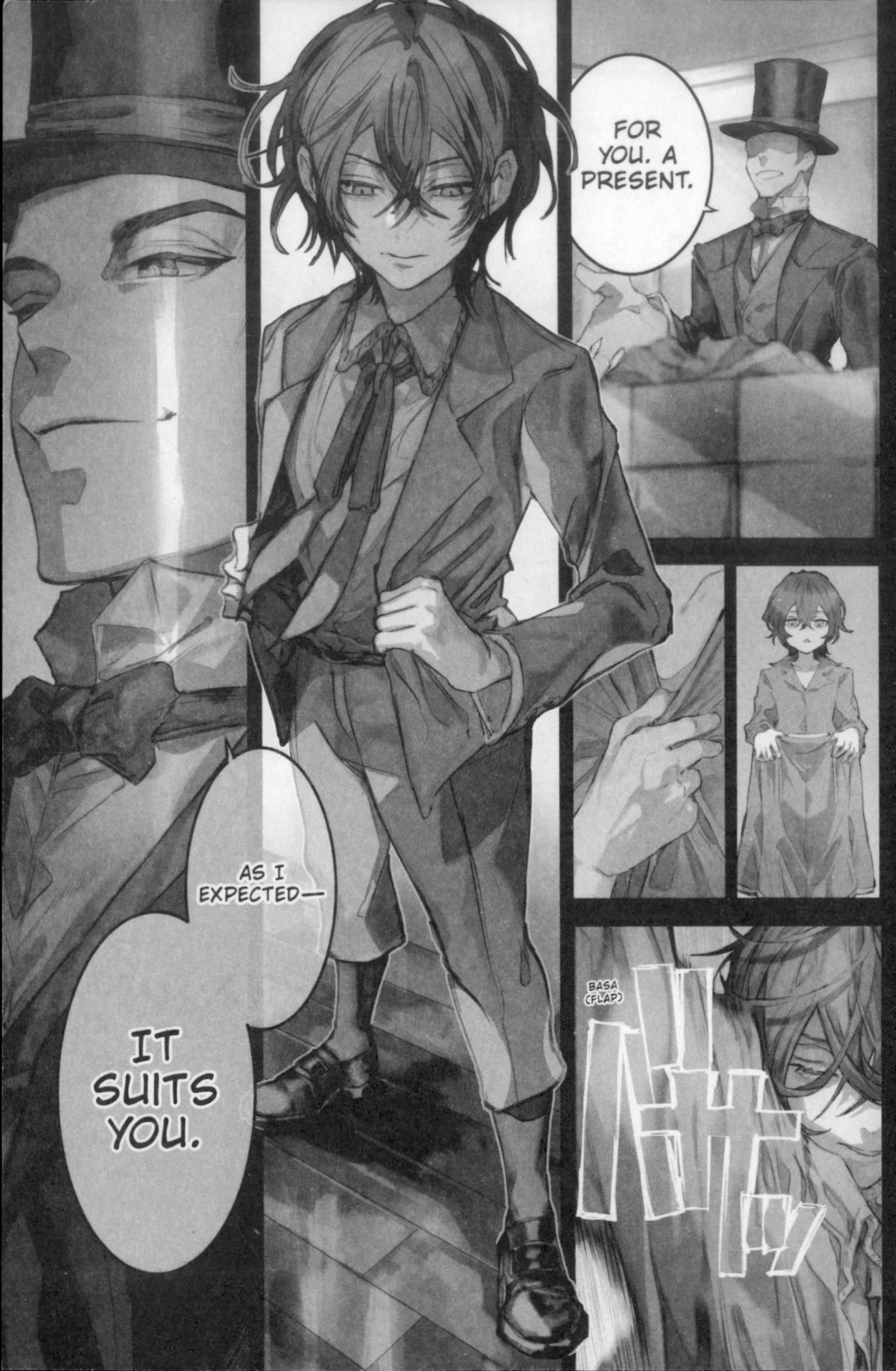
FOR YOU. A PRESENT.
BASA (FLAP)
AS I EXPECTED—
IT SUITS YOU.

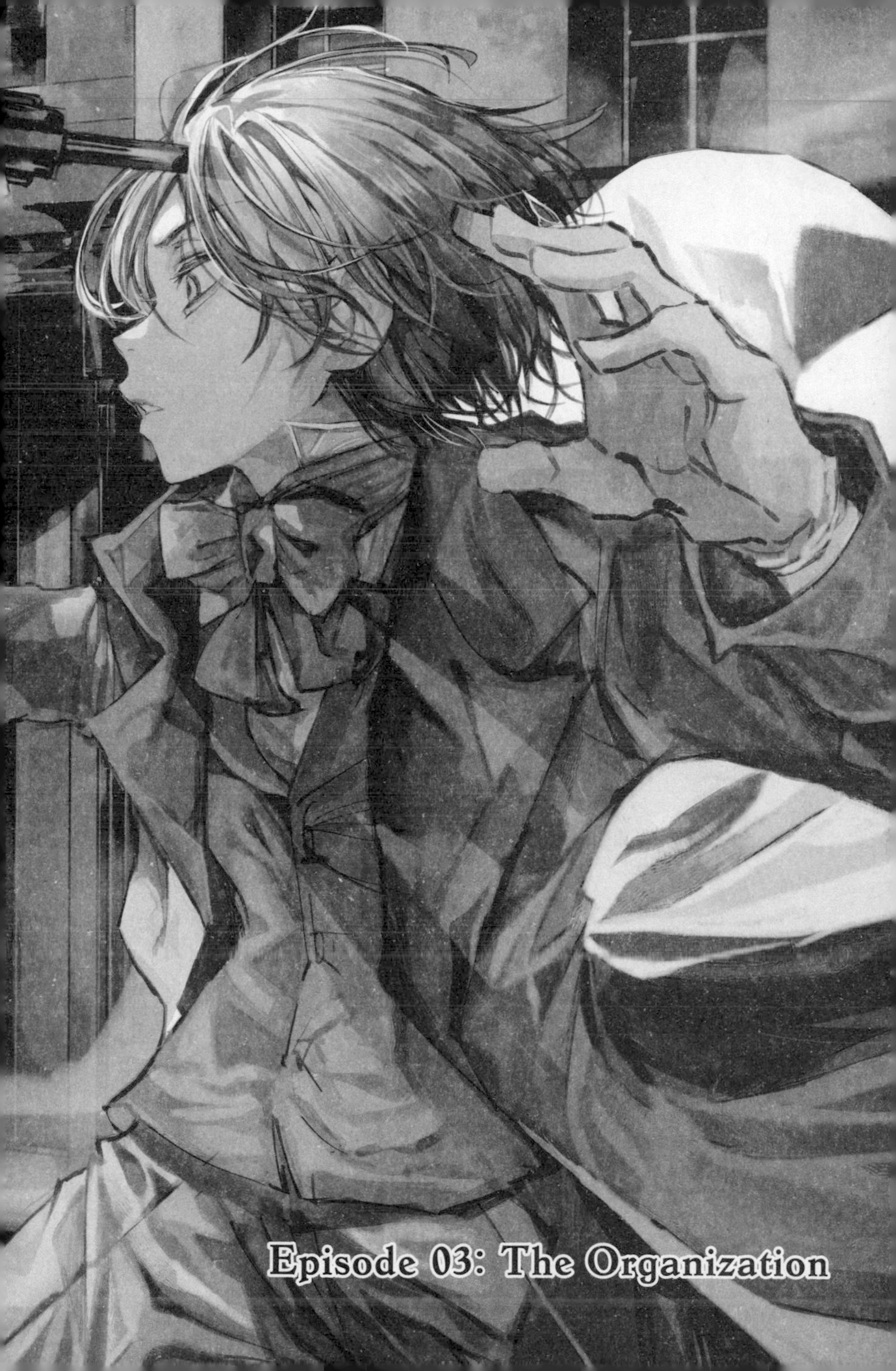
Episode 03: The Organization

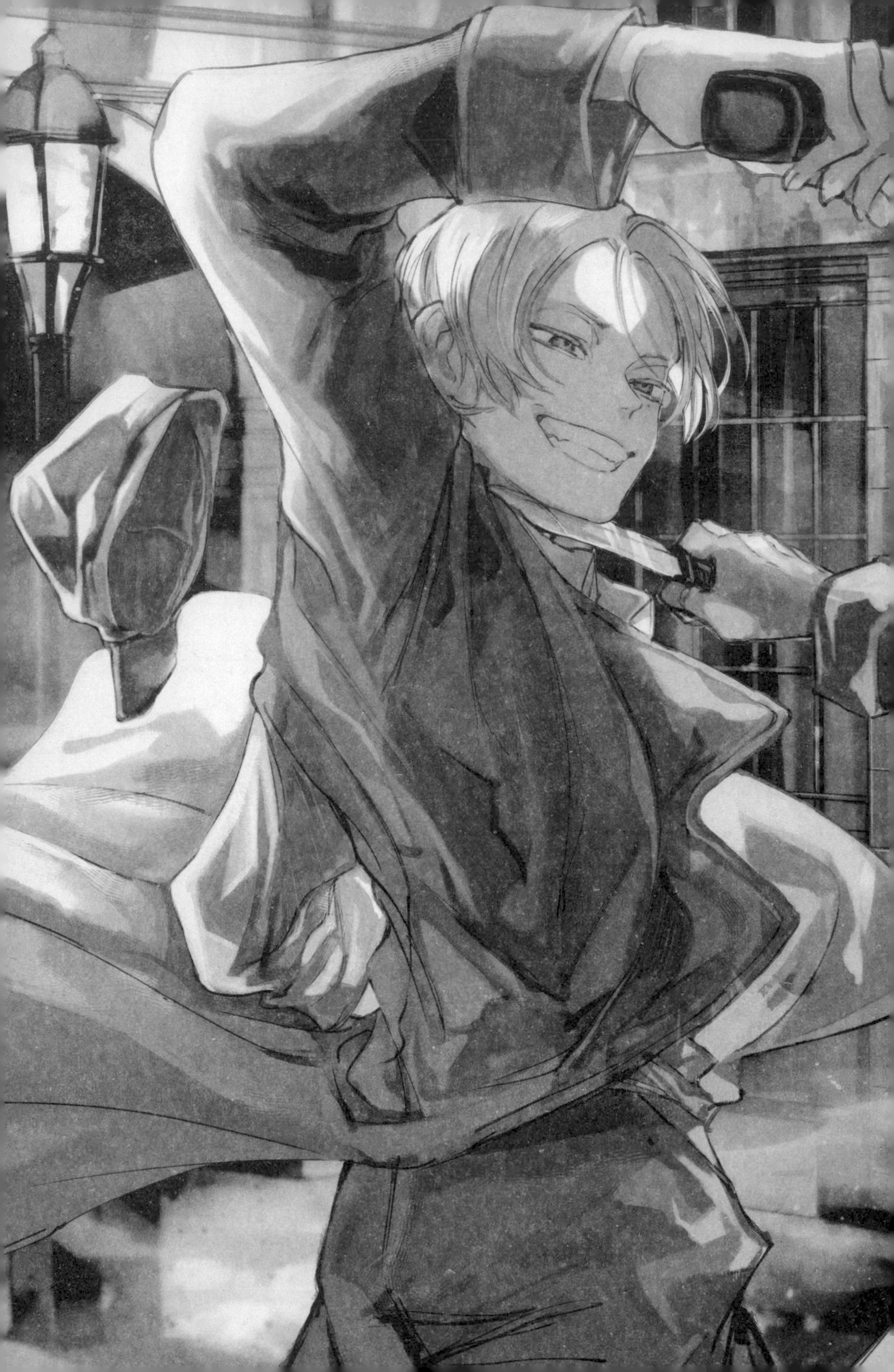

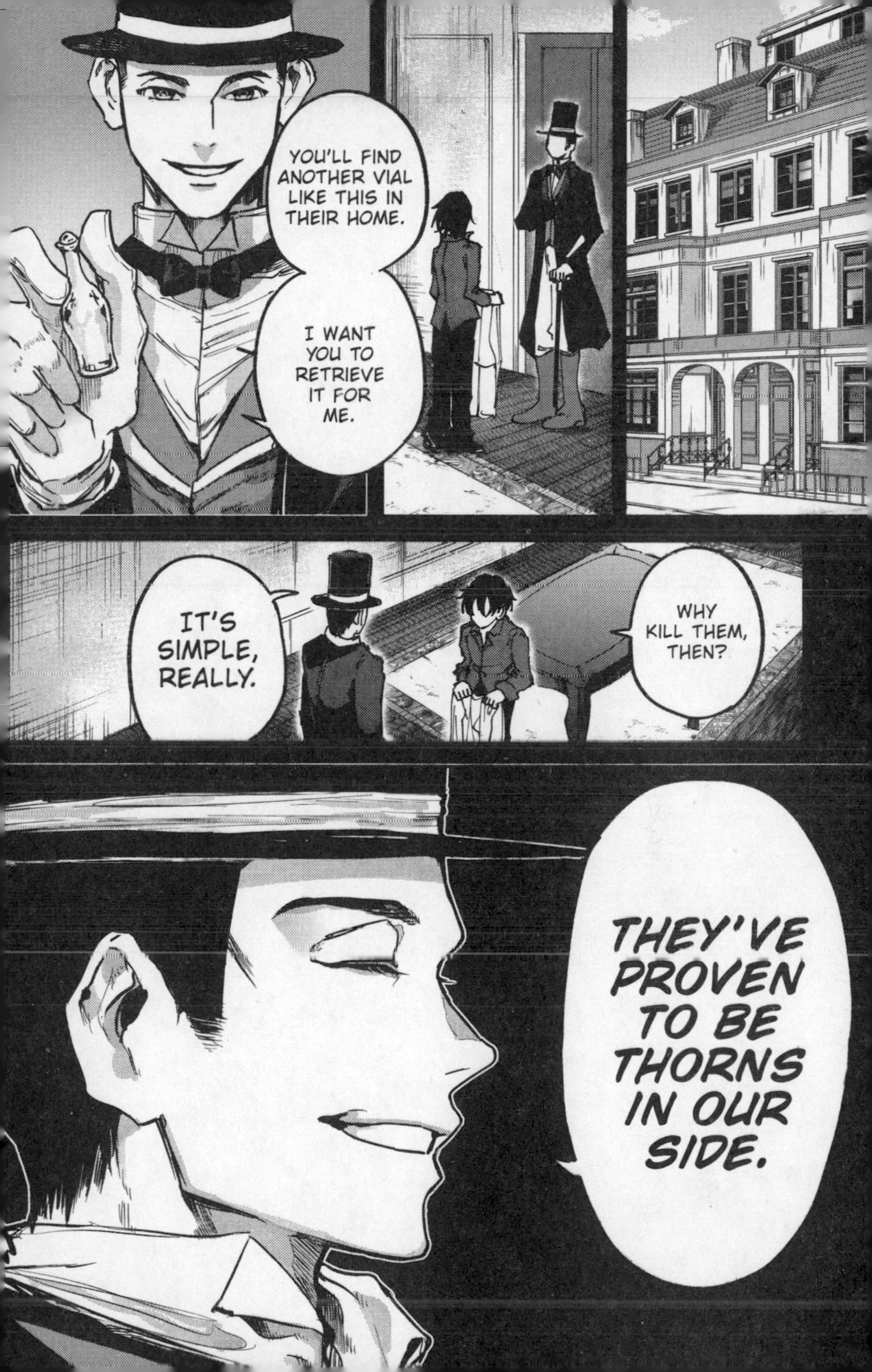
YOU'LL FIND ANOTHER VIAL LIKE THIS IN THEIR HOME.
I WANT YOU TO RETRIEVE IT FOR ME.
WHY KILL THEM, THEN?
IT'S SIMPLE, REALLY.
THEY'VE PROVEN TO BE THORNS IN OUR SIDE.

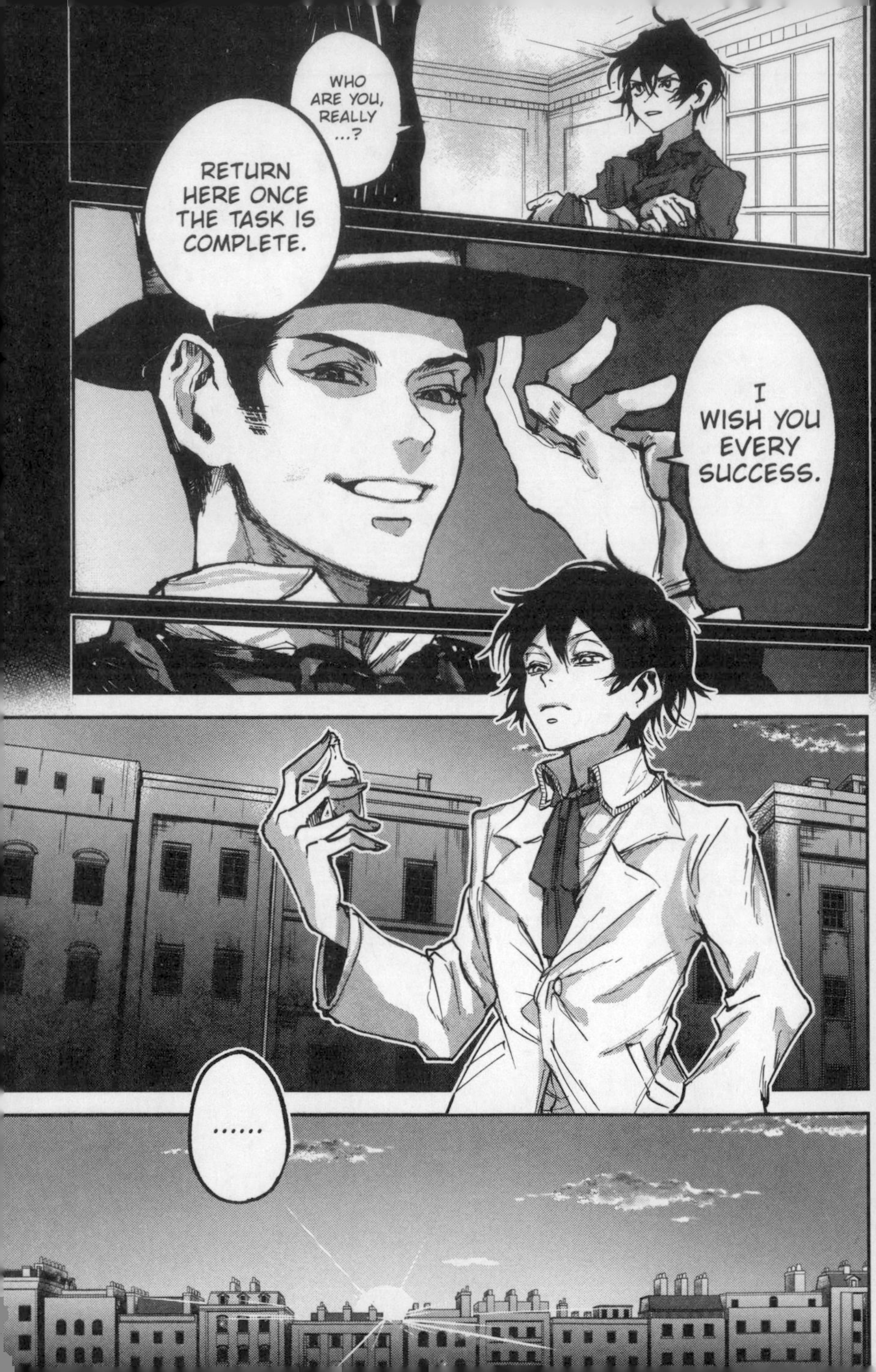
WHO ARE YOU, REALLY ...?
RETURN HERE ONCE THE TASK IS COMPLETE.
I WISH YOU EVERY SUCCESS.
......

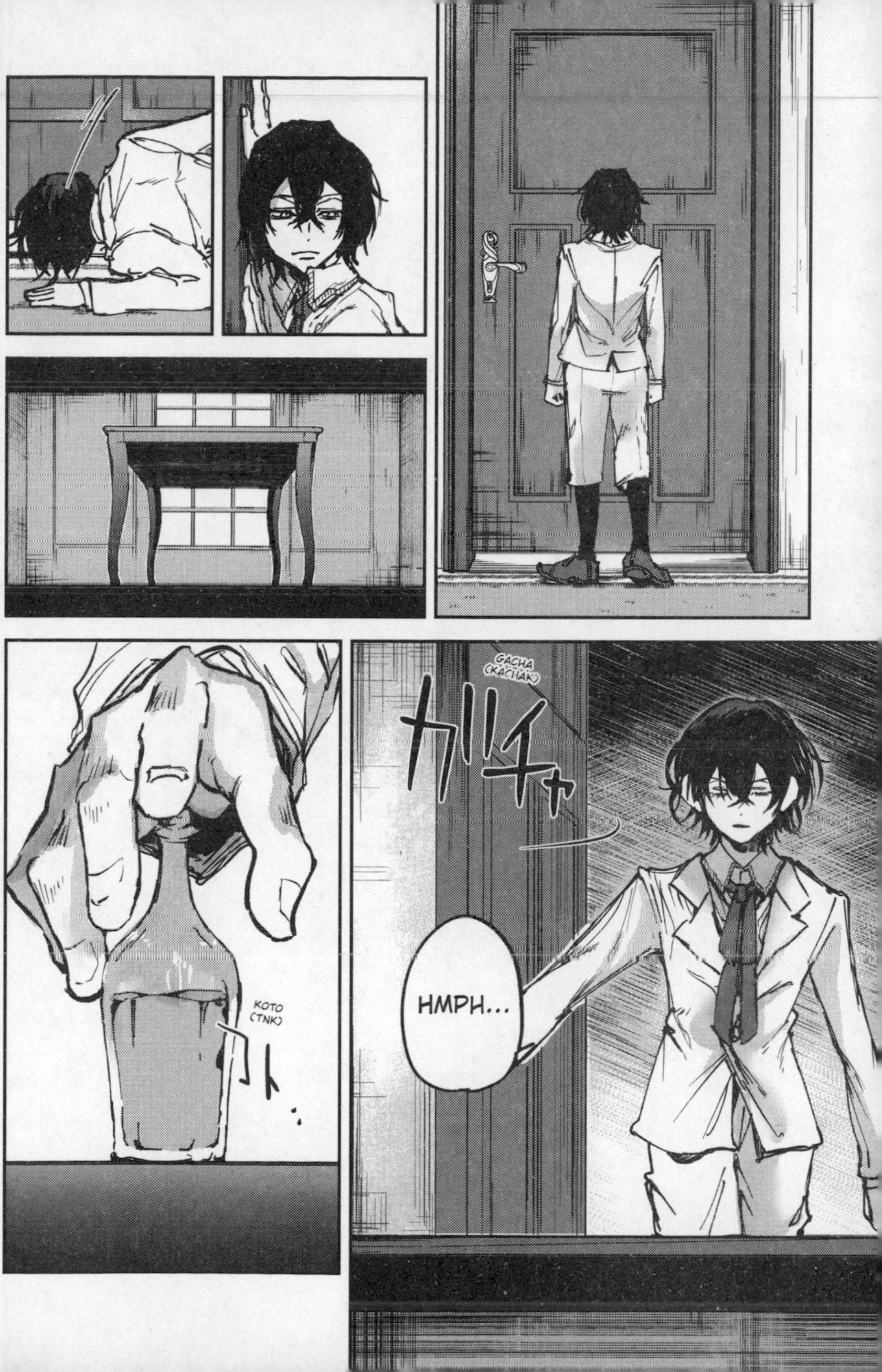
GACHA (KACHAK)
HMPH...
KOTO (TNK)

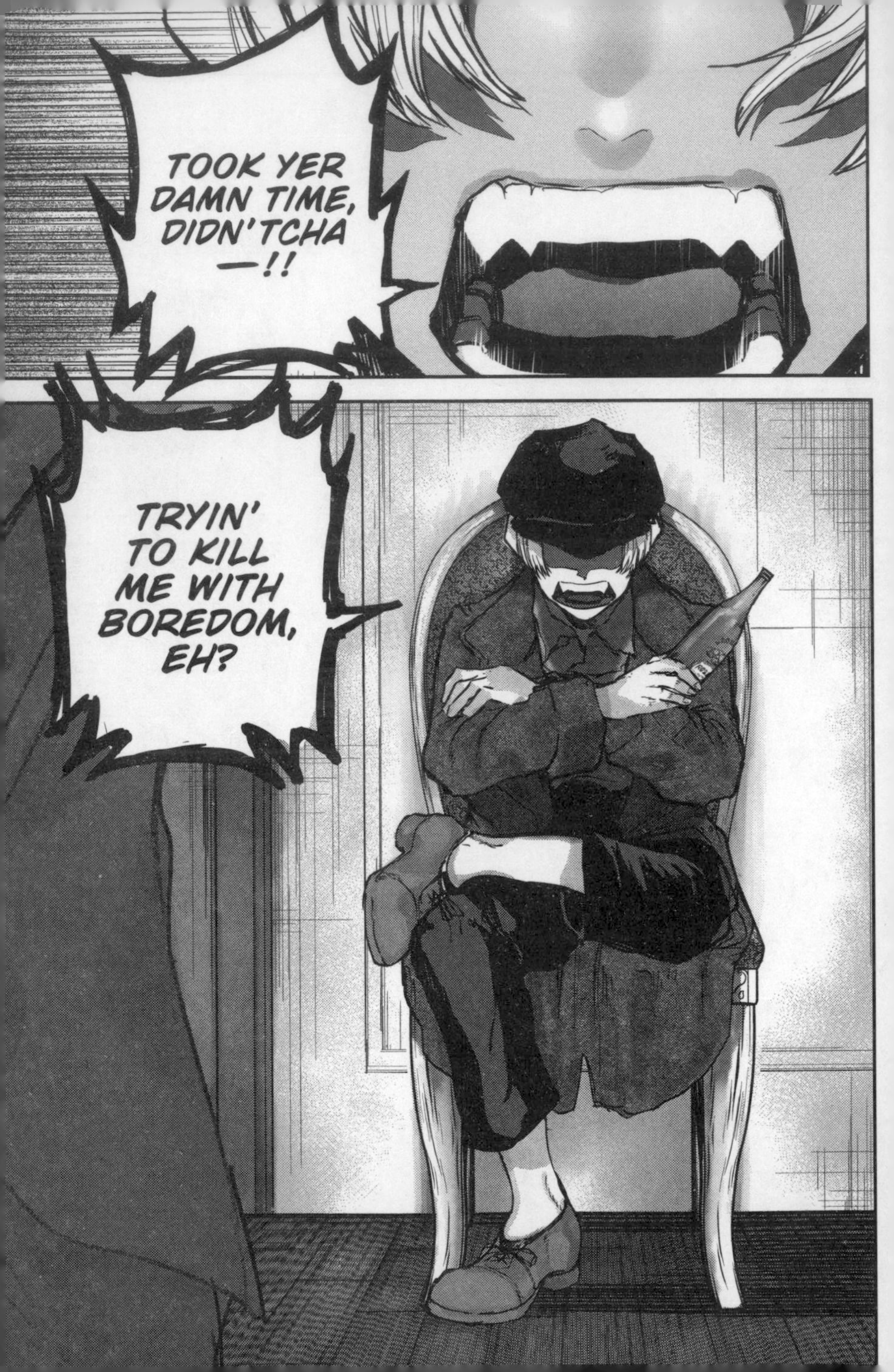
TOOK YER DAMN TIME, DIDN'TCHA—!!
TRYIN' TO KILL ME WITH BOREDOM, EH?

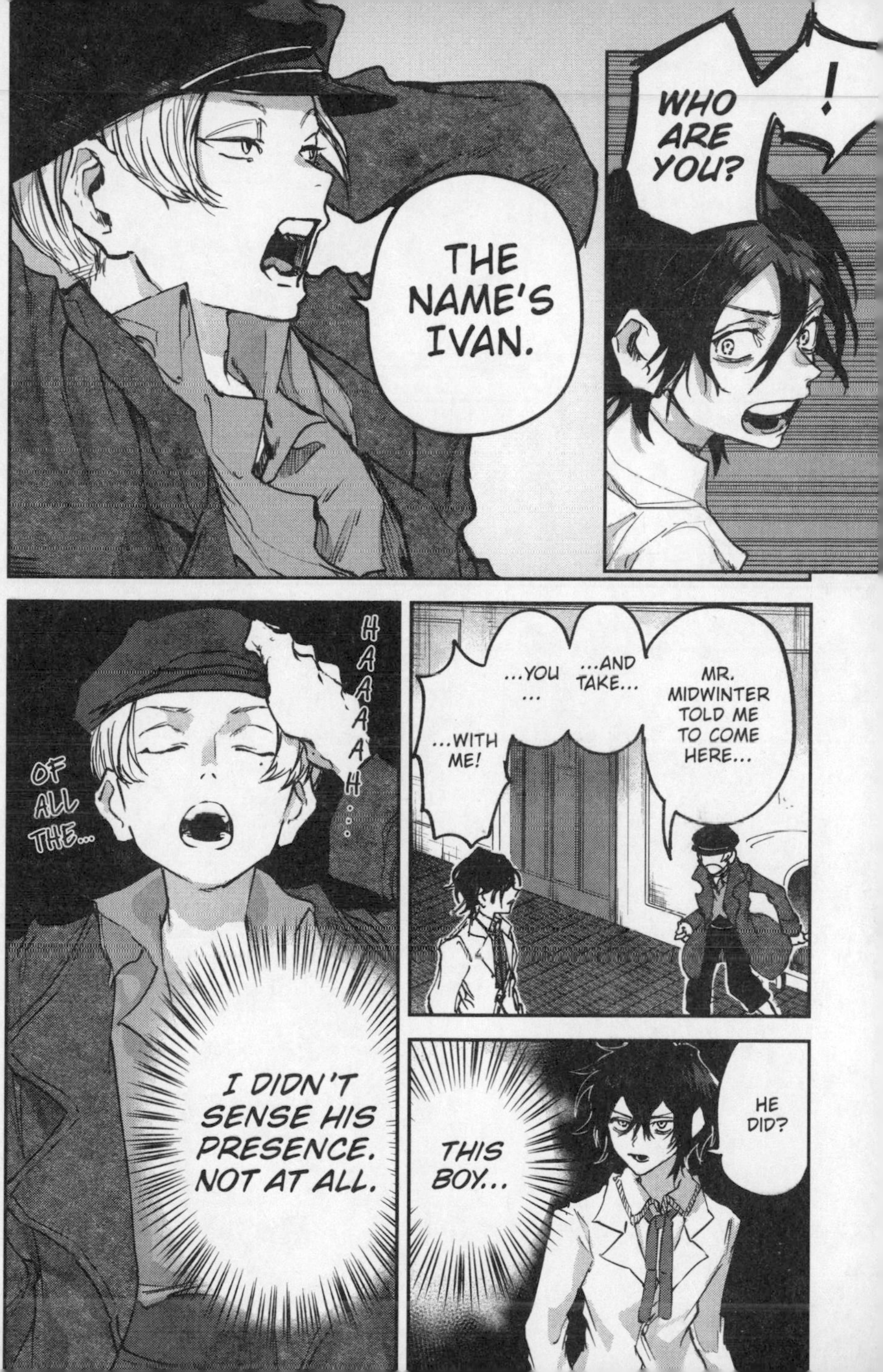
!
WHO ARE YOU?
THE NAME'S IVAN.
MR. MIDWINTER TOLD ME TO COME HERE...
...AND TAKE...
...YOU ...
...WITH ME!
HE DID?
THIS BOY...
HAAAAAH...
OF ALL THE...
I DIDN'T SENSE HIS PRESENCE. NOT AT ALL.

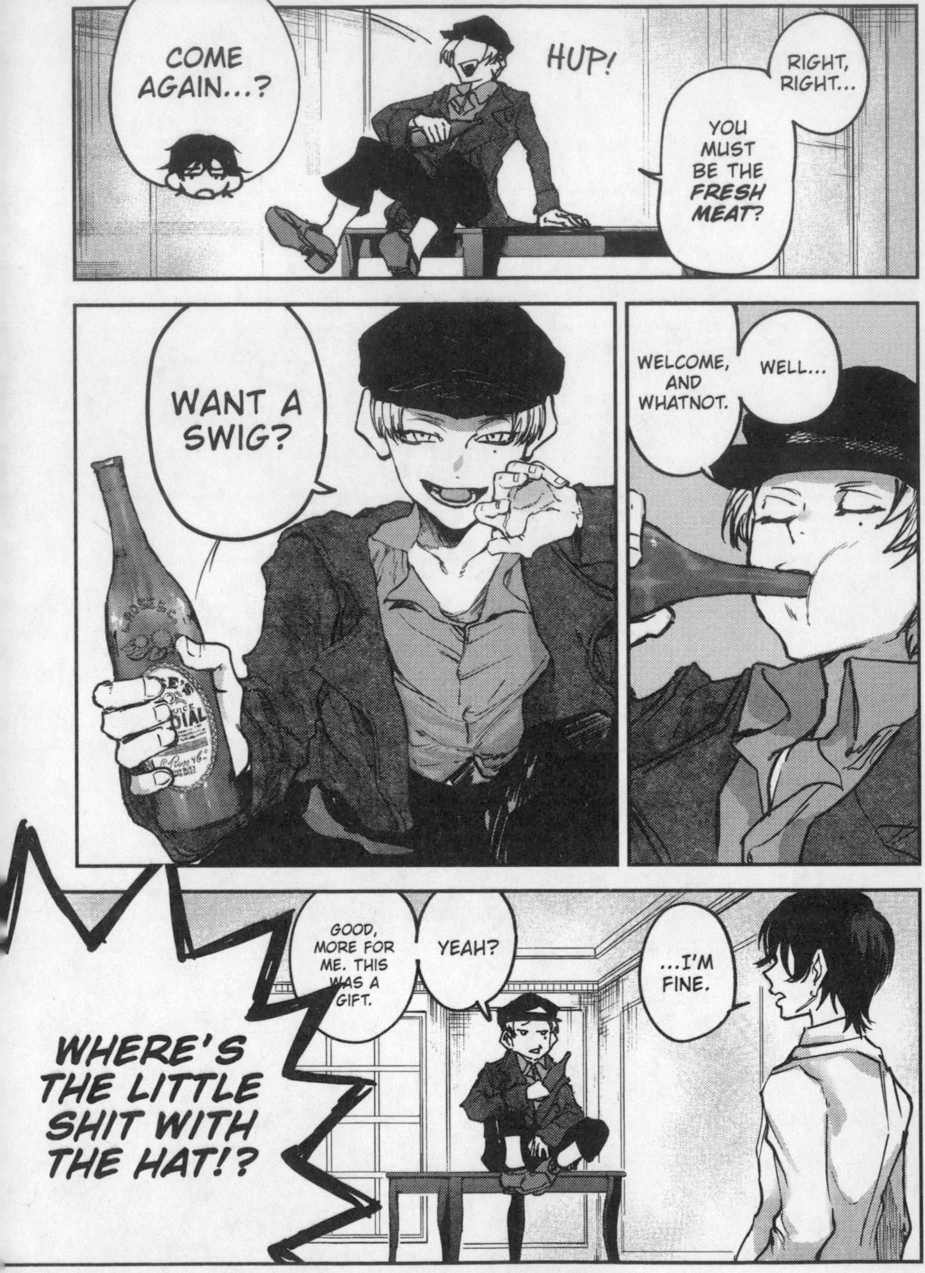
RIGHT, RIGHT... YOU MUST BE THE *FRESH MEAT*?
HUP!
COME AGAIN...?
WELL...
WELCOME, AND WHATNOT.
WANT A SWIG?
...I'M FINE.
YEAH?
GOOD, MORE FOR ME. THIS WAS A GIFT.
WHERE'S THE LITTLE SHIT WITH THE HAT!?

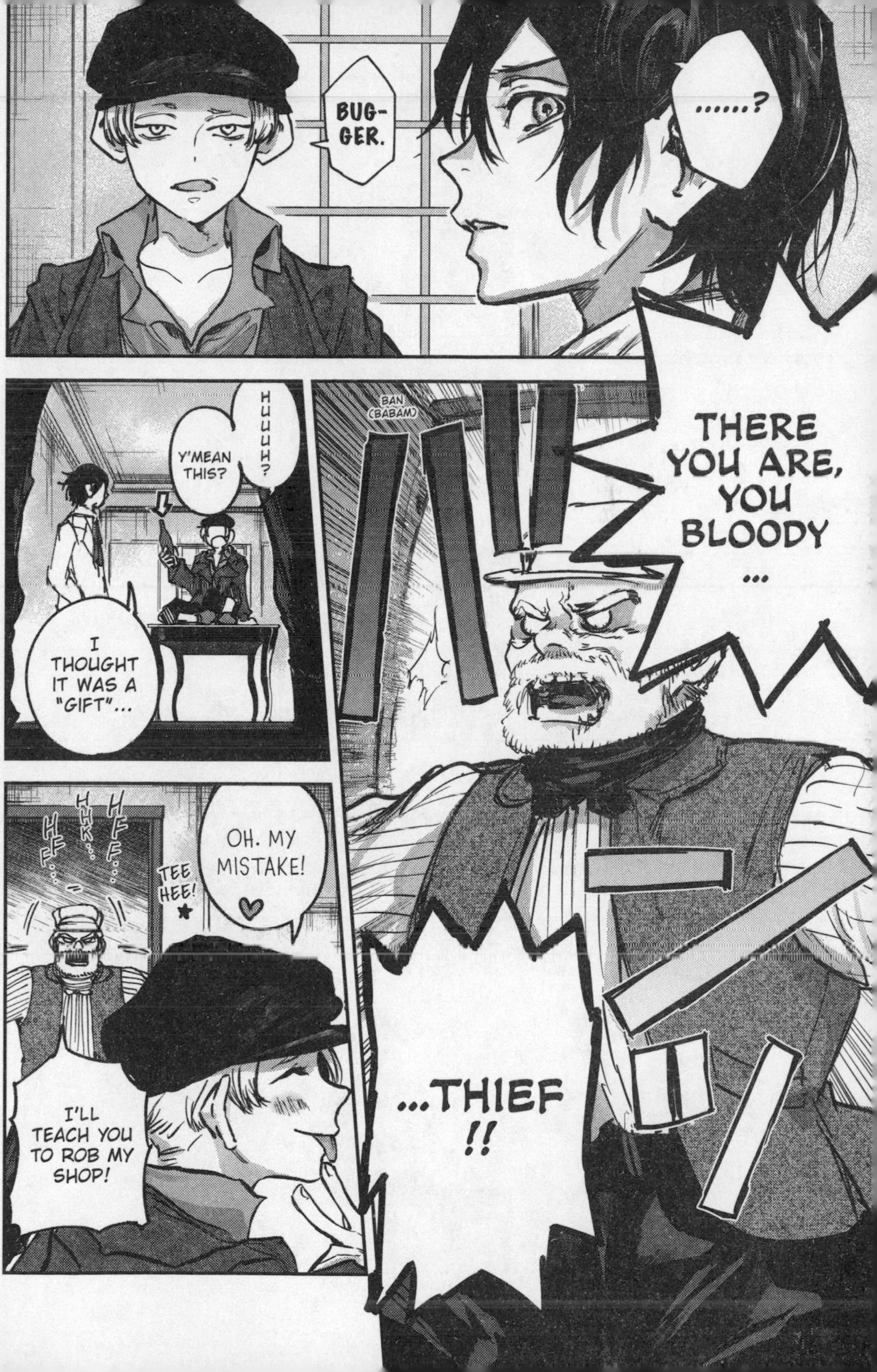
......?
BUG-GER.
BAN (BABAM)
THERE YOU ARE, YOU BLOODY ...
...THIEF !!
HUUUUH?
Y'MEAN THIS?
I THOUGHT IT WAS A "GIFT"...
OH. MY MISTAKE!
TEE HEE!
HFF... HHK... HFF...
I'LL TEACH YOU TO ROB MY SHOP!

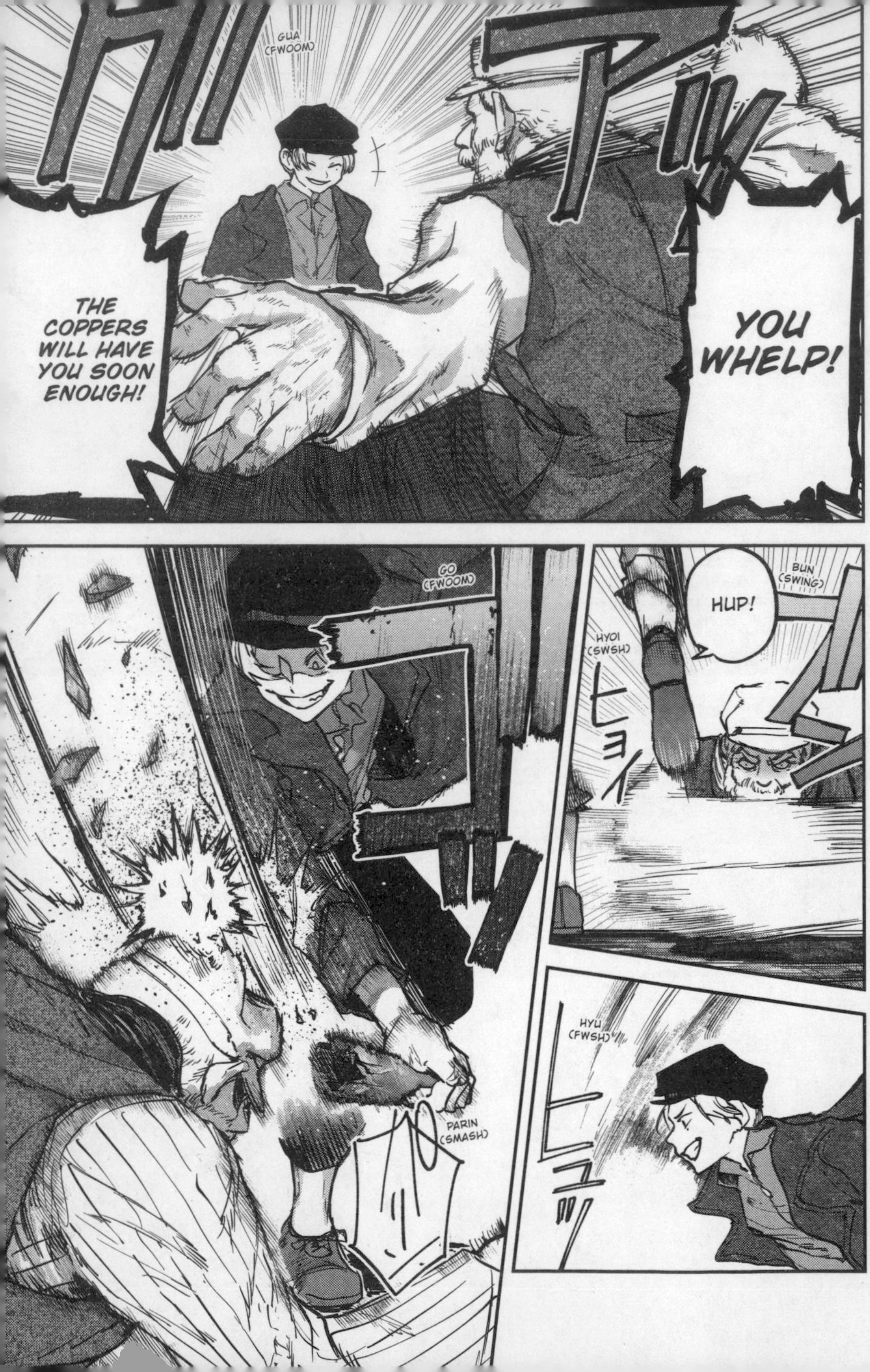
GUA (FWOOM)
YOU WHELP!
THE COPPERS WILL HAVE YOU SOON ENOUGH!
BUN (SWING)
HUP!
HYOI (SWSH)
HYU (FWSH)
GO (FWOOM)
PARIN (SMASH)

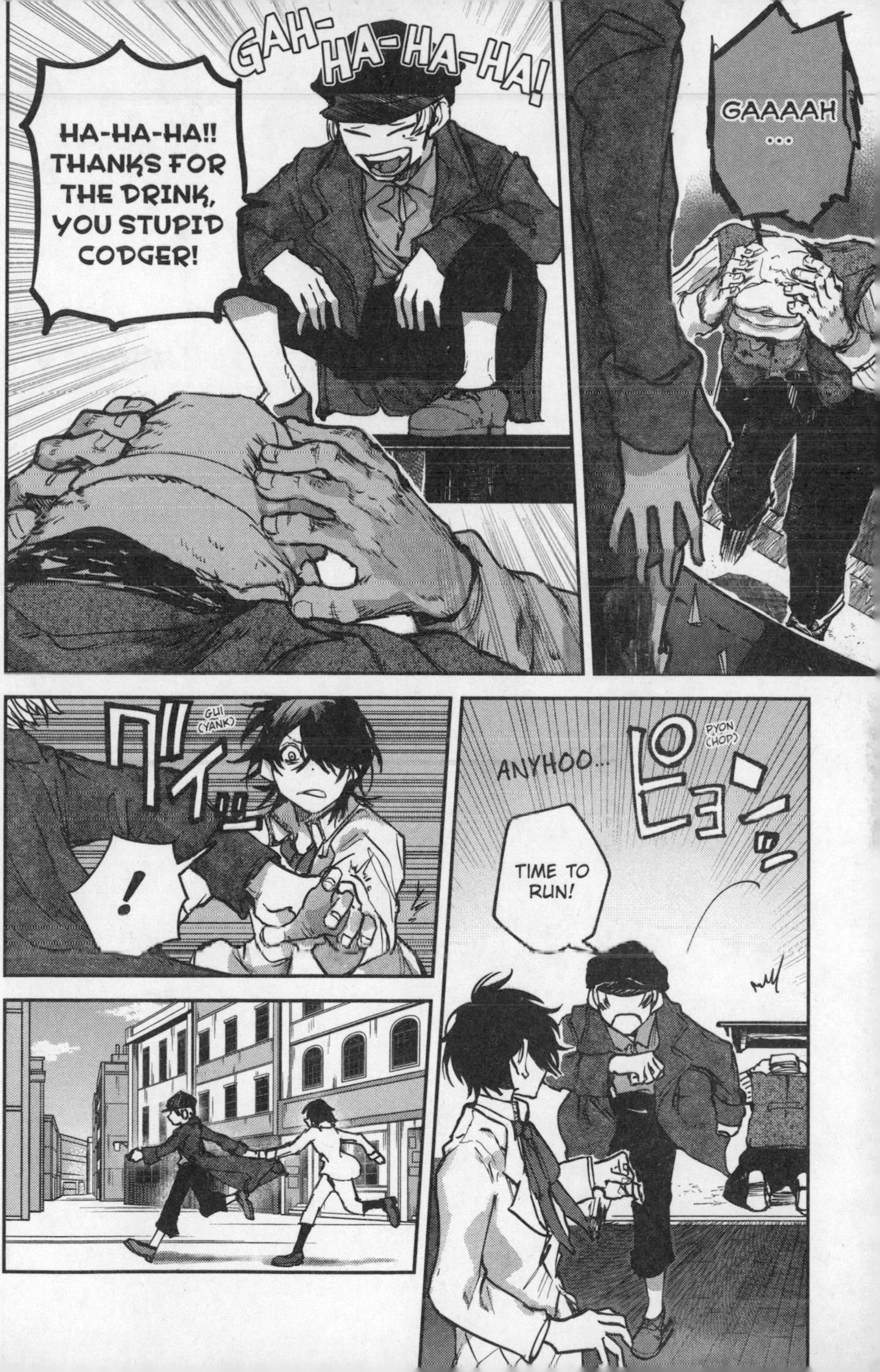
GAAAAH
...
GAH-HA-HA-HA!
HA-HA-HA!! THANKS FOR THE DRINK, YOU STUPID CODGER!
ANYHOO...
PYON (HOP)
TIME TO RUN!
GUI (YANK)
!

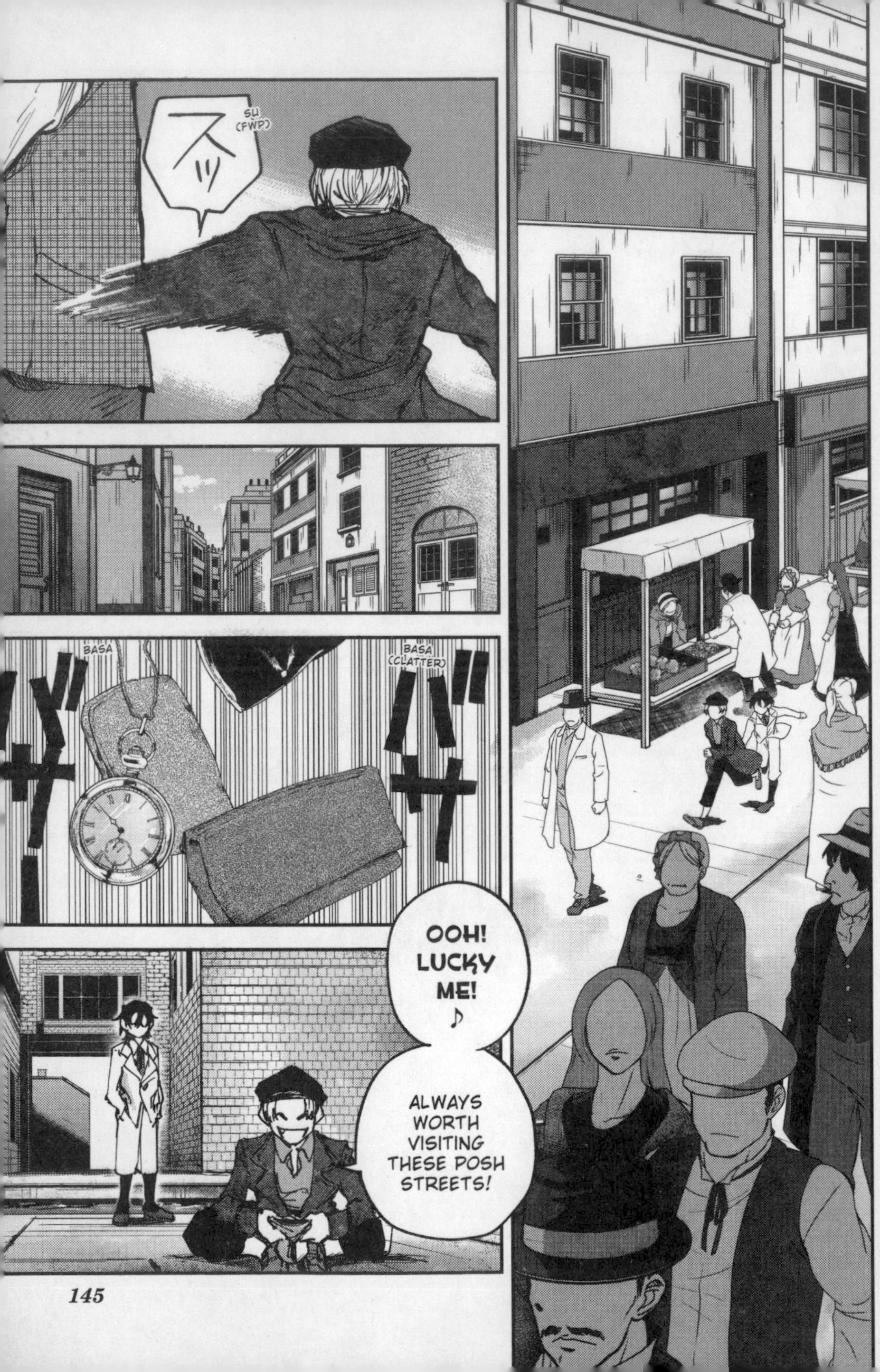
スッ
SU (FWP)
バサ
BASA (CLATTER)
バサ
BASA
OOH! LUCKY ME! ♪
ALWAYS WORTH VISITING THESE POSH STREETS!

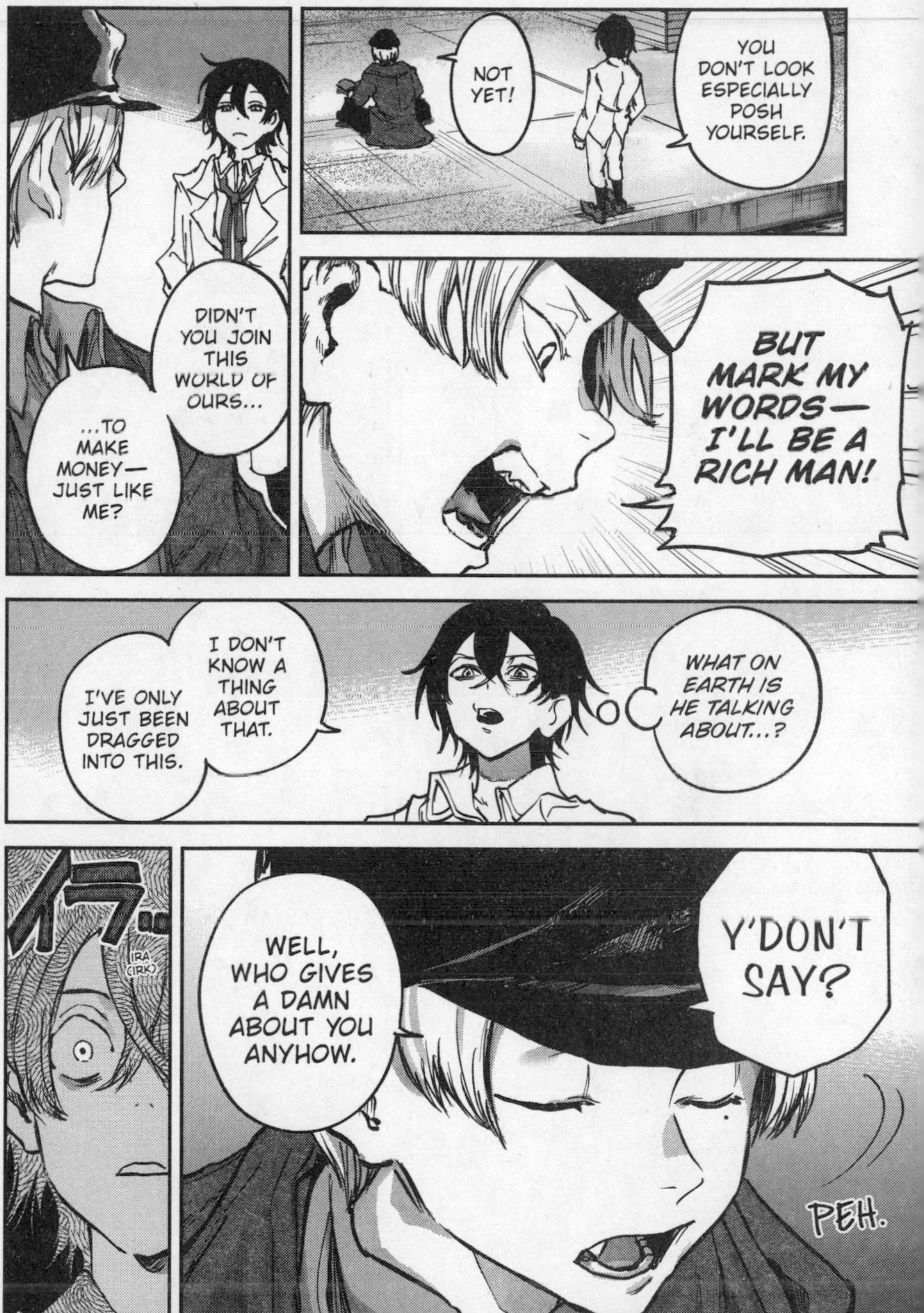
YOU DON'T LOOK ESPECIALLY POSH YOURSELF.
NOT YET!
BUT MARK MY WORDS— I'LL BE A RICH MAN!
DIDN'T YOU JOIN THIS WORLD OF OURS...
...TO MAKE MONEY— JUST LIKE ME?
WHAT ON EARTH IS HE TALKING ABOUT...?
I DON'T KNOW A THING ABOUT THAT.
I'VE ONLY JUST BEEN DRAGGED INTO THIS.
Y'DON'T SAY?
WELL, WHO GIVES A DAMN ABOUT YOU ANYHOW.
PEH.
イラ…
IRA (IRK)

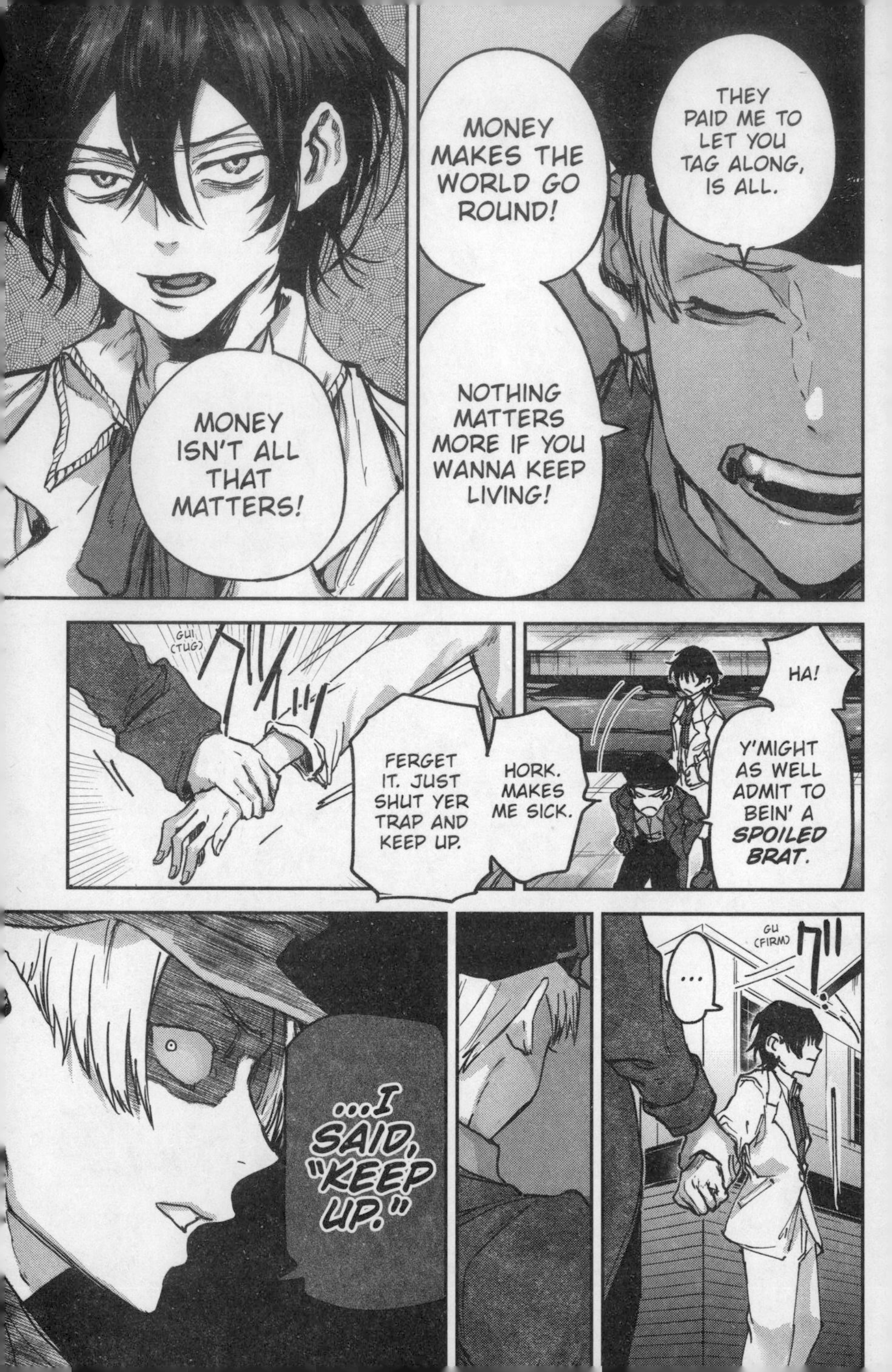
THEY PAID ME TO LET YOU TAG ALONG, IS ALL.
MONEY MAKES THE WORLD GO ROUND!
NOTHING MATTERS MORE IF YOU WANNA KEEP LIVING!
MONEY ISN'T ALL THAT MATTERS!
HA!
Y'MIGHT AS WELL ADMIT TO BEIN' A *SPOILED BRAT.*
GUI (TUG)
HORK. MAKES ME SICK.
FERGET IT. JUST SHUT YER TRAP AND KEEP UP.
GU (FIRM)
...
...I SAID, "KEEP UP."

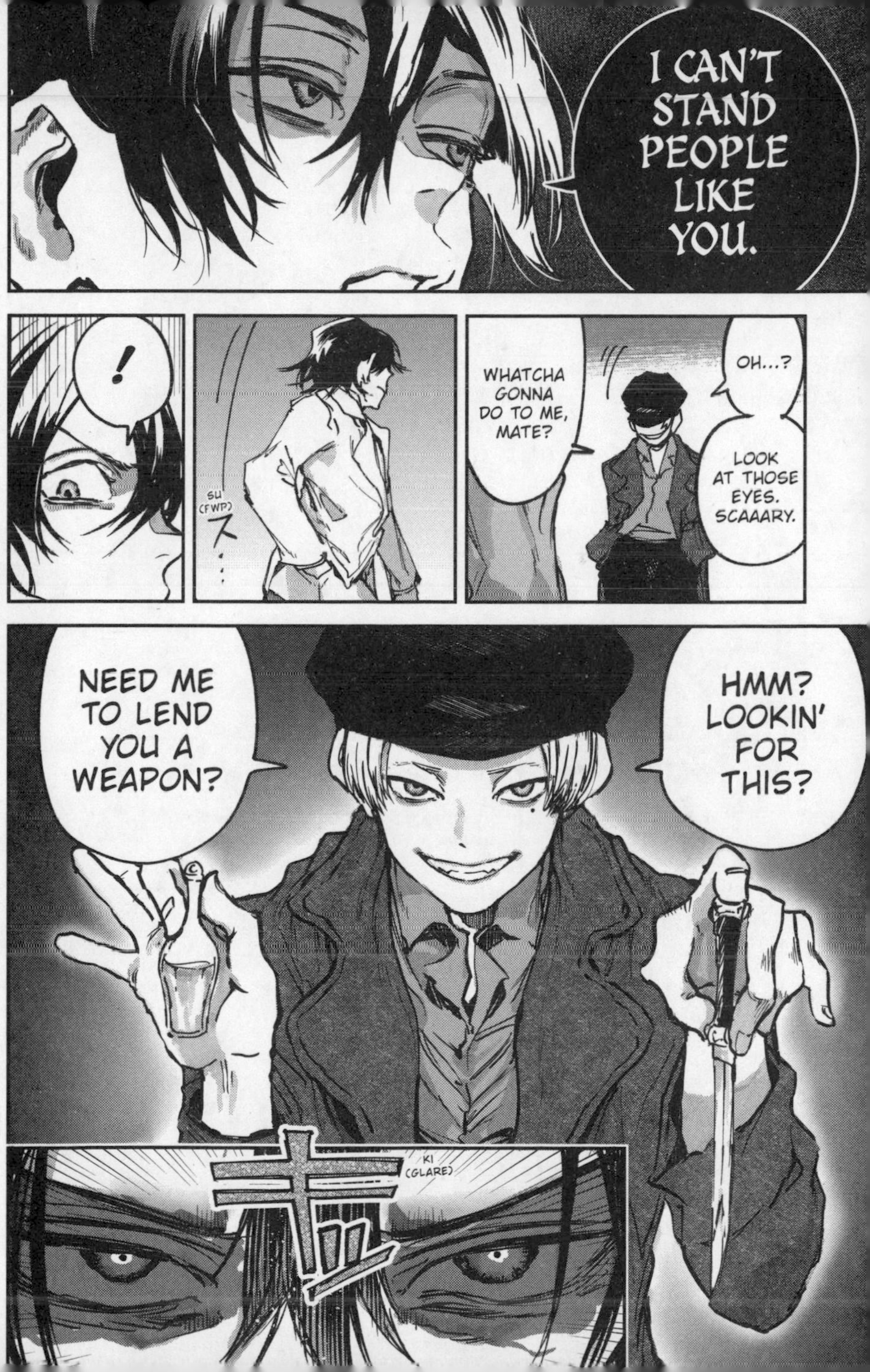
I CAN'T STAND PEOPLE LIKE YOU.
OH...?
LOOK AT THOSE EYES. SCAAARY.
WHATCHA GONNA DO TO ME, MATE?
SU (FWP)
!
HMM? LOOKIN' FOR THIS?
NEED ME TO LEND YOU A WEAPON?
KI (GLARE)

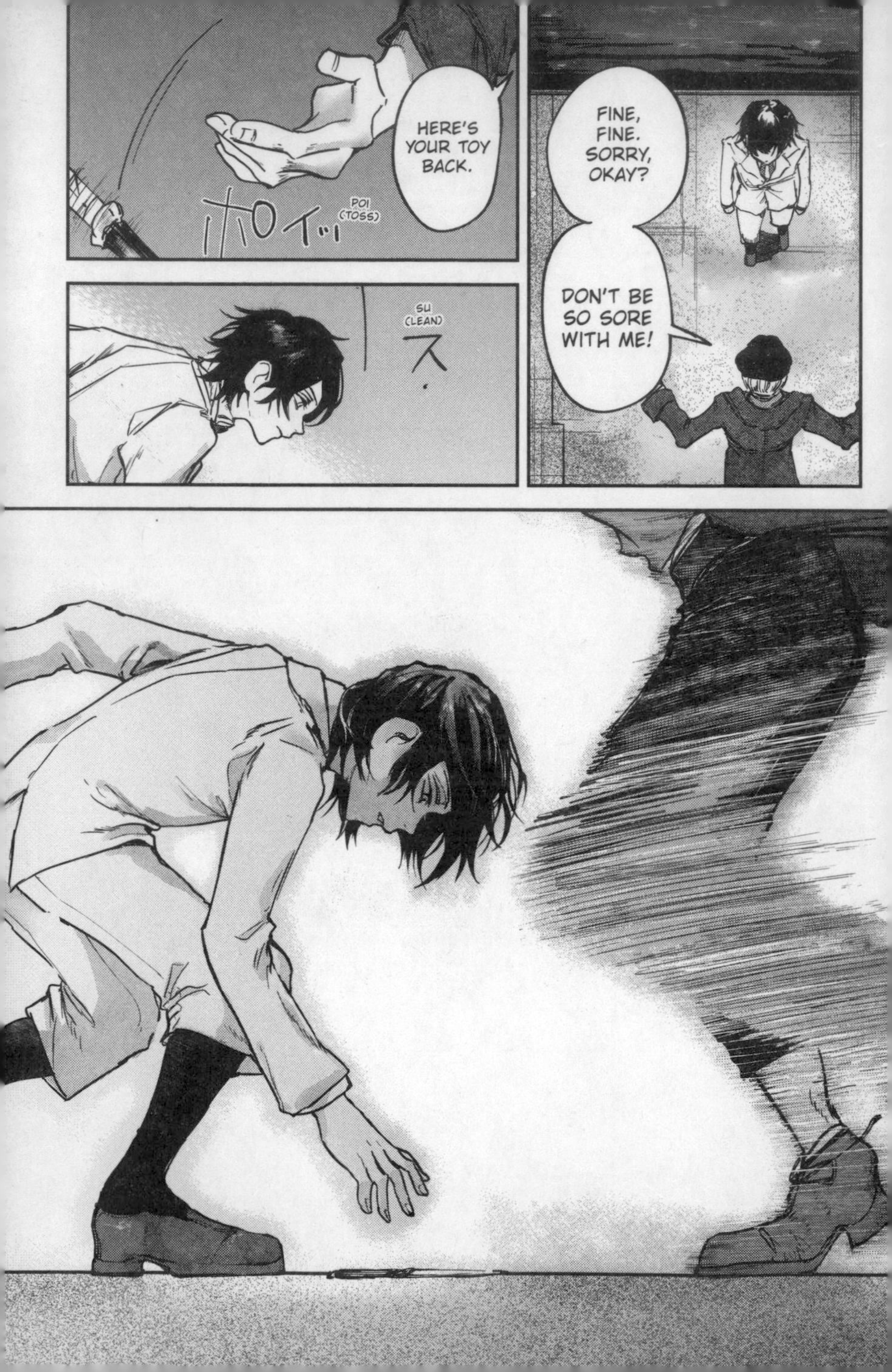
FINE, FINE. SORRY, OKAY?
DON'T BE SO SORE WITH ME!
HERE'S YOUR TOY BACK.
ポイッ
POI (TOSS)
ス
SU (LEAN)

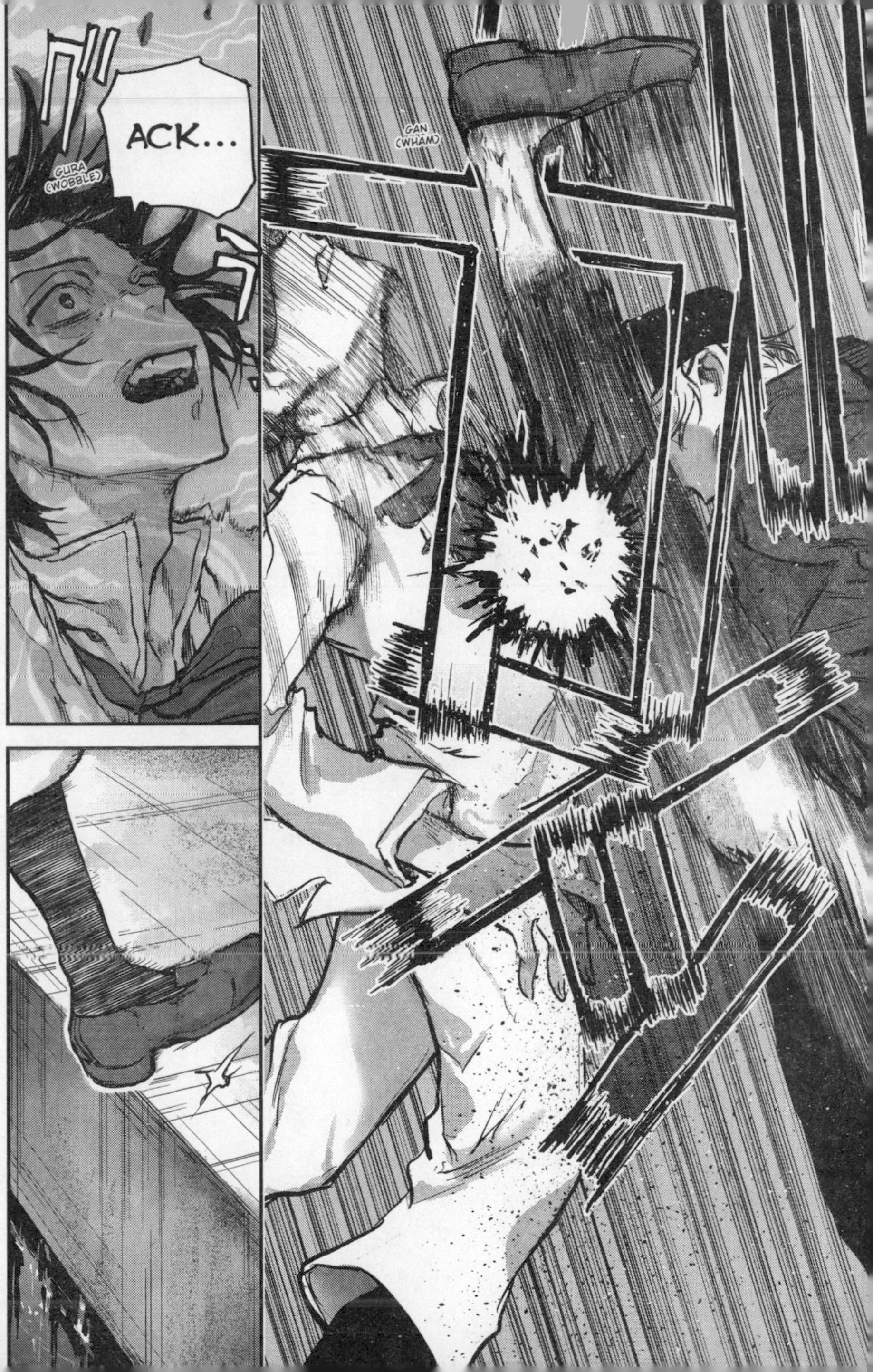
GAN
(WHAM)
ACK...
GURA
(WOBBLE)

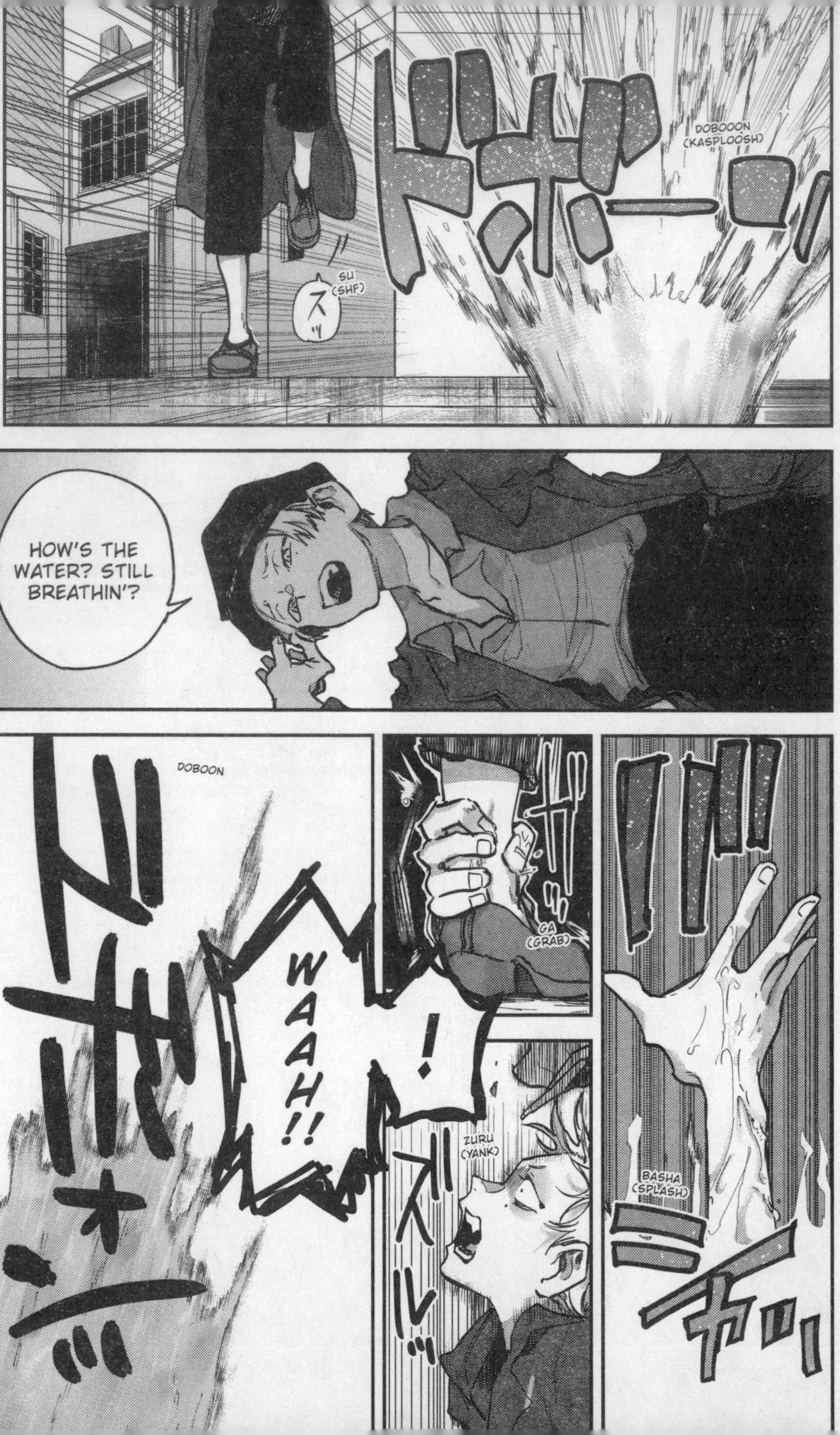

ドボーン
DOBOOON (KASPLOOSH)
スッ
SU (SHF)
HOW'S THE WATER? STILL BREATHIN'?
ガッ
BASHA (SPLASH)
GA (GRAB)
ズルッ
ZURU (YANK)
WAAAH!!
DOBOON

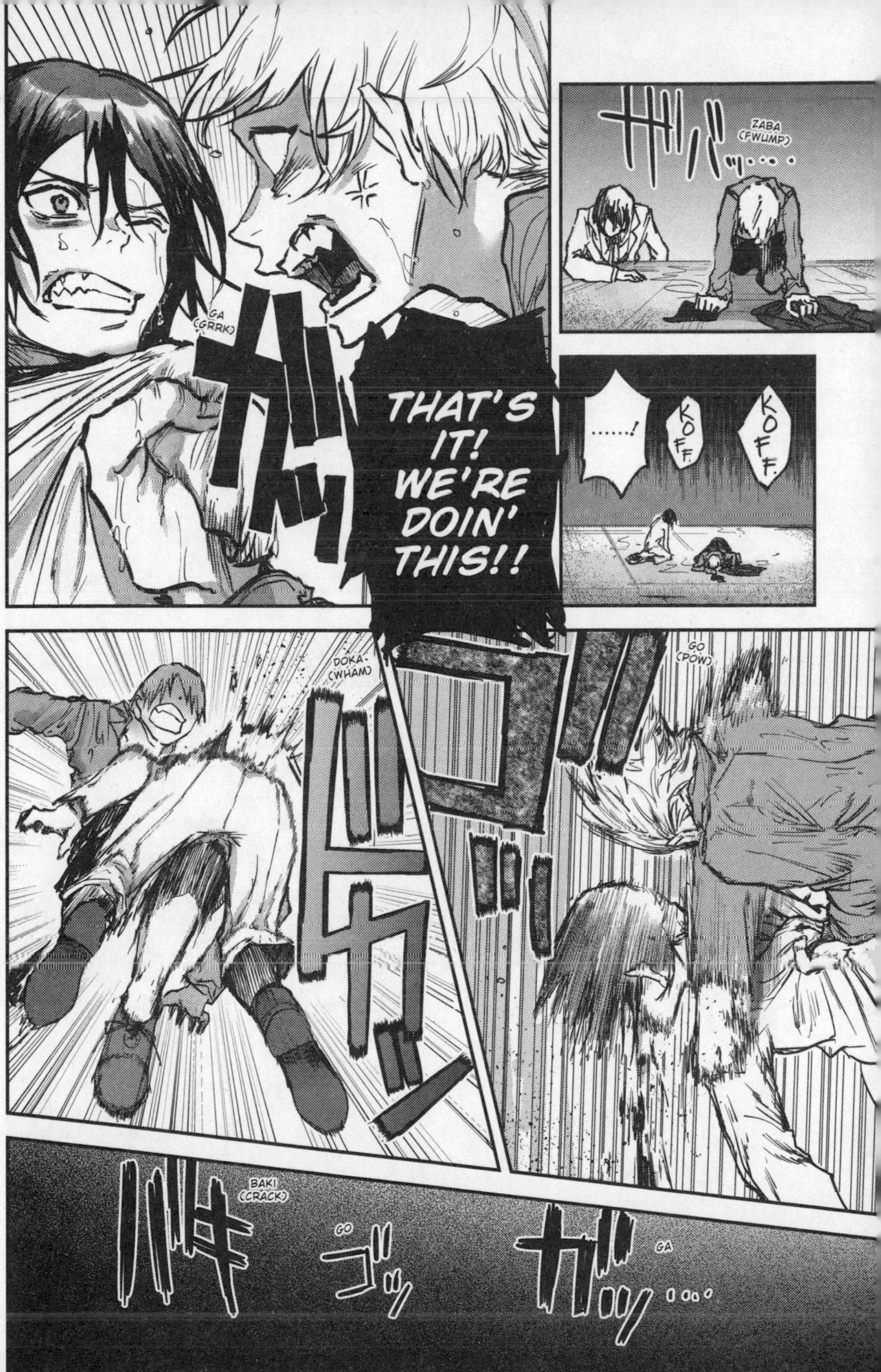
ZABA
(FWUMP)
KOFF.
KOFF.
......!
THAT'S IT! WE'RE DOIN' THIS!!
GA
(GRRK)
GO
(POW)
DOKA
(WHAM)
BAKI
(CRACK)
GO
GA

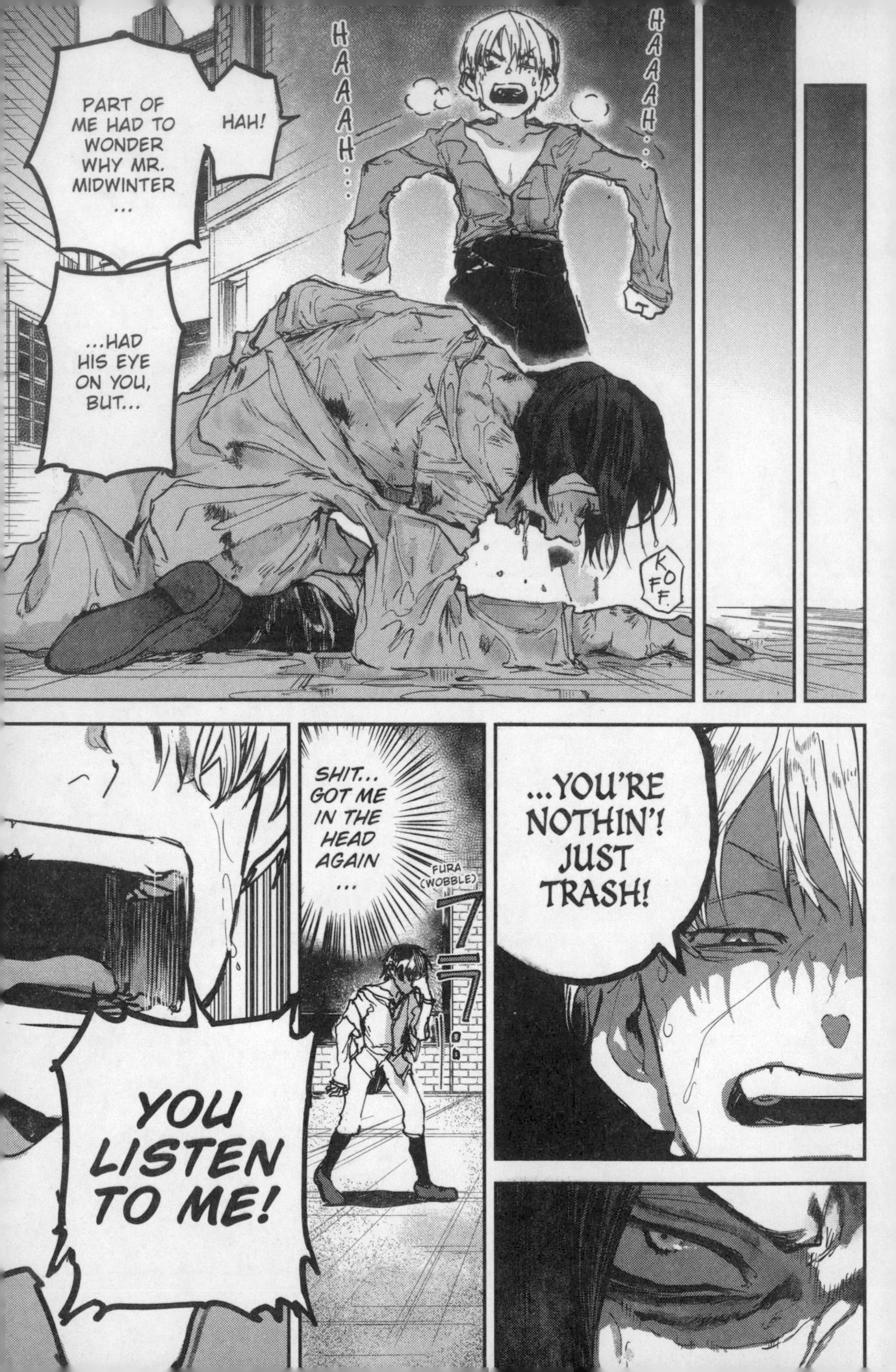
HAAAAH...
HAAAAH...
HAH!
PART OF ME HAD TO WONDER WHY MR. MIDWINTER...
...HAD HIS EYE ON YOU, BUT...
KOFF.
...YOU'RE NOTHIN'! JUST TRASH!
SHIT... GOT ME IN THE HEAD AGAIN...
FURA (WOBBLE)
YOU LISTEN TO ME!

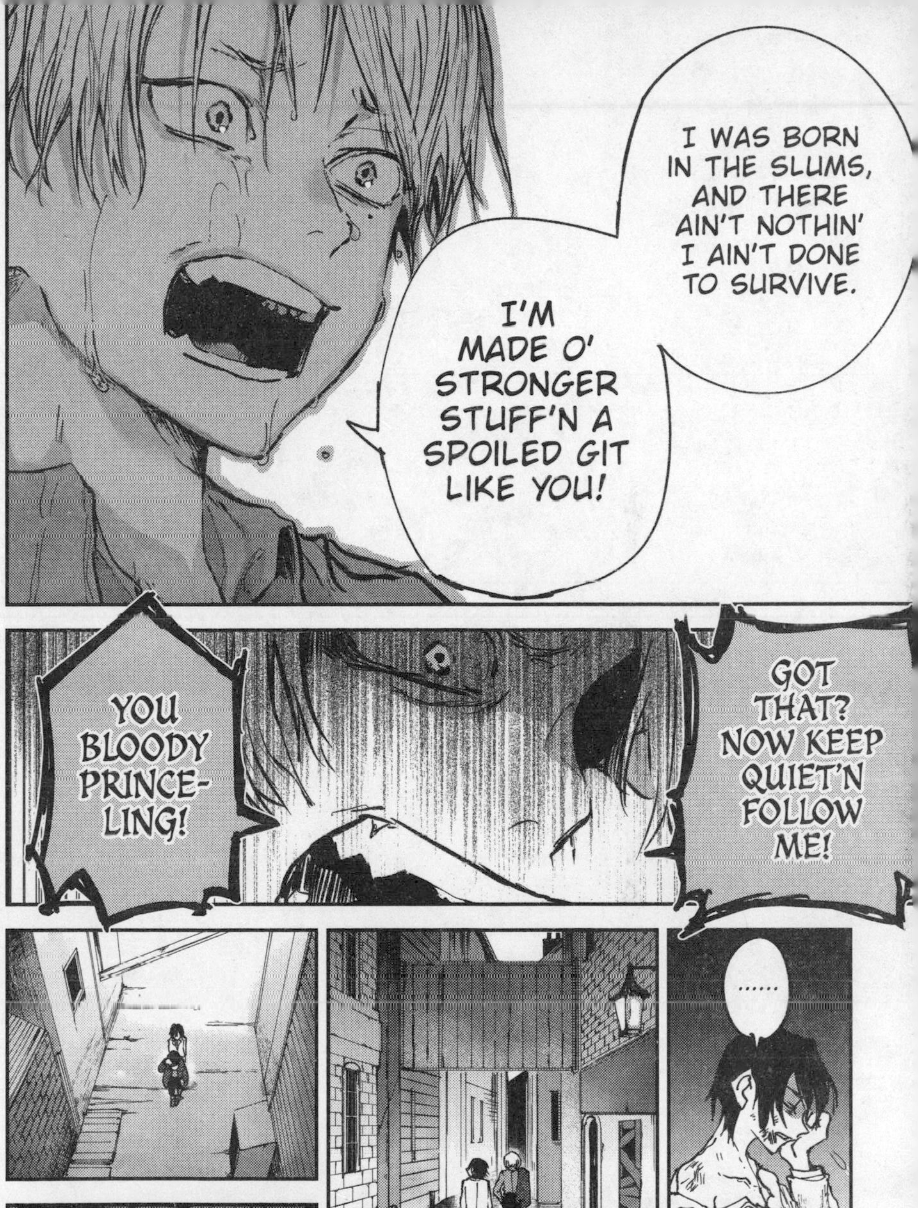
I WAS BORN IN THE SLUMS, AND THERE AIN'T NOTHIN' I AIN'T DONE TO SURVIVE.
I'M MADE O' STRONGER STUFF'N A SPOILED GIT LIKE YOU!
YOU BLOODY PRINCE-LING!
GOT THAT? NOW KEEP QUIET'N FOLLOW ME!
......

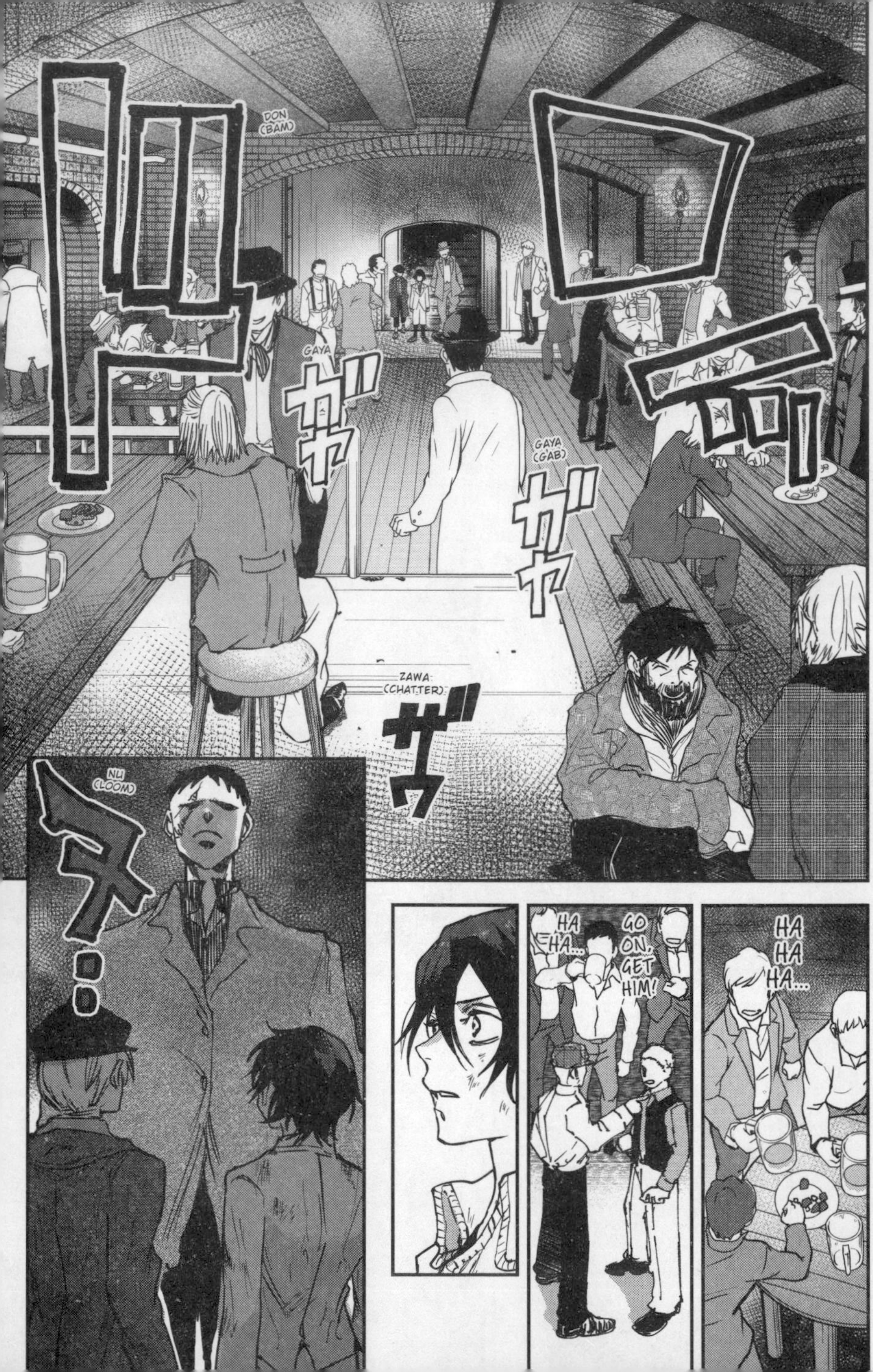
DON (BAM)
GAYA (GAB)
GAYA
ZAWA (CHATTER)
HA HA HA...
GO ON, GET HIM!
HA HA...
NU (LOOM)

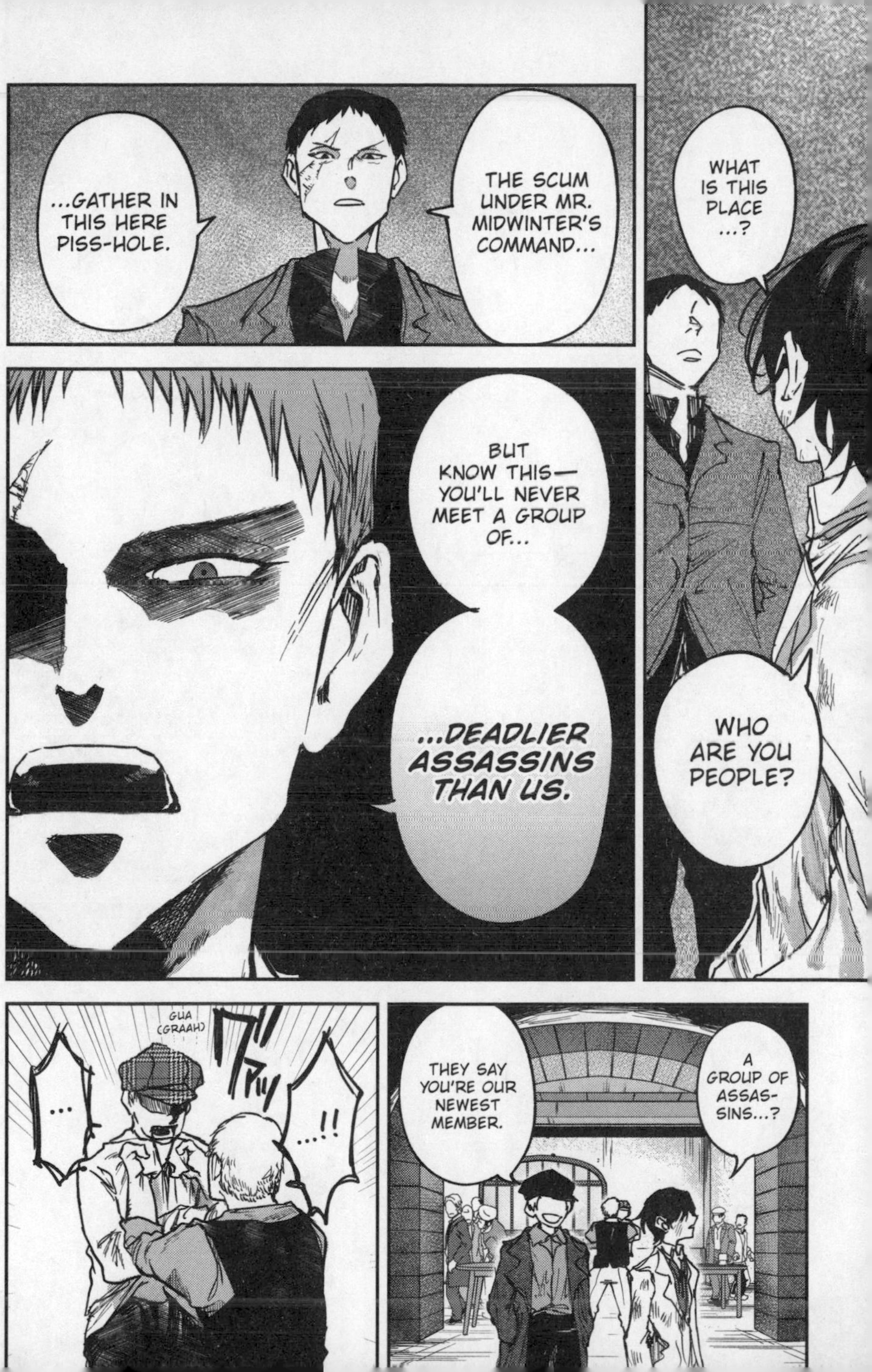
WHAT IS THIS PLACE ...?
WHO ARE YOU PEOPLE?
THE SCUM UNDER MR. MIDWINTER'S COMMAND...
...GATHER IN THIS HERE PISS-HOLE.
BUT KNOW THIS— YOU'LL NEVER MEET A GROUP OF...
...DEADLIER ASSASSINS THAN US.
A GROUP OF ASSAS-SINS...?
THEY SAY YOU'RE OUR NEWEST MEMBER.
...!!
GUA (GRAAH)
...

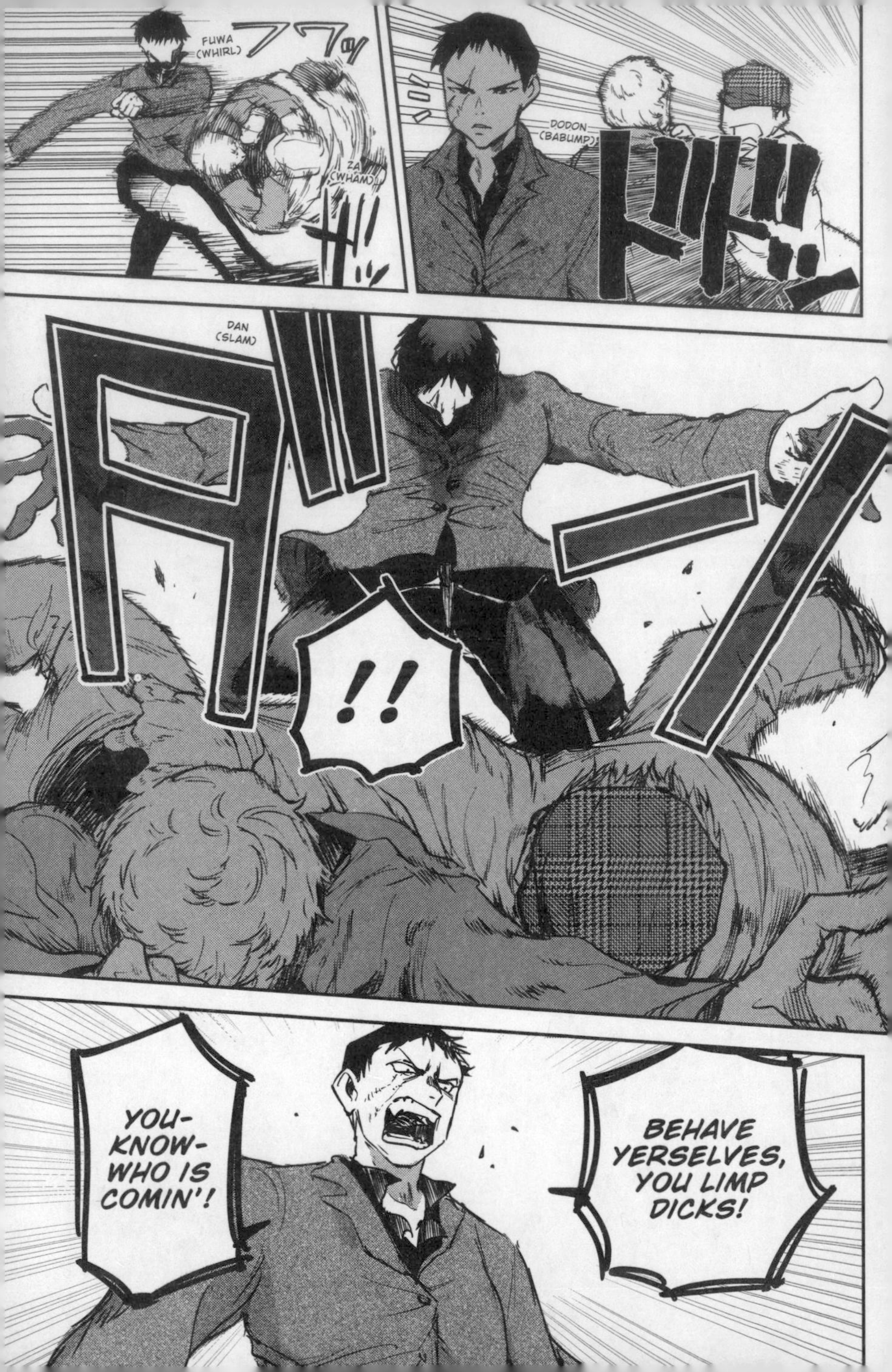
DODON (BABUMP)
FUWA (WHIRL)
ZA (WHAM)
DAN (SLAM)
!!
BEHAVE YERSELVES, YOU LIMP DICKS!
YOU-KNOW-WHO IS COMIN'!

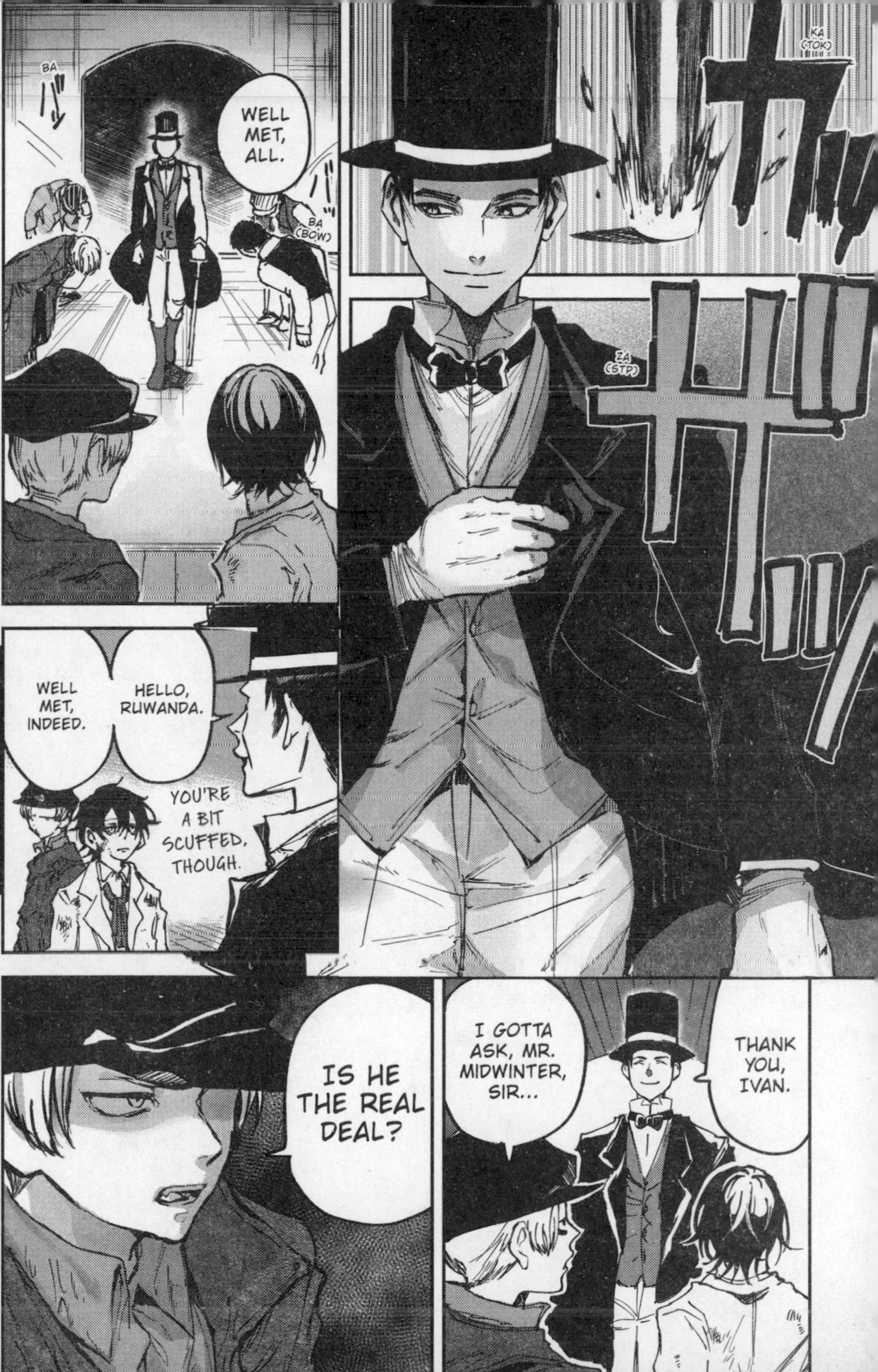
KA (TOK)
ZA (STP)
WELL MET, ALL.
BA (BOW)
BA
HELLO, RUWANDA.
WELL MET, INDEED.
YOU'RE A BIT SCUFFED, THOUGH.
THANK YOU, IVAN.
I GOTTA ASK, MR. MIDWINTER, SIR...
IS HE THE REAL DEAL?

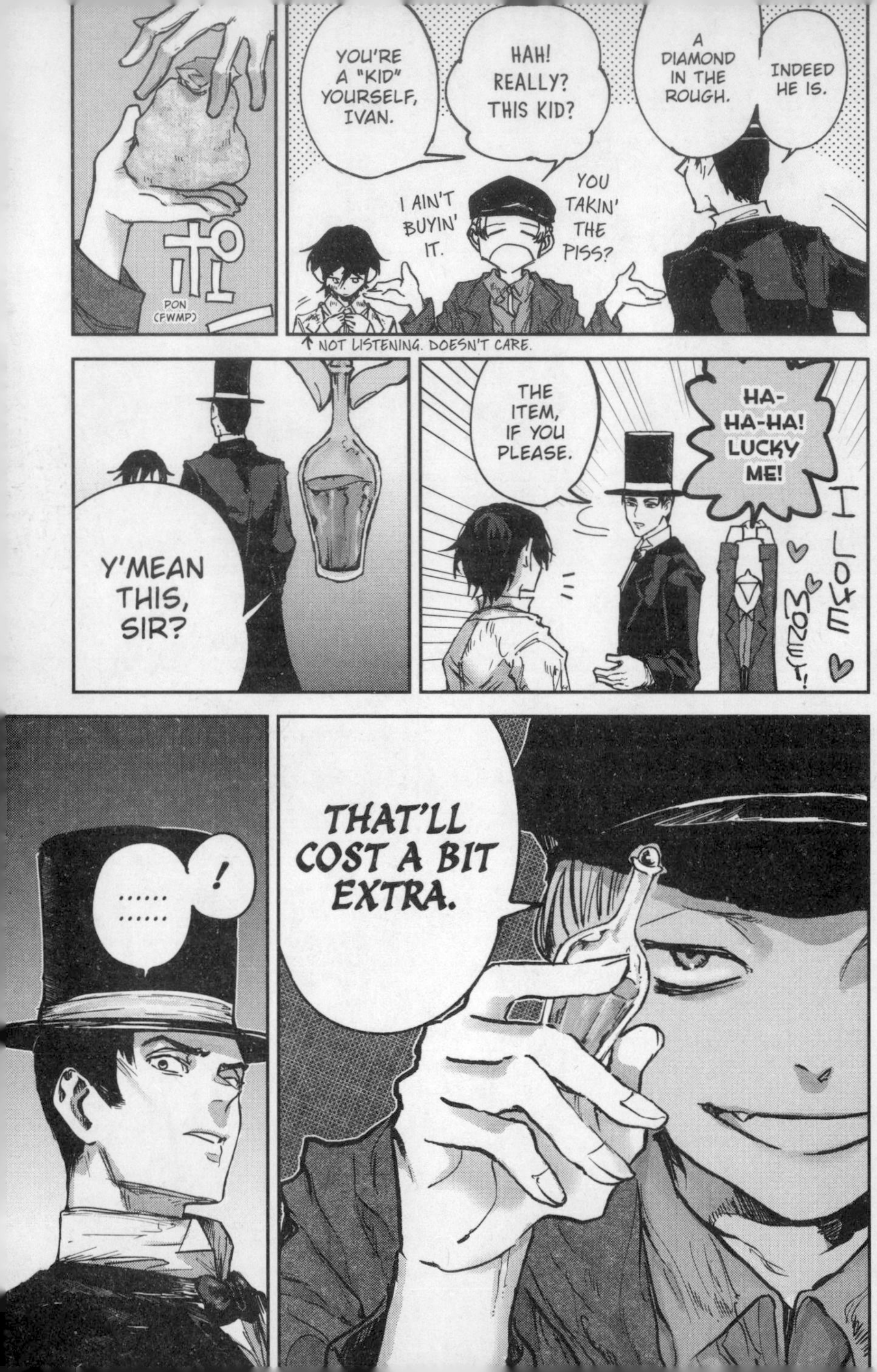
INDEED HE IS.
A DIAMOND IN THE ROUGH.
HAH! REALLY? THIS KID?
YOU'RE A "KID" YOURSELF, IVAN.
YOU TAKIN' THE PISS?
I AIN'T BUYIN' IT.
NOT LISTENING. DOESN'T CARE.
PON (FWMP)
HA-HA-HA! LUCKY ME!
I LOVE MONEY!
THE ITEM, IF YOU PLEASE.
Y'MEAN THIS, SIR?
THAT'LL COST A BIT EXTRA.
......
......
!

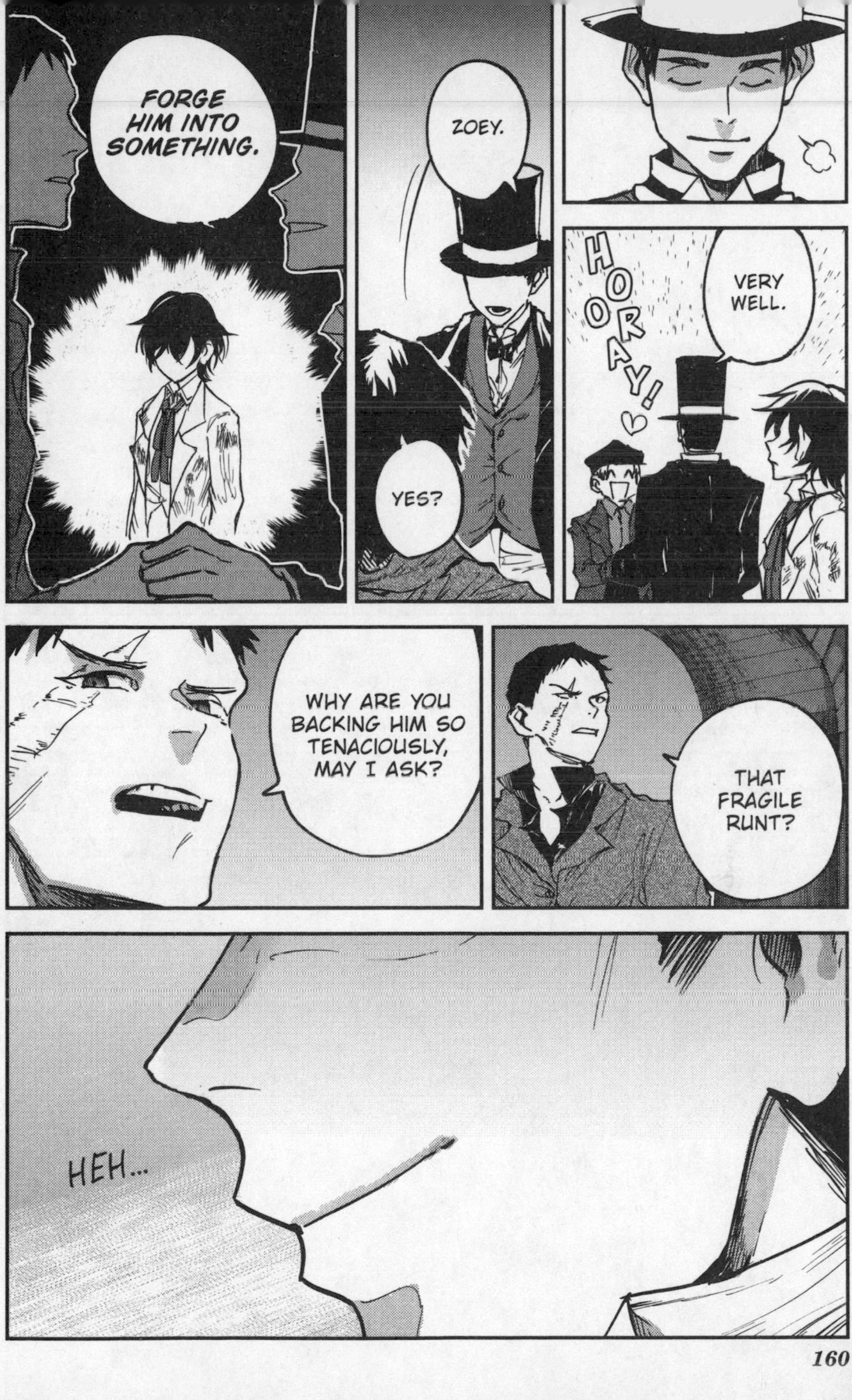

VERY WELL.
HORAY!
ZOEY.
YES?
FORGE HIM INTO SOMETHING.
THAT FRAGILE RUNT?
WHY ARE YOU BACKING HIM SO TENACIOUSLY, MAY I ASK?
HEH...

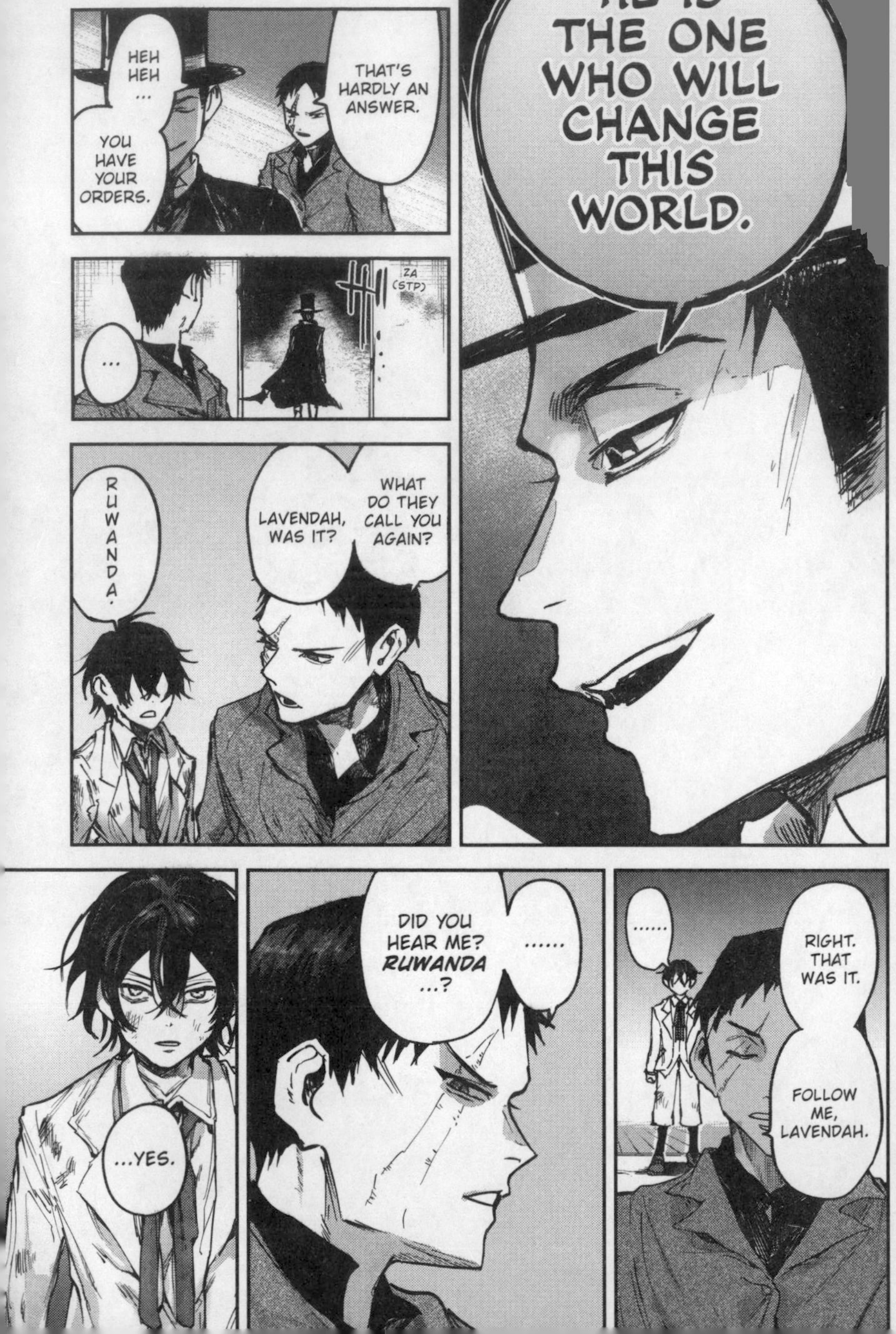
HE IS THE ONE WHO WILL CHANGE THIS WORLD.
THAT'S HARDLY AN ANSWER.
HEH HEH ...
YOU HAVE YOUR ORDERS.
ZA (STP)
...
WHAT DO THEY CALL YOU AGAIN?
LAVENDAH, WAS IT?
RUWANDA.
RIGHT. THAT WAS IT.
......
FOLLOW ME, LAVENDAH.
......
DID YOU HEAR ME? *RUWANDA* ...?
...YES.

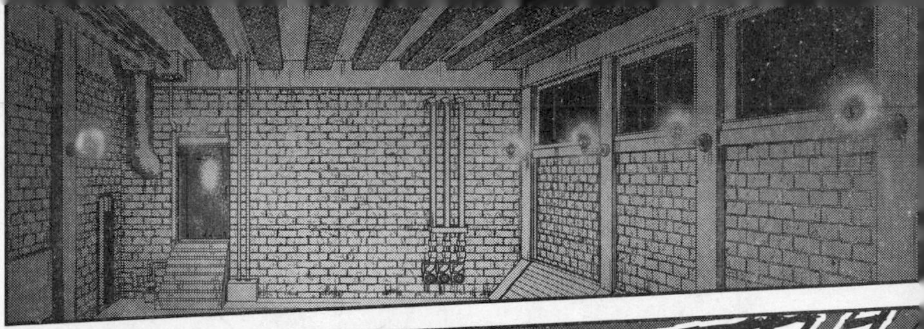

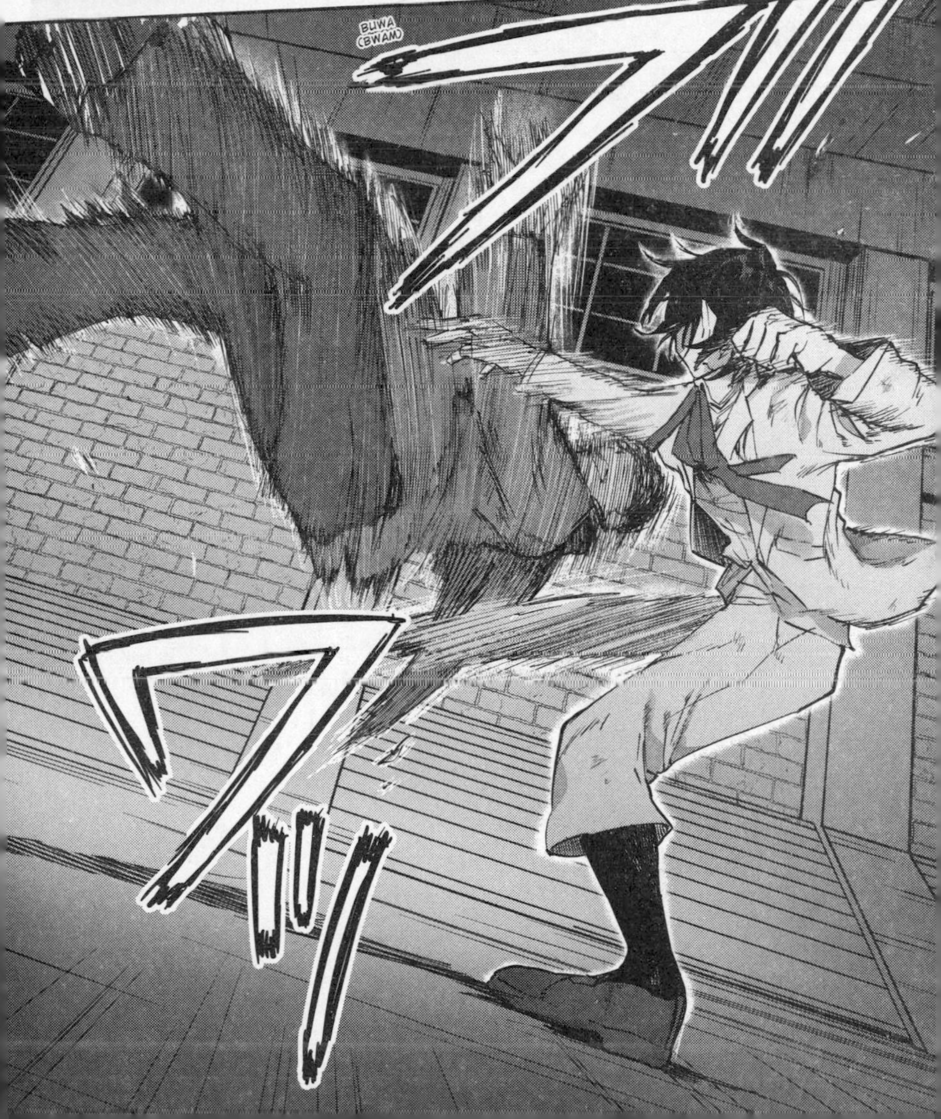
BUWA
(BWAM)

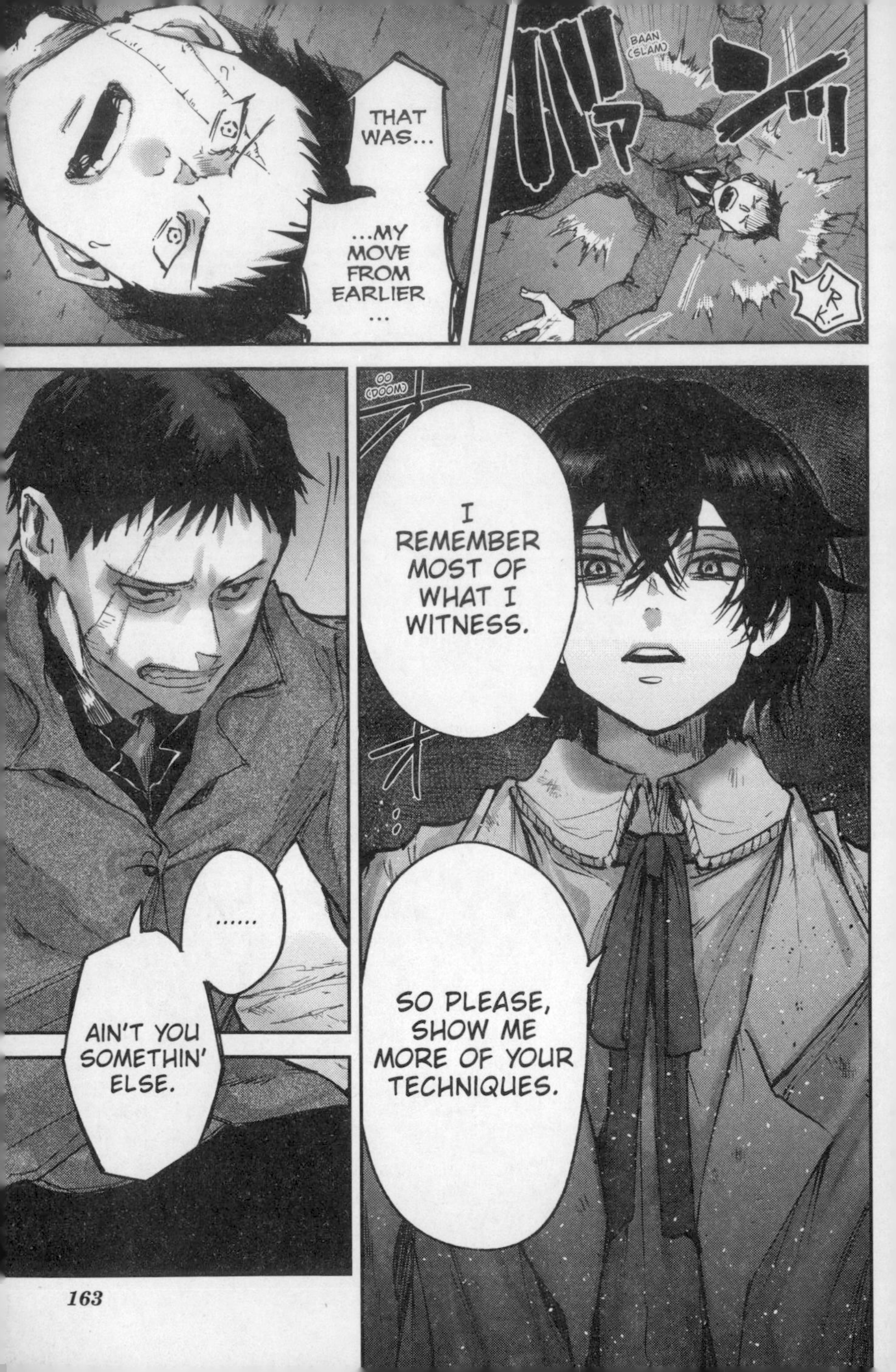
BAAN (SLAM)
URK!
THAT WAS...
...MY MOVE FROM EARLIER...
OO (DOOM)
I REMEMBER MOST OF WHAT I WITNESS.
SO PLEASE, SHOW ME MORE OF YOUR TECHNIQUES.
......
AIN'T YOU SOMETHIN' ELSE.

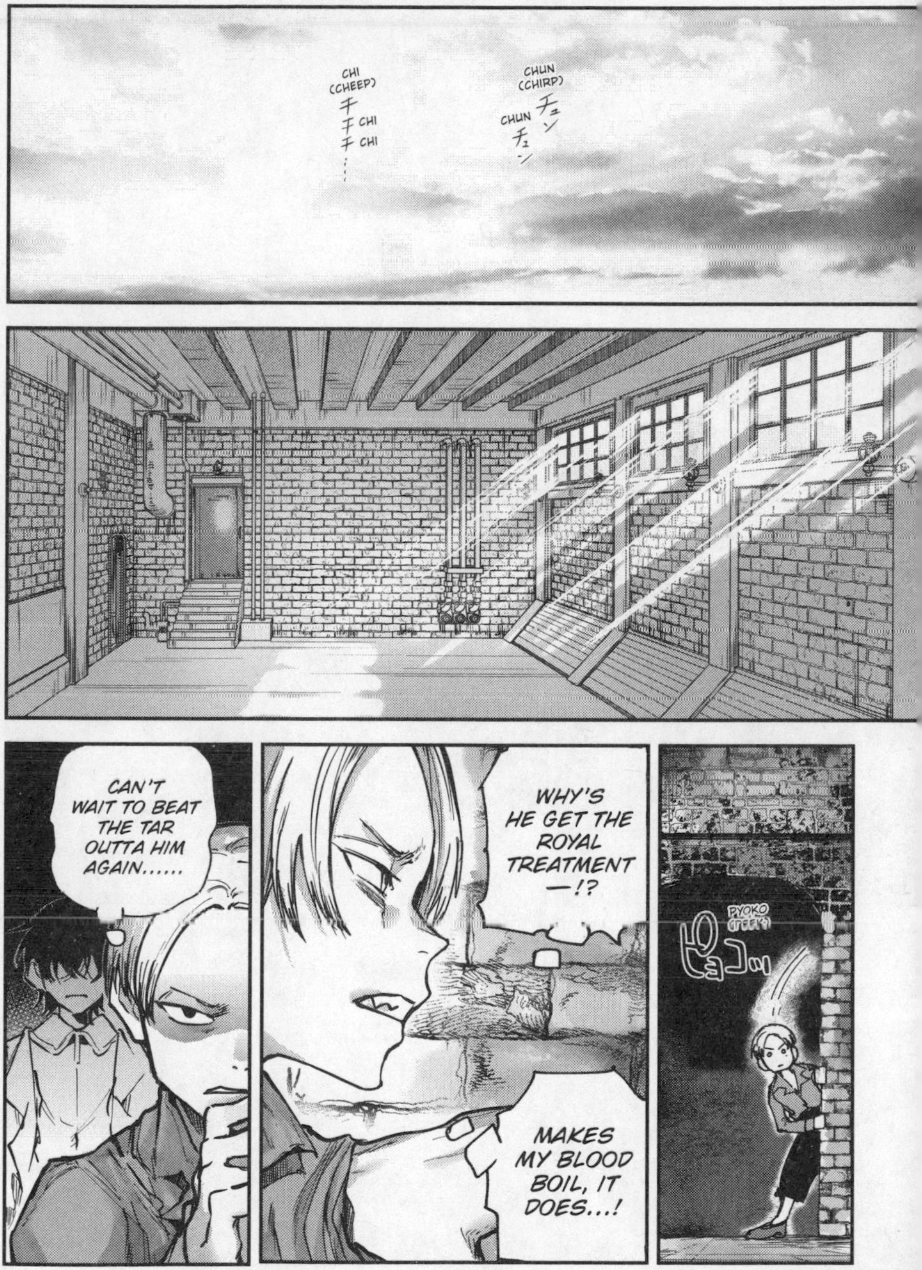
CHUN (CHIRP)
チュン
CHUN
チュン
CHI (CHEEP)
チチチ…
CHI
CHI
PYOKO
ピョコッ
WHY'S HE GET THE ROYAL TREATMENT—!?
MAKES MY BLOOD BOIL, IT DOES…!
CAN'T WAIT TO BEAT THE TAR OUTTA HIM AGAIN……

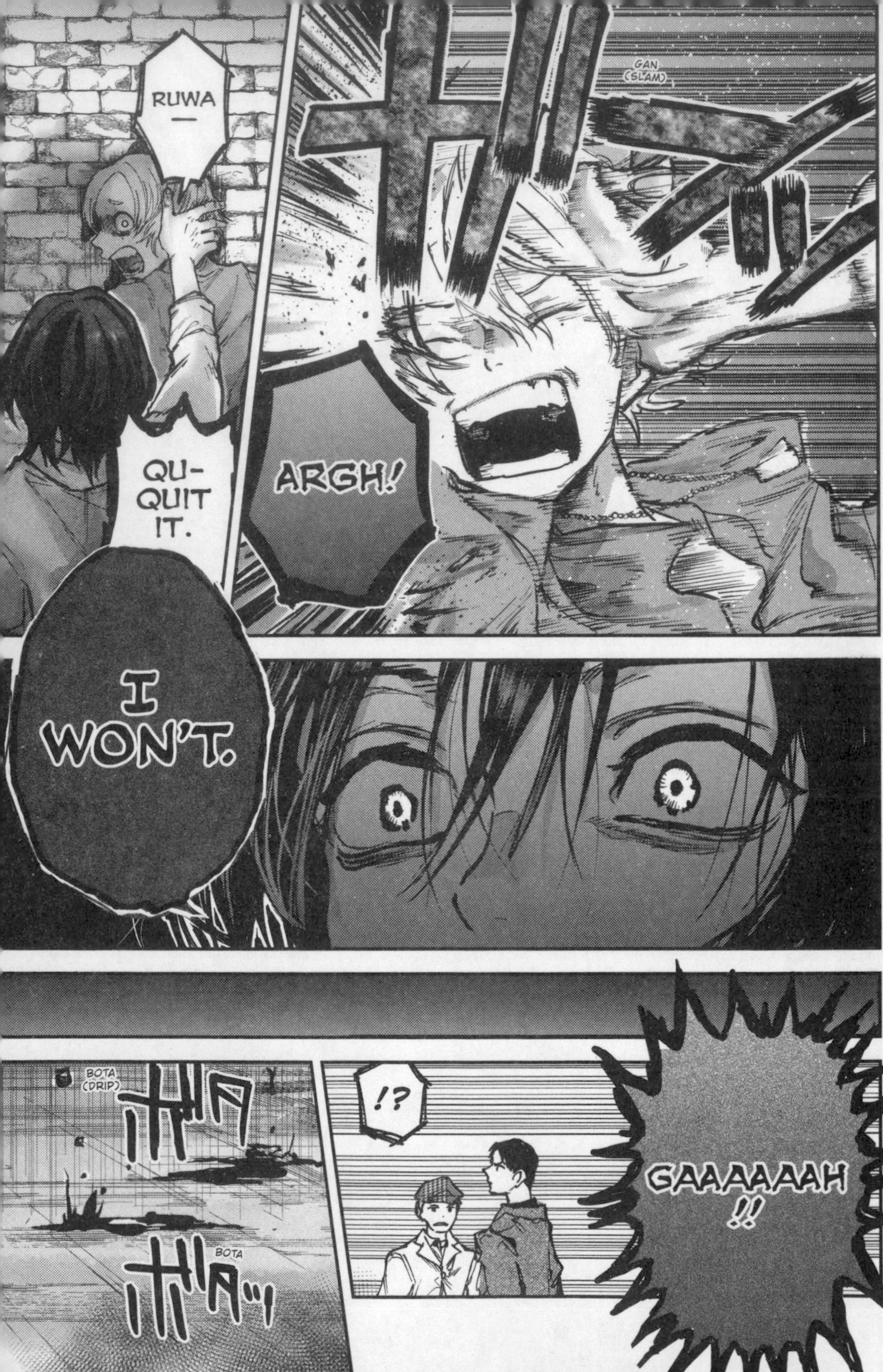
GAN (SLAM)
ARGH!
RUWA —
QU-QUIT IT.
I WON'T.
GAAAAAAH!!
!?
BOTA (DRIP)
BOTA

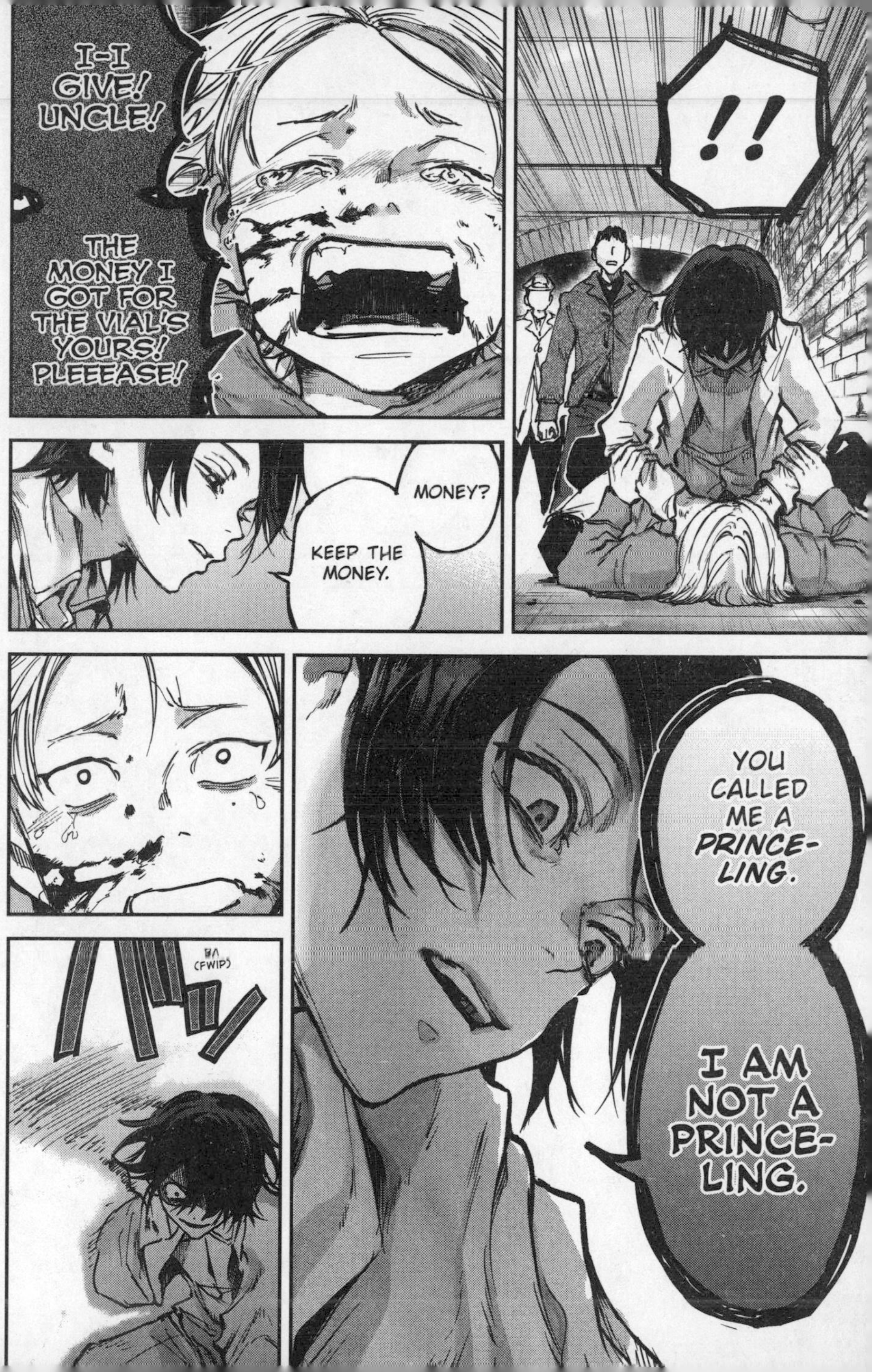
!!
I-I GIVE! UNCLE!
THE MONEY I GOT FOR THE VIAL'S YOURS! PLEEEASE!
MONEY?
KEEP THE MONEY.
YOU CALLED ME A *PRINCE-LING*.
I AM NOT A PRINCE-LING.
(FWIP)

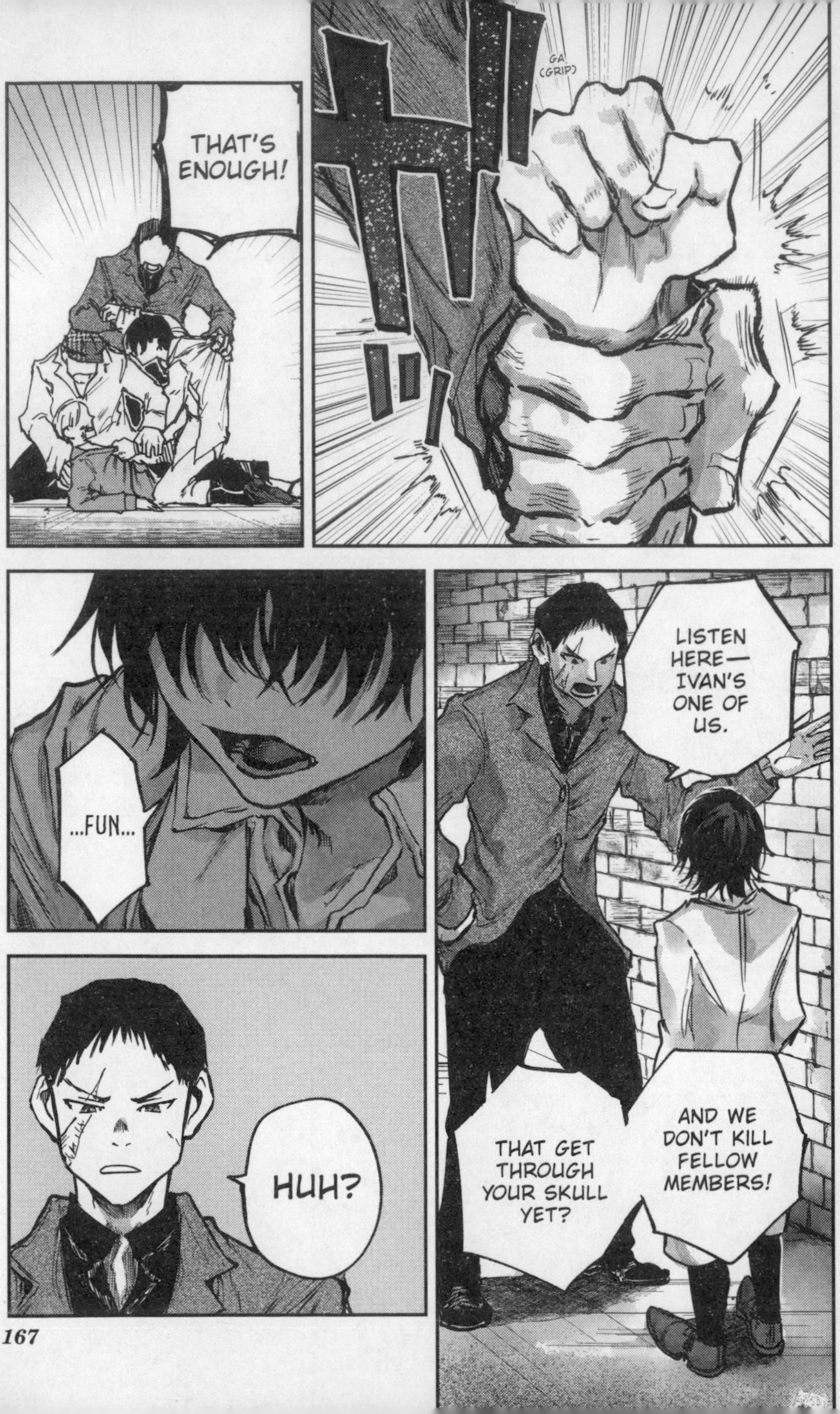
GA (GRIP)
THAT'S ENOUGH!
LISTEN HERE— IVAN'S ONE OF US.
AND WE DON'T KILL FELLOW MEMBERS!
THAT GET THROUGH YOUR SKULL YET?
...FUN...
HUH?

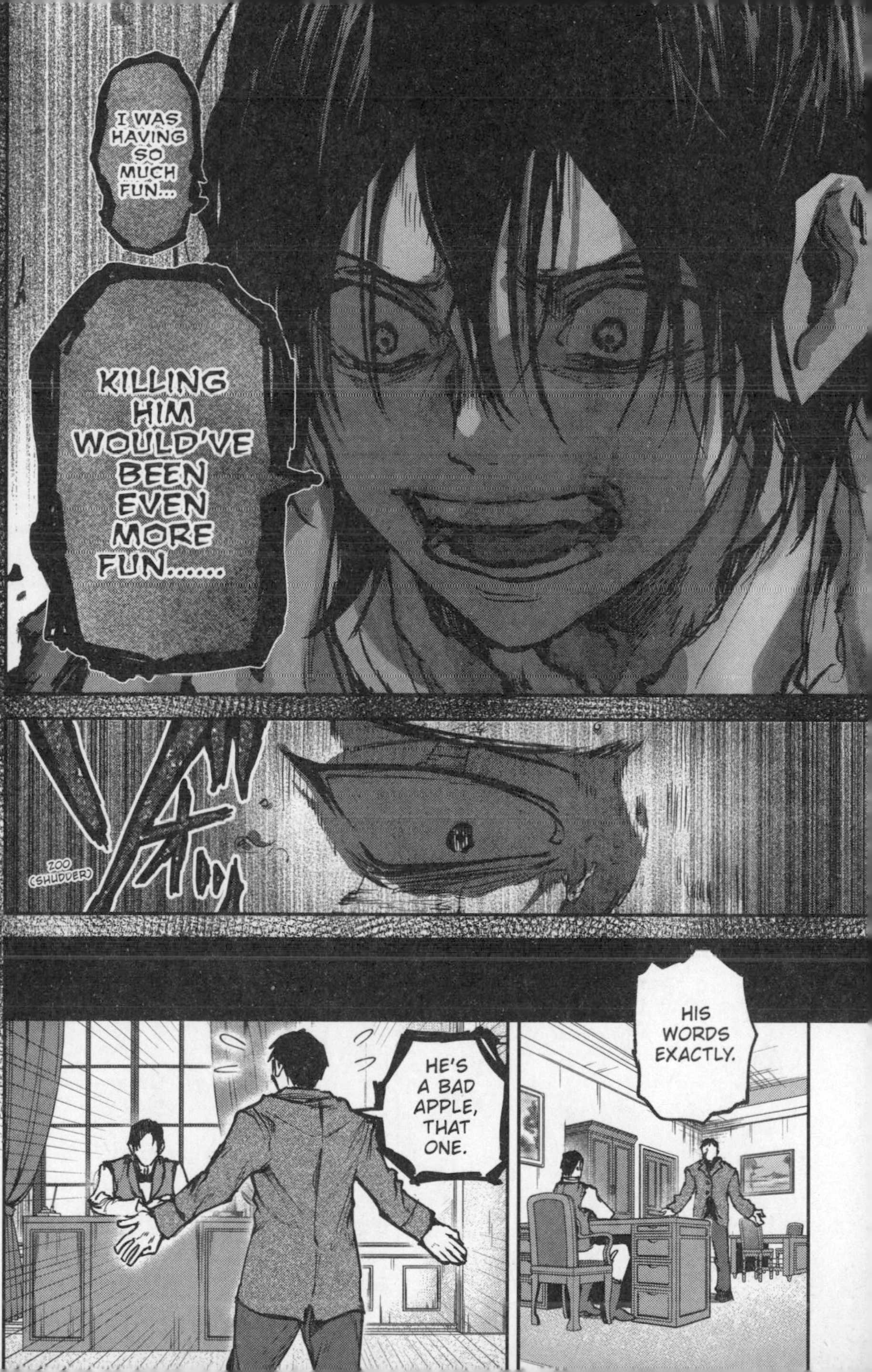
I WAS HAVING SO MUCH FUN...
KILLING HIM WOULD'VE BEEN EVEN MORE FUN......
ZOO (SHUDDER)
HIS WORDS EXACTLY.
HE'S A BAD APPLE, THAT ONE.

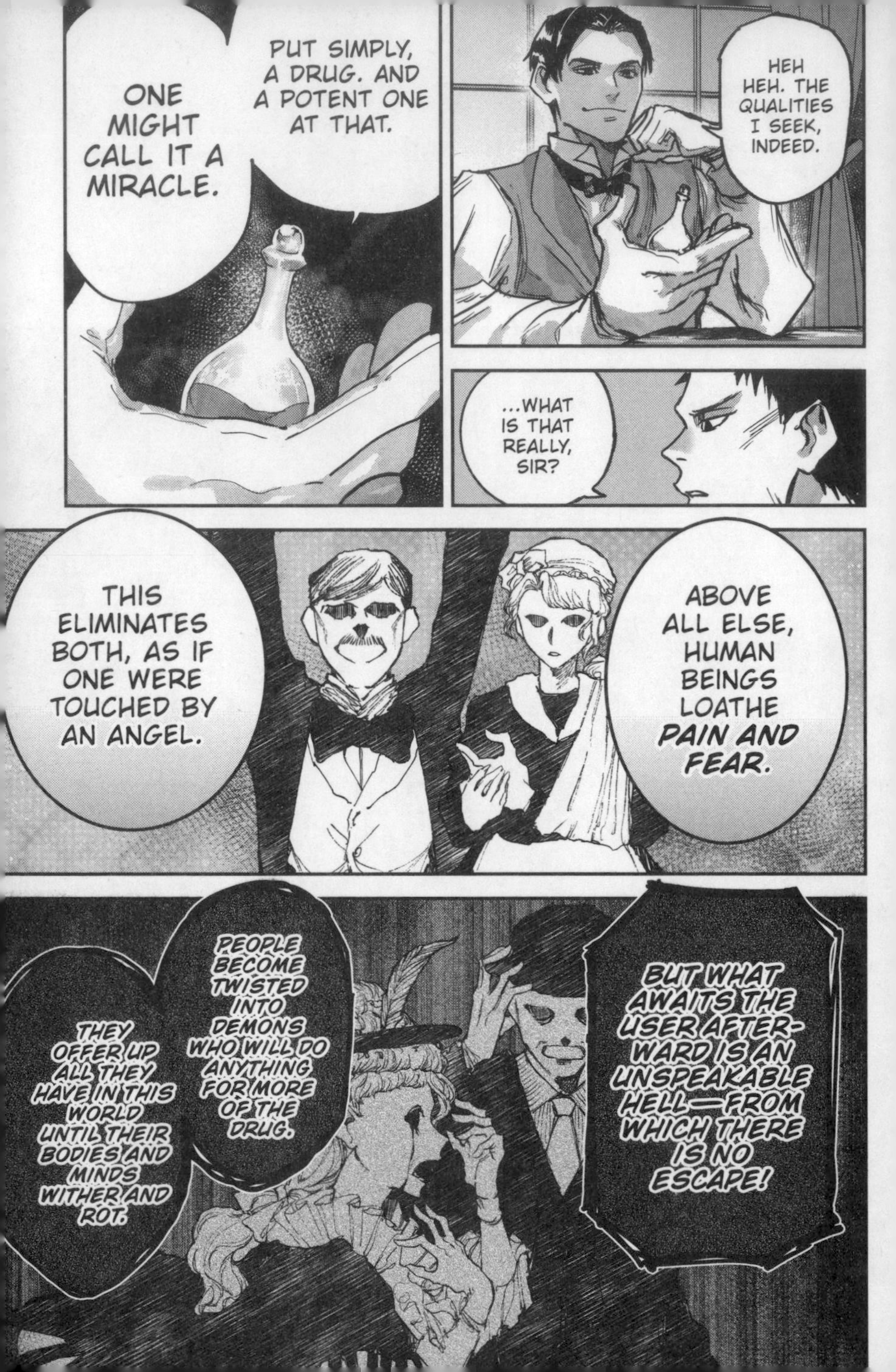
HEH HEH. THE QUALITIES I SEEK, INDEED.
...WHAT IS THAT REALLY, SIR?
PUT SIMPLY, A DRUG. AND A POTENT ONE AT THAT.
ONE MIGHT CALL IT A MIRACLE.
ABOVE ALL ELSE, HUMAN BEINGS LOATHE *PAIN AND FEAR.*
THIS ELIMINATES BOTH, AS IF ONE WERE TOUCHED BY AN ANGEL.
BUT WHAT AWAITS THE USER AFTER-WARD IS AN UNSPEAKABLE HELL—FROM WHICH THERE IS NO ESCAPE!
PEOPLE BECOME TWISTED INTO DEMONS WHO WILL DO ANYTHING FOR MORE OF THE DRUG.
THEY OFFER UP ALL THEY HAVE IN THIS WORLD UNTIL THEIR BODIES AND MINDS WITHER AND ROT.

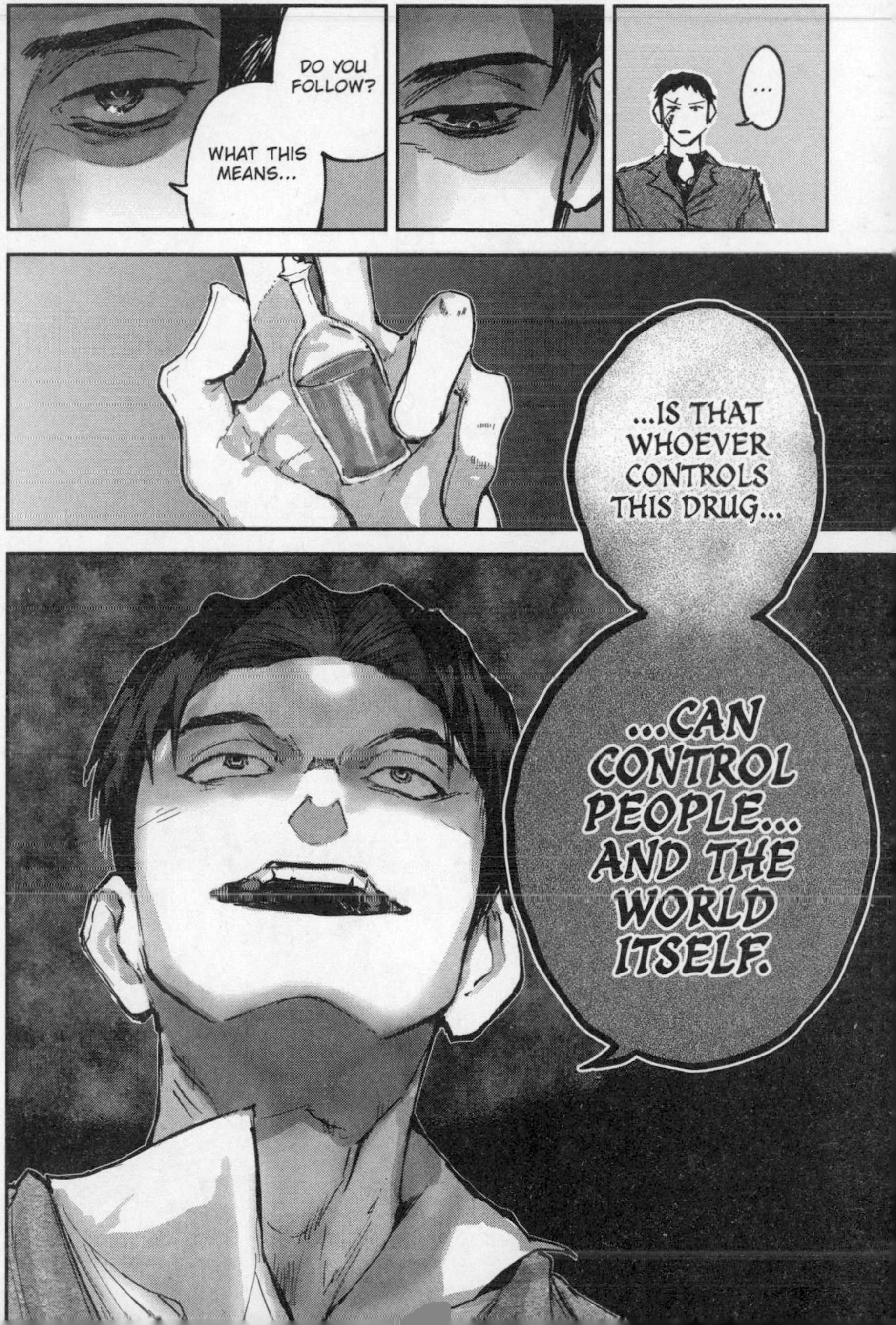
...
DO YOU FOLLOW?
WHAT THIS MEANS...
...IS THAT WHOEVER CONTROLS THIS DRUG...
...CAN CONTROL PEOPLE... AND THE WORLD ITSELF.

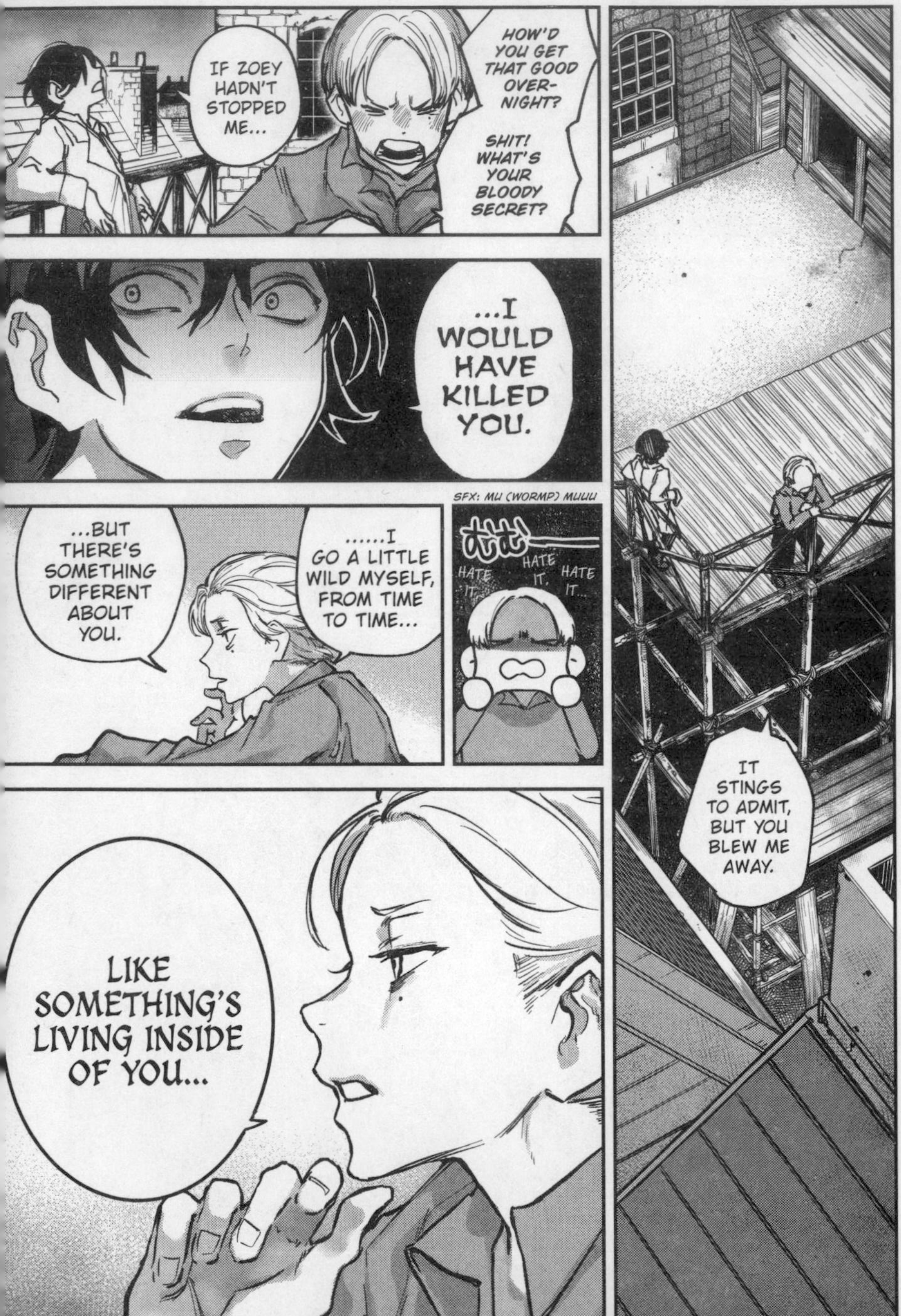
IT STINGS TO ADMIT, BUT YOU BLEW ME AWAY.
HOW'D YOU GET THAT GOOD OVER-NIGHT?
SHIT! WHAT'S YOUR BLOODY SECRET?
IF ZOEY HADN'T STOPPED ME...
...I WOULD HAVE KILLED YOU.
SFX: MU (WORMP) MUUU
HATE IT... HATE IT. HATE IT.
......I GO A LITTLE WILD MYSELF, FROM TIME TO TIME...
...BUT THERE'S SOMETHING DIFFERENT ABOUT YOU.
LIKE SOMETHING'S LIVING INSIDE OF YOU...

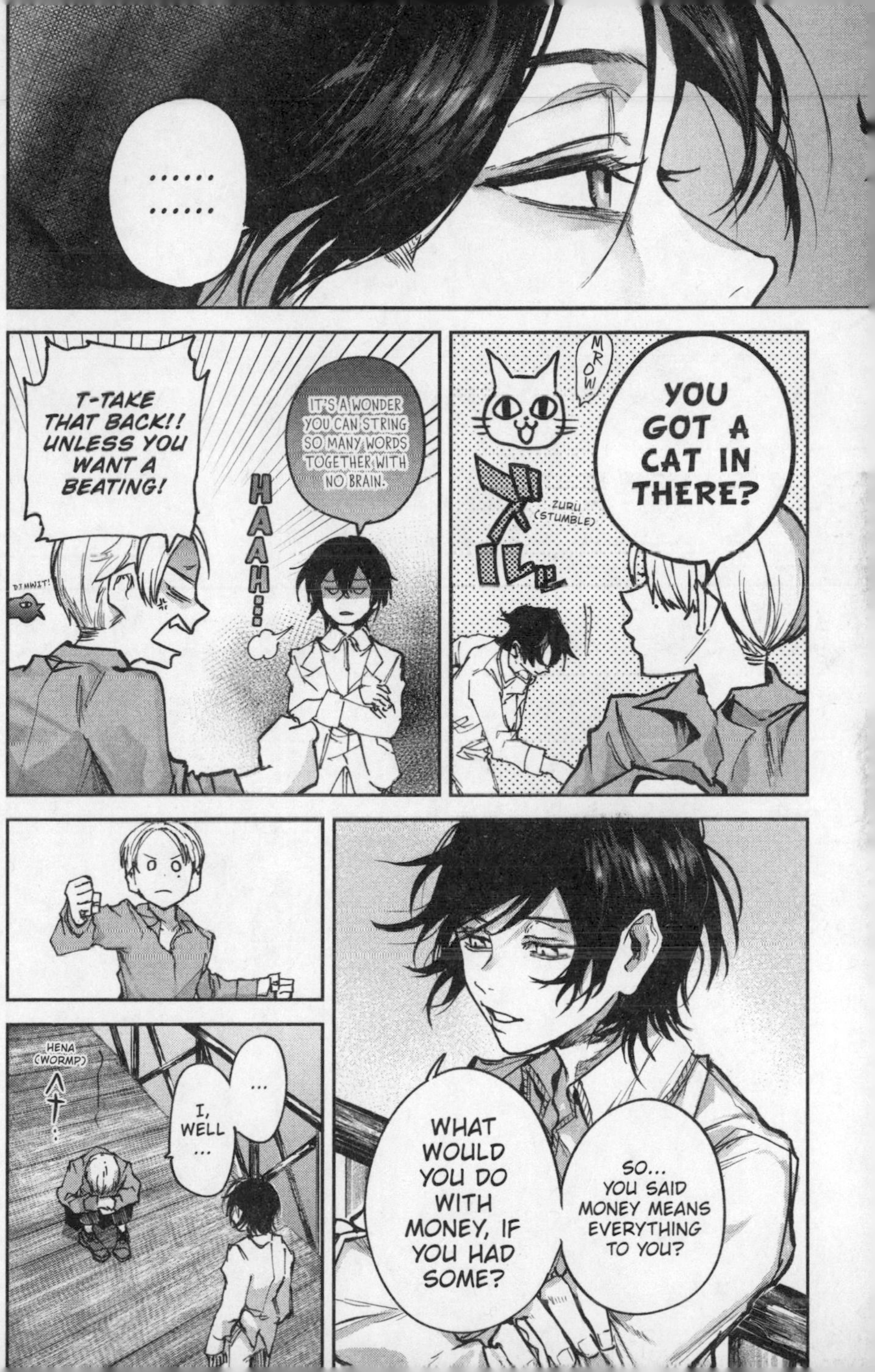
......
......
YOU GOT A CAT IN THERE?
MROW!
ZURU (STUMBLE)
IT'S A WONDER YOU CAN STRING SO MANY WORDS TOGETHER WITH NO BRAIN.
HAAAH...
T-TAKE THAT BACK!! UNLESS YOU WANT A BEATING!
DIMWIT!
SO... YOU SAID MONEY MEANS EVERYTHING TO YOU?
WHAT WOULD YOU DO WITH MONEY, IF YOU HAD SOME?
...
I, WELL ...
HENA (WORMP)

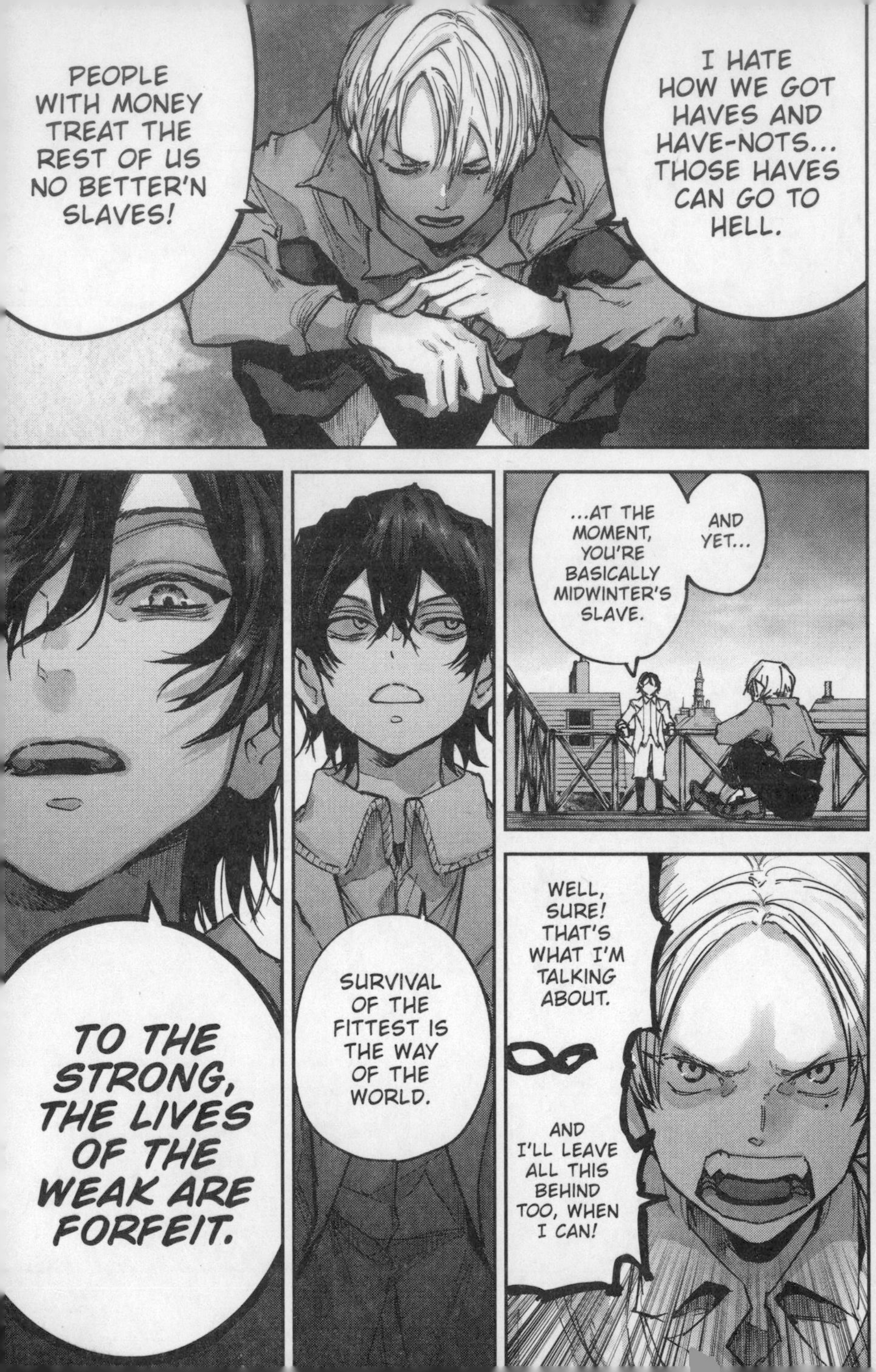
I HATE HOW WE GOT HAVES AND HAVE-NOTS... THOSE HAVES CAN GO TO HELL.
PEOPLE WITH MONEY TREAT THE REST OF US NO BETTER'N SLAVES!
AND YET...
...AT THE MOMENT, YOU'RE BASICALLY MIDWINTER'S SLAVE.
WELL, SURE! THAT'S WHAT I'M TALKING ABOUT.
AND I'LL LEAVE ALL THIS BEHIND TOO, WHEN I CAN!
SURVIVAL OF THE FITTEST IS THE WAY OF THE WORLD.
TO THE STRONG, THE LIVES OF THE WEAK ARE FORFEIT.

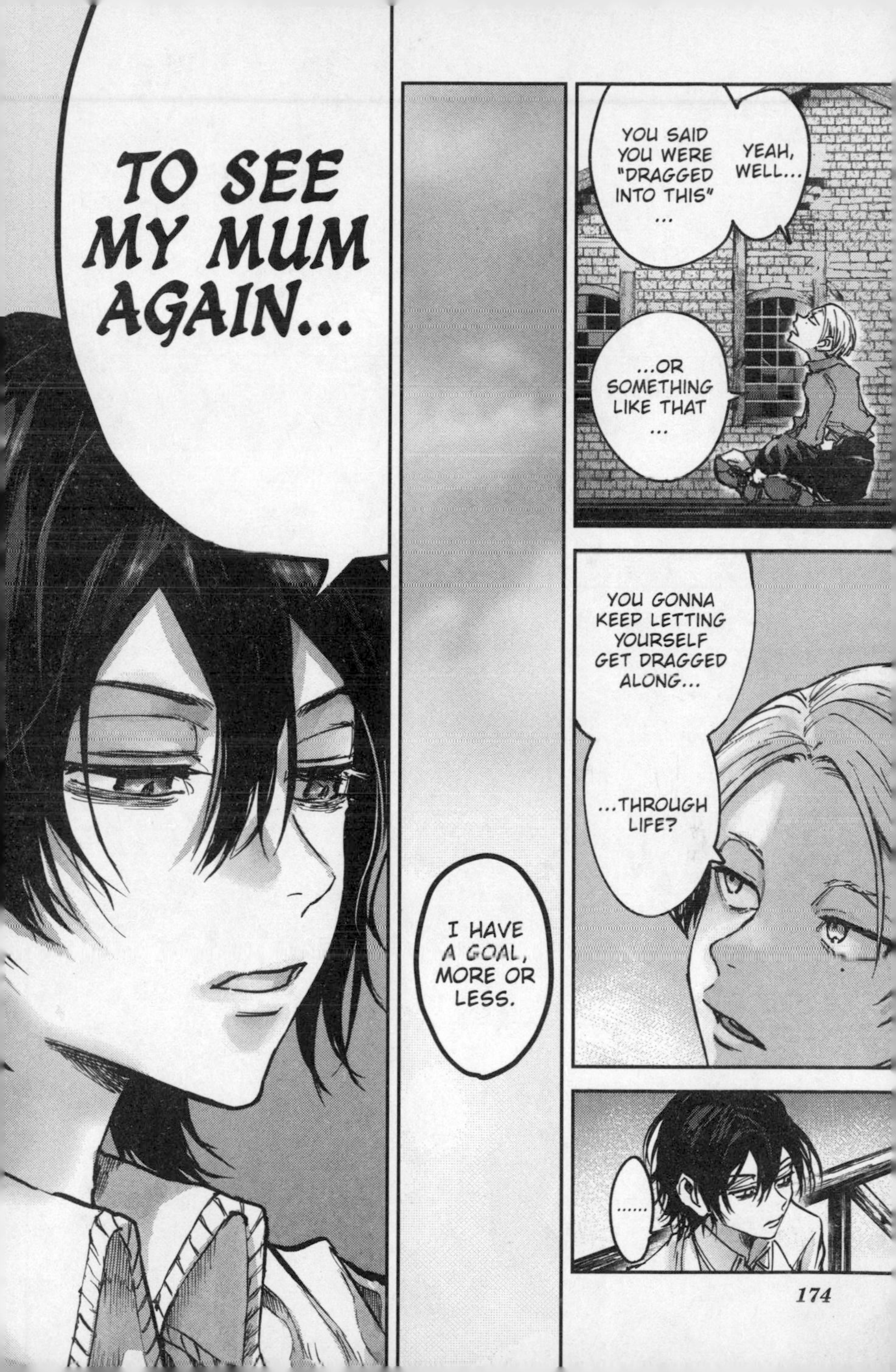
YOU SAID YOU WERE "DRAGGED INTO THIS" ...
YEAH, WELL...
...OR SOMETHING LIKE THAT ...
YOU GONNA KEEP LETTING YOURSELF GET DRAGGED ALONG...
...THROUGH LIFE?
......
I HAVE A GOAL, MORE OR LESS.
TO SEE MY MUM AGAIN...

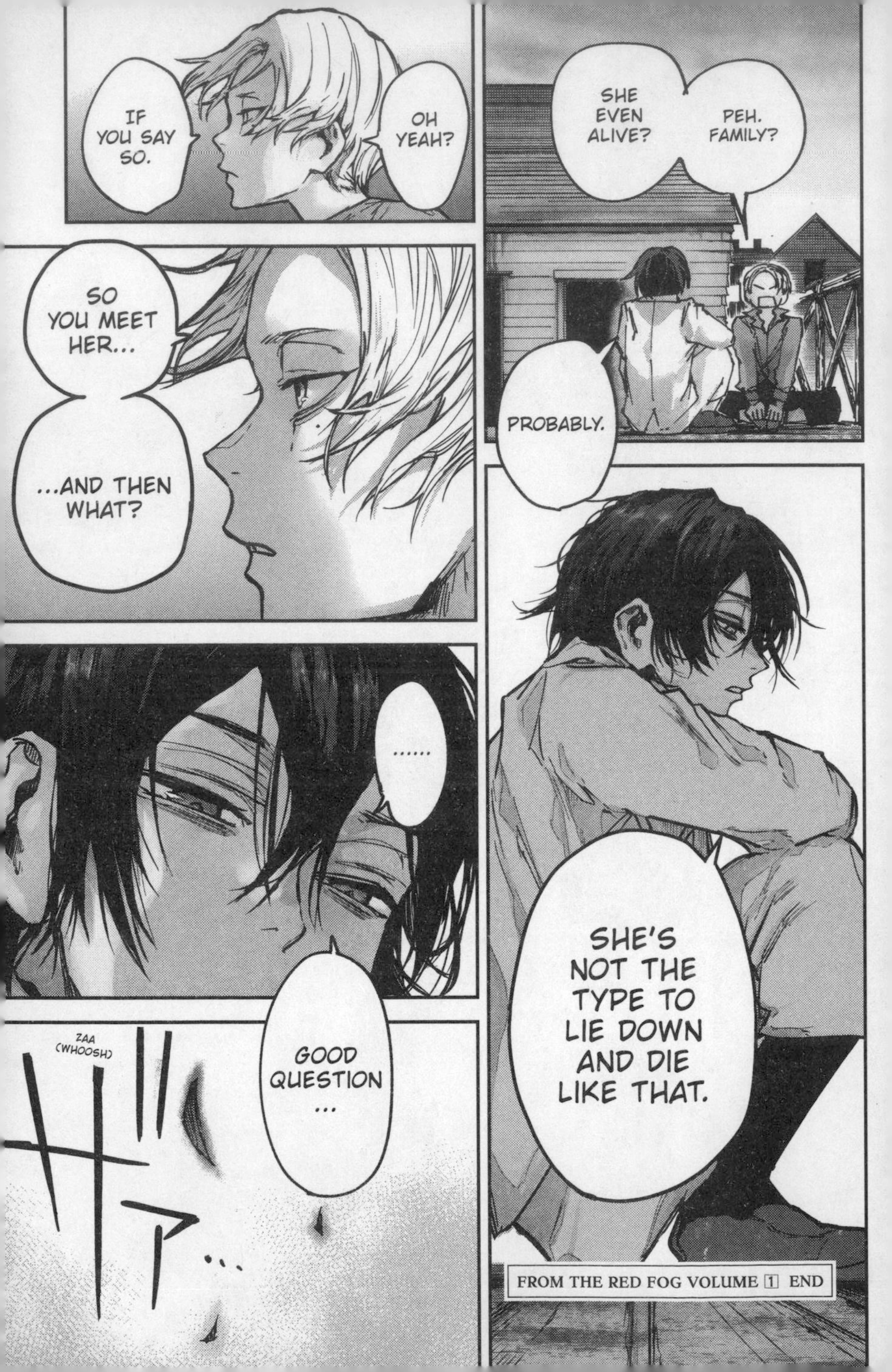
PEH. FAMILY?
SHE EVEN ALIVE?
PROBABLY.
SHE'S NOT THE TYPE TO LIE DOWN AND DIE LIKE THAT.
FROM THE RED FOG VOLUME 1 END
OH YEAH?
IF YOU SAY SO.
SO YOU MEET HER...
...AND THEN WHAT?
......
GOOD QUESTION ...
ZAA (WHOOSH)

Character File

Ruwanda Bailey

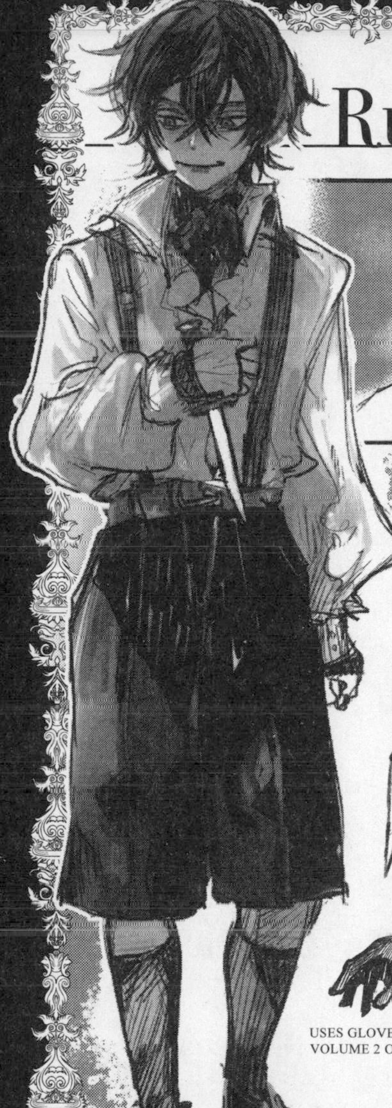

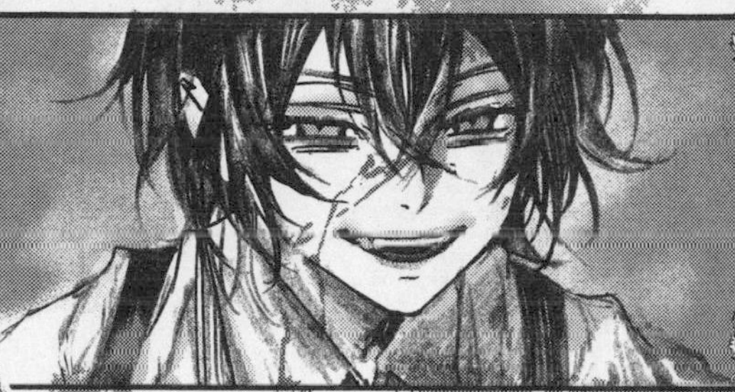

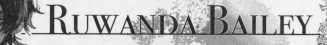

AGE: 12

BIRTHDAY: DECEMBER 22

◆Regarding his first-person pronouns in Japanese: When speaking to older people and those who don't know his true nature, he uses *boku*. When speaking to those of a similar age and status or to those he's decided to be blunt and honest with, he uses *ore*.

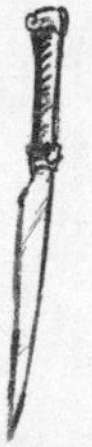

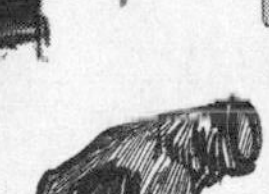

USES GLOVES FROM VOLUME 2 ONWARD

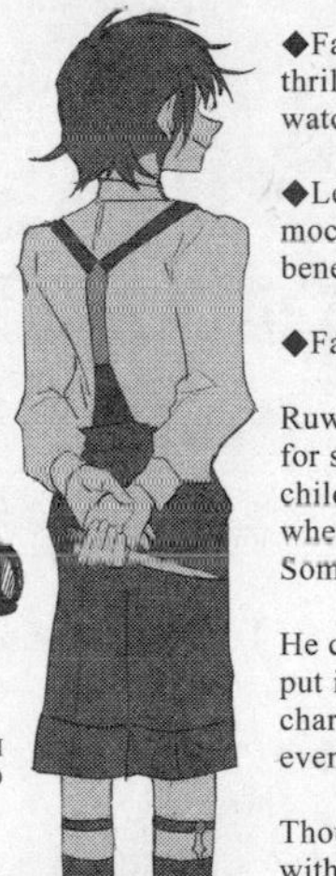

◆Favorite things: Murder, the thrill of anticipation, people-watching

◆Least favorite things: Being mocked by those he considers beneath him

◆Favorite weapon: Knife

Ruwanda has had a low capacity for sympathy and empathy since childhood. He will readily lie whenever necessary.
Something of a narcissist.

He comes off as rather mature, to put it charitably. Or, to put it less charitably, cruel, cold-hearted, and even demonic.

Though he seeks out connections with other people, forging relationships is not his forte. His relationship with his mother is nothing but a source of trauma (as of now).

*MURDER IS A CRIME, AND RUWANDA IS A FICTIONAL CHARACTER. GOOD BOYS AND GIRLS SHOULDN'T VIEW HIM AS A ROLE MODEL!